Critical Thinking

CRITICAL THINKING

ROBERT H. ENNIS
University of Illinois

Prentice Hall, Upper Saddle River, NJ 07458

Library of Congress Cataloging-in-Publication Data

Ennis, Robert Hugh, (date)
    Critical thinking / Robert H. Ennis.
        p.   cm.
    Includes Index.
    ISBN 0-13-374711-5
    1. Critical thinking. 2. Reasoning. 3. Logic. I. Title.
BC177.E66   1995   95-6243
160—dc20   CIP

Acquisitions editor: Ted Bolen
Manufacturing buyer: Lynn Pearlman
Cover art: R. Wahlstrom/The Image Bank
Editorial assistant: Meg McGuane

© 1996 by Prentice-Hall, Inc.
Simon & Schuster/A Viacom Company
Upper Saddle River, New Jersey 07458

Printed in the United States of America

10 9 8 7 6 5 4 3 2 1

ISBN: 0-13-374711-5

Prentice-Hall International (UK) Limited, *London*
Prentice-Hall of Australia Pty. Limited, *Sydney*
Prentice-Hall Canada Inc., *Toronto*
Prentice-Hall Hispanoamericana, S.A., *Mexico*
Prentice-Hall of India Private Limited, *New Delhi*
Prentice-Hall of Japan, Inc., *Tokyo*
Simon & Schuster Asia Pte. Ltd., *Singapore*
Editora Prentice-Hall do Brasil Ltda., *Rio de Janeiro*

Contents

NOTE: A PLUS (+) INDICATES MORE ADVANCED AND DIFFICULT MATERIAL.

5 Deduction: Class Logic 89

6 Deduction: Propositional Logic 119

7   **Applications of Deductive Logic: Necessary and Sufficient Conditions, Straight Deduction, Loose Derivation, and Assumption Attribution   151**

9   Best-Explanation and Causal Inference: Argument and Writing Strategy   217

10 Generalization: Meaning, Sampling, Typicality, Tables, Graphs, and Correlations   264

11 Making Value Judgments   293

12 Reported Definition and Definition Forms   320

13   Arbitrary Stipulative Definition, Positional Definition, and Definition Strategy   344

14   Applying Critical Thinking: FRISCO, Overview, and Critical Thinking in Conversation and Presentation   364

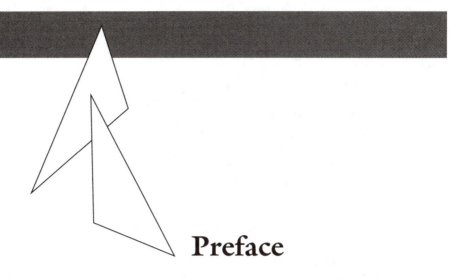

Preface

Critical thinking is a process, the goal of which is to make reasonable decisions about what to believe and what to do. Because we all are continually making such decisions, critical thinking is important to us in personal and vocational, as well as civic, aspects of our lives. Some of these decisions are about whether to believe someone else, or to act in accord with that person's recommendations. For example, an editorial in a newspaper urges that a particular candidate is the best choice for the presidency, and that we should vote for that candidate. We have a decision to make. A friend informs us that taking vitamin E and potassium is an effective way to prevent muscle cramps in the legs. Is the friend right? An author alleges that the Soviet Union was seeking world domination in the period 1945–1990. Is this author correct?

These decisions call for some creativity in our critical thinking, but other decisions can call for more creativity. For example, we might want to decide what path to follow at some crucial point in our lives, when the paths are not clearly laid out. Then we must at least to some extent develop the possibilities as well as choose among them. Not all decisions are so significant, but if they matter at all, and we want to make the best decision, then critical thinking is important.

Critical thinking is also important to the survival of a democratic way of life. If the people in a democracy do not make reasonable decisions in voting and the conduct of their everyday public lives, then the democracy in which they live is threatened. Given current conditions, once democracy is lost, it will be very difficult to recover. This is because modern technology (TVs, computers, etc.) makes available superbly efficient techniques for monitoring and controlling people's activities and thoughts. Unfortunately, these techniques are readily available for use by any totalitarian government. So the reestablishment of democracy, if lost throughout the world, would, I fear, be unlikely. Assuming that democracy should be encouraged and preserved, we then have an additional responsibility. We have a public responsibility to try to make reasonable civic decisions—that is, to try to think critically in civic matters, and to help others do so as well.

Critical Thinking Dispositions and Abilities

Most of the discussion in this book is about how to think critically. This includes observing, making judgments, planning experiments, and developing ideas and alternatives. But underlying the development of the abilities to do these things are certain important critical thinking dispositions, which are combinations of attitudes and inclinations. You might also call them *virtues*. One is the disposition to care about "getting it right" or, more broadly, to care about coming up with the best, most unbiased answer that you feasibly can in the circumstances. Even if you develop all sorts of high-powered skills and abilities, if you do not care about this, then your prowess will probably be wasted.

Another is the disposition to care to be honest and clear about what is written, thought, and said. If you do not care about getting things clear, then your thinking might well be unfocused and confused, leading nowhere.

A third is the disposition to care about the worth and dignity of every person. If you do not have this care, then you might well be a dangerous person, even if you might otherwise be a good critical thinker.

I mention these three basic dispositions because it is so easy to neglect them. They are elaborated in Chapters 1 and 14. I hope that you agree on their importance.

Although everybody is already at least somewhat proficient at critical thinking, the material here should help you to improve your abilities, to be reflective about them, and to develop your critical thinking dispositions. When facing a real situation, you must combine these abilities and dispositions, although they are often discussed separately in this book. There will be a number of opportunities to practice. But you must bear a major responsibility for the actual combining of these interdependent aspects of critical thinking in real situations, taking everything into account—no easy task. Nobody can do it for you, although your instructor and I can help.

A Brief Summary

After an introductory chapter, which sets the scene, this book deals with argument analysis, credibility of sources, observation, deduction, assumption identification, induction, value judging, definition, verbal clarity and consistency, fallacies, discussion, and presentation of your views orally and in writing. There is much emphasis on writing, as well as deciding what to believe or do.

The sections dealing with *either–or* reasoning, types of assumptions, causation, relativism, and equivocation (the latter parts of Chapters 6, 7, 9, 11, and 13) are somewhat more difficult than the other materials. They are marked with a plus sign (+). If time is short, these parts might be omitted, although depth of treatment of critical thinking abilities and principles will consequently be reduced.

At the end of the book, there is a glossary of key terms in critical thinking. Many of these terms are used in different and often technical senses in other fields, and some terms, such as *argument* are used in a limited sense in the field of critical thinking. If in doubt, check the glossary and the part of the text in which the term is discussed. The extensive index provides leads for investigating a concept.

Using This Book

Practice

It is important to apply what you learn in a variety of situations, and to do it often. Real situations are often preferable to hypothetical ones because real situations seem more important to people and because they introduce the complexities that hypothetical situations tend to hide. However, practice in hypothetical situations is also helpful because it can give insight into particular aspects of critical thinking and allow you to focus on one thing to facilitate understanding and competence. In any case, much practice is required.

Both kinds of practice (with real and hypothetical examples) can be found in doing the Check-Up items throughout the book. Do a large number of these items, the more the better, because the application to particular cases does not, for most people, flow automatically from the reading. You improve with practice.

Another Project, Writing a Position Paper

I strongly recommend that you also try to apply the principles and insights in this book to another project, as you are reading and coming to understand this book. This other project could be any significant activity in your daily life in which you have to decide what to do or believe, and need to set forth reasons for your decision. One good activity when this book is used as a text for a course in critical thinking is to write a position paper on an issue of interest to you. (A *position paper* is one in which you take a position and defend it.) After writing a draft, you should revise it, revise it again, and revise it some more—in the light of comments from a friend or associate, and from your instructor.

This paper should include a statement of your thesis, reasons in support of your thesis, the definitions of key terms where needed, subheadings, and a summary. It should pay due attention to the credibility of sources, reliability of observations, the strength of your inferences, counterarguments to your thesis, and word meanings. It should be documented where appropriate, and should be based on as good a grasp of the relevant facts, principles, and insights as you can muster. More details follow in Chapter 1 and periodically throughout the book.

Order of Study

Those of you whose learning style calls first for a broad look at critical thinking (combined with application to examples) might well profit from starting out by reading the last chapter (Chapter 14). For this procedure to do the most good, you should, with a friend, practice using the variety of questions of clarification and challenge and the variety of responses and strategies suggested in that chapter. On the other hand, if you learn best by a step-by-step approach to a subject, and are confused by encountering a wide array of concepts with which you are not familiar, you might find it best to start with Chapter 1, proceeding in order.

Significant Features of This Book

Another way for you to see what this book is about is to consider some of the significant features that I shall discuss next. You have already encountered some.

Flexibility

The book can be used in a variety of ways. You can omit the more difficult parts, as indicated earlier, for an easier-to-grasp approach to critical thinking. You can include an emphasis on writing, as I think most people should. You can do a number of the more difficult items in the Check-Ups that periodically appear, if you are so inclined. You can select and emphasize areas of special interest. Possibilities include verbal questioning and probing, definition and conceptual clarity, the application of general principles of critical thinking in your special field, the nature of causality and causal relations, the accommodation of deductive logic to natural language, and the dilemmas provided by overemphasizing the relativistic insight that there are often many different, equally good ways to do something. More will occur to you as you proceed.

There is also flexibility in the ordering of your reading and engaging these materials. You can do some skipping around, or you can proceed methodically. You can start at the beginning, or you can read the last chapter first.

One area in which there is no flexibility is the need for practice in the application to examples. You must do this.

FRISCO: A General Guide to Critical Thinking

In order to provide a reminder of the big ideas, I have developed an acronym, *FRISCO,* which stands for *Focus, Reasons, Inference, Situation, Clarity,* and *Overview.* The ideas represented by these letters provide a useful checklist, whether you are judging an already stated idea, or trying to develop a new one. If you thoughtfully consider all the ideas represented by FRISCO, you will have considered most of the major concerns in making a decision in that situation. Although it is impractical to methodically and consciously consider all of these ideas for every decision, it is often useful to do so. Furthermore, practice in doing so will sensitize you so that you will automatically notice problems and strengths without the explicit consideration of all of the FRISCO ideas.

Writing, Discussing, and Presenting

Because much of the critical thinking that we do is in the context of interacting with others in writing, discussing, or presenting, I have emphasized these three activities. Writing has been especially emphasized because much of the writing we need to do calls for critical thinking. A memo suggesting and defending a solution to a problem, for example, calls for critical thinking, as does a note to a friend suggesting and defending an interpretation of the friend's reaction to some event.

Credibility of Sources

Much of what we believe comes from other people and books. Some of these are not reliable sources for the topic (for example, the football player who endorses a breakfast cereal). Therefore, it is well to raise the question of the credibility of a source. This concern has been increasingly recognized recently among those interested in critical thinking, and is included in this book.

A Large Number of Examples

Because the improvement of one's critical thinking requires considerable practice, this book provides a large number of examples on which to practice. Some are simplified in order to introduce and provide focus; some are rich in the complexities of real life. But practice with examples is needed. Many opportunities are provided here.

Feedback

I have provided suggested responses to most of the Check-Up items. These suggested responses enable you to get immediate feedback, and give you some responsibility in evaluating your own work, because you must decide about the significance of the difference, if any, between your work and the suggested resources. Furthermore, they enable your instructor to assign more of the open-ended kinds of tasks than would be possible if your instructor were doing all the evaluating of your work. You are thus able to receive a greater amount of supervised practice on challenging tasks.

Challenge

Not all items have a suggested response. You are on your own on some. But be sure that someone else gets a chance to react to what you do.

Independent Study

This book can be used for independent study in which you are the instructor—a self-instructor. Several features make this possible: It contains extended discussions—with examples—of the critical thinking topics considered. There are many examples for practice. And there are suggested answers to most of the review items provided in the Check-Ups. Do these items, and check the suggested answers until the items in a particular section are busywork. Then go on to another section. Be sure to have a practical project, such as a position paper, to which you can apply your critical thinking insights, abilities, and dispositions.

Basis: A Coherent Overall Conception of Critical Thinking

The content of this book is based on a conception of critical thinking that I have developed over the years. It has been subjected to criticism by others, and has been improved as a result. The most recent published version of this overall conception of critical thinking appeared in *Teaching Philosophy,* if you care to examine it.[1]

---

1. "Critical Thinking: A Streamlined Conception," *Teaching Philosophy,* 14 (1), 1991, pp. 5–25.

An Extended Real and Important Example

Much of the discussion of various aspects of critical thinking is tied to an experience I had as a juror in a murder trial. One thing that struck me then was the relevance of all aspects of critical thinking to making the decisions the jury had to make. Not only were all aspects relevant, but they were interdependent. In considering this extended example, you will be able to see this applicability and interdependence.

Like all examples, the jury example is to some extent unique, even for a murder trial. Little or none of the lives of most people is spent being a juror in a murder trial. But the time that is so spent is quite significant. And the situation is an interesting one, raising many general issues that reach way beyond the trial. I hope that you will be able to see how many of the decisions you commonly face are very similar to those the jury had to make, and thus how significant features of the example apply to your own situation. For example, every day you have to decide whether someone is a credible source on a topic. You have to identify an assumption made by a friend, partner, or associate. You need to ask probing questions and to clarify what someone is saying. We jurors had to do all these things. There are many other similarities.

Natural Language

To the extent feasible, everyday language has been used and technical terms have been kept to a minimum. In particular, where deductive logic is discussed, I have tried to adapt the basic ideas of logic to our natural language, instead of the reverse, as is often done (with such words as *some, if,* and *or*).[2]

Fallacies

There are a large number of terms (such as *circular argument*) that are used to identify fallacious thinking. Knowing them can be helpful because they can save time in communicating with those people who know them, and because they are reminders of common errors that people make. They are dangerous, though. They can easily be used superficially, and can intimidate people who do not know them. Furthermore, in some cases, a fallacy term can apply even though the thinking is not fallacious. An example is *appeal to authority.* Often, appeals to authority are perfectly appropriate. Much of what we know is from authorities. When we cite a source in a research paper, we are appealing to an authority, and are often justified in doing so.

The treatment of these terms in this book is in accord with what I have just said about them. Beware of fallacy labels and use them with discretion.

Definition

The system for categorizing and discussing definitions presented here makes sense of what otherwise seems to be a morass. Definitions have three dimensions: form, function, and content. All labels for definitions, such as *persuasive definition,* fit into this structure in a way that makes sense, facilitates clarity, and helps avoid equivocation.

---

2. See P. F. Strawson's *Introduction to Logical Theory* (London: Methuen, 1952) for a discussion of this topic.

Assumption Identification

Identifying assumptions is a standard goal in critical thinking at all levels of our education system. But most treatments are theoretically and practically confusing. The treatment presented here is based on an approach I developed a number of years ago.[3] It has been subjected to scrutiny by many colleagues and has received their approval.

Application to Specific Subject Matter Concerns

This book provides a general approach to critical thinking. In each field of operation or study, there are additional things to consider. But I have found that the ideas contained here are widely applicable in all subject matter areas with which I am familiar. Of course, the ideas are not a substitute for being well-informed in an area. That is necessary as well, as are many other things, such as self-confidence. There are many necessary ingredients to successful operation in life. Critical thinking is one of them.

I wish you success in critical thinking, and ask you to join me in thanking these people for their help in formulating, writing, and producing this book: Ted Bolen, Anthony Calcara, Helen Ennis, Sean Ennis, Susan Finsen, Ray Langley, James Macmillan, Richard Morrow, Stephen Norris, Carol Peschke, William Rapaport, Antonio Rodriguez, Ilene Sanford, Michael Scriven, Anita Silvers, Thomas Tomko, Frances Wagner, Bruce Warner, and my many unnamed wonderful and thoughtful critical thinking students over the years.

ROBERT H. ENNIS

---

3. "Identifying Implicit Assumptions," *Synthese,* 51, 1982, pp. 61–86.

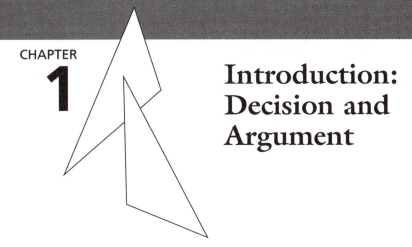

Introduction: Decision and Argument

How can you decide what to believe and what to do?

Should you believe everything you hear and read? Should you even believe everything you read in your local newspaper? Obviously not. Which of the things that you hear and read should you believe? Do you have a guess, or a theory, or an idea about something? Should you believe it? How can you investigate to find out? In short, how can you decide what to believe?

Suppose you are trying to decide how to vote, what kind of orange juice to buy (if at all), whether to see a doctor, or whether to take a class. How can you decide what to do?

The primary purpose of this book is to help you decide in a reasonable way what to believe and what to do. Sometimes decisions are easy. Sometimes they are difficult. Sometimes you have no way to decide with any confidence, and you just have to do the best you can. Fortunately, there are guidelines that are helpful in making decisions.

This book is going to help you learn to use some of the most important of these guidelines. Do not expect the guidelines to do the whole job for you. In decisions about what to believe and do, you also need reliable information and understanding of the topic or field of study. Then, after considering all these things, you must make a reasonable judgment. The guidelines and the facts do not automatically produce an answer.

Other people are often involved. You engage in discussions with them in order to gather information, ideas, and understanding for your own decisions. You ask questions. Sometimes you engage in discussions with others simply to persuade them about something. Sometimes you need to present your ideas to others so that they can make good decisions. These things are not easy to do well. This book attempts to advise you about these ways of interacting with other people. Again, these are only guidelines. The rest is up to you.

You depend on your beliefs, whether you are deciding what to do or deciding what to believe. Decisions about belief, then, are fundamental. A key feature in decisions about belief is often an argument. You will be examining others' arguments and developing your own. So let us start by looking at arguments.

Argument

Basically, an *argument* is an attempt to prove or establish a conclusion. It has two major parts: a conclusion and the reason or reasons offered in support of the conclusion. The general idea is that if the conclusion of an argument is well-supported by good reasons, you should probably believe it. An argument in this sense is not a hostile disagreement (although it could be part of one).

The conclusion in an argument is the part that the arguer is trying to get someone to believe. A word of warning: By *conclusion* I do not mean the ending of a story or set of events. The conclusion is whatever someone is trying to prove or establish.

If there is no conclusion, there is no argument. Similarly, if there is no reason given, there is no argument.

The following is an argument in this logical sense of the word:

My client is innocent of the charge of murder because she was defending herself against an attack.

This is an argument because there is a conclusion (italicized here) and a reason offered in support of the conclusion. The following similar passage is basically the same argument, with the reason and conclusion in opposite order:

She was defending herself against an attack, so *my client is innocent of the charge of murder.*

Again, there is a conclusion and a reason offered in support of the conclusion. The order of the reasons(s) and conclusion does not matter.

The following is not an argument in this logical sense:

You are a fool.
I'm not.
You are.

Each of the speakers is offering a conclusion ("You are a fool" and "I'm not"), but there is no argument here (in the logical sense of *argument*) because there are no reasons offered.

Check-Ups

So that you can get feedback and practice, there will be frequent questions and problems. They will help you to review and check your understanding. It is very important that you do these and check your answers against the suggested answers at the end of the chapter. If your answers disagree with the suggested ones, think twice before you decide that yours is wrong; there can often be more than one reasonable answer to a question. If one of your answers is different from the one suggested, then either try to satisfy yourself that yours really is all right or try to figure out why it is not.

Sometimes the check-up and practice items involve controversial issues. I do not necessarily agree (or disagree) with the opinions or arguments in the examples in this book.

Some of the check-up items are true–false. Generally, these serve as a broad review of the main points. If the statement is false, you will also be asked to revise the statement to make it true. Wherever possible, do this in an interesting way that shows that you understand what is wrong. Try to avoid just inserting the word *not* or some similar device. For example, the first one reads as follows:

> **1:1** As defined here, an argument is a hostile disagreement.

This is false, but should not be changed to read as follows:

> **1:1** As defined here, an argument is not a hostile disagreement.

A change like this does not give a strong enough indication of understanding. Rather, it should be changed to read something like the following:

> **1:1** As defined here, an argument is an attempt to prove or establish a conclusion.

This sort of revision more clearly shows that you understand.

Do not give in to the temptation to look up the suggested answer before you try to figure it out. Try it first, then look it up. Also, resist the temptation to abandon your own answer automatically when it is different from the one given. Make sure that you know a good reason before you change your answer. Yours might be just as good as the suggested answer—perhaps better.

In some cases, answers are not supplied. This is to help you think independently while still giving you the help you can get from seeing the acceptable answers that are supplied.

Often, the last item in a series is more difficult, sometimes asking you to think ahead—to go beyond the material already presented; for example, see Item 1:13 in the first set of check-up items. These items are intended to challenge you and to help you think critically about thinking critically!

Check-Up 1A

True or False?
If false, change it to make it true. Try to do so in a way that shows that you understand.

> **1:1** As defined here, an argument is a hostile disagreement.
> **1:2** The main purpose of this book is to help you decide reasonably what to believe and do.
> **1:3** This book gives some advice for interacting with other people on decisions about what to believe and do.

1:4 If a person follows the guidelines offered in this book exactly as they are written, that person does not need to attend to the irksome details in the situation calling for the thinking.

1:5 Something can be both an argument in the logical sense and part of a dispute.

Short Answer

For each of the following, write *A* if it is an argument (in the logical sense of the word *argument*). Write *N* if it is not. Do not try to judge whether an argument is a good one. Just decide whether each item is an argument at all. If you need to add a word of explanation, do so.

1:6 Mayor Martin will not be reelected because she has raised taxes.

1:7 Because zoning interferes with freedom, it is unjust.

1:8 It is absolutely clear that the future holds more promise than the past.

1:9 Although the sun is shining now, it will be raining before nightfall.

1:10 Whenever the streets are wet, they are slippery, so you should drive carefully.

1:11 "Turn down the volume, please." "Why should I?" "Don't argue with me!"

1:12 The streets are wet. Therefore, they are slippery.

1:13 Whenever the streets are wet, they are slippery.

Six Basic Elements in Critical Thinking: The FRISCO Approach

It helps to have a mental checklist for critical thinking. The one recommended here has six basic elements: Focus, Reasons, Inference, Situation, Clarity, and Overview. The first letters of these words make the easy-to-remember acronym *FRISCO*.

Sometimes you will go through these elements in order when thinking critically, but often you will skip around—and back and forth. In any case, you can use these six elements as a checklist to make sure that you have done the most important things. Generally, you should start by working on the focus and end with an overview, but you should do these two things at other times, too. Often, you should remind yourself of and reconsider the focus at points in your thinking other than the beginning. Furthermore, you should continually do the reviewing called for in the overview step. In later chapters, I shall say more about each of these elements, but my purpose here is just to give you an introduction to FRISCO, using a very short argument as an example.

Focus

The first thing to do in approaching any situation is to figure out the main point, issue, question, or problem. Without knowing this (the focus), you will waste much of your time. Ask yourself such questions as "What is going on here?," "What really matters here?," "What is this all about?," "What is this person trying to prove?," and "What am I trying to prove?"—to make sure that you know what to focus on. Sometimes there are several features on which to focus. Be ready for that.

In an argument, the focus is ordinarily the conclusion. Consider the following argument, given earlier as an example:

> My client is innocent of the charge of murder because she was defending herself against attack.

The conclusion—and the focus—is "My client is innocent of the charge of murder." This is the conclusion because this is the point that the speaker (the defense attorney in a murder trial) was trying to get the jury to believe. Unless you know where the argument is going, it is difficult to see how the pieces fit together and to decide whether, or how much, some part matters. So it is generally wise to try to identify the conclusion right away. (You will see that identifying the conclusion can sometimes be difficult, although it might seem easy now.)

When you are offering an argument, make sure that you know and can state your conclusion. It is usually a good idea to begin your presentation by stating your conclusion.

Reasons

You should also try to get a fairly good idea of the reason or reasons. You must know the reason(s) offered in support of a conclusion and decide whether the reasons are acceptable before you can make a final judgment about an argument. In the argument we have been considering, there is only one reason given: "She was defending herself against attack." It alone is offered in direct support of the conclusion.

When you are formulating your own argument, you must offer your own reasons. When you are making a decision, you should look for reasons for and against deciding in a certain way (pro and con reasons). Sometimes, when you are investigating something or doing an experiment, you are looking for evidence, and the evidence will become a reason or reasons for your conclusion. (You still must judge whether to accept the reasons because they are a basis for making a decision.) Lastly, when you are reviewing your own argument, you should identify and judge the acceptability of your reasons. All of these activities of argument formulation come under this second element, Reasons.

Chapter 2, which deals with argument analysis, is concerned with identifying the reasons other people have and seeing their role in a total argument. Chapters 3 and 4, which deal with the credibility of sources and with observation, are concerned with deciding whether two major types of reasons are acceptable.

I was on the jury that had to judge the reason "She was defending herself against attack." Most of the jurors believed that this reason, as offered by the defense attorney, was not true and we decided that the argument was not a good one. But realize that the fact that an argument is bad does not prove the conclusion to be false. She might have been innocent for other reasons, even though she was not defending herself against attack. In fact, for other reasons, the jury did find her not guilty of murder.

Inference

Suppose that the reason were true. Would it have been sufficient to establish the conclusion? This is a different question from the question under *R*, "Is the reason acceptable?" The question under the *I* in *FRISCO* is whether the reason, if it is acceptable, would support the conclusion, and how strongly. In the jury situation, it seemed to me that the reason, even though it was not acceptable, would have been sufficient; that is, that the inference is a good one. To say that an inference is a good one is to say that the step from the reason(s) to the conclusion is a reasonable one; in other words, that it is one we are entitled to make. In still other words, the reasoning (though not necessarily the reason) is acceptable.

Judging the inference is different from judging the acceptability of the reason(s). We must do both. We must judge whether the reason(s) are acceptable and we must also judge whether the reason(s) would be sufficient to establish the conclusion if the reason(s) are acceptable (that is, we also have to judge the inference). I have said this in different ways because it is a difficult distinction until you see it.

Although we shall be looking in more detail at the process of judging different kinds of inferences, one good general question to ask is this: "Is there a plausible alternative to this conclusion?" Applied to our sample argument, the thinking might go like this: "Suppose that it is true that she was defending herself against an attack. An alternative to the conclusion is that she was still guilty. Is this plausible, given that we accept the reason?" I thought not, but it was still important to consider that alternative. It would be plausible, by the way, if the attack were merely a verbal attack. Often, good alternatives go unnoticed if we do not make an effort to find them.

Because the alternative I suggested is so obvious, the strategy of looking for alternatives might not seem especially helpful in this argument. But there was another argument in that situation where looking for alternatives was a very important strategy. One of the jurors concluded that the defendant was guilty because it was agreed that it had not been proved beyond a reasonable doubt that she was innocent. But an alternative conclusion was that neither her guilt nor her innocence had been proven beyond a reasonable doubt. It was very helpful to point out this fact to that juror.

Look at this juror's comment in a different way: through the identification of an unstated assumption. The juror apparently was assuming that a defendant is guilty unless proven innocent. He was wrong about this, and we told him so. The identification and appraisal of such assumptions is part of the process of judging an inference because inferences usually depend on unstated assumptions. Identifying unstated assumptions is discussed in Chapter 7.

Unfortunately, the word *inference* has a confusing feature. It is *ambiguous*. That is, it has more than one meaning. Sometimes the word *inference* is used to mean *conclusion,* so that the conclusion of an argument would then be an inference. In our example, the proposition "My client is innocent of the charge of murder" is an inference in the conclusion sense of the word *inference*. Usually, however, the word *inference* is used as I am using it here: to refer to the step in going from the reason(s) to the conclusion. In this book, the word is used in the "step" sense (the reasoning sense) rather than the "conclusion" sense.

Incidentally, I have just exemplified an important critical thinking ability: drawing distinctions in order to avoid confusion. That is, I drew a process–product distinction between two senses of the word *inference:* inference as a process (the "step" sense) and inference as a product (the "conclusion" sense). Process–product distinctions are often helpful, but the more general point is that drawing distinctions can often help to clear up confusions and disagreements.

In judging inferences, we take into account the other parts of FRISCO. The Focus is important because it is the product of the inference. The Reasons are important because the inference starts with them. The Situation is important because it determines a number of important factors to consider in judging an inference. As you will see, the trial situation had a bearing on the kind of inferences one can make. You will also see that the meaning of the words used (particularly the word *attack*) has a bearing on the inference that can be made. All of this illustrates the interdependence of the parts of FRISCO.

Situation

When thinking is focused on belief and decision, it takes place in some broad situation that gives it significance and provides some of the rules. The situation includes the people involved and their purposes, histories, allegiances, knowledge, emotions, prejudices, group memberships, and interests. It includes the physical environment and the social environment, which in turn includes families, governments, institutions, religions, employment, clubs, and neighborhoods. These things are relevant not only to the significance of the thinking activity and some of the rules that guide it, but also to the meaning of what the thinker is doing or judging.

A crucial feature of the courtroom situation was that the burden of proof was on the State, not the defense attorney. The State had to prove its case beyond a reasonable doubt. The defense attorney had to show only that his case was a reasonable possibility. That was all that he needed in order to show that the State had not proven its case beyond a reasonable doubt.

The jurors in that situation needed to realize this difference. At first, some were tempted to hold the defense attorney to the same standard as the State's attorney. An example was the juror who wanted to conclude that the defendant was guilty because the defense attorney had failed to prove beyond a reasonable doubt that she was innocent. We had to point out to him the crucial feature of the situation: The burden of proof was on the State. It was important for us to be aware of this feature of the situation.

Clarity

When you write and speak, it is important to be clear in what you say. If others are not clear, try to get them to be clear. Make sure that you understand what they are saying.

Let us go back to the argument I was considering earlier. The defense attorney's conclusion ("My client is innocent of the charge of murder") and reason ("She was defending herself against attack") seemed clear to me in that situation. But in judging the inference from the reason to the conclusion, it was important to know what he meant by the word *attack*. If he had meant the word broadly, so that verbal abuse counted as an attack, then I believe that the inference would not have been a good one. That is, the reason, if true, would not have been enough to establish the conclusion. Why should defending herself against verbal abuse justify the killing?

On the other hand, if by the word *attack* he meant attempted physical violence, then the inference from reason to conclusion seems to be more plausible. So it is important to be clear about what he meant by the word if we are to judge fairly the inference from reason to conclusion, as well as to judge fairly the acceptability of the reason. In short, it is important to be clear about the meaning of terms and the way in which you and others are using them.

I have just drawn a distinction between physical and verbal violence in order to avoid possible confusion. Earlier, I drew a distinction between the process and product senses of the word *inference*. Drawing distinctions that avoid confusion is an important feature of the *C* in *FRISCO*.

A good clarity slogan is "*Say what you mean, mean what you say,* and try to get others to do so as well." Four good questions to use in implementing this slogan are these: "What do you mean?," "Will that confuse people who use the word(s) in a different way?," "Can you give me an example?," and "Can you give me a case that comes close, but is not an example?" More such questions are considered in Chapter 14. I urge you to be always ready to use these questions. You will find me asking and answering questions like these throughout the book. Can you remember a case that I have already offered that comes close, but is not an example?

Overview

The sixth element in critical thinking, overview, calls for you to check what you have discovered, decided, considered, learned, and inferred. Put it all together and see whether it all still makes sense. This should be done not only at the end, but continuously as you go along. Monitor your own thinking. Even though you have made a judgment about the inference at the inference phase, you do it again here as part of checking everything.

The First Five Elements: FRISC

As I review the defense attorney's argument in the Overview phase, I check each of the other five elements, the Focus, the Reason (and its acceptability), the Inference (and its acceptability), the Situation, and the Clarity of meaning of the terms and the attorney's use of them. But note some ways in which these elements are interdependent in my discussion of the defense attorney's argument: The strength of the inference depended on what the defense attorney was talking about when he used the word *attack* (I depends on C). The real focus depended on the situation (that is, ascertaining the focus depended on what we knew to be the defense attorney's interest in that situation. F depends on S.) Whether the reason should be believed depends on what he meant by *attack* (R depends on C). Determining the actual inference depends on the nature of the reason (I depends on R). I could go on, but you get the idea. The important thing to see is that it is necessary to review and put all these interdependent things together by stepping back to overview your thinking.

Critical Thinking Dispositions

Another key feature of the overview is to make sure that you have been exemplifying the critical thinking dispositions mentioned in the Preface. In more detail, ideal critical thinkers are disposed to do the following:

1. Care that their beliefs are true and that their decisions are justified; that is, care to "get it right" to the extent possible, or at least care to do the best they can. This includes the interrelated dispositions to do the following:

   A. Seek alternatives (hypotheses, explanations, conclusions, plans, sources), and be open to them.
   B. Endorse a position to the extent that, but only to the extent that, it is justified by the information available.
   C. Be well-informed.
   D. Seriously consider points of view other than their own.

2. Represent a position honestly (theirs as well as others'). This includes the dispositions to do the following:

   A. Be clear about the intended meaning of what is said, written, or otherwise communicated, seeking as much precision as the situation requires.
   B. Determine, and maintain focus on, the conclusion or question.
   C. Seek and offer reasons.
   D. Take into account the total situation.
   E. Be reflectively aware of their own basic beliefs.

3. Care about the dignity and worth of every person. This includes the dispositions to do the following:

   A. Discover and listen to others' views and reasons.
   B. Take into account others' feelings and level of understanding, avoiding intimidating or confusing others with their critical thinking prowess.
   C. Be concerned about others' welfare.[1]

Actually, these dispositions are embedded in FRISCO, but it sometimes helps to make them more explicit. For example, the disposition to try to be well-informed

---

1. A few interpretive comments: Several of the dispositions (1 D, 2 E, and 3 A) contribute to being well-informed (1 C) but are separate dispositions in their own right. The expressed concern with true belief accepts the view that our concepts and vocabulary are constructed by us, but also that (to oversimplify somewhat) the relationships among the referents of our concepts and terms are not constructed by us. We can have true or false beliefs about these. The disposition (#3) to care about the dignity and worth of every person is not required of critical thinking by definition, but in order that it be humane. I call it a correlative disposition, by which I mean that, although this disposition is not part of the definition of *critical thinking,* it is desirable for all critical thinkers to have it, and the lack of it makes the critical thinking less valuable, or perhaps of no value at all.

is needed for the evaluation of the reasons. The disposition to be open-minded and to seriously consider other points of view than one's own is needed for judging the inference. However, a few of the dispositions are explicit in FRISCO. The disposition to be clear about the meaning of the words is explicitly stated under the C. The disposition to determine and maintain the focus is explicitly stated under the F. In any case, make sure in the Overview that you are exemplifying these dispositions.

Writing a Position Paper Using Critical Thinking

As you work your way through this book, there is a danger that you will understand the separate parts without being able to put them together and apply them to your own life. One way to help deal with this danger is for you to write a short position paper and revise it as you proceed through the book, making use of any new insights you acquire. Doing so will also give you an opportunity to use what you learn in an area that matters to you.

A *position paper* is an essay in which you state and defend a thesis by giving an argument. It is often called an argumentative essay. A *thesis* is an assertion consisting of a subject and predicate. It is the conclusion (the *F* in *FRISCO*). Your defense of the thesis should consist of reasons that are relevant to and support the conclusion. It should acknowledge, and respond to, opposing points of view and weaknesses in your argument. Furthermore, it should be sensitive to word meanings and should avoid verbal confusion and be well-organized. Lastly, it should evidence such critical thinking dispositions as sensitivity to the feelings and thoughts of others (especially your audience).

Organization

Although there are many possible ways to organize a position paper, the simplest and usually most effective way in practical situations is to state your thesis early in the paper, sketch out your plan for the rest of the paper, give your reasons (and often your reasons for your reasons, if appropriate), and summarize your position, providing a restatement of your thesis and a summary of your reasons. In a paper of any length, it is often helpful to the reader to provide headings (perhaps one for each major reason) and sometimes subheadings. Ordinarily, the reasons make up the longest part of the paper.

This simple approach is conducive to clarity and ensures that the major elements are there. Some people might feel that it is an imposition on their creativity and aesthetic sensibility to be forced into this mold. No doubt that is true in some circumstances, but if you cannot follow this approach effectively, then you probably cannot be effective in other approaches, such as leaving it up to your reader to figure out what your conclusion is.

Everyday practical situations in which this approach is useful include a presentation to a committee, a letter to the editor, an attempt to get an organization to take a stand, and an answer to an examination question that asks you to defend an approach or point of view. Although here I am talking about written arguments, this approach is also useful in such verbal situations as open meetings devoted to the discussion of controversial proposals and motions. I have seen so many confusing and thereby ineffective attempts to defend a position that I urge this simple basic approach for most practical situations. Just examine the letters to the editor of your local newspaper to find examples of confusion that could have been avoided. Making this routine habitual is especially useful in situations when you are under pressure because it frees your mind to think about the issues and what others are saying.

Good organization for most people does not come automatically. Generally, I first write down as fast as I can the ideas I want to get across—in any order. Then I examine them to see what patterns among them might be found or constructed. Next, I develop a few major categories that together go somewhere and can be sequenced naturally. Then I try to fit the assorted ideas into one of the major categories and write down the result in the form of an outline. There is much trial and error about this. I try something, see how it goes, revise it, and try again. The result never is perfect, but some organization plans flow more smoothly and make more sense than others. Ultimately, you must select one and use it, subject to modification.

Revision

Very few people write a good position paper on the first draft. Expect to revise and revise and revise your work if it is to be good. I often revise papers twenty times or more before they are published. You are reading at least the twentieth revision of this chapter.

When you revise, ask yourself the following question about each sentence: Is this sentence relevant to my thesis? If the answer is negative, discard the sentence. Relevance is a broad criterion, however. A sentence can be relevant if it states a reason, defends a reason, states or responds to an opposing position, clarifies meaning, or offers background information to make the situation (S) clear.

Apply FRISCO to each draft. It is also a good idea to get opinions from your friends or associates. Ask one or more of them to apply FRISCO to your work.

Citations

If you have cited sources, be sure that you know why you have done so and that your purpose is legitimate. Some legitimate purposes include giving credit for an idea you have expressed, proving that a person really said what you claim the person said (often needed when you are challenging what someone has said), and appealing to a legitimate authority to establish one of your reasons or subreasons. A danger is to act as if you are citing someone as an authority who does not meet the criteria for credibility (discussed in Chapter 3). More specifically, it is dangerous to cite someone as an authority for a proposition when other people equally qualified hold the opposite position.

Audience

When you write a position paper—and, in general, when you express yourself—keep your intended audience in mind. Focusing on your intended audience should help you decide what information you can assume in your paper and need not state, what terms need definition, and whether you need to provide citations. For example, a letter to an editor, or virtually anything to go in a local newspaper, does not need citations. On the other hand, a position paper for your local board of education or city council needs citations. Write for your audience.

A Checklist

Here is a nineteen-item checklist to use to ensure that the principal considerations in a position paper are satisfied. An affirmative answer to each question is desirable. You might want to adjust the checklist to your own situation.

1. Is there a thesis?
2. Is the thesis clear enough for the situation?
3. Is the thesis stated at the beginning of the paper (usually desirable)?
4. Is there a title?
5. Does the paper adequately address the intended audience with respect to level of sophistication, assumed background knowledge, use of citations, definition of terms, etc.? (Also, have you made clear who is the intended audience and what is the intended medium of communication so that your commentator will have a basis for helpful comments?)
6. Is the paper sensitive to political and social contexts?
7. Are the reasons identifiable?
8. Are the reasons acceptable?
9. Do the reasons support the thesis to the degree claimed?
10. Are opposing points of view adequately represented?
11. Is every sentence relevant to the thesis?
12. Are terms defined where necessary?
13. Is the writing clear?
14. Is the paper well-organized?
15. Do transitions flow smoothly (sentence to sentence, paragraph to paragraph, section to section)?
16. Is the paper sufficiently concrete?
17. Are there headings (unless the paper is very short) and subheadings (for a long paper)?
18. On the whole, are the critical thinking dispositions (such as being open-minded, seeing things from others' points of view, and being aware of one's own basic assumptions) exemplified?
19. Is the summary adequate?

Responsibility for the Wise Exercise of Your Knowledge

When you are through with this book, you will have some powerful tools that are not only useful, but also dangerous. You will learn about some methods of discussion and persuasion that you could use to make mischief. You will learn some new words that can be used to intimidate people. You will learn to see better what is right and wrong with an argument, and will have more power that results from your understanding. You will have learned about some techniques that are often effective in deceiving people. You will then have a responsibility to use your knowledge wisely.

There is another danger: A little knowledge, because it can induce unjustified confidence, is sometimes worse than no knowledge. While you are learning the techniques, distinctions, and vocabulary of critical thinking, you should practice. But the danger is that you will flaunt your partial knowledge with more confidence than you should have. Remember these three things:

There is always more to a situation than you know.

The principles of critical thinking have exceptions and require good judgment in their application.

Information, knowledge, and understanding of the topic or field of study are crucial.

Chapter Summary

In this book, the primary concern is how to decide what to believe or do. A related concern is reasonable interaction with other people in situations calling for such decisions.

Initially, we will be concerned with the judging of arguments (in the logical sense of the word *argument*). An argument in this logical sense is an attempt to support a conclusion with one or more reasons. A conclusion is not the ending of something; rather, it is a proposition that someone is trying to prove or establish. The basic idea in judging arguments is that both the reasons and the inference (the reasoning) must be acceptable. This basic idea is expanded into FRISCO.

The six basic elements in the FRISCO process of judging arguments are Focus, Reasons, Inference, Situation, Clarity, and Overview. This list of interdependent elements is not a sequence of steps; rather, it is a checklist to use to ensure that you have done the major things. The word *FRISCO* is a device to help you remember them.

Because realistic practice is helpful, you are urged to develop, and revise—and revise—a position paper as you read this book. Apply FRISCO to each revision. As you wend your way through the book, you will learn things to improve your position paper.

Chapter 2 deals with argument analysis. In it, you will concentrate on the identification aspects of the first three elements of FRISCO. You will consider how to identify conclusions and reasons and will learn to clarify how the parts of an argument relate to each other to make an inference. Later chapters will look at the judgments you need to make in developing and appraising positions and arguments.

Check-Up 1B

True or False?
If false, change it to make it true. Try to do so in a way that shows that you understand.

1:14 One often needs to deviate from the given order of the six elements of critical thinking.

1:15 When examining an argument, it is generally a good idea to try to identify the conclusion right away.

1:16 Suppose that one has determined the writer's conclusion. Then, in judging the argument, one does not need to ask whether there are alternative possible conclusions that are better supported.

1:17 Asking whether the reasons are themselves believable is generally confusing and a waste of time.

1:18 The main point of the overview element of critical thinking is to make sure that you can tell others how you have reached your decision.

1:19 The ideas in this book, if properly understood, can be used only for good purposes.

1:20 If an argument is bad, the conclusion must be wrong.

1:21 In deciding whether to believe a conclusion, the primary issue is whether the reasons are acceptable.

1:22 A reason in one argument can be the conclusion in another.

Medium-Length Answer

1:23 Here is an argument:

You should not bother to do your homework in this course because critical thinking is difficult to learn.

Imagine that a friend of yours has just offered this argument. Also imagine and specify more details in the situation—enough for it to be realistic to you. Then apply the six basic elements of critical thinking to this argument. Briefly report your results for each element in some convenient order, perhaps this one (note that I have not put them in the original FRISCO order; you choose the order you prefer):

1. Identify the Focus.
2. Describe the Situation.
3. Discuss and judge the Clarity of the meaning of the terms.
4. Identify the Reasons and make and justify your judgments about whether they are acceptable (not about whether they are sufficient to establish the conclusion—that goes under Inference).
5. Identify the Inference step, and make and justify your judgment about it.
6. Give an Overview in which you review your decisions about whether to accept the conclusion. Check for your use of your critical thinking dispositions throughout. Come to a final decision.

1:24 Suppose that the defense attorney had been using the word *attack* to mean the giving of either verbal or physical abuse, and that he had shown that the victim was calling the defendant nasty names. How would that affect your judgment as a juror about whether the reason was sufficient to establish the innocence? Why?

1:25 Find a real (but very short) argument that you have heard someone offer or that you have read somewhere (perhaps in a newspaper, a book, or a magazine—perhaps an editorial, a letter to the editor, or a "Dear Abby" argument). Write it down or photocopy it. Apply the six basic elements of critical thinking to this argument. Briefly report your results in writing. If the argument you consider is only part of the total argument, then indicate that part and label it. Remember that an argument is an attempt to establish or justify a conclusion. Before you start working on your selection, ask yourself, "Is someone trying to establish or justify a conclusion here?" If not, look further.

1:26 Develop a plan for a position paper. Suggest a tentative thesis and a rough idea of your argument in the form of an outline.

Suggested Answers for Chapter 1

Reminder: If used wisely, a set of suggested answers can be of great help to you in your study and practice. Wise use calls for you to do the items, problems, and questions first, and then look up the suggested answers. Do not peek at an answer before making a reasonable effort. If a suggested answer does not agree with yours, then try to figure out why. Perhaps yours is wrong, but perhaps yours is just different, but quite good. In any case, try to make sure that you understand why the suggested answer is what it is. Ask your instructor for help, if necessary.

For the True–False items, I shall first list the True–False answers and then suggest acceptable revisions of the False items. Remember that there are other acceptable revisions, and sometimes other acceptable answers, depending on how you interpret the question and the situation.

Check-Up 1A

1:1 F   1:2 T   1:3 T   1:4 F   1:5 T

1:1 As defined here, an argument is an attempt to prove or establish a conclusion, and consists of a conclusion and one or more reasons offered in support of the conclusion. (Just the first part of this definition would have been enough, but I chose here to give more.)

1:4 The details of the situation are always important in making decisions.

1:6 A   1:7 A   1:8 N   1:9 N   1:10 A   1:11 N

1:12 A   1:13 N

Check-Up 1B

1:14 T   1:15 T   1:16 F   1:17 F   1:18 F   1:19 F

1:20 F   1:21 F   1:22 T

1:16 It is generally a good idea to ask whether there are alternative possible conclusions that are as well, or better, supported.

1:17 To ask whether the reasons are themselves believable is often a good idea.

1:18 The main points of the overview are to check to catch any errors made previously, to see how everything fits together, and to make sure that you have evidenced the critical thinking dispositions.

1:19 The ideas in this course can be misused.

1:20 Showing that an argument is bad does not by itself show that the conclusion is wrong.

1:21 In deciding whether to believe a conclusion, the primary issues are whether the reasons are acceptable and whether they give sufficient support for the conclusion.

1:23 This is up to you. I hope you were brief.

1:24 That would be reason to judge the support insufficient, because calling somebody nasty names is not sufficient reason for killing.

1:25 This is up to you. I hope you had an easy time finding a short, interesting argument.

1:26 This is up to you. Please continue to develop this as you proceed through this book.

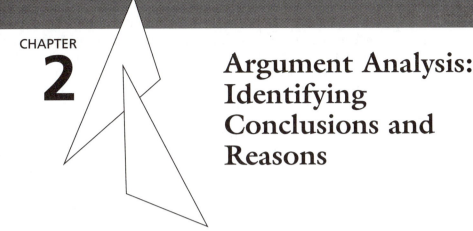

CHAPTER 2

Argument Analysis: Identifying Conclusions and Reasons

Before you can be confident in your judgment about an argument, you must know what the argument is. The first thing to do is to determine the focus (the *F* in *FRISCO*). In an argument, the focus is the conclusion—the thing that the arguer is trying to get us to accept. So the first thing to do is to identify the conclusion.

Generally, the second thing to do is to identify the reasons (the "R") offered in support of the conclusion. In preparation for judging the inference (the "I"), it is also usually helpful to make a deliberate effort to see how the conclusion and the reasons fit together. These activities of argument analysis are not always as easy as they seem, and they are the concerns of this chapter. In later chapters, we will look at deciding whether to accept reasons and inferences. Here our concern is just to figure out what are the reasons and conclusions and to figure out their relationships to each other.

The Murder Trial

The murder trial I mentioned earlier will be the source of a number of my examples, so I shall give some more background about it. I have changed some features in order to protect privacy and have unavoidably omitted a number of details of the situation.

Arlene Burr was on trial for the murder of her boyfriend, Al Hamilton. Arlene, 22, was living with her parents that cold night in January when it happened. Arlene and Al had been out in his car, and returned at about 11 P.M. According to the prosecutor, Arlene was jealous because Al was going with another woman, and she lured him into the dining room and stabbed him in the heart. He died within five minutes of the stabbing. There were no witnesses to the stabbing, although there were people in nearby rooms.

Although he agreed that there were no witnesses, the defense attorney had a different account. He claimed that Al Hamilton chased Arlene into the dining room after threatening to kill her, and she simply tried to defend herself with a carving knife that happened to be lying on the table.

Arlene was charged not only with murder, but also with the lesser charge of voluntary manslaughter. The prosecutor thought that if he could not get a murder conviction, he could at least get a conviction for voluntary manslaughter. The jury had to decide about each charge. We were told that if she was guilty of murder, then she was also guilty of voluntary manslaughter. We were also told that it was possible for her to be guilty of voluntary manslaughter without being guilty of murder. Later I will state what was involved in each charge. For now, I will only note that for each it was required that the State prove beyond a reasonable doubt that Arlene performed the act that caused the death of Al Hamilton. This was the first of several things to be proven to establish that it was murder. It was also the first of several things to be proven to establish voluntary manslaughter. A complete specification of the conditions for each charge appears in Chapter 6.

At the end of the trial, the prosecuting and defense attorneys each had a chance to summarize their cases for the jury. As one might expect, one of the prosecutor's conclusions in his summary argument was that Arlene performed the act that caused Al's death. Here is a portion of his summary argument for this conclusion (with the paragraphs numbered for reference):

1. Members of the jury, it is clear that Arlene performed the act that caused Al's death. Let me remind you of some of the important facts that establish this conclusion.

2. The most important fact is that on the witness stand she admitted stabbing him. She said that she picked up the knife and stabbed him in the chest with it. Obviously she would not have admitted it if she had not done it, so she did stab him.

3. The pathologist who examined the body said that there was only one knife wound, and that was in Al's chest. The pathologist also said that this one knife wound was the cause of death. Arlene's knife stroke must have caused his death.

4. You might think that Arlene is not strong enough to stab someone that seriously, but remember that the knife stroke was not a powerful one. This is because the knife stroke went in only about 2.5 inches and did not touch any bones. The pathologist testified to this.

5. There was no one else in the dining room at the time of the stabbing. It is clear that Arlene did not mention anyone else. Neither did her parents. Because they did not mention anyone else, obviously there was no one else.

6. The first person to touch the body after the stabbing was the ambulance driver, who reported that he arrived to find Al dead five minutes after Arlene's father called in. Her father said that he called as soon as Arlene came into her parents' bedroom with a bloody knife in her hand. Her father also said that he prevented anyone from entering the dining room until the ambulance driver did so.

7. We must therefore conclude that, although she loved him, Arlene did perform the act that caused Al Hamilton's death.

Conclusions and Reasons

The final conclusion in this part of the prosecutor's summary speech is this proposition: "Arlene performed the act that caused Al's death." There are several reasons for picking this one. I will consider these reasons and talk about various criteria for identifying conclusions and reasons. (By *criteria* I mean rules or guides for making a judgment.)

Criteria (or Cues) for Identifying Conclusions

One excellent criterion for something's being a conclusion is the author's (or speaker's) calling it a conclusion. In the prosecutor's Paragraph 1, he did just this.

In the first sentence of Paragraph 7, the prosecutor used two other clear conclusion indicators: "therefore" and "conclude." The use of either of these indicator words is a very reliable criterion for identifying a conclusion. (He did not need two indicators here. Sometimes people use more than one for emphasis.)

Here is a list of some words that we often use to indicate that a conclusion is coming next:

therefore	it follows that
hence	the following is my conclusion
thus	here is my conclusion
so	we must conclude that

These indicators are not always present, but when they are present you should take advantage of them. They introduce something that the speaker or writer wants to conclude. Furthermore, you should use one of these or some other clear indicator when you want to be absolutely sure that your audience knows what your conclusion is.

The word *because* (and sometimes the word *since*) is also a valuable indicator. It tells us that a reason comes next. This often means that the *other* part of the sentence is a conclusion. The last sentence of Paragraph 5 starts with the word *because*. This word introduces a reason: "they did not mention anyone else." The other part of the sentence, "there obviously was no one else," is a conclusion. Note, however, that it is not the main conclusion of the whole passage. It is only the conclusion of the fifth paragraph. The prosecutor's argument then consists of one main conclusion, supported by a number of subconclusions, or intermediate conclusions.

Often, the conclusion appears at either the beginning or the end of a paragraph or passage, and sometimes at both the beginning and the end. The prosecutor's main conclusion appears at the beginning of the passage and at the end of the passage.

Writers and speakers often put the conclusion at the beginning in order to get your attention and to enable you to see why they are saying the things they do. This is a good practice, especially when the topic and the reasoning are complex. On the other hand, sometimes people put the conclusion at the end to make it clear what they hope to have accomplished. It is often a good idea to do both—to put the conclusion at both the beginning and the end.

However, placement is not a thoroughly reliable criterion. People sometimes put their conclusions in the middle, and sometimes they do not even state them explicitly at all, leaving it up to you to figure it out. But searching around at the beginning and at the end of a passage is helpful. The conclusion is often in one place or the other (or both).

Conclusion-Suggesting Emphasis Terms: Must, Should, Etc.

Often, when there is no clear conclusion indicator, the conclusion has an emphasis term such as *must* or *should* in it, suggesting that it is the conclusion. This happens at the end of Paragraph 3: "Arlene's knife stroke must have caused his death." One of the signs suggesting that this is the conclusion is the word *must*, which is used for emphasis here. The prosecutor is saying that the evidence forces us to accept the conclusion that Arlene's knife stroke caused the death. Unfortunately, the word *must* (and others like it) have other functions, so they are not very reliable indicators.

Check-Up 2A

True or False?

If a statement is false, change it to make it true. Try to do so in a way that shows that you understand.

2:1 The conclusion rarely comes at the beginning or end of a passage.

2:2 The word *because* introduces a reason.

2:3 The word *because* often indicates that the part of the sentence not introduced by this word is a conclusion.

2:4 If a sentence does not appear at the beginning or end of a passage, then it is not the conclusion.

2:5 The word *therefore* introduces a conclusion.

2:6 The word *so* introduces a reason.

2:7 A criterion is a guide for making a decision.

Short Answer

2:8 At the end of Paragraph 2, the words "she did stab him" appear. Is this a conclusion? Why?

2:9 In Paragraph 4, the word *because* does not introduce a conclusion; it introduces a reason. Write out the conclusion this reason supports. Pick this conclusion from the same paragraph, and pick one that is actually stated in the paragraph.

2:10 Write out a short argument of your own containing at least one reason and a conclusion. Use some indicator word that enables others to know that the conclusion comes next. Draw a circle around this indicator word and underline your conclusion twice.

2:11 What is the prosecutor trying to prove in Paragraph 4, taken by itself? Why do you think this is the conclusion of Paragraph 4?

Identification

For each of the following arguments (2:12 through 2:23), (a) underline the conclusion twice and (b) if there is a word that indicates that a conclusion comes next, draw a circle around it. Then (c) underline once each reason offered to support the conclusion and (d) make a box around any words that indicate that a reason comes next. The first two are done as examples:

2:12 Jane's baseball glove is missing. (So) she went to the park today.

2:13 Jane went to the park today. I know this because her glove is missing.

Before you do these things, be clear about what pieces of paper you will use to show the results to your instructor. If your instructor has not made a suggestion, then I suggest that you photocopy these items and do the suggested work on the copy, to be given to your instructor. You have permission to photocopy these items for this purpose. If you do not have access to a photocopier, write out the sentences on a separate piece of paper.

2:14 Because Arthur plays chess slowly and carefully, this will be a long game.

2:15 Eggs boiled at high altitude take much longer to cook. Therefore, you should boil this egg for a longer time.

2:16 The unexamined life is not worth living. I know this to be true because Socrates said so.

2:17 It is obvious that she loved him. So she did not kill him.

2:18 Because the pathologist found only one wound on the victim's body, that wound must be the one she caused.

2:19 A twenty-two-year-old woman could not do such a thing to someone she loved. She could not even have struck at him with a knife. Therefore, someone else did it.

2:20 Rooms with light-colored walls are well-lighted. Because Mr. Martinez says that Monique's room is not well-lighted, we can conclude that it does not have light-colored walls.

2:21 Because Charles Dickens describes people and events in great detail, Jonathan will no doubt be reading that book for a long time.

2:22 She must have hated him. He was going with another woman, wasn't he?

2:23 Tom Jeffers could not have killed Al Hamilton. Tom was in the local hospital from 10 P.M. to midnight and Al was killed at about 11:05 P.M.

Reasons and Intermediate Conclusions

Often a conclusion serves as a reason for another conclusion. Then it is called an intermediate conclusion. For example, the conclusion of Paragraph 5, "There was no one else in the dining room at the time," is in turn a reason for the conclusion of the part of the prosecutor's speech that you read, "Arlene performed the act that caused Al Hamilton's death." This conclusion, given the rest of the prosecutor's summary speech, was a reason for the prosecutor's ultimate conclusions, "Arlene is guilty of murder" and "Arlene is guilty of voluntary manslaughter."

In order to avoid confusion, let us limit the use of the label *intermediate conclusion* to any conclusion supporting another conclusion that is part of the passage under consideration. Otherwise, almost every conclusion would be called an intermediate conclusion.

Nonindicators

Some Words that Signal Importance

One set of words in the first paragraph, although it does introduce the main conclusion, is not a reliable indicator that what comes next is a conclusion of the reasoning that is presented. Those words are "it is clear that." Sometimes, such words are used instead to introduce a reason that is not defended in the surrounding line of reasoning. Note their use in Paragraph 5 to introduce a reason. Other words that can introduce either a conclusion or a reason are *obviously* and *there is no doubt that*. Note the word *obviously* in the last sentence in Paragraph 2 and in the last sentence of Paragraph 5. In one place it introduces a reason; in the other, a conclusion. These kinds of words, although they generally introduce statements that are important, are not reliable indicators of a conclusion. They express the speaker's (or author's) self-confidence and sometimes serve to intimidate people. Beware of being intimidated by such words.

Because I have so often seen such terms used to introduce statements that are not at all obvious, I make a practice of deliberately checking to see whether things called obvious really are obvious. I recommend this practice to you. It applies to expressions such as *it is obvious, it is clear that, there is no doubt that,* and *of course.* (Do not use such terms to hide the weaknesses in your own arguments or to intimidate people. Instead, have good arguments!)

Contrast Words

The word *although* is an important word in arguments. Note that the prosecutor used it in the last paragraph when he said, "although she loved him." Usually, the word *although* indicates something that is neither a reason nor a conclusion. It usually introduces something that contrasts with what the person is trying to show. Other language that does the same thing is the phrase *despite the fact that*.

It is often good persuasive strategy to admit something that you realize is clearly true and that might be used in an argument against you. When you admit such a thing, you reduce the dramatic element that someone arguing in the other direction might try to use against you. You also make clear that you have considered the bearing of this fact on your case and have decided that it is not enough to make you change your mind. If you had not considered it, you might be faulted for having overlooked something important. Contrast words provide a good way to introduce such an admission.

For example, when the prosecutor conceded, "although she loved him," he showed that he was aware that Arlene's loving Al could be used to argue that she would not kill him. He showed that he had considered this argument and decided that it was not strong enough to counteract the powerful argument he offered for his case. He conceded what he had to concede, and showed the jury that someone offering the argument (the prosecutor himself) had given consideration to this possibly damaging fact.

Starting a paragraph or a presentation with *although* also has the value of helping to make your presentation more interesting. It sets up a paradox, or a conflict that the listener will often want resolved. Consider this strong beginning of another speech given by the prosecutor (made at the beginning of the trial, not the end):

> Members of the jury, although Arlene loved Al Hamilton, she murdered him. In fact, she murdered him because she loved him.

Note the contrast and concession at the beginning of Paragraph 4: "You might think that Arlene is not strong enough to stab someone that seriously, but remember that the knife stroke was not a powerful one." The phrasing "You might think that . . ., but . . . ," often suggests that the opposite (or the denial) of what you might think is really the conclusion. In Paragraph 4, this is so. That is, "Arlene is strong enough to stab someone that seriously" is the conclusion of Paragraph 4. (I will consider this example in greater detail later on.)

There are a variety of other devices that indicate something important that a speaker wants to get across without necessarily indicating a conclusion. Trying to list them all is unnecessary because you probably have the idea by now. To check this, I ask you to think about whether the words *but* and *however* are conclusion indicators. Always? Sometimes? Never? Can you give some examples to support your answer?

The "Therefore" Test

When there are no clear conclusion indicators, it is sometimes helpful to use the "therefore" test. To do this, you take each proposition you are considering as a possible conclusion (one at a time), move it to the end of the passage, insert the word "therefore" in front of the proposition, and see which result makes the most sense. Consider this example:

Example 2:1

The streets are very slippery. Lynn should not ride her bike.

Assuming that this is an argument, which is the conclusion? First take the slippery streets proposition, put it last, and insert *therefore* in front of it:

Example 2:2

Lynn should not ride her bike. Therefore, the streets are slippery.

Now do it the other way:

Example 2:3

The streets are slippery. Therefore, Lynn should not ride her bike.

Example 2:3 makes the most sense to me in the situation as I imagine it, so I pick as the conclusion, "Lynn should not ride her bike."

However, the "therefore" test does not always give the answer. Consider this example, offered by the defense attorney:

Example 2:4

She did not intend to kill him. The knife stroke was delivered with only moderate force.

Here are the two possible results in applying the test:

Example 2:5

The knife stroke was delivered with only moderate force. Therefore, she did not intend to kill him.

Example 2:6

She did not intend to kill him. Therefore, the knife stroke was delivered with only moderate force.

Both results make sense to me before we take the Situation (the *S* in *FRISCO*) into account. Consider the situation: Who said the sentences in Example 2:4 and what was his role in the trial? Assuming that the selection is intended to be an argument, it makes more sense for the defense attorney to have 2:5 in mind because it argues for a conclusion that he wanted us to accept. Considering the situation in which the argument arises helps us then to decide which is the conclusion.

Even though the "therefore" test does not always give the answer by itself, it is a useful device. It often clearly reveals the conclusion, and usually is at least of some help. Because it is the writer's intended conclusion that we are trying to determine in this chapter, we often cannot be sure that we have determined it. Sometimes writers themselves are not sure what they are trying to prove, and often what they say can legitimately be interpreted in different ways. For some examples, look at the letters to the editor in your local newspaper. However, despite this difficulty, the "therefore" test is often very helpful.

Check-Up 2B

True or False?

If a statement is false, change it to make it true. Try to do so in a way that shows that you understand.

2:24 The word *although* often introduces a conclusion.

2:25 The word *obviously* often introduces something that is not obvious.

2:26 The word *obviously* generally indicates that a conclusion comes next.

2:27 The word *must* is sometimes used to introduce a conclusion.

2:28 When using the "therefore" test, select as the conclusion the statement that makes most sense when it follows the word *therefore*.

2:29 A conclusion can also be a reason for another conclusion.

Short Answer

For each of the following arguments, (a) underline the conclusion twice and (b) draw a circle around any words that clearly indicate that a conclusion comes next. Then (c) underline once each reason offered to support a conclusion and (d) make a box around any words that indicate that a reason comes next. If any proposition is both a reason and conclusion in the passage (an intermediate conclusion), it would then be triple-underlined. If you have any doubt that you have identified the conclusion, use the "therefore" test. Remember that because you are trying to figure out the writer's intentions, there are sometimes legitimate alternative interpretations, especially because these examples appear out of context. As before, either do all this on a photocopy of these pages or copy the items by hand if your instructor has not made an alternative suggestion.

2:30 Although he died, the knife stroke was delivered with only moderate force. We can conclude this because the knife penetrated only 2.5 inches and did not touch any bone.

2:31 She must not have intended to kill him. The knife stroke was delivered with only moderate force. So she is not guilty.

2:32 Obviously she was strong enough to do the job, although she is not very strong. The knife stroke was delivered with only moderate force.

2:33 Although Martine was on the scene, she did not see the accident. Here's how I know: Martine always tells us when important things happen, and she did not even mention the accident.

2:34 Traffic on Poplar Road must be changed from two-way to one-way. There is too much traffic on this road now and there are frequent collisions.

2:35 Because the prosecuting attorney proved conclusively that the defendant killed the victim, it has been proven beyond a reasonable doubt that the defendant performed the act that caused the death of the victim. The first condition for a murder verdict is satisfied.

2:36 There is no doubt that a very important feature of our legal system is that a defendant is considered innocent until proved guilty. But the public does not seem to believe this. Obviously we need a broad public-information campaign about that feature of our system.

2:37 Jones can never be elected to the presidency. She has a questionable background and has a habit of irritating people with her penetrating questions. This is obvious to me, although I realize that she would make an excellent president. However, we need her on our side. So let's make her Chair of the Rules Committee.

More Short Answer

2:38 Write out an argument in which you use the words *although, obviously,* and *must*.

2:39 Are the words *but* and *however* conclusion indicators? Give examples to support your answer.

Propositions with Two or More Parts

A proposition is a complete thought that can be asserted separately and meaningfully by itself. *Jane's baseball glove is missing* is a proposition in this sense. So is *She went to the park today.*

Although reasons and conclusions are not always simple separate propositions, they are simple and separate in the following argument:

Example 2:7

Jane's baseball glove is missing. So she went to the park today.

But in the following example, the two propositions that are the reason and the conclusion are combined to make a larger proposition.

Example 2:8

Because Jane's baseball glove is missing, she went to the park today.

One important thing to notice about the combination is that the writer is still asserting the two separate propositions: that Jane's glove is missing and that Jane went to the park today. The writer is also asserting the complex proposition that is the whole of Example 2:8. But consider this complex proposition:

Example 2:9

If Jane's baseball glove is missing, then she went to the park today.

Here the writer is not claiming that Jane's baseball glove is missing, nor that Jane went to the park today. Rather, the writer is only claiming one thing, the whole thing. In Example 2:9, the second part ("she went to the park today") is not a conclusion for which the writer is arguing. Neither is the first part ("Jane's baseball glove is missing") a reason that the writer is offering in support of a conclusion. The writer is only saying that the first part (the "if" part) would, if true, be enough to establish the second part. Although the two propositions can be meaningfully asserted by themselves, they are not separately asserted in Example 2:9.

One practical consequence of this is that in identifying reasons and conclusions, you generally do not break *if–then* propositions into their separate parts. But you do break *since, because, although,* and other similar propositions into their separate parts because both parts are asserted. Generally, the whole *if–then* proposition is a reason, or even sometimes the conclusion, but it is always treated as a whole. Often the arguer does in addition want to assert one part or the other of an *if–then* proposition. But in asserting only the *if–then* proposition, the arguer is not thereby asserting one or both of its parts.

This leads us to the second practical consequence: When you assert an *if–then* proposition, you ordinarily commit yourself to a relationship between the parts, but you generally do not commit yourself to the truth of the parts. For example, if you asserted the sentence in Example 2:9, you would not thereby commit yourself to Jane's glove's being missing, nor to her being in the park. Rather, you would commit yourself to the idea that her glove's being missing would be sufficient to establish that she went to the park. Furthermore, you would commit yourself to the idea that her not having gone to the park would be enough to establish that her glove is not missing. This last commitment is more difficult to grasp, and will be discussed in Chapter 6.

How would you apply these ideas to sentences containing the word *when* or *whenever*? Here is an example of such a sentence: "When the Dodgers win, I am happy." Another: "Whenever it rains, the streets are wet." Think about it.

Figuring Out the Conclusion

Earlier in this unit, we considered some conclusion indicators that are right before your eyes, such as *therefore, so,* and placement in a passage. Sometimes, however, you must figure out the conclusion that was intended when the clues are less obvious and the "therefore" test does not settle it. The general question to ask is this one: Given the things that the author said and the situation (the *S* in *FRISCO*) in which they were said, what makes the most sense for the author to be concluding? I shall suggest three loose criteria to help decide. The first two of these criteria really are just an expansion of the "therefore" test.

Three Criteria for Identifying Conclusions

Consider Paragraph 4 of the prosecutor's speech:

> You might think that Arlene is not strong enough to stab someone that seriously, but remember that the knife stroke was not a powerful one. This is because the knife stroke went in only about 2.5 inches and did not touch any bones. The pathologist testified to this.

The conclusion is, "Arlene is strong enough to stab someone that seriously." Let us see how this choice satisfies three criteria for figuring out what the conclusion is. Here is the first criterion:

1. Usually the conclusion somehow contributes to the author's goals, the more directly the better.

Here is the reason for this first criterion: If a conclusion did not in any way contribute to the author's goals, then we would wonder why the author bothered to offer it. (This contribution need not be a narrow one, by the way. The conclusion might just satisfy the author's curiosity.)

One of the prosecutor's goals was to make a good case. If Arlene were not strong enough to have done the job, then the case would be very weak, so the conclusion contributed to his goal.

Here is the second criterion:

2. A proposition that is the conclusion is probably supported by one or more others.

Here is the reason for this second criterion. People offering arguments try to make the conclusion follow from, or at least be supported by, the rest of the argument. They usually succeed, so one likely characteristic of a conclusion is that it is supported in the passage. People do not always succeed in supporting their conclusions, so we cannot insist that the conclusion follow from the rest of the argument, or even be supported by it. Furthermore, often several propositions follow from or are supported by the rest of the argument. So this criterion is just a rough one. It gives us a rough necessary condition for something's being a conclusion.

Consider again the proposition "Arlene is strong enough to stab someone that seriously." Although it does not necessarily follow from the rest, it follows in the sense that the rest of the paragraph is enough to establish the conclusion.

Suppose that we are considering the proposition "The pathologist testified to this" as a possible alternative conclusion. This proposition does not seem to follow from or be supported by the rest of the paragraph. So we do not pick "The pathologist testified to this" as the conclusion, even though it comes at the end of the paragraph. Note that the "therefore" test gives the same result.

Remember that this criterion does not say that the conclusion must actually receive support from the rest of the passage. It says only that if a proposition is not supported by other things in the passage, then it might well not be the conclusion. Here is a case in which a proposition is a conclusion, although it receives little or no legitimate support from the reason that is offered:

"Because the Prime Minister uses Shino Toothpaste, you should use it."

The conclusion, "You should use it," is not well-supported, but that does not show that it is not the conclusion. The author of the statement *intended* it to be the conclusion.

Here is the third criterion:

3. Generally a conclusion of a passage should use most or all of the passage for its support. If two propositions are supported in a passage, then the one using the greater amount of the passage is probably the conclusion.

Can you see the basis for this criterion? I assume that arguers generally have a reason for what they do. If there is a sentence in an argument that does not contribute to the conclusion, then we wonder why that sentence is there. If we pick as the conclusion something that makes that sentence part of the argument, then we no longer have to explain away the presence of that sentence.

Note that this criterion assumes that people do not include irrelevant material in their arguments. This assumption is sometimes wrong, so this criterion is also a rough one, requiring you to use your judgment.

Suppose that the two candidates for the conclusion of Paragraph 4 are:

A. Arlene is strong enough to stab someone that seriously.
B. The knife stroke was not a powerful one.

Each of these follows from other things said in the paragraph. However, we choose A as the conclusion of the paragraph because it uses for its support all of the support that B uses (the last two sentences) and B itself. A uses more of the paragraph for its support than B, so A is the conclusion.

Let us apply these three criteria to another example. Assuming that the following is an argument, what is its conclusion? Why?

Defense Attorney: "She did not mean to kill him. She loved him."

Let us call the first sentence C and the second sentence D:

C. She did not mean to kill him.
D. She loved him.

Which is the conclusion? C satisfies the first criterion better than D. It would contribute to the defense attorney's goals more directly than D. If C is accepted by the jury, that helps to get Arlene acquitted. If D is accepted by the jury, that only helps to get C accepted.

Applying the second criterion, each could be used to support the other, but D supports C better than C supports D in this situation. So, by the second criterion, C comes out ahead, though not overwhelmingly. C is better supported in the passage. (Can you think of a situation in which Criterion 2 would support the choice of D?)

On the third criterion, they come out equal. Each could use the other for its support, so each has one other idea in the passage to support it. Each could use all of the rest (in this case "the rest" is only one sentence) for its support.

Putting the results together, we should choose C as the conclusion, given the trial situation. Note the important role played by the situation (the *S* in *FRISCO*) in deciding what the conclusion is.

Apply these criteria to another example, which is part of Item 2:37 in Check-Up 2B:

> Jones can never be elected to the presidency. She has a questionable background and has a habit of irritating people with her penetrating questions. This is obvious to me, although I realize that she would make an excellent president.

What is the conclusion? Even if you know already, please work through it with me. First of all, the material following the word *although* is probably not the conclusion, because *although* is a contrast word. So the proposition "I realize that she would make an excellent president" is not the conclusion. That leaves the first two sentences as possibilities. Let us label them E and F:

E. Jones can never be elected to the presidency.
F. She has a questionable background and has a habit of irritating people with her penetrating questions.

Which one is the conclusion, if either? The fact that E comes at the beginning counts in favor of its being the conclusion, but that does not settle the matter. Let us apply the three criteria. Because we do not know the situation or the author, we cannot be sure what would contribute to the goals of the author, but E is more likely to contribute directly to someone's goals than F, so E is slightly favored.

The most important consideration here is the second criterion. It calls for us to decide which supports which. Could E plausibly be used to support F? Could F plausibly be used to support E? The answers are probably "No" and "Yes," respectively. E more plausibly follows from the other part than does F. Hence, the selection of E is strongly supported.

Next, let us attempt to apply the third criterion. Because only one part of the argument (E) is supported by the rest, it uses more of the rest for its support than any other part, so E is again preferred.

All the signs point to E's being the conclusion, and the second criterion points to it very strongly. There is no reason to think that the conclusion has been left unstated. So we should choose E.

Unstated Conclusions

Sometimes people do not explicitly state their conclusions. You must figure them out by making one or more intelligent guesses and checking them with the "therefore" test or the three conclusion-identification criteria just discussed. The conclusion in Example 2:10 is not stated. Can you figure it out?

Example 2:10

If Sean were in school, then the soccer ball would be in the box. But the soccer ball is not in the box.

The one conclusion that occurs to me is that Sean is not in school. It satisfies the "therefore" test. In the situation in which I heard the argument, it also satisfied the three criteria for identifying conclusions. In that situation, it quite probably was the conclusion.

+ *Because* in Explanations That Try to Account for Something

The word *because* (or *since*) does not always indicate that the other part of the sentence is a conclusion. Sometimes it introduces something that is supposed to account for something else. Then, instead of introducing reasons for conclusions in arguments, it introduces explanatory factors. Here is an example (quoted earlier):

She killed him because she loved him.

In the trial, this was an explanation, not an argument. Here the prosecutor was not directly trying to prove that she killed him. Instead, he was trying to explain why she killed him. *She loved him* was not a reason offered to show that a conclusion is true. Rather, the prosecutor was assuming that she killed him, and was using the proposition "She loved him" to explain why.

This distinction between arguments and explanations is sometimes a tricky one, so be wary. Actually, there are several kinds of explanations, and this is only a distinction between arguments and causal explanations. Causal explanations try to account for something. The prosecutor in the example gave a causal explanation of her killing Al. The proposed cause was her love for Al.

A practical test to distinguish arguments from causal explanations goes as follows: If the consequence is assumed to be true in the situation, then you probably have a causal explanation. If, in the situation, the speaker is trying to prove the consequence, then it is probably an argument. In our example, the consequence (that she killed Al) was assumed to be true, so it was a causal explanation, not an argument.

In a way, of course, the whole explanation was part of an argument offered in support of the conclusion that she is guilty. If the prosecutor could not have produced an explanatory motive (a cause or partial cause), then it would have been harder for the jury to believe that she did the deed. In Chapters 8 and 9, we shall look more deeply at the role of explanation in arguments.

The main point for now is that sometimes passages that look like arguments for a particular conclusion are not that at all. Rather, they are attempts to account for a consequence. In such a situation, the goal is not to prove a proposition that might look like a conclusion. Rather, the truth of that proposition (for example, "She killed him") is taken for granted and the passage tries to account for it (that is, to explain why the event happened).

If you try to apply FRISCO to an explanation and treat the consequence as the conclusion, you will run into trouble. This is because FRISCO is aimed at deciding whether to accept the conclusion. Generally, in the account-for type of explanation, the proposition that looks like a conclusion is already assumed to be true, so the decision about that proposition is already made.

Summary So Far

So far in this chapter, the primary concern has been with the first two elements of the FRISCO approach to argument judgment: 1) Focus (identifying the conclusion) and 2) Reasons (identifying the reasons, though not judging them). You have considered indicators that point to the conclusion and reasons in an argument. These include *therefore, so, because,* and placement in a passage. You have seen and used the "therefore" test. You have also considered three criteria that are more precise than the "therefore" test:

1. A conclusion is likely to contribute to the author's goals.
2. A proposition that is the conclusion is probably supported by one or more others.
3. Generally, a conclusion should use most or all of the passage for its support. If two propositions are supported in a passage, then the one using a greater amount of the passage is probably the conclusion.

The "therefore" test and the three criteria can also be used in identifying conclusions that are not explicitly stated. Make one or more intelligent guesses, and apply the test or criteria.

You have seen that the two parts of an *if–then* proposition are generally treated as one whole unit, although those parts are often asserted or denied at another point. You have seen that *if–then* propositions can be reasons and conclusions of arguments.

+You have also seen that the words *because* and *since* do not always introduce reasons in arguments. Sometimes, they introduce propositions that are intended to explain why something occurred. That is, they introduce propositions that are intended to account for something else, not prove it.

As a result of your study of this chapter so far, you should be more adept at picking out conclusions and the reasons offered to support them. When it is not your own conclusion that you are identifying, it is not always possible to be confident that you have succeeded in identifying it. The intentions of other people are sometimes difficult to discern, and some writers and speakers are just not clear. So the identification of someone else's conclusion is a matter about which reasonable people might differ. For example, you might reasonably differ with some of the proposed answers at the end of this chapter. Still, you should have more justified confidence in your ability to identify the parts of an argument.

This identification of conclusions and reasons is related to the other elements of critical thinking. That is, you sometimes need to judge the inferences in order to guess what it would have been reasonable for the author to have concluded. So you also had a little practice in this chapter at making decisions about whether to accept the reasons and the inferences in an argument. The rest of this book focuses on these decisions.

Check-Up 2C

True or False?
If false, change it to make it true. Try to do so in a way that shows that you understand.

2:40 The conclusion is likely to contribute somehow to the author's goals.

2:41 If two propositions are supported in a passage and both contribute to the author's goals, then the one using a greater amount of the passage for its support is probably the conclusion.

2:42 The parts of an *if–then* proposition are generally not asserted separately in the proposition, although they might elsewhere be asserted separately.

2:43 An *if–then* proposition can be the conclusion of an argument.

2:44 An *if–then* proposition can be a reason in an argument.

2:45 The word *because* always introduces a proposition that serves as a reason in an argument.

2:46 The "if" part of a proposition is a reason in an argument containing the proposition.

2:47 The "because" part of a proposition generally cannot be separated off and called a reason.

Short Answer
For each of the following arguments, underline, circle, and box as before. If the final conclusion is not explicitly asserted on its own, add what you think is the final conclusion and underline it twice. As before, either photocopy these pages and present the marked photocopies or copy them by hand if your instructor has not made other arrangements.

2:48 If you boil an egg at high altitude, then it takes much longer to cook it. Therefore, you should boil this egg for a long time.

2:49 If Monique's room has light-colored walls, then it is well-lighted. Because Mr. Martinez says that her room is not well-lighted, we can conclude that it does not have light-colored walls.

2:50 If the public does not realize that people are to be considered innocent until proven guilty, then there will continue to be mistreatment of perfectly innocent people. Hence we need a broad public-information campaign about this feature of our system.

2:51 Men generally have difficulty being sensitive to others. If it is desirable for our society to consist of fully developed human beings, then people who are sensitive should make a special effort to help those who are not. Generally, this means that women should make a special effort to help men to be more sensitive. I say this even though some might feel that it places an unfair burden on women.

2:52 Women generally do not have confidence in themselves, or else they find it difficult to maintain confidence. Therefore, if we are to achieve true equality, hiring preference should be given to women in cases where men outnumber women. To some people this might at first appear to be unfair to men, but I think that on reflection they will change their minds.

More Short Answer

For each of the following arguments, pick the conclusion of the whole argument and tell why you think it is the conclusion.

2:53 Prosecutor: Tom Jeffers did not do the deed. He was in the hospital at the time.

2:54 Defense Attorney: She was defending herself against attack. He threatened to kill her.

2:55 Juror: She said that he said that he would kill her. But if he had wanted to kill her, he would have done so before they got in the house. He had plenty of time and a good opportunity. (Note: This argument was used in convicting her of voluntary manslaughter.)

2:56 Another juror: The pathologist testified that the knife stroke was only of medium strength. Arlene did not think that she would cause him great bodily harm. She did not commit murder. (Note: The possibility that this is a good argument persuaded the jury to decide that she was not guilty of murder.)

Longer Answer

2:57 Pick the argument of either 2:51 or 2:52 and in about one page apply the six-element FRISCO approach, defending your decision with your reasons. Except for judging the reasons, you have already done the "FR" part. Be prepared to present your analysis, decision, and reasons to the rest of the class.

2:58 Find a very short argument on a newspaper editorial page. Cut it out and do the standard underlining, circling, and drawing of rectangles. If you need to add the conclusion, do so. Then apply the rest of the FRISCO approach to the argument (as well as you can at this time) and report your results in writing. Be sure to include your reasons in defense of your decision. Be prepared to present your analysis, decisions, and reasons to the class.

Still More Short Answers for More Practice

Here are some more arguments. Identify, underline, circle, box and report your results just as before, remembering that you might have to state the conclusion yourself if it is not explicitly asserted in the passage.

Remember that because you are trying to figure out writers' intentions, there might be several legitimate interpretations. Sometimes, there is more than one good answer. For some of the odd-numbered items, proposed answers are deliberately omitted in order to give you more realistic practice.

2:59 Although the sun is shining brightly now, it will be raining before nightfall. Mr. Roberts, our dependable TV weatherman, said so. So we had better postpone our picnic.

2:60 So many kids are getting high school diplomas even though they cannot read. College graduates do not understand percentages. Adults cannot read directions. The solution is simple: The schools should attend to their primary job, the development of basic skills and the intellectual virtues. Because they cannot both do this job well and devote all the resources that are currently devoted to athletics, busing, music, and making students happy, we must conclude that such things should be dropped. Homes, neighborhoods, and religious institutions are able to perform these functions.

2:61 Too many parents are not equipped to provide students with these necessities in development. For various reasons, neighborhoods and religious institutions cannot do the job. The schools, then, must assume these tasks. If not, these educational tasks will not be performed.

2:62 If I do my homework now, I'll miss band practice. If I do it later, my friend's feelings will be hurt. Both of these consequences are unacceptable. The conclusion is obvious.

2:63 Shakespeare never intended Iago to be a melodramatic villain. If he had, then Iago's wife would have been neither so trusting throughout the play *Othello* nor so surprised when she found out the evil things he had done.

2:64 The signers of the Declaration of Independence did not intend to claim that men and women should be considered equal. For one thing, they used the word *men* in the statement, "All men are created equal." For another, it is a historical fact that men and women were not considered equal in 1776 and nothing was done in those days to ensure equal treatment. Women were not even guaranteed the right to vote in the United States until 1920.

2:65 With these dim streetlights, there is a greater chance of crime. The accident rate is clearly higher than it should be. Furthermore, these streetlights, being easy to break, are often damaged by vandals. Mercury-vapor cobra-type streetlights would cost the city very little because the state and federal governments would pay most of the bill. Such streetlights would provide much more light and be vandal-proof. Need I say more?

2:66 NO TO S.B. 833: As the parent of a six-year-old with cystic fibrosis, I urge you to oppose Senate Bill 833 because it would make research on diseases such as cystic fibrosis, cancer, AIDS, and nephrosis much more expensive. Consequently, less research would be done. The bill requires that animals used in research be bred and raised for that purpose, and prohibits the use in research of stray dogs and cats (who would otherwise be put to sleep anyway). It is time to choose between human beings and animals. I choose human beings.

Note: Underlining reasons and conclusions and circling and boxing indicators are complicated tasks for this one, so do not be surprised if you find it frustrating. The alternate system that you are about to encounter is, I believe, easier to use for such complex arguments. In any case, in practical situations some simplification is in order. You might want here simply to identify the main conclusion, the indicators, and the reasons, without distinguishing intermediate conclusions.

Medium Answer

For each of the following arguments (included with permission of the *New York Times*), identify the conclusion and write a paragraph or two defending your belief that the proposition you have identified is actually the conclusion intended by the writer.

> 2:67 PERFORMANCE IS UP, BUT NOT REPUTATION: The public perception is that public schools are flunking. Magazine covers picture an enterprise in disarray. University professors complain, from a safe distance, of an educational wasteland. And why not? Have not reading and Scholastic Aptitude Test scores declined steadily for 18 years?
>
> But most public perception about those things, including education, tends to lag behind reality. It ignores the indicators that for more than a year have been showing an encouraging upward trend in school performance. Reading scores in New York and a number of other cities have taken a decided turn for the better. New Jersey recently reported improvements throughout its entire system.
>
> Nationally, last year's SAT scores have held steady for the first time after almost two decades of decline. But it is fair to suggest that a new emphasis on good teaching and diligent study has had some effect. So, perhaps, has the shelving of pedagogical theory that accorded value to anything students found relevant, or fun.
>
> The nation's schools still have a long way to go to deserve unqualified cheers. But they are starting to succeed again. What a terrible time for people to perceive public education as a lost cause and withdraw adequate support.
>
> 2:68 DISQUALIFIED: Donald Lan is the Secretary of State of New Jersey, which means that he must review the returns of Tuesday's still-undecided election for governor. Mr. Lan is in a curious position, since he was not only an early contender in the Democratic gubernatorial primary, but later became deputy campaign manager for the Democratic candidate, James Florio.
>
> Mr. Florio and the Republican contender, Tom Kean, agree that every effort should be taken to ensure the legitimacy of the ultimate result. That means Mr. Lan ought to step aside. We do not question his honesty, only the appearances. With a near-dead heat for the top office of the state, the appearances of having a partisan certify the results are dead wrong.

An Alternative:
Diagramming the Whole Argument

Sometimes it helps to draw an arrow diagram of an argument in order to make sure you know how the parts are related to each other. The steps are as follows:

1. Enclose each assertion in angle brackets. Then label each assertion with a letter and circle the letter when you put it in the diagram.
2. Start a diagram by putting the letter for the conclusion at the top.
3. Put the letter(s) for the reason(s) underneath and arrange them in a way

that shows what supports what. Show the connections with arrows pointing in the direction of support (up).

Here is an example, using the defense attorney's argument for her innocence (I have inserted the letters A and B).

(A) <My client is innocent of the charge of murder> because (B) <she was defending herself against an attack>.

In the diagram of this simple argument, we put the letter A above the letter B and draw an arrow from B up to A. This shows that B is offered in support of A.

If two or more reasons are offered in support of a conclusion, they all appear below it with arrows going up to it showing their support, as in the following example:

Paragraph 3: (A) <The pathologist who examined the body said that there was only one knife wound> and (B) <that was in Al's chest>. (C) <The pathologist also said that this one knife wound was the cause of death>. (D) <Arlene's knife stroke must have caused his death>.

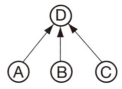

In drawing this diagram, I omitted a refinement that I shall soon discuss.

If one thing supports another, which in turn supports a third, then they make a chain, as in the following argument:

(A) <He threatened to kill her>. (B) <She was defending herself against attack>. (C) <She must be innocent>.

Here is a more complicated one. Check to make sure that you see why each part of the diagram is the way it is.

Paragraph 2: (A) <The most important fact is that on the witness stand she admitted stabbing him>. (B) <She said that she picked up the knife and stabbed him in the chest with it>. Obviously (C) <she would not have admitted it if she had not done it>. Hence, (D) <she did stab him>.

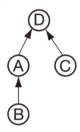

Note that in judging that B was offered in support of A, I neglected the first six words in A. Do you think I was justified in doing so? I again omitted the refinement that I shall soon discuss.

This system for diagramming arguments can be changed or made more elaborate, if it suits your taste. You could even turn the diagrams upside down and call them tree diagrams. This is often done. The main thing is to use it as a tool to represent what you think are the intentions of the writer. Feel free to modify it in whatever way seems helpful. If you want to leave out such unnecessary words as *obviously*, then do so. If it helps you to combine or separate different assertions, then do so. One refinement I like is to distinguish between two ways in which a pair of propositions can support another: jointly (in cooperation) or separately (independently), as in the following diagrams, in which A and B support C jointly and independently:

In my suggested diagrams, I shall use this refinement, and recommend it to you. However, one difficulty with using this refinement is that it is sometimes difficult to tell whether the person making the argument intended the reasons to join together to support the conclusion. A suggestion: If in doubt, diagram them as independent reasons.

Using this joint system, the previous argument from Paragraph 2 in the prosecutor's speech would look like this:

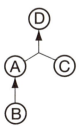

Another refinement is to add what you think are unstated assumptions. However, it is often difficult to identify unstated assumptions in a way that is fair to the arguer, so beware. The process of identifying assumptions is discussed in Chapter 7, but here is an example:

Example 2:11 (based on Item 2:15)

Argument:

(A) <Eggs boiled at high altitude take much longer to cook>. Therefore, (B) <you should boil this egg for a longer time>.

Possible unstated assumption:

(C) <We are at a high altitude>.

A diagram might look like this, using the joining-together system and using square brackets to indicate the unstated assumption:

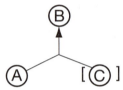

In general, if you do add something that is not explicitly there, mark it with square brackets ([,]).

Feel free to use any other refinement that you find helpful. But make sure that you make clear what your refinement means. Also remember that you cannot separate *if–then* sentences and treat the parts as asserted separately unless the author did so, or intended to do so.

This system only gives a picture of an argument. It does not tell you how strong the argument is. But such a diagram can often help you decide whether to accept an argument because the picture makes the argument more clear. For example, when the reasons join together, if one is false, the other loses its force.

The way to learn to make arrow diagrams is to practice. Do the first set in the Check-Up and compare it with my suggested answers. Then do the second set and compare, and so on. Some answers are deliberately omitted because discussion of arrow diagrams without an "authoritative" answer can be valuable to you. If some seem like busywork, then skip them. The ones at the end will be challenging. Remember that there are different ways of diagramming the same argument because you are trying to represent the writer's intentions, and there are often legitimately different interpretations of people's intentions, especially when you do not know the writer or the situation.

Check-Up 2D

True or False?
If false, change it to make it true. Try to do so in a way that shows you understand.

2:69 Making an arrow diagram of an argument does not tell you how strong the argument is.

2:70 In the system described here, the letter for the conclusion always goes at the top.

2:71 In a three-part argument chain, the intermediate conclusion goes in the middle (in the system described here).

Short Answer

For Items 2:72 through 2:83, make an arrow diagram for each of the arguments in Items 2:12 through 2:23. Label the propositions in order of appearance, with A, B, etc. The first is done as an example:

2:72 (A) <Jane's baseball glove is missing>. So (B) <she went to the park today>.

More Short Answer

For Items 2:84 through 2:91, do the same thing with Items 2:30 through 2:37.

Still More Short Answer

For Items 2:92 through 2:100, do the same thing with Items 2:48 through 2:56.

Still More

For Items 2:101 through 2:107, do the same thing with Items 2:59 through 2:65. Write out the final conclusion if it is not explicitly asserted.

Even More

For Items 2:108 through 2:109, do the same with Paragraphs 5 and 6 of the prosecutor's summary argument.

And Finally

For Items 2:110 through 2:112, do the same thing for Items 2:66 through 2:68. These are difficult but realistic. They are a real test of your diagramming ability and of the value of arrow diagrams to you. If you need to simplify in order to see the big picture, do so.

Longer Answer

2:113 Find an argument in a short editorial, a "Dear Abby" selection, or a letter to an editor. You may use one that you have previously used in this course. Cut it out or copy it.

    a. Underline the final conclusion twice.

    b. Bracket the propositions and assign letters to them.

    c. Represent the argument pictorially in an arrow diagram.

Suggested Answers for Chapter 2

Reminder: In some cases, different answers are as good as the ones given. If one of your answers is different from the one suggested, then either try to satisfy yourself that yours really is all right, or else try to figure out why it is not.

Check-Up 2A

2:1 F   **2:2** T   **2:3** T   **2:4** F   **2:5** T   **2:6** F   **2:7** T

2:1 The conclusion often comes at the beginning or end of a passage.

2:4 If a sentence does not appear at the beginning or end of a passage, it still might be the conclusion.

2:6 The word *so* often introduces a conclusion.

2:8 It is preceded by the word *so* and the rest of the paragraph supports this statement.

2:9 The knife stroke was not a powerful one.

2:10 One possible example: She killed Al. So she performed the act that caused Al's death.

2:11 "Arlene is strong enough to stab someone that seriously." This conclusion must be true if the prosecutor is to get a conviction. Also, the rest of the paragraph supports this conclusion.

2:14 Because Arthur plays chess slowly and carefully, this will be a long game.

2:15 Eggs boiled at high altitude take much longer to cook. Therefore, you should boil this egg for a longer time.

2:16 The unexamined life is not worth living. I know this to be true because Socrates said so.

2:17 It is obvious that she loved him. So she did not kill him.

2:18 Because the pathologist found only one wound on the victim's body, that wound must be the one she caused.

2:19 A twenty-two-year-old woman could not do such a thing to someone she loved. She could not even have struck at him with a knife. Therefore, someone else did it.

2:20 Rooms with light-colored walls are well-lighted. Because Mr. Martinez says that Monique's room is not well-lighted, we can conclude that it does not have light-colored walls.

2:21 Because Charles Dickens describes people and events in great detail, Jonathan will no doubt be reading the book for a long time.

2:22 She must have hated him. He was going with another woman, wasn't he?

2:23 Tom Jeffers could not have killed Al Hamilton. Tom was in the local hospital from 10 P.M. to midnight and Al was killed about 11:05 P.M.

Check-Up 2B

2:24 F   2:25 T   2:26 F   2:27 T   2:28 T   2:29 T

2:24 The word *although* rarely introduces a conclusion.

2:26 The word *obviously* can be used to introduce conclusions, reasons, insults, etc.

2:30 Although he died, the knife stroke was delivered with only moderate force. We can conclude this because the knife penetrated only 2.5 inches and did not touch any bone.

2:31 She must not have intended to kill him. The knife stroke was delivered with only moderate force. So she is not guilty.

2:32 Obviously she was strong enough to do the job, although she is not very strong. The knife stroke was delivered with only moderate force.

2:33 Although Martine was on the scene, she did not see the accident. Here's how I know: Martine always tells us when important things happen, and she did not even mention the accident.

2:34 Traffic on Poplar Road must be changed from two-way to one-way. There is too much traffic on this road now and there are frequent collisions.

2:35 Because the prosecuting attorney proved conclusively that the defendant killed the victim, it has been proven beyond a reasonable doubt that the defendant performed the act that caused the death of the victim. The first condition for a murder verdict is satisfied.

2:36 There is no doubt that a very important feature of our legal system is that a defendant is considered innocent until proved guilty. But the public does not seem to believe this. Obviously we need a broad public-information campaign about that feature of our system.

2:37 Jones can never be elected to the presidency. She has a questionable background and has a habit of irritating people with her penetrating questions. This is obvious to me, although I realize that she would make an excellent president. However, we need her on our side. (So) let's make her Chair of the Rules Committee.

2:38 One possibility: Obviously argument analysis can be difficult. Although some examples are easy to analyze, one must realize that practicing with these can develop one's skills.

2:39 No. The following examples refute the suggestion: 1) "He is old, but not wise. So we cannot depend on him." 2) "She is young. However, she is not wise. So we cannot depend on her."

Check-Up 2C
2:40 T   **2:41** T   **2:42** T   **2:43** T   **2:44** T   **2:45** F
2:46 F   **2:47** F

2:45 Sometimes *because* introduces a reason in an argument, sometimes it indicates an explanation containing the proposition.

2:46 The "if" part of a proposition is often asserted at some other place as a reason in an argument containing the proposition.

2:47 The "because" part of a proposition is generally intended to be asserted on its own.

2:48 If you boil an egg at high altitude, then it takes much longer to cook it. (Therefore,) you should boil this egg for a long time.

2:49 If Monique's room has light-colored walls, then it is well-lighted. Because Mr. Martinez says that her room is not well-lighted, (we can conclude that) it does not have light-colored walls.

2:50 If the public does not realize that people are to be considered innocent until proven guilty, then there will continue to be mistreatment of perfectly innocent people. Hence, we need a broad public-information campaign about this feature of our systems.

2:51 Men generally have difficulty being sensitive to others. If it is desirable for our society to consist of fully developed human beings, then people who are sensitive should make a special effort to help those who are not. Generally, (this means that) women should make a special effort to help men be more sensitive. I say this even though some might feel that it places an unfair burden on women.

2:52 Women generally do not have confidence in themselves, or else they find it difficult to maintain confidence. (Therefore,) if we are to achieve true equality, hiring preference should be given to women in cases where men outnumber women. To some people this might at first appear to be unfair to men, but I think that on reflection they will change their minds. (Possible added final conclusion: "Hiring preference should be given to women in cases where men outnumber women." If this is added, then it is double-underlined and the *if–then* statement is triple-underlined.)

2:53 "Tom Jeffers did not do the deed." This is the conclusion because it is supported by the other part of the sentence and because this proposition more directly helps the prosecutor to achieve his goals.

2:54 "She was defending herself against attack." This is the conclusion because it is supported by the other sentence and because it more directly aids the goals of the defense attorney.

2:55 Answer deliberately omitted as a challenge to you.

2:56 "She did not commit murder." This is the conclusion because this is the only thing supported by all the other parts of the argument and because it was our ultimate concern at the time.

2:57 and 2:58 These are up to you. Make sure that you are clear, brief, and well-organized.

2:59 Although the sun is shining brightly now, it will be raining before nightfall. Mr. Roberts, our dependable TV weatherman, said so. So we had better postpone our picnic.

2:60 So many kids are getting high school diplomas even though they cannot read. The solution is simple. The schools should attend to their primary job, the development of basic skills and the intellectual virtues. Because they cannot both do this job well and devote all the resources that are currently devoted to athletics, busing, music, and making students happy, we must conclude that such things should be dropped. Homes, neighborhoods, and religious institutions are able to perform these functions.

2:61 Deliberately omitted.

2:62 If I do my homework now, I'll miss band practice. If I do it later, my friend's feelings will be hurt. Both of these consequences are unacceptable. The conclusion is obvious. (Added conclusion: I should not do my homework.)

2:63 Deliberately omitted.

2:64 The signers of the Declaration of Independence did not intend to claim that all men and women should be considered equal. For one thing, they used the word *men* in the statement "All men are created equal." For another, it is a historical fact that men and women were not considered equal in 1776 and nothing was done in those days to ensure equal treatment. Women were not even guaranteed the right to vote in the United States until 1920.

2:65 Deliberately omitted.

2:66 NO TO S.B. 833: As the parent of a six-year-old with cystic fibrosis, (I urge you to) oppose Senate Bill 833 because it would make research on diseases such as cystic fibrosis, cancer, AIDS, and nephrosis much more expensive. (Consequently,) less research would be done. The bill requires that animals used in research be bred and raised for that purpose and prohibits the use in research of stray dogs and cats (who would otherwise be put to sleep anyway). It is time to choose between human beings and animals. I choose human beings.

2:67 Deliberately omitted.

2:68 The final conclusion is that Mr. Lan ought to step aside and not review the returns. This conclusion passes the "therefore" test. We do not know all of the purposes of the editorial writer, but getting a political person to step aside in making a judgment about election returns when the person has a conflict of interests is a plausible purpose for an editorial writer. This conclusion is supported in the editorial. It makes use of all the other material in the editorial for its support, and as far as I can see, nothing else does.

Check-Up 2D
2:69 T   **2:70** T   **2:71** T
2:73 (2:13) (A) \<Jane went to the party today>. I know this because (B) \<her glove is missing>.

2:74 (2:14) Because (A) <Arthur plays chess slowly and carefully>, (B) <this will be a long game>.

2:75 (2:15) (A) <Eggs boiled at high altitude take much longer for the egg to be cooked>. Therefore, (B) <you should boil this egg for a longer time>.

2:76 (2:16) (A) <The unexamined life is not worth living>. I know this to be true because (B) <Socrates said so>.

2:77 (2:17) It is obvious that (A) <she loved him>. So (B) <she did not kill him>.

2:78 (2:18) Because (A) <the pathologist found only one wound on the victim's body>, (B) <that wound must be the one she caused>.

2:79 (2:19) (A) <A twenty-two-year-old woman could not do such a thing to someone she loved>. (B) <She could not even have struck at him with a knife>. Therefore, (C) <someone else did it>.

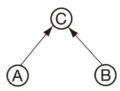

2:80 (2:20) (A) <Rooms with light-colored walls are well-lighted>. Because (B) <Mr. Martinez says that Monique's room is not well-lighted>, we can conclude that (C) <it does not have light-colored walls>.

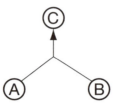

2:81 (2:21) Because (A) <Charles Dickens describes people and events in great detail>, (B) <Jonathan will no doubt be reading that book for a long time>.

2:82 (2:22) (A) <She must have hated him>. (B) <He was going with another woman>, wasn't he?

2:83 (2:23) (A) <Tom Jeffers could not have killed Al Hamilton>. (B) <Tom was in the local hospital from 10 P.M. to midnight> and (C) <Al was killed at about 11:05 P.M.>

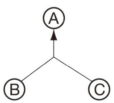

2:84 (2:30) Although (A) <he died>, (B) <the knife stroke was delivered with only moderate force>. We can conclude this because (C) <the knife penetrated only 2.5 inches and did not touch any bone>.

2:85 (2:31) (A) <She must not have intended to kill him>. (B) <The knife stroke was delivered with only moderate force>. So (C) <she is not guilty>.

2:86 (2:32) Obviously (A) <she was strong enough to do the job>, although (B) <she is not very strong>. (C) <The knife stroke was delivered with only moderate force>.

2:87 (2:33) Although (A) <Martine was on the scene>, (B) <she did not see the accident>. Here's how I know: (C) <Martine always tells us when important things happen>, and (D) <she did not even mention the accident>.

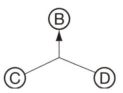

2:88 (2:34) (A) <Traffic on Poplar Road must be changed from two-way to one-way>. (B) <There is too much traffic on this road now> and (C) <there are frequent collisions>.

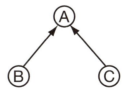

2:89 (2:35) Because (A) <the prosecuting attorney proved conclusively that the defendant killed the victim,> (B) <it has been proved beyond a reasonable doubt that the defendant performed the act that caused the death of the victim>. (C) <The first condition for a murder verdict is satisfied>.

2:90 (2:36) There is no doubt that (A) <a very important feature of our legal system is that a defendant is considered innocent until proved guilty>. But (B) <the public does not seem to believe this>. Obviously, (C) <we need a broad public-information campaign about that feature of our system>.

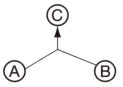

2:91 (2:37) (A) <Jones can never be elected to the presidency>. (B) <She has a questionable background and has a habit of irritating people with her penetrating questions>. (C) <This is obvious to me>, although (D) <I realize that she would make an excellent president>. However, (E) <we need her on our side>. So (F) <let's make her Chair of the Rules Committee>.

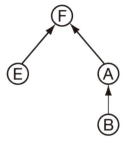

(Note: On some readings, D also supports F.)

2:92 (2:48) (A) <If you boil an egg at high altitude, then it takes much longer for the egg to be cooked>. Therefore, (B) <you should boil this egg for a long time>.

2:93 (2:49) (A) <If Monique's room has light-colored walls, then it is well-lighted>. Because (B) <Mr. Martinez says that her room is not well-lighted>, we can conclude that (C) <it does not have light-colored walls>.

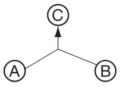

2:94 (2:50) (A) <If the public does not realize that people are to be considered innocent until proved guilty, then there will continue to be mistreatment of perfectly innocent people>. Hence, (B) <we need a broad public-information campaign about this feature of our system>.

2:95 (2.51) (A) <Men generally have difficulty expressing their emotions>. (B) <If it is desirable for our society to consist of fully developed human beings, then people who do find it easier to express their emotions should make a special effort to draw out those who do not>. (C) <Generally this means that women should make a special effort to encourage men to express their inner feelings>. I say this, even though (D) <some might feel that it places an unfair burden on women>.

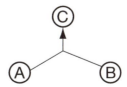

2:96 (2:52) (A) <Women generally do not have confidence in themselves, or else they find it difficult to maintain confidence>. Therefore, (B) <if we are to achieve true equality, hiring preference should be given to women in cases where men outnumber women>. (C) <To some people this might at first appear to be unfair to men>, but I think that (D) <on reflection they will change their minds>. (Added final conclusion: (E) <Hiring preference should be given to women in cases where men outnumber women.>)

2:97 (2:53) Prosecutor: (A) <Tom Jeffers did not do the deed>. (B) <He was in the hospital at the time>.

2:98 (2:54) Defense Attorney: (A) <She was defending herself against attack>. (B) <He threatened to kill her>.

2:99 (2:55) Deliberately omitted.

2:100 (2:56) Juror: (A) <The pathologist testified that the knife stroke was only of medium strength>. (B) <She did not think that she would cause him great bodily harm>. (C) <She did not commit murder>.

2:101 (2:59) Although (A) <the sun is shining brightly now>, (B) <it will be raining before nightfall>. (C) <Mr. Roberts, our dependable TV weatherman, said so>. So (D) <we had better postpone our picnic>.

2:102 (2:60) (A) <So many kids are getting high school diplomas even though they cannot read>. (B) <College graduates do not understand percentages>. (C) <Adults cannot read directions>. The solution is simple: (D) <The schools should attend to their primary job, the development of basic skills and the intellectual virtues>. Because (E) <they cannot both do this job well and devote all the resources that are currently devoted to athletics, busing, music, and making students happy>, we must conclude that (F) <such things should be dropped>. (G) <Homes, neighborhoods, and religious institutions are able to perform these functions>.

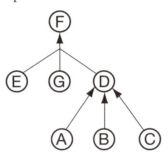

Explanatory note regarding the previous item: In case you are wondering why the previous item is diagrammed that way, here is a word of explanation: A, B, and C seem fairly obviously to be offered in support of D. E and G seem to be offered in support of F. The question about which some people wonder is whether D is offered in support of F, or F in support of D. To answer this question try the "therefore" test: Which sounds right in the situation in which this argument probably appears: 1) "The schools should attend to their primary job, the development of the basic skills and the intellectual virtues; therefore athletics, busing, music, and making students happy are things that should be dropped" or 2) "Athletics, busing, music, and making students happy are things that should be dropped; therefore the schools should attend to their primary job, the development of the basic skills and intellectual virtues"? Even though the dropping of the indicated things might cause the schools to focus on the intellectual virtues, it is probable that the claimed primacy of the intellectual virtues is offered as a supporting reason for the dropping of the indicated things. So D is probably offered in support of F.

2:103 (2:61) Deliberately omitted.

2:104 (2:62) (A) <If I do my homework now, I'll miss band practice>. (B) <If I do it later, my friend's feelings will be hurt>. (C) <Both of these consequences are unacceptable>. The conclusion is obvious. (Probable final conclusion: (D) <I should not do my homework>.)

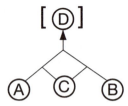

2:105 (2:63) Deliberately omitted.

2:106 (2:64) (A) <The signers of the Declaration of Independence did not intend to claim that men and women should be considered equal>. For one thing, (B) <they used the word *men* in the statement "All men are created equal">. For another, (C) <it is a historical fact that men and women were not considered equal in 1776> and (D) <nothing was done in those days to ensure equal treatment>. (E) <Women were not even guaranteed the right to vote in the United States until 1920>.

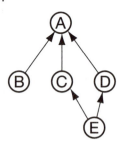

2:107 (2:65) Deliberately omitted.

2:108 (Paragraph 5) (A) <There was no one else in the dining room at the time of the stabbing>. It is clear that (B) <Arlene did not mention anyone else>.

(C) <Neither did her parents>. Because (D) <they did not mention anyone else>, obviously (A) <there was no one else>.

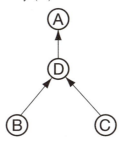

2:109 (Paragraph 6) Deliberately omitted.

2:110 (2:66) NO TO S.B. 833: As the parent of a six-year-old with cystic fibrosis, I urge you to (A) <oppose Senate Bill 833> because (B) <it would make research on diseases such as cystic fibrosis, cancer, AIDS, and nephrosis much more expensive>. Consequently, (C) <less research would be done>. (D) <The bill requires that animals used in research be bred and raised for that purpose> and (E) <prohibits the use in research of stray dogs and cats> (F) <(who would otherwise be put to sleep anyway)>. (G) <It is time to choose between human beings and animals>. (H) <I choose human beings>.

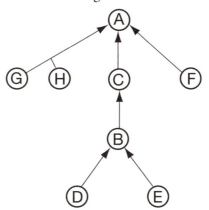

2:111 (2:67) Deliberately omitted.

2:112 (2:68) DISQUALIFIED: (A) <Donald Lan is the Secretary of State of New Jersey>, which means that (B) <he must review the returns of Tuesday's still-undecided election for governor>. (C) <Mr. Lan is in a curious position> because (D) <he was not only an early contender in the Democratic gubernatorial primary, but later became deputy campaign manager for the Democratic candidate, James Florio>.
(E) <Mr. Florio and the Republican contender, Tom Kean, agree that every effort should be taken to ensure the legitimacy of the ultimate

result>. That means (F) <Mr. Lan ought to step aside>. (G) <We do not question his honesty>, (H) <only the appearances>. (I) <With a near–dead heat for the top office of the state>, (J) <the appearances of having a partisan certify the results are dead wrong>.

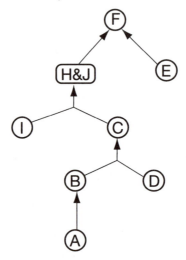

3

The Credibility of Sources

Suppose that you hear the basketball coach of the University of Illinois say on television that the Chevrolet is a good car. Should you take his word? Suppose that you are on the jury when the pathologist says that the knife stroke was not a powerful one. Should you take her word? I am not asking whether what they said is true, although we are interested in that too. Instead I am asking whether their saying those things in those circumstances was sufficient reason to believe what they said. Another way of putting that question is, "Were those people *credible* on that topic in those circumstances?"

This sort of question is important to consider because a great many of our beliefs come from other people. Often, someone else's word is all we have to go on. Think, for example, of how often in your daily life you accept something on the word of the newspapers and magazines, your teachers, your textbooks, your friends, etc. Think of the times when writing position papers (of the sort suggested in Chapter 1) that you need to cite sources to support your reasons (the *R* in *FRISCO*). Are your sources credible on the matter at hand?

We jurors had to make credibility judgments many times. One example was our judgment about the credibility of the pathologist in her testimony that the knife stroke was only of moderate force. Another was our judgment about the credibility of the defendant in her claim that the victim threatened to kill her.

Remember that the immediate question is not whether what the person said was correct, although that is our ultimate interest. The question here is whether, in the circumstances, the person deserves to be believed about the topic at hand. What the person says might in fact be correct, even though we should not take the persons word on it. Furthermore, a very credible source might be mistaken.

Judging the credibility of a source is most useful when we do not have any other way to tell whether what the person says is correct. When the person's word is all we have to go on, a common situation, we should pay close attention to that person's credibility. But because the credibility of a source does not guarantee the truth of what the source says, we must keep an open mind about it. We can usually proceed as if what a credible source says is true, but we cannot be absolutely certain.

How can you tell whether to take another person's word? This is often a difficult question, but there are criteria that can help you answer it—even though there is no guarantee that your judgment based on them is correct. In this chapter, you will first examine four basic criteria for judging the credibility of a source, and then consider some refinements, four additional criteria, and some standard labels applied to sources of information, sometimes called fallacy labels. One basic theme of this chapter is that not all *appeals to authority* (a fallacy label) are fallacious. In fact, most are legitimate. Our job is to figure out which ones are legitimate.

Credibility comes under the *R* part of the FRISCO approach to critical thinking because judging the credibility of sources is relevant to determining the acceptability of reasons. The *I* part of FRISCO, the degree to which the reasons support the conclusion, is a topic we shall not start to consider in a careful organized manner until Chapter 5. However, you should be thinking about it now, because in actual acts of critical thinking, in judging yours and others' arguments and decisions, all of these aspects of FRISCO are interdependent.

Four Basic Criteria for Credibility

1.   *Background Experience and Knowledge*

Perhaps most important of all is whether the person has sufficient experience and knowledge to know what he or she is talking about. Often, but not always, this requires formal training. I did not take the Illinois coach's word on automobiles because I had no reason to think that he was an expert on automobiles. I defer to him in basketball, but not automobiles. One trap in deciding about someone's credibility is transferring our respect for someone's expertise in one area to another area. To invite you to fall into this trap is to commit the fallacy called *transfer.*

The pathologist seemed to us on the jury to be an expert in the area of her testimony. She was a medical doctor regularly employed by the civil authorities to do autopsies. She testified that she had performed over 200 of them, and this testimony was not challenged by either the defense or prosecuting attorney. (So we, to some extent, depended on the expertise of the attorneys to turn up information that might have been damaging to the credibility of the witnesses. By not challenging the witness' expertise, they gave us some reason to accept it.)

Having background experience and knowledge does not guarantee that a person will be right about something. It only helps to make the person's statements more credible. The person, we then think, is at least in a position to make accurate statements. This criterion can be stated as follows: *The person should have background training and experience appropriate for making the statement.*

Be aware that this criterion applies not only to statements requiring expertise. It also applies to gossip and other information you receive from your friends and acquaintances. My friend Jim told me that he saw Martine out with Karl at The Blue Cloud. If I am to take his word, then Jim's background (training and experience) should have enabled him to recognize Martine and Karl. It should also enable him to recognize a case of their being out together. In particular he should know what kind of place it is and he should know the difference between a chance encounter and a case of their being out together. Suppose that The Blue Cloud were a coffee shop where people regularly drift in and out alone and join anyone with whom they are acquainted, rather than a formal restaurant where people sit only with people with whom they came. He should know which type of place it is and be able to apply to this case the distinction between a chance encounter and their being out together. This background experience and knowledge, although it is not expertise, is necessary if he is to be credible on this matter.

2. *Lack of Apparent Conflict of Interest*

Probably the basketball coach had a conflict of interest. That is, he presumably stood to gain (in this case, probably financially) from saying what he said about Chevrolets. It is standard practice for sports figures to be paid for endorsing products. So the basketball coach presumably did not satisfy the criterion of lack of apparent conflict of interest when he made his statements about Chevrolets.

The pathologist, on the other hand, seemed to have no conflict of interest. That is, she did not seem to stand to gain from saying that the knife stroke was not a powerful one (as opposed to saying that it was a powerful one). So the pathologist did appear to satisfy this criterion when she made the statement about the strength of the knife stroke.

In my comments about the degree of satisfaction of the conflict of interest criterion by the two speakers, I hedged by using such terms as *presumably* and *seemed to*. I did this because I am not certain of either judgment. There is good reason to believe that the basketball coach was paid to endorse Chevrolets and no reason, as far as I know, to believe that the pathologist received an incentive for testifying one way rather than the other. But I did not see the coach receive money for the endorsement. Furthermore, if the pathologist had received an incentive to say one thing rather than the other, those involved would have made every effort to keep the jurors (and everyone else as well) from knowing this. If the pathologist took money for saying one thing rather than another, then she might well have lost her job.

So, in stating this criterion, it is best to include the word *apparent: The person should have no apparent conflict of interest.*

Conflict of interest need not be merely financial. Sometimes people get deeply involved in and attached to a cause (for example, one side or the other on the issue of gun control, or the issue of what hockey team is better). Because they believe so strongly in their positions, saying things that help their side are in their interests. So, if someone deeply committed to a cause says something that affects the success of his or her interest, that person has a conflict of interest. This does not mean that the person is wrong, nor does it mean that the person has actually let his or her special interest affect a judgment. It is only a warning that there might be some undue influence (possibly even a subconscious influence) and that the person's credibility is thereby lessened.

Other sorts of interests that might result in a conflict of interest include receiving an award or a prize, making the team, being popular, avoiding punishment, getting an "A," being elected president, and securing power. Can you think of any others?

3.   *Agreement with Others Equally Qualified*

If two people satisfy equally the other criteria for credibility but disagree with each other, then which one is more credible? Putting the question this way suggests the answer: We generally should take the word of neither. One of them might well be right, but given that they are otherwise equal, the disagreement calls for us to take the word of neither. We would have to find other ways to decide which statement to believe, if any.

On the other hand, if people who come out well on the other criteria also agree with each other, then that is all the more reason to take their word. But this is no guarantee that they are correct. It sometimes happens that all the people who satisfy the other criteria are wrong. For example, at one time all the authorities held that the earth is flat (not roughly spherical) in shape. But they were wrong.

The basketball coach is in disagreement with others who satisfy the other criteria as well as he does (which is not very well). For example, he is in disagreement with the football player who endorses Fords (and who similarly does not do well on the other criteria). So their disagreement with each other further disqualifies each as an authority on car quality.

Because these two already come out poorly on the other criteria, it does not make so much difference to note that they come out poorly on this criterion. But there are cases where coming out poorly on this criterion does make a difference. Suppose that two experts who satisfy the other criteria disagree with each other about whether a particular nuclear power plant is safe. Even though one of them might well be right, we cannot take one's word over the other. Considering only these two, we cannot treat one as more credible than the other. Hence, if we are to have a reasonable belief about the matter, we must go further than seeking their word about it. This is a common situation with current controversial issues. Even though it helps to develop ways to be wise in our selection of people to believe, we have to develop other techniques for judging. More about these other ways as we proceed in this course. (I am not promising to produce a magic formula for deciding what to believe about difficult issues such as nuclear power plants. Life is not that simple!)

This criterion can be stated as follows: *The person should be in agreement with other people who satisfy the other criteria as well or better.*

4.   *Reputation*

A fourth basic criterion for judging the credibility of a person is the person's reputation. Ordinarily, a person who has a reputation for lying or being wrong is less credible than a person with a reputation for being right and for telling the truth. One's general reputation is important, but one's reputation in the specific area of the statement is also important. Some people I know are notoriously and commonly mistaken in some areas and are very dependable in other areas, where they have good reputations. For example, a friend of mine has a poor reputation for information about good places to shop, but a good reputation for her judgments about academic talent. This is so even though she has studied both areas.

The Illinois basketball coach had a good reputation (at the time) in the area of basketball. As far as I know, he had no reputation, good or bad, in the area of automobile judgment, so he comes out weakly positive on this criterion. The pathologist probably had a good reputation in the area of pathology. Neither attorney attempted to challenge her reputation, and she retained her job as a pathologist, so she also came out positively on this criterion.

This criterion, then, is as follows: *The person should have a good reputation for being right and telling the truth in general, and especially in the area of concern.*

Tabulating the Results

One way to organize your results in applying the four basic criteria to a statement is to assign a rating on each criterion. Then tentatively summarize your judgments. In Table 3.1, I report the results of my having done this for the statements of the basketball coach and the pathologist. As you can see, making a tentative overall judgment requires balancing the importance of each of the subjudgments. There is no mechanical way to do this. Even so, it helps to consider these credibility criteria. Often that is the best we can do in a situation in which we have incomplete knowledge.

TABLE 3.1   A Summary Of My Judgments, Using Four Basic Credibility Criteria

Criterion	Basketball coach about automobiles	Pathologist about the knife stroke
1. Background experience and knowledge	Probably weak	Strong
2. Lack of conflict of interest	Very weak	Strong
3. Agreement with others who come out as well as, or better, on other criteria	Very weak	No judgment
4. Reputation	Satisfactory	Strong
Tentative overall judgment	Probably not credible on this statement	Probably credible on this statement

Check-Up 3A

True or False?
If false, change it to make it true. Try to do so in a way that shows that you understand.

3:1 If a person stands to profit financially from saying one thing rather than another, that person has a conflict of interest.

3:2 Only people who are experts can satisfy the background-experience-and-knowledge criterion.

3:3 The criteria for credibility more directly apply to judging whether to take someone's word than to judging whether the person is correct.

Short Answer

    3:4 Find a particular assertion in a newspaper. Cut out the selection in which it appears, identify the assertion explicitly (perhaps by highlighting or underlining), making sure that you identify only one assertion. Explicitly identify the source. Attach the selection to a paper on which you report the results of your attempt to apply the four basic criteria of credibility to the source of the assertion. Make an overall judgment about the assertion, answering the question, "Should I take this person's word on this?" Suggestion: Use the tabulation method I described. Another suggestion: Because your judgment probably will not be at one extreme or the other ("a fully credible source for this statement" or "a totally incredible source for this statement"), you might need qualifying words such as *probably, it seems,* or *presumably.*

    3:5 Do the same thing for an assertion you find in a magazine.

    3:6 Do the same thing for a serious assertion made by a friend. Write it down and describe the situation before you report your results.

Further Criteria

In addition to the four basic criteria for credibility, certain other less basic ones should be taken into consideration, if possible. They too are important, though often not so important as the first four. Like the first four, these criteria require good judgment in application. Judgment is required in deciding whether each criterion is satisfied and in deciding the importance of each criterion in a given situation.

5. *Established Procedures*

Although established procedures sometimes give incorrect results, it usually is best to follow them, if such procedures exist. In the trial, one of the expert witnesses testified that the type of blood found on the knife was type A, the same as Al Hamilton's blood type. Among other things, the expert testified that she had used the established procedures for determining blood type. If she has used anything but the established procedures, her testimony would have been less credible.

On the other hand, we all know of cases in which the established procedures have produced incorrect answers. For example, the established procedures for determining the weather at an airport I know are as follows: An observer emerges from a building ten minutes before every hour and makes a ceiling and visibility observation. If a flight of the airline employing (and thus paying) the observer is expected, additional observations are made on request of the pilot of that flight or on the initiative of the observer. If no airline flight is expected and if there is a significant change in the weather at half after the hour, this change would probably go unreported. So a pilot of a nonairline aircraft would probably be given incorrect information until the next hourly report because until that time, the old information would still be on the weather report network. The established procedure would probably yield an incorrect report.

Because of such exceptions, the word *ordinarily* is included in the statement of the criterion: *Ordinarily the person should have used established procedures, if any exist.*

6. *Known Risk to Reputation*

Experts are well aware that they must guard their reputations so that they can continue to play the role of experts. This is an extra reason for them to try to be accurate about what they say. Experts I know are usually more careful about what they say when they know that their reputations can be hurt if they are discovered to be wrong. If you think about it, I believe that you will agree that most people tend to be more careful in situations in which their errors would be discovered.

The blood analyst knew that the blood could be reanalyzed by someone else. If she turned out to be wrong, she knew that this would hurt her reputation. This in turn would hurt her capacity to earn a living as a technician and testifier. (Experts who testify in the courtroom are generally paid one way or another.) So she satisfied this criterion of known risk to one's reputation.

In several kinds of situations, one's reputation is at little or no risk. In such situations, this criterion is not satisfied, or not well satisfied. For example, a friend told me that he saw a pileated woodpecker while on a solitary walk through the woods on Connecticut Hill near Ithaca, New York. Though rare, pileated woodpeckers do live in that area, but there was no way of checking whether my friend actually saw one. So his reputation was not at risk and he knew it. This is a situation in which there is no way of gathering further evidence to check the original statement. The evidence cannot be gathered because the event has already occurred and is no longer accessible. (I believed him, by the way, but he did not satisfy this criterion in making this report.)

Another kind of an occurrence inaccessible for others is a person's feeling or sensation, such as a backache. It is often very difficult for someone else to tell whether you have a backache, so people who report backaches generally do not satisfy this criterion. Their reputations for honesty are often not at risk, because generally no one else can tell whether they really do have a backache.

Sometimes a reputation is not at risk because the statement is too vague. For example, I found the following prediction in my horoscope in the local newspaper: "Some situation connected to travel, legalities, publicity may bring upsets." The reputation of the astrologer who wrote that prediction was not at risk because there is no way to check the truth of the prediction. It is too vague. It says "may bring upset," so if there are no upsets, the prediction is not shown wrong. It would not even be cast under a veil of suspicion if there are no upsets. Furthermore, the three categories cover so much of life's interests that there is bound to be some degree of upset in at least one on almost any given day. Can you think of any other sources of vagueness?

The astrologer's reputation was not at risk. Presumably, the astrologer knew this, so the astrologer does not satisfy the sixth criterion: *The person should know that his or her reputation can be helped or hurt by the statement's being discovered to be correct or incorrect.*

7. *Ability to Give Reasons*

If we are to take someone's word, that person should have good reasons for what he or she says. Otherwise, we should be suspicious.

Depending on the content, the reason might simply be that the person saw something clearly. Jim's reason for *saying* that Martine was at The Blue Cloud might simply be that he saw her there.

On the other hand, my physician's reason for saying I had appendicitis cannot be that he saw it. Inflamed appendixes are not seen during the diagnosis stage. Instead, he reasoned that I had appendicitis. His reasons were that I had a fever, had abdominal pain aggravated by pressing, and had a rapidly increasing above-normal white corpuscle count, among others. He was able to tell me these reasons and explain their significance. This ability helped make him credible.

We cannot always insist on the person's giving understandable reasons. Sometimes people are too busy to give reasons to us, and sometimes the reasons are so complicated that an ordinary person cannot understand them. But generally, an expert who understands the topic well also understands it well enough to give an understandable explanation. Such an explanation might be simplified and might neglect some important refinements, but it should be intelligible. One mark of the better experts is that they can generally do this.

One possible reason a person might have for not doing this is that he or she is trying to hide something—perhaps ignorance, perhaps worse. You must judge these things on the basis of what you know about the situation. Unfortunately, you usually cannot be sure.

The seventh criterion is as follows: *The person should be able to give understandable reasons in support of the statement. It is also generally desirable that the person actually do so, especially if asked for reasons.*

8. *Careful Habits*

People do not always show the same amount of care from one activity to the next. But carelessness of one sort is often an indication of carelessness of a similar sort. A statement made by a person known to be careless in one area is suspect if the area is similar to that of the statement.

If Jim were known to be careless in identifying people at The Cha Cha Restaurant, then he might well be careless in identifying people at The Blue Cloud. If the blood technician were known to be very careful in mixing chemicals, then that counts in her favor for care in testing blood.

Here is the criterion: *The statement maker should have careful habits in areas similar to the area of the statement.*

Summary

In summary, these four additional criteria are concerned with established procedures, known risk to reputation, ability to give reasons, and habits of care in similar areas. I realize that these criteria are somewhat vague and difficult to apply. You might think of them as suggestions for questions to ask yourself about someone making a statement. Again, in making an overall judgment you must decide how important each is in a given situation. This is what I had to do in Table 3.2 when applying these four additional criteria to the coach's and pathologist's statements.

I assigned *unknown* to the coach on established procedures because, although I think that he did not use them, I am not sure enough of this to make a judgment.

TABLE 3.2   A Summary Of My Judgments, Using Four Additional Credibility Criteria

Criterion	Coach about automobiles	Pathologist about knife stroke
5. Established procedures	Unknown	Probably strong
6. Known risk to reputation	Satisfactory	Strong
7. Ability to give reasons	Strong	Strong
8. Careful habits	Satisfactory	Strong
Summary (using all eight criteria)	Probably not credible on this statement	Probably credible on this statement

On the established procedures category, I rated the pathologist's statement *probably strong* because, although she used some established procedures for measuring the depth of the wound and the bones for damage, I suspect that there are no established procedures for determining as a whole how forceful the blow was. (I might be wrong about this, but there was no way a juror could tell. We were not allowed to ask any questions.)

On the known-risk-to-reputation criterion, I rated the coach's statement satisfactory because other people can drive and check the Chevrolet automobile. I did not rate it strong on this criterion because there is so much disagreement about automobiles and about criteria for judging them, making it difficult to prove him wrong.

I rated both strong on ability to give reasons because both gave reasons that I understand. On careful habits, I rated the coach satisfactory because I would guess that he has careful habits in judging automobiles. I rated the pathologist strong on careful habits because she seemed quite careful about what she said on the witness stand and because her habits in the area under consideration would probably have to be careful for her to keep her job. My overall judgments then, taking all eight criteria into account, are *probably not credible* for the coach, and *probably credible* for the pathologist. My principal concerns about the coach's statement about automobiles were his probable conflict of interest and probable lack of special expertise about automobiles. I weighted them most heavily among the eight criteria.

Be aware that this summary credibility judgment I have just reported is not based on an exhaustive investigation of each of the speakers and their statements. Rather, it is based on a realistic amount of effort given the situations in which I found myself. One always has to make a compromise between the amount of time one spends and the amount of certainty one can have. Given my decision about what was a realistic amount of effort, I judged that I should not take the coach's word on automobiles and that I should take the pathologist's word about the strength of the knife stroke.

These eight credibility criteria must be applied with good judgment, both in deciding whether each criterion is satisfied and in deciding how much weight to give to each. While applying these criteria, and after you have applied them, you should be open to new information about sources and ready to change your mind about their credibility, if need be. Always attempt to see things from others' points of view.

Be alert for alternatives and be well-informed. In other words, although there are no mechanical rules for good judgment, your judgment is improved by the critical thinking dispositions presented in Chapter 1.

Check-Up 3B

True or False?

If false, change it to make it true. Try to do so in a way that shows that you understand.

3:7 If a procedure is an established one, then it is correct.

3:8 For credibility purposes, it is best for the statement maker to know that his or her reputation is at risk.

3:9 For credibility purposes, the vaguer the statement, the better, because vague statements cannot be proved wrong.

3:10 If a statement maker knows that there is no way to check his or her statement, then he or she is probably not credible.

3:11 A person making a credible statement should generally be able to give understandable reasons in support of the statement.

3:12 If a person is careless in one kind of activity, then that person is not likely to be credible in any other kind of activity.

Short Answer

3:13 Go back to the newspaper statement you evaluated for 3:4 and apply the four additional criteria to it. (Suggestion: Use the tabulation method again.) Then make and report an overall judgment about the credibility of this statement based on your application of all eight criteria.

3:14 Do the same for the statement you found in the magazine (3:5).

3:15 Do the same for the statement by your friend (3:6).

Fallacy Labels

A fallacy is an error in thinking or reasoning. *Transfer, appeal to authority, testimonial,* and *personal attack* are labels used for fallacies in the area of credibility of sources. But is it always wrong to do the things so labeled? Let us consider them one at a time.

Transfer

Earlier in this unit, I suggested that it is generally a mistake to take an authority's word in some other area than that in which the person is an authority. That is, it is often a mistake to *transfer* the assumption of expertise from one area to another. Although this is generally true, it depends on how similar the areas are. If the basketball coach told me that a particular person is a good football player, I would be inclined to believe him because the areas are similar enough and because there is much personal contact between experts in the two fields. On the other hand, I am not ready to transfer the coach's expertise to automobiles, as I said before. So even though transfer is generally a fallacy, it is not always so.

Appeal to Authority

Because much of our knowledge comes from other people and is based on the statements of someone else, it would be foolish to condemn all appeals to authority. The defense attorney did a reasonable thing in appealing to the authority of the pathologist about the strength of the knife stroke. The pathologist was an expert and an appropriate source of knowledge about what happened. There were a number of other statements in that trial that were justified by appeal to authority, including statements about fingerprints, blood type, the cause of death, and the position of the body. Without appeals to authority, our court system would collapse. We are often justified in taking someone else's word, including the word of experts—not always, as we all know, but often.

Appeal to authority is not necessarily wrong, but it is not necessarily right either. Each appeal to authority must be judged on its own merits. You are already familiar with this process of judging sources for their credibility.

Testimonial

The coach's claim that the Chevrolet is a good car would be called a *testimonial* for Chevrolet. In this case, primarily because of probable conflict of interest and presumed lack of expertise, one should probably not take his word on the matter. But there are many cases of testimonial that we do accept and that should be believed. Eyewitness testimony should of course generally be believed if it satisfies credibility criteria. But eyewitness testimony is not really properly called testimonial. Rather, a *testimonial* is testimony *in support of* some particular idea, thing, or person.

When one of my colleagues assured me that a particular person I was thinking of hiring for a writing job was a well-organized, clear, coherent writer, that was a testimonial. When a friend told me that a particular movie was well worth seeing, that was a testimonial. In both cases, the testimonial satisfied very well the credibility criteria. I believed the testimony, acted on it, and was glad that I had.

In both cases, it was very important to know well the source of the testimony in order to apply the criteria of credibility. In the case of the job-related testimony, it was important to know something about the writing standards of the testifier (my colleague) and especially important to know the extent of conflict of interest, if any. I have repeatedly found that teachers and advisers give misleading, overgenerous testimonials about their own students and advisees. I suppose that this is partly because of strong concern for the welfare of the student and partly because it is to the teacher's credit for the student to be well-placed. In the case in question, there was no strong conflict of interest, as far as I could see, and the colleague struck me as a scrupulously honest person. He also knew me well and realized that his reputation with me would be damaged if I discovered him to be wrong about the person. So I took his word and did not regret doing so.

The principal danger with movie testimonials from friends is the possible difference in taste, as we all well know. We must take the friend's taste reputation into consideration. This danger exists even for testimonials by professional critics. But they also have the possibility of conflict of interest (which is not generally found for friends' testimony about movies). Critics are under pressure from their employers and the newspapers that carry their syndicated columns, and they might well be trying to please someone or do a favor for a friend in the motion picture industry. Recently, a local critic panned a local opera production. The critic's commentary angered some local people and the critic was fired. Critics know that their jobs are dependent to some extent on such political pressures and as a result have a continual conflict of interest.

It should be clear, then, that there are cases of testimonial that we should not trust, but there are also cases that we should trust. Testimonial is not automatically a fallacy. The criteria for judging the credibility of sources are useful in judging whether to believe testimonials.

Personal Attack

A *personal-attack* argument is an attack on the character or qualifications of a person rather than a challenge to the merits of the person's argument. Suppose you present an argument in support of the view that your volleyball team needs more practice. Suppose that someone challenges your argument on the ground that your religious preference differs from hers or that you are selfish and do not share food the way others do. Whether or not these are reasonable attacks on your character, they do not affect your argument, nor do they show anything about whether your team needs more practice. In such cases, a personal-attack argument is a fallacy.

On the other hand, an attack on the character of a witness is a standard and often appropriate maneuver by an attorney in a courtroom. This is simply the application of the criterion of reputation. If someone has repeatedly lied, and if that can be shown in court, then that is good reason for us to be dubious about the person's testimony. Using the witness' reputation for being a liar is a reason for suspecting the testimony would be a personal-attack argument.

If a physician has taken a bribe for illegal drug prescriptions, then we have a right to be suspicious about his recommendation that he perform an expensive operation. Noting the bribe in an argument against the physician's recommendation is a personal-attack argument, but it is not necessarily a fallacy.

The important thing is whether the attack on the person is relevant, that is, whether it bears on the matter at hand. A person's reputation for lying is relevant to our decision whether to take the person's word. A person's reputation for bribery is relevant to whether we should accept the person's recommendation about something from which he or she would profit. This is so even if the person's argument in support of the recommendation looks good. There are many ways in which a person can slant things or deliberately ignore evidence without our realizing it.

In summary, these supposed fallacies of credibility (transfer, appeal to authority, testimonial, and personal attack) are sometimes fallacies and sometimes not. For the first three, you should apply the criteria for credibility and judge on that basis. For personal attack, you must also decide whether the attack is relevant.

Chapter Summary

The ideas in this chapter apply to judging the acceptability of reasons (part of the *R* in *FRISCO*). The focus has been on judging the credibility of sources of reasons. If a reason comes from a credible source, that helps to make the reason acceptable.

You have considered eight criteria for judging the credibility of sources, the first four of which are basic. These criteria are background experience and knowledge, lack of apparent conflict of interest, agreement with others equally qualified, reputation, established procedures, known risk to reputation, ability to give reasons, and careful habits in similar areas. The set is not exhaustive. You will probably think of others in specific situations.

These criteria apply to personal, public, and vocational situations in which you are trying to decide whether to believe what someone says or what you have read. They also apply to position-paper-writing situations, when you want to cite credible sources to support your reasons. If your sources are not credible, they do not provide legitimate support.

The eight credibility criteria do not automatically yield a judgment about the credibility of a source. Your own good judgment is also needed to determine the application of the criteria and their weighting. Good judgment depends heavily on the basic critical thinking dispositions, including being alert for alternatives, looking at things from others' points of view, being tentative, and trying to be well-informed.

You have also considered some of the fallacy labels people sometimes use when judging the credibility of sources. It is important to understand the meaning of these terms when they are used so that you will not be intimidated and so that you will be able to respond to the implied accusation. Sometimes these things are fallacies and sometimes not:

1. *Transfer* is an attempt to transfer acceptance of someone's expertise in one area to some other area. This is usually a fallacy, but not always.
2. *Appeal to authority* is an attempt to get someone to believe something on the basis of the expertise of someone else. Whether this is a fallacy depends on whether the criteria of credibility are satisfied.
3. *Testimonial* is a source's testimony in support of a position. Whether this is a fallacy depends on the degree of satisfaction of the criteria of credibility.
4. *Personal-attack argument* is an argument against a statement that points out some defect in the maker of the statement. Whether this is a fallacy depends in part on whether the defect is relevant to the content of the statement.

Check-Up 3C

True or False?

If false, change it to make it true. Try to do so in a way that shows that you understand.

3:16 To appeal to an authority is to commit a fallacy.

3:17 It is generally foolish to accept testimonials as a basis for action.

3:18 Personal attack arguments are almost always fallacious.

3:19 In judging an argument, it can be relevant to show that the person offering the argument would profit from your accepting the conclusion.

Short Answer

For each of the following items, apply one or more of these labels (remember that in applying the label you are *not* committed to calling the item a fallacy):

- **A.** Transfer
- **B.** Appeal to authority
- **C.** Testimonial
- **D.** Personal-attack argument
- **E.** No reason for thinking that it is any of the above

3:20 A friend says, "The early-morning Amtrak train is the best way to get to Chicago, all things considered."

3:21 Another friend says, "My sister, who should know because she sometimes rides that train, tells me that the early morning train is not the best way to get to Chicago."

3:22 The first friend says, "Don't pay any attention to her—she is prejudiced."

3:23 A football quarterback, who won the best-player-of-the-year award, advises us that Glittering Oats has more nutritive value than any other cereal and that it is responsible for his football prowess.

3:24 Sarah Steinfeld, a Grand Master chess player, advises us that Glittering Oats has more nutritive value than any other cereal and that it is responsible for her skill in chess.

3:25 A juror says, "You can't believe the defendant. He even looks like a liar."

3:26 A famous movie director tells us that the president's economic ideas are foolish.

3:27 A defender of the president's economic ideas tells us that a noted economist supports the president's economic ideas.

3:28 A teacher says, "The preferred spelling of the plural of *bus* is *buses,* according to Webster's dictionary, so you should spell it that way."

3:29 A professional football player reports, "I drink Hugh's Brew because it's good for me and I like it. You'll like it too."

3:30 A letter to an editor of a newspaper reads, "You are bound to have a biased view of the importance of protecting local business. After all, your employer is a member of the business-oriented country club. You should mention this when you advocate increased police protection downtown and your readers should be duly skeptical of what you say."

3:31 The defense attorney says, "My client is innocent of the charge of murder because she was defending herself against attack."

3:32 A friend advises, "When you limber up your muscles, you should stretch them and hold them stretched without inducing a lot of pain. You should not make a series of painful stretches of short duration. That's what the coach says."

Medium Answer

3:33 In the jury room, one of the jurors said about the prosecutor's argument, "We have to be wary because it is to the prosecutor's interest to win the case. In his presentation, therefore, he might well have left out some important facts. Besides, he slurred his words and was practically shouting at us. I don't trust people who do that." What do you think of the juror's reasons for being wary of the prosecutor's argument? Why?

3:34–3:37 For each of the following items, find an example in a newspaper or magazine. Referring to relevant criteria of credibility, defend your judgment in writing and attach a copy of the item. You might find that you can use an item more than once. You may do so.

3:34 An appeal to authority that you accept.

3:35 A testimonial that you accept.

3:36 A testimonial that you do not accept.

3:37 A case that you would label as fallacious transfer.

Suggested Answers for Chapter 3

Check-Up 3A

3:1 T   3:2 F   3:3 T

3:2 People other than experts can satisfy the background-experience-and-knowledge criterion if the statement is in the everyday realm and the speaker has sufficient everyday knowledge and experience.

3:4, 3:5, and 3:6 These are up to you. Review what you have said.

Check-Up 3B

3:7 F   3:8 T   3:9 F   3:10 F   3:11 T   3:12 F

3:7 If a procedure is an established one, the chances are that it is correct, but it might not be.

3:9 For credibility purposes, vagueness has both advantages and disadvantages.

3:10 Even if a statement-maker knows that there is no way to check his or her statement, the statement might be credible, depending on the satisfaction of the other criteria.

3:12 If a person is careless in one kind of activity, this carelessness is suggestive of possible carelessness in similar kinds of activity.

3:13, 3:14, and 3:15 Again, these are up to you. Review what you have said. Make sure that your overall judgment is clearly stated.

Check-Up 3C

3:16 F   3:17 F   3:18 F   3:19 T

3:16 To appeal to an authority is to commit a fallacy if the authority is not qualified on the topic.

3:17 It is foolish to accept testimonials as a basis for action if the source is not qualified.

3:18 Personal attack arguments are sometimes fallacious.

3:20 C	**3:21** B	**3:22** D	**3:23** A & C	**3:24** A & C
3:25 D	**3:26** A	**3:27** B	**3:28** B	**3:29** A & C
3:30 D	**3:31** E	**3:32** B

Note: As is, 3:31 is not a testimonial, but would be if the attorney said, "My client is innocent of murder because I know her well and know that she would never murder anyone."

3:33 Each reason is a case of personal attack. However, the juror's first precaution is well taken. The prosecutor has a conflict of interest, so we could not depend on him to present both sides of the matter. (We could not depend on the defense attorney to present both sides, either.) The attack on the prosecutor's argument that was based on the prosecutor's speech habits was not legitimate. Those traits were not relevant to the strength of his argument.

3:34–3:37 Again, these are up to you. Be sure to review what you have said.

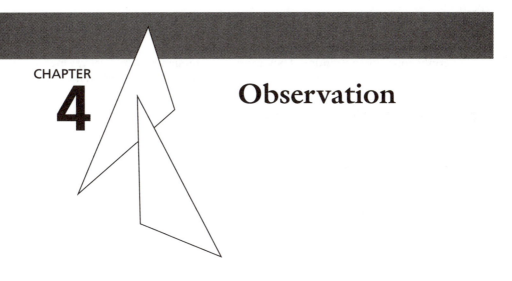

Observation

Have you ever been sure that you saw or heard something, and then learned that someone else saw or heard something different? This happens to me. For example, when I am playing tennis with one particular person, I sometimes see the ball land on the line and he says it landed outside of the line.

There are criteria that are useful in such situations. You can apply them to your own observations and to the reports of others. Although they do not guarantee correctness, they can help. Like the criteria for credibility, these are used in the *R* element of the FRISCO approach to critical thinking: judging the acceptability of the reasons (including evidence). Observation statements usually serve as reasons in an argument. The pathologist's observations, for example, served as reasons for her conclusion that the knife stroke was of only moderate force.

The discussion of observation in this chapter is applicable to your papers in which you defend a position (and to narrative papers in which you simply try to report an occurrence). Some of your reasons in position papers will be observations made by you or by others. These reasons will be justified roughly to the extent that they satisfy the criteria of observation statements presented here. In particular, (to give a summary in advance) they will be justified as observations roughly to the extent that they come from a credible source, are really observations (as opposed to being conclusions), are based on the use of appropriate technology, were made by a competent, careful, unbiased observer under good conditions, are directly reported by the observer, and are based on or corroborated by records of the observation.

Credibility Criteria

Whether the report of the observation is made by you or by someone else, the eight criteria for credibility apply. You are already familiar with these criteria (and should realize that both my opponent and I in the tennis match have a conflict of interest). But these eight criteria are not enough. There is also a set of criteria that apply especially to observation, whether you or someone else is doing it. Again, the criteria are only approximate guides. They cannot be applied automatically. One must use good judgment and pay close attention to the situation (the *S* in *FRISCO*).

Conclusions Versus Observations

An acquaintance reported that he saw a stranger stealing a friend's bicycle. Actually, all that the acquaintance observed was that a person he did not know took the bicycle out of the rack and rode off with it. Because the friend had given the person permission, it was not a case of stealing. My acquaintance concluded that the bike had been stolen, but only observed its removal. The observation that the bike was removed was more dependable than the conclusion that the bike had been stolen. In general, observations are more dependable than the conclusions based on them.

In the courtroom, witnesses (except experts) are not allowed to offer their conclusions. They are allowed to say only what they have observed. For example, in Arlene's trial, a police officer reported that he saw a depression in the snow by the passenger side of Al's automobile. He was asked whether the depression was caused by someone falling down. The defense attorney objected on the ground that the question called for a conclusion. The judge sustained the objection and the question was withdrawn. The police officer observed the depression in the snow, but he was not allowed to report his conclusion about its cause. The policy of prohibiting conclusions is supposed to protect the jury from undue influence and to minimize the errors in the testimony. (The jurors are expected to infer conclusions, however.)

Although the preference of observations over conclusions is usually a good idea, in this particular situation, I thought it was unfortunate that we could not benefit from the police officer's conclusion. Without a photograph, his conclusion about the depression was likely to be helpful in finding out about its shape and its cause. Although an ingenious attorney could have drawn more observational information out of the police officer, the officer's conclusion would have been helpful too. Other people's interpretations are often helpful in developing our own, provided that we are careful. How would you have felt in this case?

This prohibition of conclusions by witnesses in the courtroom does not extend to experts drawing conclusions in their own specialties. The pathologist was permitted to state her conclusion about the strength of the knife stroke. The assumption is that experts are better able to draw conclusions in their own fields than are jurors.

Why Distinguish Observations from Conclusions?

Despite my discomfort with the rigid courtroom prohibition of inferring by (nonexpert) witnesses, there are good reasons for the rule. Furthermore, it is well for us all to be sensitive to the problem out of court. When someone witnesses something, we should be alert for any conclusions in the report of the event, as in the report of the alleged bicycle theft.

A witness reports: "Right after the accident, the driver emerged from the car in a drunken stupor." But possibly the driver was dizzy from the shock of the accident. The proposition that the driver was drunk is a conclusion, and is less dependable than the observation on which it was based. This does not mean that we should totally ignore the witness' conclusion. The witness did see the circumstances, and might have taken much into account in drawing the conclusion. But we should be careful not to accept the witness' conclusion without asking the witness further questions about the situation, which is what the courts call cross-examination. I hesitate to use the term in everyday circumstances because it suggests a hostile confrontation, but a mild version of cross-examination is almost always in order when we face a witness' conclusion.

Jim reported that he saw Martine out with Karl in the Blue Cloud. His seeing Martine and Karl at The Blue Cloud was an observation. But his report that they were out together, given that he glimpsed them only briefly, was a conclusion in that situation. They might have accidentally met at The Blue Cloud, and not have been "out together" at all. In this case, if it matters to us whether Martine was out with Karl, it can be quite important to distinguish the observation from the conclusion. We should generally be more ready to accept the observation than the conclusion based on it. Jim might be a very careful concluder, and might well be right, but many people are not careful concluders and everyone makes mistakes sometimes in drawing conclusions from accurate observations. So there is an important distinction here. Do not claim to have observed what actually is a conclusion.

This is an area to exhibit the critical thinking dispositions "try to be well-informed" and "withhold judgment when the evidence and reasons are insufficient." In other words, be careful, though not overly skeptical.

+ Making the Distinction Between Observations and Conclusions

Beware. In discussions of observations and conclusions, it is easy to fall into the trap of thinking that there really are no observations, only conclusions. Some challenger might claim, for example, that Jim's apparent observation statement, "I saw Karl at the Blue Cloud last night," was really only a conclusion. The challenger might hold that Jim saw someone who looked, talked, and danced like Karl, but who might not really have been Karl. So, the challenger might claim that the statement "I saw Karl at the Blue Cloud last night" was inferred from the fact that the person looked, talked, and danced like Karl, and so could only be a conclusion. The challenger could go on: "Jim was only inferring that it was The Blue Cloud, because all he really could observe was that it had the appearance and atmosphere of the Blue Cloud and a sign outside saying 'Blue Cloud.'" Once a challenger gets going this way, there is no place to stop, if the challenger wants to carry on and neglects the practical features of the situation.

There is at least a two-part response possible, the first part of which depends heavily on the situation (the *S* in *FRISCO*): Jim knows Karl well and could not have failed to recognize him in that situation, and to deny the existence of observations is to destroy our ability to make and apply in a readily understandable way the point that observations are generally more reliable than the conclusions that are based on them. This is an important point to be able to make and apply, as is shown by the great emphasis it receives in the courts and by numerous examples from our own personal experiences.

However, the way the distinction between observations and conclusions is actually drawn in a particular case depends on the situation. Some statements are obviously conclusions in any situation. For example, "The best things in life are free," "The same side of the moon always faces the earth," and "Arlene is not guilty of murder" would be conclusions under any circumstances that I can imagine. But some statements that in a given situation are observations could, in another situation, be conclusions. Consider Jim's statement, "I saw Karl at The Blue Cloud last night." This was an observation statement when I heard it. But imagine a different situation. Suppose that Karl had an identical twin brother who had just arrived in town, and that Jim knew this. Suppose that Jim knew Karl very well, being familiar with the ring he wears, his speech habits, and his clothing. Suppose further that Jim, after seeing this person in a dimly lit Blue Cloud, approached him, noted his ring and clothing, and engaged him in conversation. Suppose that Jim then said to himself, "This must be Karl, not Karl's brother." Then his report to me that he saw Karl was not an observation statement, but was a conclusion.

Sometimes just a challenge can make a conclusion out of what seemed to be an observation statement. Suppose that my companion, while looking routinely at the speedometer in a car, says, "We are going 55 miles per hour." This could justifiably pass as an observation. Suppose that I challenge the statement. If he defends it by saying that the speedometer was recently checked, that the tires are new, and that he is compensating for being off to the side, then a repeat of his statement would be a conclusion because it is now being supported. So the observation–conclusion distinction depends on what is known and acceptable without defense in the situation (the *S* in *FRISCO*). There is not a sharp line separating observations from conclusions.

Summary

On the face of it, there is an obvious distinction between observation statements and conclusions. Observation statements report what is observed. Conclusions state what is inferred from what is observed and other things. Generally, there is more room for error in inferring conclusions than in securing the observations on which they are based. That is why it is often good practice, when someone offers a conclusion, to ask for the observations and other evidence on which it is based. That is, ask, "Just what exactly did you see?" or "What exactly did you hear?" Be careful, though not overly skeptical.

+Under special situations, a statement that looks like an observation report might actually be a low-level conclusion. Then it must be judged as a conclusion. The reasons and inferences supporting it must be judged for their adequacy, or its actual observational source must be judged for credibility and satisfaction of reasonable criteria for an observation (some criteria will be provided later in this chapter). The distinction between observations and conclusions is not precise, and often depends on the situation (the *S* in *FRISCO*).

Check-Up 4A

True or False?
If false, change it to make it true. Try to do so in a way that shows that you understand.

4:1 Observations are generally more reliable than conclusions inferred from them.

4:2 In decisions about whether to believe an observation report by someone else, the eight credibility criteria apply, as well as special criteria for observation.

Short Answer

Classify each of the italicized statements as an observation report (O) or a conclusion (C). If in doubt, imagine and describe in writing a situation in which your doubt would be resolved, and then make your judgment.

4:3 *The barometer now reads 30.10 inches and it is 11 A.M.*

4:4 *The barometer read 29.92 inches at 7 A.M.*

4:5 So *the weather will clear up.*

4:6 The ambulance driver said, *"I arrived at 11:10 P.M."*

4:7 The ambulance driver said, *"He was dead when I arrived."*

4:8 The ambulance driver said, *"He could not have been dead very long."*

4:9 The director said, *"On page 65 of my script, these words appear: 'A rose by any other name would smell as sweet.'"*

4:10 The director said, *"That means that you don't change something just by changing its name."*

4:11 My companion, while looking at the speedometer, said, *"This vehicle is traveling at 60 miles per hour."*

4:12 My companion, while still looking at the speedometer, said, *"I observe that you are exceeding the speed limit."*

The Process of Observing

So far, we have considered the distinction between conclusions and observations and the importance of minimal concluding in an observation report. Let us turn now to the actual process of observing, and some criteria for making judgments about observations. As with the credibility criteria you considered in the previous chapter, these criteria do not apply themselves automatically. Good judgment and sensitivity are required in applying them.

Appropriate Technology

Some observations, like the observation of Saturn's rings from a space ship, require elaborate technology. Others, like Jim's seeing Martine and Karl at the Blue Cloud, require only Jim's eyes (which, though not high technology, were the appropriate technology for that situation). Space ship or television technology was not only unnecessary for the observation of Martine and Karl, but it would have interfered with the actions of the subject of the observation. Martine and Karl might well have gone somewhere else if they knew there was a television camera at the Blue Cloud.

The general rule here is vague: The technology of the observation should be appropriate for the subject being observed and for the information required. In order to apply this criterion, you must know something about the subject and the available technology. Otherwise, you must place your faith in someone else's judgment about these. Then you must depend on your application to the other person of the criteria of credibility. This is because in effect you would be taking someone's word that the technology was appropriate.

Observation Conditions

If the Blue Cloud had been very smoky, it would have been much more difficult for Jim to identify Martine. Identification of the North Star can be made difficult or impossible by clouds, haze, moonlight, and sunlight. The conditions must be conducive to observation.

Observer's Ability

Observer's ability is generally crucial to the making of a reliable observation. This holds for such diverse activities as recognizing people, tracking animals, reading barometers, and determining the composition of the sun by using a spectroscope. Observer ability involves background knowledge (for example, knowing what Karl looks like, knowing what a raccoon track looks like, knowing that elevation above sea level affects barometers, knowing the spectroscopic display of sodium, etc.). It also involves doing certain things well (for example, focusing and aiming a telescope, lining up the line across the top of the mercury's surface with some point on the scale, estimating the correct reading on the basis of the position of a point between the lines on a scale, etc.). It involves knowing to check and recheck the observed phenomenon and the condition of the equipment and surroundings by answering such questions as these: Is the barometer straight up and down? Am I avoiding parallax distortion? (Parallax distortion comes from the observer's eyes being off to the side, or too high or low, so that the reading on the scale is different from the one that would be obtained from a position directly in front. I mention parallax distortion because it can interfere in so many different situations that one should generally be aware of it.) Am I reading the scale right (misreading a scale being another widespread enemy of accuracy)? Do I get the same reading when I observe again? Is there enough light for me to be sure?

Lastly, observer ability includes having the senses needed by the observer (that is, sight, hearing, etc.) in good enough condition. To read a barometer, for example, one's eyes must be functioning well (though, perhaps with help, such as eyeglasses).

Because the important features of observer ability vary from situation to situation, the most that can be required for all cases is this: The observer's ability must be adequate for the observation. However, things such as parallax, misreading, failure to check and recheck, and defective senses are often important enough to rate special mention as dangers.

Observer Attention, Lack of Bias, Care

Inattentive, biased, and careless observers are a significant source of error, as we all well know from our own errors when inattentive, biased, or careless. Fatigue, drugs, alcohol, and distractions often cause inattention. However, when under such influences, observers often do not realize their reduced dependability, even when we ourselves are the observers.

Often observers tend to "see" what they want to see or expect to see, even if it does not occur. You need only to survey the news media today to find examples. Protections against such bias should be used, such as obtaining observers who have no conflict of interest and who are open to seeing what actually occurs rather than what they are sure is going to occur. In experiments where human beings are identifying different products, it is best that the judgers do not know what they are identifying (as in Coke vs. Pepsi identification tests, which require such a "blind" procedure).

In some situations, even double-blind procedures are appropriate. For example, in the testing of medicines, it is often best for the person dispensing the medicines (as well as the patients) not to know whether the material they are dispensing is the thing being tested or a placebo. This is because the dispensers of the medicine might communicate the nature of the dose to the patient, often inadvertently. The term *double-blind* is used to indicate that neither the subjects nor the persons dealing with the subjects know what is being dispensed.

Summary

The process of observation should use appropriate technology, be conducted under good conditions, and be done by an observer who is skilled enough for the type of observation being made and who is attentive, unbiased, and careful. If the actual observation is not done well, any inferences we draw from the observations are suspect.

Observation Reports

In general, the closer the observation report to the observation, the better. This closeness is not only closeness in time but also closeness of the reporter to the observation. Rejection of hearsay evidence and emphasis on records are attempts to maintain this closeness.

Hearsay

The prohibition of hearsay is another fairly rigid rule in the courts. Roughly speaking, *hearsay* is testimony that reports what someone else said with the intention of persuading the listener of the truth of what was said. Rumors are standard examples of hearsay. Babette reported to Sarah, who has an interest in Jon, "Manuel told me that he saw Jon out with Martine at the Blue Cloud." That is hearsay, and Sarah should be careful in accepting such a report.

When people report what other people say, they often do not get the words exactly the same. Manuel actually said that he saw Jon and Martine at the Blue Cloud. But Babette did not quote him exactly and produced a statement ("out with") different in meaning from Manuel's, perhaps getting Jon in trouble with Sarah.

Not every report of what someone else has said is hearsay. If a person yelled "Fire!" in a theater, and someone reported that fact in a trial of the person for negligent behavior (because there was no fire), the testimony would not be hearsay. In order to be hearsay, there must also be the intention that someone will take the testimony as support for the original person's assertion (in this case, that would be the assertion that there was a fire). But the point of the testimony was not to show that there was a fire, but rather to show that the person yelled "Fire" and might therefore have been responsible for the ensuing riot.

In Arlene's trial, the prosecuting attorney asked a police officer who was stationed in front of the house whether another police officer said he saw footprints in the back of the yard. The prosecutor then asked for more details about what the other police officer said about the footprints. The defense attorney objected. Understandably, the judge sustained the objection, so the question was withdrawn. Its answer would have been hearsay, as was the answer to the previous question, which was stricken from the record.

One reason for the courtroom prohibition of hearsay is that people are often wrong about what other people say they saw. They are wrong about this more often than the original observer is wrong. Another reason is that a witness giving hearsay cannot be confronted, cross-examined, or questioned for more details about the event. For example, the police officer stationed in the front of the house would have been unable to give more details than he himself was given about the footprints in the snow around Al's car. He could not be cross-examined about those footprints.

John H. Wigmore, a standard authority on legal evidence, defends the importance of the possibility of cross-examination this way:

> Why this insistence on the opportunity to cross-examine? Because the experience of the last three centuries of judicial trials has demonstrated convincingly that in disputed issues one cannot depend on the mere assertion of anybody, however plausible, without scrutiny into its basis. All the weaknesses that may affect a witness' trustworthiness—observation, memory, bias, interest, and the like— may otherwise lurk unrevealed; modifying circumstances omitted in his tale may give his facts an entirely different effect, if disclosed; and cross-examination is the best way to get at these.[1] (Note Wigmore's emphasis on the importance of the situation—the *S* in *FRISCO*.)

A good example of the utility of confrontation and cross-examination arose in Arlene's trial. She and Al were the only ones in the dining room at the time of his stabbing. So she was the only available source of a first-hand account. Although the defense attorney had the right not to have her called to the stand, he chose to call her. It looks suspicious if the defendant refuses to testify and be cross-examined.

She testified that when trying to escape from him, she grabbed the knife from the cabinet top and, in desperation, swung it around behind her without even looking at him. If she had not been on the stand, then her attorney would presumably have said something to that effect. That would have been hearsay. He could not have been cross-examined about it. Even if he had been, oddities in the story could not have been explored because the best he could do is simply repeat what she had told him.

---

1. John H. Wigmore, *A Student's Textbook of the Laws of Evidence* (Brooklyn: The Foundation Press, 1935), 238–239.

In choosing to call her to the stand, he exposed her to the risk of cross-examination, though he protected her from the embarrassment of refusing to testify. The prosecuting attorney proceeded to ask her whether she is left- or right-handed. She said she is right-handed. The placement of the knife, the cabinet, and the wall required her to swing at him with her left hand, if her swing was backhanded, as she said. When the attorney pointed this out, she agreed and said she swung with her left hand. On request she demonstrated the action. The prosecutor then showed her a diagram of the room and the furniture and contended that the victim could not have been in a place where he could be hit in the way he was hit if she swung the way she said. This could not have come out, if we had been given only the defense attorney's account of what she said, without cross-examination. Incidentally, the jury later acted out the stabbing in accord with her description and found the description implausible.

Although there are good reasons for the prohibition of hearsay in the courts, exceptions are allowed. Reporting someone's dying words (such as Al's saying, "Arlene stabbed me," to Arlene's father) is often allowable.

In daily life, we often offer and accept hearsay. Often, this is perfectly all right. For example, in marking a checklist, a copilot records what the pilot says he sees. The copilot asks, "Gear-down lights [on]?" The pilot says "Check" or something like that, meaning that the lights that show that the landing gear is down are lit. The copilot, without actually looking at the lights, checks the box by that item and thus makes a hearsay record. The procedure is quite appropriate.

Although there are legitimate exceptions, hearsay is often still dangerous. Generally, it is better to get closer to the observation than to use an intermediary. Much gossip is hearsay, and often is distorted, as we all well know.

An interesting way to show the unreliability of second-hand, third-hand, and even more remote observation reports is to play a game called "Telephone." Have a friend write down in two sentences a description of something the friend has seen, allowing no one else to see the writing at that time. Then the friend, unheard by the rest of the group, tells a second friend what is written. The second friend, unheard by the rest, tells a third, then on to a fourth. This should be enough, but more can be added. The last in the line gives aloud the report as he or she believes it to be. Discrepancies from the original are usually interesting.

Records

We are all familiar with the phenomenon of bad memories. Mine is particularly bad. The longer the time since an event, the more likely it is that I have forgotten the details—often the entire event. For most people, reports of long-ago events are less dependable than recent reports.

There are exceptions. For example, distant events that were particularly significant to the observer can be better remembered than more recent events of lesser significance. Furthermore, older people sometimes remember long-ago events much more clearly than recent ones.

Generally, the safest way to ensure accuracy is to make a record. Although introducing a system of records brings in another possible source of error, records are generally much better than memory, although they can be altered. When I record the car mileage at the beginning of a trip, my numbers are occasionally difficult to read, but my record is almost always better than my memory.

Great emphasis on records is found in the courtroom, and for good reason. On things that can be recorded, records are less prone to simple error than memories and there is usually less opportunity to alter a record without getting caught than to alter one's report of something one remembers. For example, an erasure of my mileage number might well show, but a switch in what I decide to report from my memory would go undetected.

There is an elaborate set of guidelines used in courtrooms to help us have confidence in the observation records offered in evidence. They are not rigid rules; they depend on the particular situation. Roughly speaking, they try to ensure that the correct observation was recorded in the first place and that the record was adequately protected from alteration. Among other things, they emphasize the following four guidelines:

> The record is made by the observer. (This eliminates an extra possible source of error.)

> The observer (who, it is hoped, is also the record maker) is the one who gives the report, rather than someone else. (This eliminates an extra possible source of error and enables cross-examination).

> The observer claims to remember that at the time of making the record he or she believed it to be correct, or the observer has the habit of making correct records.

> There is corroboration of the records. (*Corroboration* is agreement that comes from some other source.)

For each of these four guidelines, can you think of a case you know in which it was violated (with some sort of distortion resulting from the violation)?

Actually, there are many more guidelines used in the courts for specific kinds of situations. Legal practice depends on accuracy of observation reports. But the guidelines I have mentioned are the most important general ones. Different situations call for different emphases and kinds of application, so you must be sensitive to the situation in order to apply these guidelines properly, and (perhaps) to develop some that are special for the type of situation you find.

For example, it was important to determine whether the knife was lying out in plain view before the stabbing. If it was, then Arlene's claim that she just grabbed it without thinking much about it would be more plausible. If it was not lying in plain view, then the stabbing would have seemed to be more deliberate and to have required more thought by Arlene.

There was a written record of evidence about the knife's location: the detective's notes on Arlene's original statement about the stabbing. For this record, Arlene was the observer and the detective a hearsay recorder of Arlene's observation. Unfortunately, Arlene had an obvious conflict of interest. It was in her interest for the jury to believe that the knife was lying in plain sight. Given this conflict of interest, it was important to get and record corroborating testimony from other members of her family (who also had a conflict of interest). Other corroboration from visitors would also have been helpful, but it was not available.

Further examination of Arlene would not have been as much help as such corroboration. The question was a simple one. Was the knife on the cabinet top or not? This was a case in which the guideline calling for corroboration was more important than the guideline calling for the observer (Arlene) to make the report to the jury.

In another situation, however, it was more important to satisfy the report-by-observer guideline than the corroboration guideline. This concerned the nature of the wound. The pathologist testified that the wound did not involve bones and was clean, directed downward at about 45 degrees, and about 2.5 inches deep. Was it so clean that the knife had to go in and out at the same angle (45 degrees)? If so, the jury might conclude that the knife stroke could not have been made the way Arlene described.

The pathologist's written record merely said "clean." So, under questioning, she needed to give further details, which would come from her memory, not the written record. Corroboration by others was not especially important here. She was accepted as an expert without conflict of interest. So this was a case in which the report-by-observer guideline was more important than the corroboration guideline.

The point is that different situations call for different emphases on the guidelines. You must use your own good judgment in applying them and in developing special ones to fit particular situations. But even though there is variation in the degree of emphasis on the guidelines, the guidelines as a whole make a good basis for a judgment.

Summary

A report of an observation is generally more dependable if made by the observer. Furthermore, if the observer makes the report in person, then the observer can be questioned and unclear points clarified—an advantage.

It is generally desirable to base observation reports on records made at the time of observation. Records are usually better than memories, and are generally less susceptible to deliberate deception. But records can be altered and mistakes can creep in, making corroboration desirable.

Check-Up 4B

True or False?
If false, change it to make it true. Try to do so in a way that shows that you understand.

4:13 Any testimony in which a witness reports what he or she heard someone else say is called *hearsay*.

4:14 Hearsay testimony is always improper in a court of law.

4:15 Observation reports by the observer are generally to be preferred over others' reports of these observation reports.

4:16 Generally, records and memories are equally reliable sources of observation reports.

4:17 The guidelines for presenting and requesting observation records are equally important in each situation.

Short Answer

For the italicized material in each of Items 4:18 through 4:23, mark one or more of A, B, C, and D, or choose E for "None of these":

A. The italicized material is hearsay.

B. The italicized material is a presentation by the observer of a record of an observation, the record having been made by the observer.

C. The italicized material is a presentation by someone (not the observer) of a record of an observation, the record having been made by the observer.

D. The italicized material is a presentation by someone (not the observer) of a record of an observation, the record having been made by a third person (also not the observer).

E. None of these.

4:18 Arlene's father said "I heard Al shout, *'Arlene, you stabbed me.'*" (This served as evidence that Arlene stabbed Al.)

4:19 *"I saw Martine and Karl out together at the Blue Cloud,"* said Jim.

4:20 Jim said, "I wrote in my notebook that *I saw Martine in the Blue Cloud at 11:00 P.M.*"

4:21 The person investigating the crash of the airliner reported, "*There was a check in the box by the phrase on the checklist, 'Gear-down lights [on]'.* Presumably the copilot made the check after asking the pilot whether those lights were lit."

4.22 Sir James Cottrell-Fiske said, "I wrote in my diary for November 18 that *I saw a V-2 rocket buzzing over London.*" (This was offered by Cottrell-Fiske as evidence that V-2s were in operation by that time.)

4:23 Detective Pulaski said, "*Detective Jones found Al's keys in a pocket of Arlene's purse, with the pocket zipped closed. Detective Jones found the purse on the dining room floor.* Detective Jones wrote this information down in her report made out at 3 A.M. the next morning, and she told me about it as well. Unfortunately, Detective Jones has left the state to take a position elsewhere, so she cannot give this report in person."

Medium Answer

4:24 In a newspaper or magazine, find one observation statement. Copy or present enough of the selection in which it appears for your instructor to understand what is going on. Underline the statement. Classify the observation statement as you have just done with the previous ones (one or more of A-D or E) and tell whether you believe it and why.

Making an Overall Appraisal of an Observation Statement

For convenience in summarizing your reactions to an observation statement, you can make a chart like the credibility chart and include the credibility criteria. You can make it detailed with a line for each concern, or make fewer lines by grouping the criteria. My rough attempts to do this for the statement as uttered by Arlene, "The knife was in plain sight on the cabinet" and for the pathologist's statement, "The wound was about 2.5 inches deep," are in Table 4.1.

TABLE 4.1 Judging Observation Statements

1. Credibility of source

	Arlene's statement "The knife was in plain sight on the cabinet."	Pathologist's statement "The wound was about 2½ inches deep."
a. Background experience or knowledge	Strong	Strong
b. Lack of conflict of interest	Very weak	Strong
c. Agreement with others who come out as well as, or better, on other criteria	Satisfactory	No judgment
d. Reputation	No judgment	Strong
e. Established procedures	Strong	Strong
f. Known risk to reputation	Satisfactory	Strong
g. Ability to give reasons	Strong	Strong
h. Careful habits	Uncertain	Strong
Summary: Credibility	Weak	Strong

2. Minimal concluding involved (observation rather than inference)

	Strong	Strong

3. The process of observation

a. Appropriate technology	Strong	Strong
b. Observation conditions	Strong	Strong
c. Observer ability	Strong	Strong
b. Observation attention, bias, care	Weak	Strong
Summary: Process of observation	Satisfactory	Strong

4. The report

a. Nonhearsay	Strong	Strong
b. Records		
i Records made by observer	Weak	Strong
ii Report made by observer	Strong	Strong
iii Observer claims to remember correctness, or has habit of being correct	Strong	Strong
iv Corroboration of record	Satisfactory	None
Summary: The report	Satisfactory	Strong
Summary of all my judgments:	Uncertain	Very probably true

Although there are eighteen criterion-based judgments before the grouped and final judgments in Table 4.1, one could group the criteria to make, for example, four judgments before the final judgment. The four could be credibility, minimal concluding (observation, rather than concluding), the process of observation, and the report. If one seeks a little more detail, one could substitute three subcategories from the process of observation (technology, conditions, and observer) and two from report (nonhearsay and records), making seven crucial categories in all (credibility, minimal concluding, technology, conditions, observer, nonhearsay, and records). Other organizing arrangements of relevant factors are possible. What organizing arrangement do you like, given some situation with which you are familiar? Think about it.

No matter how the relevant factors are organized, there is no precise line that separates fully reliable from fully unreliable observation statements, and you must not simply keep score. One overall judgment must be made, taking into account the separate judgments. The final judgment must take into account the relative importance of your separate judgments, given the situation.

I would have judged Arlene's statement to be probably true if I had given roughly equal weighting to each of the four major categories that I used. But actually, I felt that she had much to gain by lying about this. Consider: The knife's being in plain sight could have suggested its use to a frightened person, making her use of it more readily interpretable as a thoughtless act. Under this interpretation, she would not have known that what she was doing "caused a strong probability of great bodily harm," which became a crucial condition for murder in this case. So the conflict of interest criterion was very important. This criterion also made the corroboration from her family less helpful because they also had a conflict of interest. So I gave the rating "uncertain" to Arlene's observation statement. On the other hand, I judged the pathologist's statement to be very probably true because that statement came out so very well on all the criteria that seemed important in that situation. (Note the importance of the situation in this process, the *S* in *FRISCO*.)

Perhaps you have noticed that there is some duplication in the criteria. Corroboration of a record (under records) might simply be achieved by agreement with others (under credibility). Because corroboration is very important, such double attention seems acceptable.

The credibility criterion "ability to give reasons" requires a special interpretation when applied to observation statements. If someone actually gives a reason to support a statement, then the statement becomes a conclusion rather than an observation. My suggestion is to let ability to give reasons here mean ability to give reasons in defense of the observation procedure that was used. This could be a simple defense of a simple procedure. For example, Jim should have been able to say, if asked, "Just looking around at the Blue Cloud was all I had to do. It is a small, well-lighted place, it was not crowded, and the air was clear."

Note that I judged both statements strong for observer's skill because I felt that each person had sufficient skill to make the observation being made. You might be tempted to judge Arlene negatively here because no special ability is required to observe a knife in plain sight. But remember all that matters is that the observer have enough ability for the type of observation being made. Arlene satisfied that requirement.

Finally, note that I judged Arlene weak on "Record made by observer."

Although the police later questioned her and secured a statement from her, she did not at the time of the killing write anything down or tape record her observations about Al's death. This is not to say that she should have done so. Not making a record at the time of observation did detract from the reliability of her observations. Therefore, I judged her observation report weak here—the same score I would give to anyone else who did not make an immediate record of an observation.

I suggest that you examine each value I have assigned and try to see why I did what I did. In my assignments, I naturally took more information into account than you can know. Knowing the situation is very important, so do not expect complete agreement between us. Rather, seek to understand roughly how I arrived at my judgments, given what you already know about the trial.

The fact that your judgments inevitably depend on your appraisal of a situation does not mean that just any judgment is acceptable. Clearly, Arlene's observation statement was not as dependable as the pathologist's statement.

Chapter Summary

In this chapter, you have considered a number of criteria for observations. When you are considering observation statements, the criteria for credibility also apply. Application of each criterion requires good judgment, as does weighting them and making an overall judgment. These criteria should be used not only for discussion and grounding of inferences in your personal, vocational, and civic situations, but for vocational or civic position papers that depend on observations for one or more reasons in support of your views.

Although loose and vague to an extent, the criteria are useful. Some statements are more dependable than others, as an application of the criteria can show. But you must keep the whole situation in mind and be flexible, vigilant, and careful.

Observation comes under the *R* in *FRISCO* and depends on the *S*. It is used in judging the acceptability of reasons (including evidence).

Check-Up 4C

True or False?
If false, change it to make it true. Try to do so in a way that shows you understand.

4:25 Skill in observing is required only where technology is involved.

4:26 All really reliable observations require special technology.

4:27 After rating an observation statement according to each of the criteria for judging observation statements, you should judge as unreliable any statement that receives less than strong ratings for at least two criteria.

4:28 Agreement by several people on an observation statement is the most important criterion for observation statements.

Medium Answer

4:29 Take the one statement you considered for 4:24, identify it, and use the suggested system for assigning judgments. Use a level of complexity of the system with which you feel comfortable for the situation. Reach a final judgment and explain why you made your final judgment. Then explain why you used the degree of complexity of the system that you did use. Was your judgment helped by the suggested system for assigning values? Why?

4:30 Do the same for an observation statement made by a friend. Be sure to quote the statement and describe the situation.

4:31 Is the full set of observation criteria too elaborate for your purposes? Why? If it is too elaborate, develop an alternative and apply it in a situation you describe. Comment on the usefulness of your system for the situation you have described.

Suggested Answers for Chapter 4

Reminder: In some cases different answers are as good as the ones given. If one of your answers is different from the one suggested, then either try to satisfy yourself that yours really is all right or else try to figure out why it is not.

Check-Up 4A

4:1 T	**4:2** T	**4:3** O	**4:4** O	**4:5** C	**4:6** O
4:7 C	**4:8** C	**4:9** O	**4:10** C	**4:11** O	**4:12** C

Check-Up 4B

4:13 F	**4:14** F	**4:15** T	**4:16** F	**4:17** F

4:13 Roughly speaking, hearsay is testimony in which a witness reports something that he or she heard someone else say (and the testimony is intended to support the claim that what was said was true).

4:14 Hearsay testimony is usually improper in a court of law.

4:16 Generally, records are more reliable than memories.

4:17 The weighting of the guidelines for presenting and requesting observation records varies with the situation.

4:18 A	**4:19** E	**4:20** B	**4:21** D	**4:22** B	**4:23** A & C

4:24 This is up to you. I will be asking you about this one again.

Check-Up 4C

4:25 F	**4:26** F	**4:27** F	**4:28** F

4:25 Skill in observing is often required even when technology is not involved.

4:26 Many reliable observations do not require special technology.

4:27 There are no precise score cutoff points for reliability of observation statements.

4:28 Corroboration of an observation statement is often very important, but not always the most important thing.

4:29 and **4:30** These are up to you. Be sure that you have taken the situation into account in making your judgment.

4:31 Check your alternative with some friends or associates.

Deduction: Class Logic

In Chapters 2, 3, and 4, our primary concerns were with analyzing arguments and appraising reasons. Now we turn to inference (*FRISCO's I*), the step from the reason(s) to the conclusion.

In Chapters 5 and 6, we shall look only at one kind of inference, basically the kind that has interested professional logicians: deductive inference. However, the approach to deductive inference in this book will be different from theirs because our purpose in critical thinking is practical and general, theirs theoretical and abstract, making theirs heavily symbolic. Although their symbolic approach is very valuable for certain purposes of philosophers, mathematicians, computer scientists, and some others, it has drawbacks when used as a guide to the practical reasoning of people actually deciding what to believe or do. One drawback is the difficulty for most people of understanding its systems at even an elementary level. A second is that most of these systems are occasionally misleading as guidelines to reasoning.[1]

Because the approach to deductive logic you will see here is simple, practical, more intuitive, and usable from the outset of your study, there is much value in it. But if you are looking for an elegant, abstract, symbolic system, you will not find it here. For that, you should go to a standard deductive-logic textbook.

In this chapter, you will be introduced to the meaning of the central question in deductive inference: Does a conclusion follow necessarily from one or more other propositions? You will also learn a few specific techniques for handling some standard kinds of deductive arguments. These will give you a good start, but realize that there are many other techniques and possible refinements.

For some people, the material in Chapters 5 and 6 is easy. For others, it is dif-

---

1. This is a controversial topic, beyond the scope of this book, but those who are interested might start with a look at C. I. Lewis' "Implication and the Algebra of Logic," *Mind,* October 1912, pp. 522–531, and P. F. Strawson's *Introduction to Logical Theory* (London: Methuen & Co., 1952), where some misleading features are elaborated. H. P. Grice, in his "Logic and Conversation," in *The Philosophy of Language* (2nd edition), edited by A. P. Martinich (Oxford: Oxford University Press, 1990), offers a defense.

ficult. If it is difficult for you, find someone for whom it is easy, and ask for help. If it is easy for you, help someone. By so doing, both parties will actually learn much more than they would otherwise.

Deductive Validity and Invalidity

Let us start with the basic concept in deductive inference: *deductive validity*. To say that an argument is *deductively valid* is to say that its conclusion follows necessarily from its reasons. That is to say, if you accept the reasons in a deductively valid argument, you are thereby automatically committed to accepting the conclusion. In a deductively valid argument, it would be contradictory to reject the conclusions if you accept the reasons. Consider this argument:

Example 5:1

Look, you do realize that if Ben is a cat, then Ben is an animal. And Ben definitely is a cat. So, it follows that Ben is an animal.

As usual, the first thing is to identify the conclusion (the *F* in *FRISCO*), which is "Ben is an animal." Then we look for the reasons (*FRISCO*'s *R*), which are *a* and *b* in Example 5:2. Reducing the argument to its minimum features, it becomes:

Example 5:2

   a. If Ben is a cat, then Ben is an animal.
   b. Ben is a cat.
   c. Therefore, Ben is an animal.

In this argument, the conclusion follows necessarily from the combination of reasons, *a* and *b*. That is, if you accept *a* and *b,* you are automatically committed to accepting *c*. There is no way to avoid it. The argument is deductively valid. Make sure that you see this utter unavoidability of the conclusion, given the reasons. It is the essential feature of deductive validity.

This concept of deduction is different from that of Sherlock Holmes. Generally, his "deduced" conclusions were based on inductive inference, a type of inference we shall consider soon, starting in Chapter 8. His conclusions generally were supported by very strong evidence, but were not absolutely unavoidable. For example, in *The Sign of the Four,* when he concluded that a man with a wooden leg had been in the victim's room, there were other possible explanations for the fact that there were marks on the floor like the marks that would have been made by a wooden leg. The marks on the floor might have been made by someone else in order to implicate the man with the wooden leg. Thus, we are not inescapably committed to Holmes' conclusion on the basis of his evidence. At best, most of his "deduced" conclusions followed "beyond a reasonable doubt," the standard used in criminal trials in contemporary courts.

Deductive validity is a much more stringent standard. Given the reasons in a deductively valid argument, there is absolutely no way to avoid the conclusion. But as you will come to see, this standard is an ideal about which we often need to make compromises in practical situations. More about these compromises later. But before you can consider the compromises, you must become familiar with the ideal.

Note that it is only the *relationship* between the reasons and the conclusion that we are talking about when we call an argument deductively valid. We are not talking about the conclusion—or the premises—in themselves. In particular, to call an argument deductively valid is *not* to say that the conclusion is true. Here is an example of a deductively valid argument with a *false* conclusion:

Example 5:3

    a. Whales are large fish.
    b. All large fish lay eggs.
    c. Therefore, whales lay eggs.

In Example 5:3, if you accept *a* and *b,* you are automatically committed to accepting *c,* so the argument is deductively valid, even though the conclusion and the first premise are false.

There is a use for deductive arguments that lead to false conclusions. Such arguments are a way to show that one or more of the reasons are false: If a deductively valid argument has a false conclusion (as in Example 5:3), then we know that at least one of the reasons is false. Otherwise, the conclusion would have to be true because the argument is deductively valid. Suppose that there are only two reasons in a deductively valid argument with a false conclusion (as in Example 5:3). Then, if one of the reasons is true, the other must be false (because at least one has to be false). In Example 5:3, if we assume that *b* is true and *c* is false, then *a* must be false. Therefore, the deductive validity and the assumptions that *c* is false and *b* is true establish that *a* is false. That is, they establish that whales are not large fish. This is the standard kind of reasoning used in rejecting hypotheses.

You will read more about this later, but I discussed the example here to show that a deductively valid argument can have a false conclusion, and that there is a practical use for deductively valid arguments with false conclusions.

Deductive Invalidity

A *deductively invalid* argument is one in which the conclusion does *not* necessarily follow from the reasons. Here is one:

Example 5:4

    a. Fish are vertebrates.
    b. Mammals are vertebrates.
    c. Therefore, fish are mammals.

The fact that fish and mammals share a common characteristic, being vertebrates, does not require that fish be mammals. Here is another deductively invalid argument:

Example 5:5

    a. Whales are vertebrates.
    b. <u>Mammals are vertebrates.</u>
    c. Therefore, whales are mammals.

In Example 5:5, even though the conclusion and the reasons are true, the conclusion does not follow necessarily from the reasons given. As in the fish argument, the fact that whales and mammals share a common characteristic does not require that whales be mammals. Whales are mammals, but this is not necessarily established by their sharing this common characteristic. If you do not see this, substitute *fish* for *whales* in Example 5:5. This substitution exhibits the deductive invalidity of the argument in Example 5:5. This sort of substitution is helpful in seeing deductive invalidity (or validity) when your beliefs about truth interfere with your judgments about deductive validity, or when the argument is too complicated or abstract for you to comprehend comfortably.

Examples 5:4 and 5:5 are helpful in several ways:

They exhibit deductively invalid relationships.

Example 5:5 shows that an argument can have a true conclusion even though it is deductively invalid.

Together, the examples exhibit one technique for evaluating an argument: constructing a similar argument, the validity or invalidity of which is easy to see.

It is important to realize that deductive invalidity is often not a fatal flaw in an argument. Many good arguments are deductively invalid. An example was presented early in Chapter 2: the prosecutor's proof beyond a reasonable doubt that Arlene performed the act that caused Al's death.

Summary

We have begun to look at one standard kind of inference: deductive inference. It is different from what Sherlock Holmes generally called "deduction," but is similar in basic spirit, though not in detail, to the deduction of symbolic logic. However, ours is the deduction of everyday reasoning. It is easier to learn this at the outset, and it avoids the occasionally misleading features of symbolic logic. It also lacks the elegance of symbolic logic, but it has practical uses, as you will see.

To say that an argument is *deductively valid* is to say that if the reasons are accepted, the conclusion must necessarily also be accepted. The truth of the reasons requires the truth of the conclusion if the argument is deductively valid. To say that an argument is not deductively valid is to say that the conclusion does not follow necessarily—although it might be true and well-established by the reasons, perhaps even proved beyond a reasonable doubt.

A deductively invalid argument can have a true conclusion, so showing an argument to be deductively invalid does not show the conclusion to be false. A deductively valid argument can have a false conclusion, if at least one of the reasons is false. It can also have a true conclusion together with false reasons. But showing an argument to be deductively valid, if the reasons are true, establishes that the conclusion is true. Furthermore, showing the conclusion of a deductively valid argument to be false establishes that at least one of the reasons is false.

In brief, any combination is possible but the combination of deductive validity, all true reasons, and a false conclusion. If you have any two of the three, you cannot have the third.

Although these points were illustrated with some examples, digesting them and feeling comfortable with them will probably require practice with and discussion of many more examples, including some that apply these basic ideas to your own specialty. Try to apply these ideas to examples in your own specialty, as well as to the examples provided here.

Check-Up 5A

True or False?
If false, change it to make it true. Try to do so in a way that shows that you understand.

5:1 A deductively valid argument is one in which the conclusion follows necessarily from the reasons.

5:2 If an argument is deductively valid, acceptance of the reasons commits you to accepting the conclusion.

5:3 Deductive validity is equivalent to proof beyond a reasonable doubt.

5:4 If the conclusion of an argument is true, then the argument must be deductively valid.

5:5 If the conclusion of an argument is false, then the argument must be deductively invalid.

5:6 If the conclusion of a deductively valid argument is false, then one or more of the reasons is false.

5:7 If the conclusion of an argument is false and the reasons are true, then the argument is deductively invalid.

Short Answer
For each of the following arguments, decide whether you think it is deductively valid or deductively invalid. Use your basic understanding of deductive validity as I have explained it: If you accept the reasons, you are thereby committed to accepting the conclusion.

5:8 a. Houses are buildings.
  b. Buildings are structures.
  c. Therefore, houses are structures.

5:9 **a.** Motorcycles are vehicles.
   b. Vehicles are mechanical contraptions.
   c. Therefore, motorcycles are mechanical contraptions.

5:10 **a.** Houses are structures.
   b. Homes are structures.
   c. Therefore, houses are homes.

5:11 **a.** Birds have wings.
   b. Ostriches are birds.
   c. Therefore, ostriches have wings.

5:12 **a.** No vehicles are permitted.
   b. Motorcycles are vehicles.
   c. Therefore, no motorcycles are permitted.

Class Logic, Using a Circle System

Next, we shall consider one common type of deductive logic—class logic—the type that deals with relationships among classes and individuals. We shall use a circle system for dealing with class logic arguments.

Inclusion

In this circle system, deductive arguments are represented by a set of circles (called Euler circles[2]) and *X*s, each circle representing a class. *X*s represent individuals.

First, I shall represent the argument in Check-Up Item 5:8 with circles, so check back and read that argument. The purpose here is to show how the system works. You already know that the argument is deductively valid.

Diagram 5:1, using one circle, represents the class of buildings:

Diagram 5:1

To show that the class of houses is included in the class of buildings, a circle for houses is put inside the circle for buildings:

Diagram 5:2

---

2. This system is largely based on one developed by Leonhard Euler, a Swiss mathematician. Professor William Rapaport has suggested useful changes.

Diagram 5:2 is a picture of the relationship stated by reason *a* in Check-Up Item 5:8. That reason is, "Houses are buildings." The fact that the circle for houses is inside the circle for buildings pictures the relationship between houses and buildings that is asserted in reason *a*. It shows that houses are buildings; that is, the class of houses is included in the class of buildings. If that picturing is not clear to you, think about it for a while. This is an example of the basic relationship in this circle approach.

Although the word *all* is not in the original proposition, we draw diagrams as if it were, that is, as if the original were "*All* houses are buildings." It is generally a good idea to do this, unless there is reason from the context not to do so.

Diagram 5:3 pictures the relationship asserted in reason *b*, "Buildings are structures."

Diagram 5:3

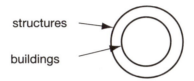

Note that Diagrams 5:2 and 5:3 have a circle in common: the circle for buildings. The diagrams can be combined, drawing the circle for buildings only once, as in Diagram 5:4, which you could form by placing Diagram 5:2 over Diagram 5:3.

Diagram 5:4

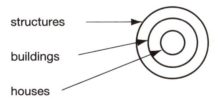

Notice that by combining the diagrams for the two reasons (*a* and *b*), I have made a diagram that shows that the conclusion is inescapable. That is, Diagram 5:4 shows that the circle for houses is unavoidably inside the circle for structures, which is to say that houses are structures. There is no way to avoid diagramming the conclusion, given the diagrams of the reasons.

The Basic Circle-System Validity Test

The circle diagram exhibits the validity of the argument of Check-Up Item 5:8. It does this by showing that diagramming the reasons forces us to diagram the conclusion. Here is the circle diagram test for deductive validity:

Can diagramming the reasons force us to diagram the conclusion? If so, the argument is deductively valid. If not, the argument is deductively invalid.

Apply this test to the next example, Check-Up Item 5:9.

a. Motorcycles are vehicles.
b. Vehicles are mechanical contraptions.
c. Therefore, motorcycles are mechanical contraptions.

Putting the two reasons in the same diagram gives Diagram 5:5. You ordinarily do not need to draw two separate diagrams when combining two reasons. One diagram is usually enough:

Diagram 5:5

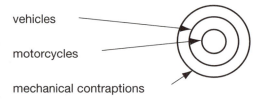

Diagram 5:5 shows the argument in Check-Up Item 5:9 to be deductively valid. Diagramming the reasons forced me to diagram the conclusion. The circle for motorcycles is unavoidably included in the circle for mechanical contraptions, which is what the conclusion asserts.

Do not be influenced by the relative size of the circles. Relative size is irrelevant. For example, do not infer from Diagram 5:5 that most mechanical contraptions are vehicles.

Next, I shall show the use of this basic circle system to exhibit deductive invalidity. Check-Up Item 5:10 is an invalid argument:

a. Houses are structures.
b. Homes are structures.
c. Therefore, houses are homes.

Diagram 5:6 shows this argument to be invalid because it shows that it is possible to diagram the reasons without diagramming the conclusion:

Diagram 5:6

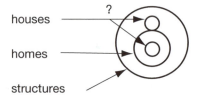

I did full justice to the reasons, but managed to avoid diagramming the conclusion. The circle for houses does not need to be inside the circle for homes, as is shown by the upper one of the alternative circles for houses. That shows the argument to be invalid.

The circle for houses could also be in the circle for homes, as is shown by the lower of the alternative circles for houses. This lower circle is not absolutely necessary to show invalidity. But in my experience, most students find that including this sort of thing helps them to feel comfortable with their diagrams.

Summary

This basic circle system is useful when we are judging the deductive validity of arguments that involve the relationships of classes. A circle represents a class, and a circle within another circle shows that the smaller is included in the larger. If, after drawing the circle relationships for the reasons in an argument in one diagram, we find that we have unavoidably diagrammed the conclusion, the argument is deductively valid. Otherwise, it is not.

The procedure for the basic type of argument we have been considering is first to draw two circles to represent one reason. Then add the other reason to the same diagram, but usually add only one circle because the other circle generally should already be there. This circle for the second reason should go inside or outside the circle that is already there, depending on whether it is included in or includes the other. (They can also overlap and there can be more classes and circles, but those are refinements I shall let you add, if you need to do so.) Then check to see whether the conclusion was also diagrammed and, if so, whether it was unavoidably diagrammed. If it was unavoidably diagrammed, judge the argument deductively valid. If not, it is deductively invalid.

The strategy in diagramming an argument is to keep the conclusion in mind and, giving the reasons every chance to show their power, to try not to diagram the conclusion. If the diagramming of the reasons does not inescapably commit us to diagramming the conclusion, the argument is deductively invalid. The strategy in doing these diagrams is to work against the conclusion, but to be fair to it. We are not trying to represent the world as we know it, but rather to represent the requirements of the reasons as stated, and to see what possibilities are still allowed.

A helpful way to show the deductive invalidity of an argument is to draw alternate circles for a crucial class, with a question mark by the junction of their arrows. One of these circles should be so placed that it denies the conclusion. The other is consistent with the conclusion.

Check-Up 5B

True or False?
If false, change it to make it true. Try to do so in a way that shows that you understand.

> 5:13 In the circle system, one circle is used to represent a whole proposition.
> 5:14 To show that Class A is included in Class B, the circle for A is put inside the circle for B.

5:15 To represent the proposition *Turtles are egg layers,* the circle for egg layers is put inside the circle for turtles.

5:16 If a conclusion is unavoidably diagrammed in the diagramming of the reasons, then the argument is deductively valid.

Short Answer

Diagram each of the following propositions. Label the diagram. Make sure that the points of the arrows touch the circles to which they point.

5:17 Harleys are motorcycles.
5:18 Canoes are boats.
5:19 Basketballs are spheres.
5:20 Bananas are magnets.
5:21 Spheres are round objects.
5:22 Magnets are pieces of fruit.

Here are some deductively valid arguments. Diagram them in a way that shows them to be deductively valid. Label each diagram completely and make sure that the arrow points touch the circles to which they point.

5:23 **a.** Harleys are motorcycles.
b. Motorcycles are vehicles.
c. Therefore, Harleys are vehicles.

5:24 **a.** Canoes are boats.
b. Boats are vehicles.
c. Therefore, canoes are vehicles.

5:25 **a.** Basketballs are spheres.
b. Spheres are round objects.
c. Therefore, basketballs are round objects.

5:26 **a.** Bananas are magnets.
b. Magnets are pieces of fruit.
c. Therefore, bananas are pieces of fruit.

Subject Class and Predicate Class

In the proposition "Houses are buildings," the subject class is *houses* because *houses* is the subject of the sentence. The predicate class is *buildings,* and is in the predicate of the proposition. In propositions like this, the circle for the subject class goes inside of the circle for the predicate class because the proposition says that the subject class is included in the predicate class (the "inside–outside" rule). You can see that this is the way it was drawn in Diagram 5:2. There are exceptions to this inside-outside rule for drawing circles, so be careful. Make sure that the diagram actually represents what is intended. Use the inside-outside rule for drawing circles only as a temporary crutch.

Sometimes these classes do not explicitly appear in a proposition, so you often have to transform a proposition in order to create explicit classes. Most often, the elusive class is the predicate class, which may be created by changing the predicate to consist of a noun or noun phrase and making sure that either the word *is* or the word *are* is used to connect the two parts of the proposition.

For example, the proposition *Houses are expensive* does not contain a predicate class. There is a subject class, *houses*, but the word *expensive* is an adjective, not the label for a class. So, we make a predicate class, perhaps *expensive things*, and leave the word *are* between the two parts. Thus, you transform *Houses are expensive* into *Houses are expensive things* in order to have two classes connected by an *is* or *are*. The new proposition is diagrammable in the circle system, as you can see:

Diagram 5:7

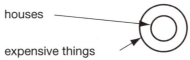

Birds have wings is an example of a sentence without an *is* or an *are*. How would you transform that proposition into an *is* or *are* relationship between two classes? Circles inside of circles can explicitly represent only an *is* or *are* relationship, not a *have* relationship.

Here are some possibilities that would work: *Birds are winged creatures, Birds are creatures with wings, Birds are things that have wings,* and *The bird is a winged creature.* The main problem is to create a predicate class that does justice to the meaning of the original sentence. I like *winged creatures* best, so would diagram *Birds have wings* as follows:

Diagram 5:8

Sometimes classes are labeled in such a way that the labels do not look like class labels, such as *the ostrich* and *a bird* in *The ostrich is a bird*. The proposition means the same as *Ostriches are birds*, and is diagrammed in Diagram 5:9.

Diagram 5:9

Now try to diagram the following argument, which is Check-Up Item 5:11:

Example 5:6

    a. Birds have wings.
    b. The ostrich is a bird.
    c. Therefore, the ostrich has wings.

If necessary, rewrite the argument, perhaps as follows:

Example 5:7

    a. Birds are winged creatures.
    b. Ostriches are birds.
    c. Therefore, ostriches are winged creatures.

In Example 5:7, each proposition consists of two class terms connected by the word *are,* so the diagram showing the argument to be deductively valid can be made using only nouns (or noun phrases) as labels. This rewriting step is not necessary, as long as you know that it is implied, and as long as you use class terms to label the circles:

Diagram 5:10

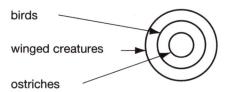

Note that in order to fit the system, the reasons and the conclusion had to be modified. This is common. You will often have to use your ingenuity.

Specific Class Members and Universal Terms

The following argument refers to a specific person, Juan:

Example 5:8

    a. All of the members of the basketball team are tall.
    b. Juan is a member of the basketball team.
    c. Therefore, Juan is tall.

It does not make sense to represent Juan by a circle because Juan is not a class. We can represent him with an *X:*

Diagram 5:11

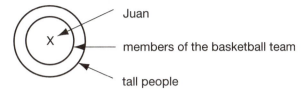

Note that a predicate class, *tall people,* had to be created out of the adjective *tall.*

Note also that the words, *all of the,* are left out of the diagramming of the noun phrase, *all of the members of the basketball team.* This is because the circle labeled with "members of the basketball team" automatically represents them all. To say *all* in the diagram would duplicate what is already said by the circle. The boundaries of a circle contain every one of the group or class that is represented by the circle, so words such as *all, every,* and *each* are generally omitted from diagrams. The boundaries do the job these words do in the sentences.

Summary

In attempting to represent a sentence by a circle, we sometimes need to transform the proposition so that it connects exactly two classes, using either the word *is* or the word *are.* Predicate adjectives must be transformed into nouns, and other verbs than *is* or *are* must be changed in a way that captures the meaning of the original proposition. Doing this often makes the result somewhat different from the ways we ordinarily speak, so the result should usually be converted back to ordinary speech.

A member of a class is represented by an *X.* Universal terms such as *all, every,* and *each* are generally left out of diagrams because their meaning is already conveyed by the boundaries of the circles.

If you do not make these transformations—at least mentally—then when things get complex, as they will, confusion will often result.

Check-Up 5C

True or False?
If false, change it to make it true. Try to do so in a way that shows that you understand.

5:27 In a standard class-inclusion proposition, the subject class is represented by the inner circle.

5:28 Putting one circle inside another indicates that the class represented by the inner circle is included in the class represented by the outer circle.

5:29 Before diagramming a proposition like *chairs can burn,* one must at least mentally transform the proposition into a proposition composed of two classes (represented by nouns or noun phrases) connected by the word *is* or the word *are.*

5:30 The proposition *Grasshoppers can fly* is in the recommended idealized form ready to be diagrammed.

5:31 The subject of the proposition *All office chairs are uncomfortable* is represented in a diagram by the words *office chairs,* the word *all* being omitted.

Short Answer

Here are some propositions to practice diagramming. Diagram each and label the parts in full with nouns or noun phrases. Make sure that the arrows touch the circles.

5:32 All the chairs in this room are wooden.

5:33 All wooden things can burn.

5:34 Raoul plays soccer.

5:35 All soccer players are in good physical shape.

Here are some more deductively valid arguments. Diagram them (using circles) in a way that shows them to be deductively valid. Label the diagrams completely.

5:36 a. All parallelograms are quadrilaterals.
  b. All quadrilaterals are plane figures.
  c. Therefore, all parallelograms are plane figures.

5:37 a. All the chairs in this room are wooden.
  b. All wooden things can burn.
  c. Therefore, all the chairs in this room can burn.

5:38 a. Raoul plays soccer.
  b. All soccer players are in good physical shape.
  c. Therefore, Raoul is in good physical shape.

5:39 a. *Magic Mountain* is by Thomas Mann.
  b. All of Thomas Mann's books are good.
  c. Therefore, *Magic Mountain* is a good book.

The following deductively valid arguments are written in more natural form. For each, (a) state the conclusion and (b) make a circle diagram of the argument to show it to be deductively valid. Make sure that the diagram is properly labeled.

5:40 All mayors are politicians. Nobody can doubt that. Furthermore, all politicians are deeply concerned about taxes. Therefore, all mayors are deeply concerned about taxes.

5:41 Because Sarah Washington is a mayor, and all mayors are deeply concerned about taxes, it must be true that Sarah Washington is deeply concerned about taxes.

5:42 All literary works that have fascinated me have had an influence on my life. Because all of Chekhov's short stories have fascinated me, they have all had an influence on my life.

5:43 All unwanted plants are weeds. We do not want the wheat in our corn field. Therefore, those wheat plants are weeds.

5:44 Anything that interferes with people's desires is unjust. Because zoning interferes with people's desires, it is certainly unjust.

5:45 Anything that promotes the good life is just. Because zoning promotes the good life, it is just.

Exclusion

Just as class inclusion is represented by one circle inside another, class exclusion is represented by two completely separate circles. For example, the proposition *No vehicles are permitted* could be represented this way:

Diagram 5:12

Diagram 5:12 says that the class of vehicles is *excluded* from the class of things that are permitted. Now try to diagram the argument of Example 5:9, which you have seen as Check-Up Item 5:12:

Example 5:9

    a. No vehicles are permitted.
    b. Motorcycles are vehicles.
    c. Therefore, no motorcycles are permitted.

Try to diagram Example 5:9 before you read further.

Diagram 5:13 exhibits the deductive validity of Example 5:9:

Diagram 5:13

In drawing Diagram 5:13, I first drew the first reason by drawing two separate circles: one for vehicles and one for things that are permitted. Then I drew the circle for motorcycles inside the circle for vehicles, as required by the second reason. This unavoidably put the circle for motorcycles totally separate from the circle for things that are permitted, which is what the conclusion says. Therefore, the conclusion is inescapably diagrammed by diagramming the reasons, so the argument is deductively valid.

Nonmembership

Like exclusion, nonmembership is shown by putting the X for an individual outside of a circle. See Diagram 5:14 for one way to diagram the proposition *Joan's bike is not permitted*.

Diagram 5:14

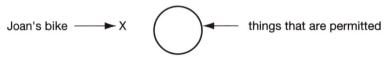

In Example 5:10, the proposition diagrammed in Diagram 5:14, *Joan's bike is not permitted*, is the conclusion:

Example 5:10

    a. No motorcycles are permitted.
    b. Joan's bike is a motorcycle.
    c. Therefore, Joan's bike is not permitted.

As shown by Diagram 5:15, this conclusion is inescapable, given the reasons, so the argument is deductively valid.

Diagram 5:15

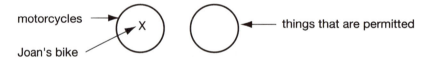

Invalid and *Valid:* Terms of Condemnation and Commendation

In deductive logic books and courses, it is common practice to use the words *invalid* and *valid* without their being preceded by the word *deductively*. This practice is confusing to many people because in everyday speech, *invalid* by itself is a general term of condemnation of arguments and statements, and *valid* by itself a general term of commendation. So, it will seem to many people that, when these words are used, general commendation or condemnation is claimed. If so, and the word *deductively* is not used, it might then seem that we are invited to condemn all *deductively* invalid arguments, even if they are good arguments (like the prosecutor's and the pathologist's). It might also seem that we are invited to commend deductively valid but circular arguments (arguments that make no progress), and deductively valid arguments that have false reasons and that are offered in support of their conclusions. These invitations should be refused.

To avoid confusion in deductive logic, I place the word *deductively* in front of the words *invalid* and *valid* (unless I actually do mean general condemnation or commendation). I urge you to do likewise, even though it is sometimes more convenient to omit the word *deductively*. Deductive validity is not automatic success and deductive invalidity is not automatic failure.

Summary and Comment

Class exclusion is represented by drawing circles separate from each other. Similarly, nonmembership can be represented by placing the *X* for the nonmember outside of the circle for the class of which it is not a member.

Because *valid* and *invalid* are in everyday speech taken to be general words for commendation and condemnation of arguments, it is best to attach the word *deductively* to them when we are talking about deductive validity and invalidity. Otherwise, confusion can result.

There are many other refinements for the circle system, including using overlapping circles.[3] But this introduction should get you started. Develop your own adaptations of these ideas. No system will answer all questions. You need to ask yourself continuously, "Does what I am doing make sense in this situation?"

Check-Up 5D

True or False?
If false, change it to make it true. Try to do so in a way that shows that you understand.

5:46 Class exclusion can be represented by drawing two circles separated from each other.

5:47 Class nonmembership can be shown by drawing an *X* inside the class of which the individual is not a member.

5:48 You will sometimes need to make adaptations of the presented circle system to fit your situation.

5:49 If it is possible to diagram the reasons without diagramming the conclusion, then the argument is deductively invalid.

5:50 In diagramming an argument, if it is possible to avoid diagramming the conclusion, then you must show this possibility.

---

3. For some possibilities, see R. L. Armstrong and L. W. Howe, "An Euler Test for Syllogisms," *Teaching Philosophy, 13* (1) (March 1990), pp. 39–46; James O. Bennett and John Nolt, "Venn/Euler Test for Categorical Syllogisms," *Teaching Philosophy, 17* (1) (March 1994), pp. 41–55; Keith Stenning and John Oberlander, "A Cognitive Theory of Graphical and Linguistic Reasoning: Logic and Implementation," *Cognitive Science, 19* (1995), pp. 97–140; and my *Natural Language Logic,* forthcoming.

5:51 If it is possible to diagram the conclusion, then the argument is deductively valid.

5:52 Any argument that is deductively valid is a good argument.

5:53 Any argument that is deductively invalid is a bad argument.

5:54 In this book, the word *valid* means *deductively valid*.

5:55 Using *invalid* to mean *deductively invalid* can be confusing to most people.

Short Answer

For each of the following deductively valid arguments, (a) state the conclusion and (b) draw a diagram of the argument that shows it to be deductively valid, making sure that the labels are perfectly clear.

5:56 No dogs are permitted in the park. Because Mike is a dog, he is not permitted in the park.

5:57 No leaded gasoline is permitted in this fuel tank. Therefore, the gasoline from this can is not permitted in this tank because the gasoline from this can is leaded gasoline.

5:58 Nobody under thirty-five years of age can be president. Because Tina is under thirty-five years of age, she cannot be president.

5:59 Twenty-year-olds are not eligible to vote. Mirabelle is twenty, so she is ineligible to vote.

5:60 It is clear that Sharon will have to pay the full admission price. This is because she is over eleven, and nobody over eleven does not pay the full admission price.

5:61 Henry, on the other hand, will not pay the full admission price because he is eleven, and nobody who is eleven (or under) pays the full admission price.

5:62 Nothing written by that bureaucrat makes any sense. Because Regulation EZCOMP will be written by that bureaucrat, it will not make any sense.

5:63 The canteen is not open today. I am sure of this because no stores are open today and

[An additional challenge for you in this item is to fill in a reason that would make the argument deductively valid. Identifying this likely assumption gives you a glimpse of this activity, which is discussed in Chapter 7.]

More Short Answer

For each of the following arguments, (a) state the conclusion and (b) make and label a diagram that shows the argument to be deductively invalid. As a reminder of a way to exhibit deductive invalidity, the first is done as an example.

5:64 Alligators are vertebrates that live in and out of water. But we know very well that amphibians are vertebrates that live in and out of water. Therefore, alligators are amphibians.

a. Conclusion: Alligators are amphibians

b.

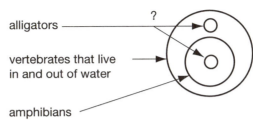

5:65 People under eighteen are not permitted to vote. Because Mark is not permitted to vote, he is under eighteen.

5:66 All good communists are opposed to the reelection of the governor. Because the members of the action committee are opposed to the reelection of the governor, the members of the action committee are good communists.

5:67 Nobody in the in-group rides a three-speed bicycle. Nobody who rides a three-speed bicycle is careless with our energy supply. From this we can see that nobody in the in-group is careless with the energy supply.

5:68 People who think critically are in favor of the new zoning law. From this, it follows that the members of the planning commission are critical thinkers because they are unanimously in favor of the new zoning law.

5:69 Propositions that have been proved beyond a reasonable doubt are true. Because the proposition that the defendant was not justified in using the force she used has not been proven beyond a reasonable doubt, that proposition is not true. (Hint: Use types of propositions for your classes, such as *true propositions* and *propositions that have been proven beyond a reasonable doubt.*

More Short Answer

For each of the following arguments, (a) state the conclusion, (b) make a labeled circle diagram of the argument exhibiting whether it is valid or invalid, and (c) report your judgment with the words *deductively valid* (or *DV*) or *deductively invalid* (or *DI*).

5:70 All squares have four right angles. Figure ABCD is a square. Therefore, figure ABCD has four right angles.

5:71 All nearsighted people have difficulty seeing things far away. John has difficulty seeing things far away. Therefore, he is nearsighted.

5:72 Birds that are unable to fly are fast runners. The penguin is a bird that is unable to fly. From this it follows that the penguin is a fast runner.

5:73 Indices used to show trends in productivity should take into account changes in the cost of living. The percent increase in the Gross Domestic Product is an index used to show trends in productivity. Therefore, that index should take into account changes in the cost of living.

5:74 The first few sentences in Marc Antony's speech to the people of

Rome should be combined because these sentences are short, and short sentences should always be combined.

5:75 The practice of lay investiture weakened the church. Practices weakening the church were opposed by the papacy. Therefore, there is no doubt that the practice of lay investiture was opposed by the papacy.

5:76 An equilateral polygon inscribed in a circle is a regular polygon. ABCDE is a regular polygon. From this we know that ABCDE is an equilateral polygon inscribed in a circle.

5:77 Electric bells in complete circuits ring loudly. The front doorbell is in a complete circuit. Therefore, although we cannot hear it from here, it must be ringing loudly.

5:78 People who are not trusted by the American people are not elected president. Marguerite Blank is trusted by the American people. Therefore, she will win the presidential election.

5:79 Blaine was not trusted by the American people. This fact follows from the fact that the American people do not elect people whom they do not trust and the fact that they did not elect him.

5:80 Complementary colors are pairs of colors that, when combined, appear to be white. Blue and yellow are a pair of complementary colors. From this, you can predict that blue and yellow, when combined, will appear to be white.

5:81 Let us assume that plants and animals that are not closely related cannot be crossed to produce hybrids. Because the two species that we have been studying (let us call them X and Y) are closely related, they can be crossed to produce hybrids.

5:82 I have concluded that Mary does not know the rules of punctuation. Here's why: People who know the rules of punctuation do well in their written compositions. But Mary does not do well in her written composition, so my conclusion follows.

5:83 All heretics were condemned, but no true believers were heretics. Therefore, no true believers were condemned.

5:84 ". . . none of woman born shall harm Macbeth." But "Macduff was from his mother's womb untimely ripp'd." Therefore, Macduff shall harm Macbeth.

Suggested Answers for Chapter 5

Note: Different diagrams from those suggested are often at least as good as the ones given. If yours differ from the ones suggested, then either try to satisfy yourself that yours are all right, or figure out why not.

Check-Up 5A
5:1 T   **5:2** T   **5:3** F   **5:4** F   **5:5** F   **5:6** T   **5:7** T

5:3 Deductive validity is not equivalent to proof beyond a reasonable doubt; the inference part of deductive validity is more demanding, but the establishment of the reasons part is much less demanding—actually not demanding at all.

5:4 Deductively invalid arguments can have true conclusions.

5:5 Deductively valid arguments can have false conclusions when they have false reasons.

5:8 Deductively valid

5:9 Deductively valid

5:10 Deductively invalid

5:11 Deductively valid

5:12 Deductively valid

Check-Up 5B

5:13 F   **5:14** T   **5:15** F   **5:16** T

5:13 In the circle system, propositions are represented by circles and *X*s.

5:15 To represent the proposition *Turtles are egg layers,* the circle for turtles is put inside the circle for egg layers.

5:17

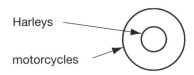

5:18

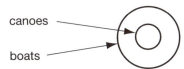

5:19

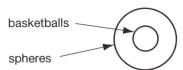

5:20

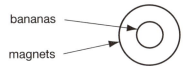

5:21

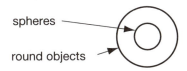

5:22

magnets

pieces of fruit

5:23

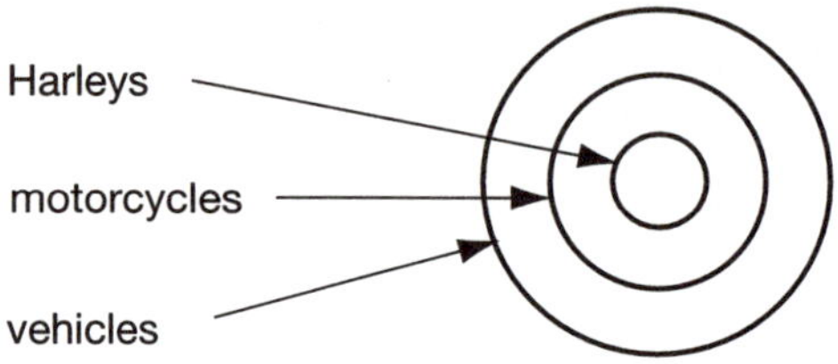

Harleys

motorcycles

vehicles

5:24

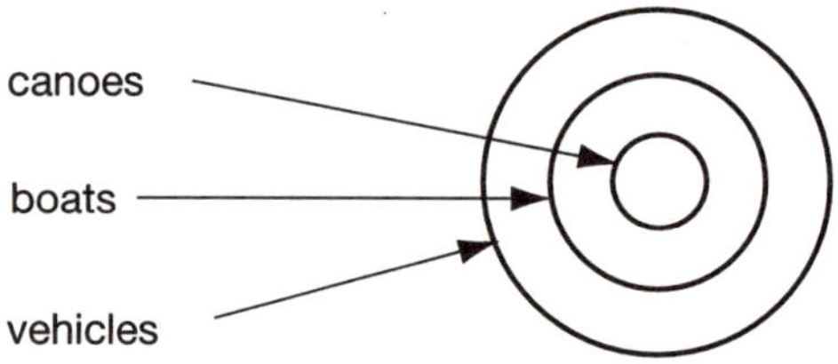

canoes

boats

vehicles

5:25

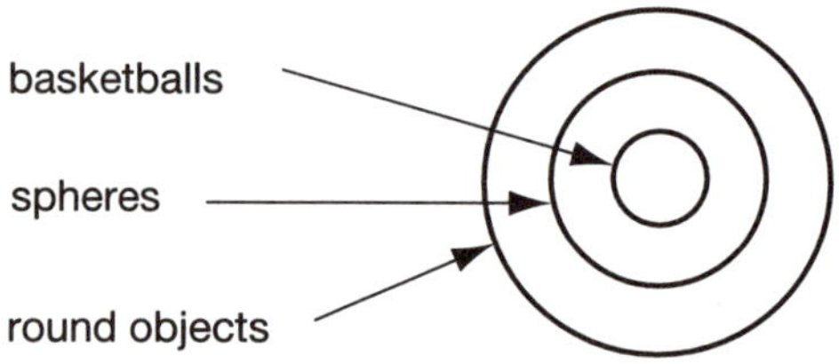

basketballs

spheres

round objects

5:26

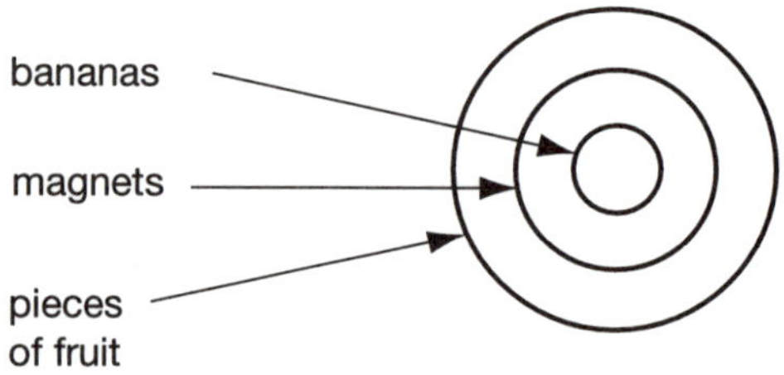

bananas

magnets

pieces
of fruit

Check-Up 5C
5:27 T   **5:28** T   **5:29** T   **5:30** F   **5:31** T
5:30 The proposition *Grasshoppers are flying creatures* is in the recommended idealized form, ready to be diagrammed.

5:32

5:33

5:34

5:35

5:36

5:37

5:38

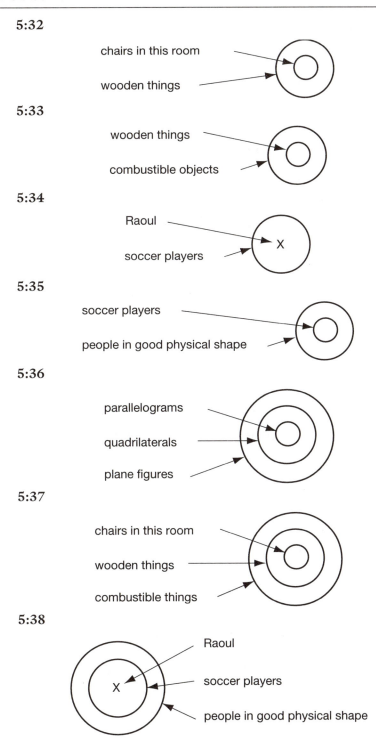

5:39

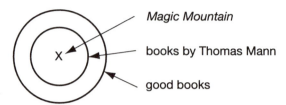

Magic Mountain

books by Thomas Mann

good books

5:40 a.   Conclusion: All mayors are deeply concerned about taxes.

b.

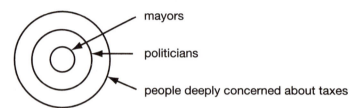

mayors

politicians

people deeply concerned about taxes

5:41 a.   Conclusion: Sarah Washington is deeply concerned about taxes.

b.

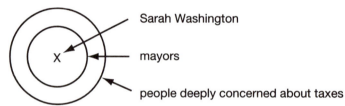

Sarah Washington

mayors

people deeply concerned about taxes

5:42 a.   Conclusion: All Chekhov's short stories have had an influence on my life.

b.

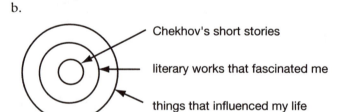

Chekhov's short stories

literary works that fascinated me

things that influenced my life

5:43 a.   Conclusion: Those wheat plants are weeds.

b.

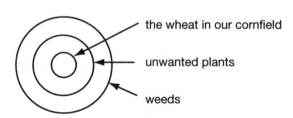

the wheat in our cornfield

unwanted plants

weeds

5:44 a.   Conclusion: Zoning is unjust.

b.

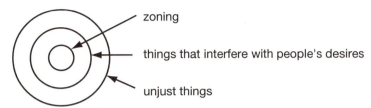

zoning

things that interfere with people's desires

unjust things

5:45 a.   Conclusion: Zoning is just.

b.

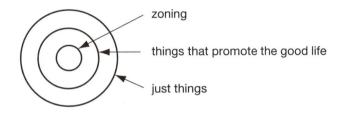

zoning

things that promote the good life

just things

Check-Up 5D

5:46 T	**5:47** F	**5:48** T	**5:49** T	**5:50** T	**5:51** F
5:52 F	**5:53** F	**5:54** F	**5:55** T		

5:47 Class nonmembership can be shown by drawing an *X* outside the class of which the individual is not a member.

5:51 The *possibility* of diagramming the conclusion does not ensure deductive validity.

5:52 Good arguments need not be deductively valid.

5:53 Some good arguments are deductively invalid.

5:54 In this book and in everyday language, the word *valid* by itself does not mean *deductively valid*.

5:56 a.   Conclusion: Mike is not permitted in the park.

b.

Things permitted in the park

Mike

X

dogs

5:57 a.   Conclusion: The gasoline from this can is not permitted in this tank.

b.

things permitted in this tank

gasoline from this can

leaded gasoline

Note: The gasoline from this can could have been represented with an *X* instead of a circle. It does not matter.

5:58 a.   Conclusion: Tina cannot be president.
       b.

5:59 a.   Conclusion: Mirabelle is ineligible to vote.
       b.

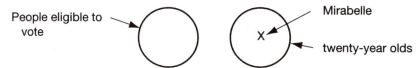

5:60 a.   Conclusion: Sharon will have to pay the full admission price.
       b.

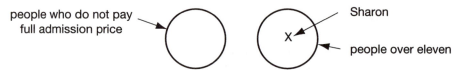

5:61 a.   Conclusion: Henry will not have to pay the full admission price.
       b.

5:62 a.   Conclusion: Regulation EZCOMP will not make any sense.
       b.

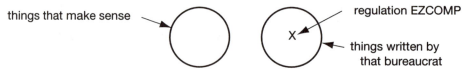

5:63 a.   Conclusion: The canteen is not open today.
       b.

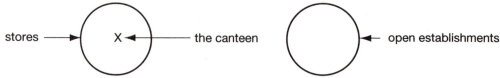

       c.   Unstated reason, or assumption: The canteen is a store.

5:64 Done in text as an example.

5:65 a. Conclusion: Mark is under eighteen.

b.

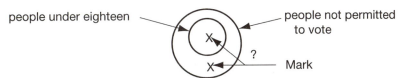

people under eighteen — people not permitted to vote

X

?

X — Mark

5:66 a. Conclusion: The members of the action committee are good communists.

b.

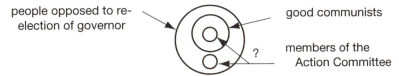

people opposed to re-election of governor — good communists

members of the Action Committee

?

5:67 a. Conclusion: Nobody in the in-group is careless with the energy supply.

b.

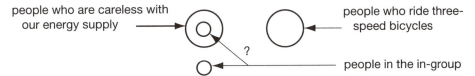

people who are careless with our energy supply — people who ride three-speed bicycles

?

people in the in-group

5:68 a. Conclusion: The members of the planning commission are critical thinkers.

b.

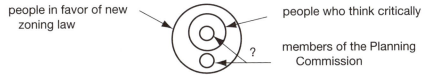

people in favor of new zoning law — people who think critically

members of the Planning Commission

?

5:69 a. Conclusion: The proposition that the defendant was not justified in using the force she used is not true.

b.

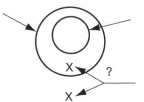

propositions that are true — propositions that have been proved beyond a reasonable doubt

X

?

X — the proposition that the defendant was not justified in using the force she used

5:70 a.   Conclusion: Figure ABCD has four right angles

     b.

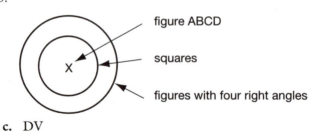

    c. DV

5:71 a.   Conclusion: John is nearsighted.

     b.

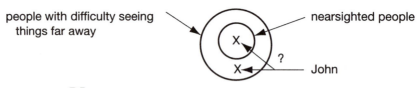

    c. DI

5:72 a.   Conclusion: The penguin is a fast runner.

     b.

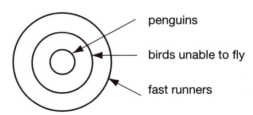

    c. DV

5:73 a.   Conclusion: The percent increase in the Gross Domestic Product is an index that should take into account changes in the cost of living.

     b.

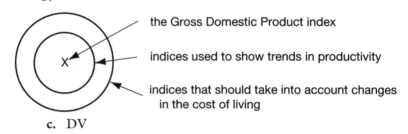

    c. DV

5:74 a. Conclusion: The first few sentences in Marc Antony's speech to the people of Rome should be combined.

b.

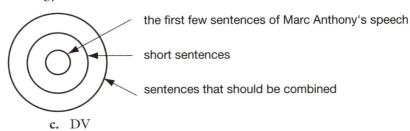

the first few sentences of Marc Anthony's speech

short sentences

sentences that should be combined

c. DV

Henceforth in this set, odd-numbered answers will be omitted. A challenge!

5:76 a. Conclusion: ABCDE is an equilateral polygon inscribed in a circle.

b.

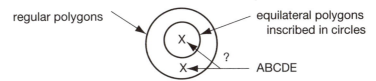

regular polygons

equilateral polygons inscribed in circles

ABCDE

c. DI

5:77 Deliberately omitted.

5:78 a. Conclusion: Marguerite Blank will win the presidential election.

b.

people not trusted by the American people

people elected president

Marguerite Blank

c. DI

5:79 Deliberately omitted.

5:80 a. Conclusion: Blue and yellow, when combined, will appear to be white.

b.

blue and yellow

complementary colors

pairs of colors which, when combined, appear to be white

c. DV

Note: For convenience, I treated *blue* and *yellow* together as a member of the class, *pairs of colors.* I hope you were able to extend the system in a way that enabled you to handle this situation in a reasonable way. You will have to do this sort of thing in the future because no system answers all the questions. You often have to be creative and sensitive in dealing with practical situations.

5:81 Deliberately omitted.

5:82 a.   Conclusion: Mary does not know the rules of punctuation.

      b.

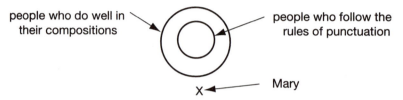

      c. DV

5:83 Deliberately omitted.

5:84 a.   Conclusion: Macduff shall harm Macbeth.

      b.

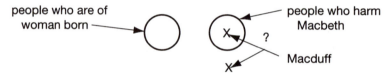

      c. DI

Thought question: What then does follow?

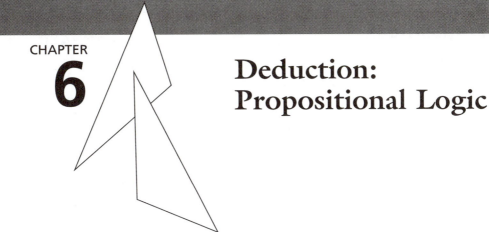

Deduction: Propositional Logic

Now that you understand deductive validity and have some techniques for handling class logic, you are ready to move on to propositional logic. Here are three examples of propositional-logic arguments.

Example 6:1

    a. If *Ben is a cat*, then *Ben is an animal*.
    b. *Ben is not an animal.*
    c. Therefore, *Ben is not a cat*.

Example 6:2

    a. Either *Arlene stabbed Al*, or *Arlene is innocent*.
    b. *Arlene did not stab Al.*
    c. Therefore, *Arlene is innocent*.

Example 6:3

If *parking is prohibited on this street* and *Sybil parked there last night*, then *Sybil is in trouble*. However, I know that *Sybil is not in trouble* and that *parking is prohibited on this street*. Therefore, *she did not park there last night*.

You can probably see that the first two arguments are deductively valid, but you might not be sure about the third. In any case, circle techniques do not work here, so we will move on to another common set of techniques. As with class logic, there are many strategies and refinements that will be omitted. But basic ideas will be presented, ideas that you can build on by yourself, or through reading other sources.[1]

---

1. Most standard elementary deductive logic texts would be helpful. For one that continues an emphasis on natural language, see my *Natural Language Logic,* forthcoming.

Propositions

According to the meaning of *proposition* that we shall use, a *proposition,* roughly speaking, is either a sentence or, if embedded in a more complex sentence, could be a sentence if isolated.[2] It is a set of concepts (or words) with a given meaning that can stand alone and make sense if asserted. Here are some examples of simple propositions that appear in italics in Examples 6:1, 6:2, and 6:3:

Example 6:4: Some Basic Propositions

    a. Ben is a cat.
    b. Ben is an animal.
    c. Ben is not an animal.
    d. Ben is not a cat.
    e. Arlene stabbed Al.
    f. Arlene is innocent.
    g. Arlene did not stab Al.
    h. Parking is prohibited on this street.
    i. Sybil parked there last night.
    j. Sybil is in trouble.
    k. Sybil is not in trouble.
    l. She did not park there last night.

Look again at the arguments in Examples 6:1, 6:2, and 6:3 to see the role that the propositions in Example 6:4 play in those arguments. Note also the role in Examples 6:1, 6:2, and 6:3 played by the words *if, then, either, or,* and *and.*

Here are some things that are not propositions because they cannot stand alone and make sense if asserted:

Example 6:5

    a. Robins
    b. People under eighteen
    c. anybody is under eighteen (in "If *anybody is under eighteen,* then that person may not enter.")

The classes that are *a* and *b* in Example 6:5 obviously do not make sense to assert all by themselves. Suppose, for example, someone came up to you and said, "Robins." What sense would you make of that? Of course it would make sense as an answer to a question, such as "What kinds of birds are those?" But then the speaker would implicitly be asserting a complete proposition, *Those are robins,* which can stand alone and make sense if asserted. But the word *Robins,* without any such implication, is not an assertion.

---

2. A more precise, theoretical definition of *proposition* would not be helpful for present purposes.

Even though Example 6:5*c* (*anybody is under eighteen*) has a subject and predicate, someone's trying to assert it does not make sense, if its words mean what they mean in the complete sentence given in parentheses in that example. What would you make of someone's coming up to you and saying, "Anybody is under eighteen," in the sense in which it is meant in Example 6:5*c*? Actually, the proposition in quotes in Example 6:5*c* fits best under class logic because its meaning is *People under eighteen may not enter.*

If–Then Reasoning

Reasoning with *if–then* propositions is the most important kind of propositional reasoning, so we shall start with it. The following argument is a case of *if–then* reasoning because it employs an *if–then* proposition:

Example 6:6

   a. If Ben is a cat, then Ben is an animal.
   b. Ben is a cat.
   c. Therefore, Ben is an animal.

The first reason, *a*, is an *if–then* proposition consisting of two shorter propositions joined by the words, *if* and *then*, in appropriate places. The second reason, *b*, is a separate assertion of the *if* part. The conclusion, *c*, is an assertion of the *then* part of *a*.

The first (the complex) proposition asserts that the second reason is enough to entitle us to draw the conclusion. The conclusion follows necessarily from the two reasons together.

This is not to say that the conclusion is true. It might very well be that Ben is not an animal. But if the reasons are true, then he must be an animal. That is, given that it is true that if Ben is a cat, then Ben is an animal, and given also that Ben is a cat, then Ben must be an animal. If those two reasons are true, there is no way to avoid the conclusion. Therefore, the argument in Example 6:6 is deductively valid.

Affirming the Antecedent

In Example 6:6, the *if* proposition has been affirmed (in *b*). This entitles us to draw as a conclusion the *then* proposition (*c*). Because the *if* part is called the *antecedent* and because the antecedent is separately affirmed (in reason *b*), the form of reasoning in Example 6:6 is called *affirming the antecedent*. Affirming the antecedent is a deductively valid form.

Antecedents and Consequents

In the first reason (*a*) of Example 6:6, the proposition *Ben is an animal* is the *then* part of the *if–then* proposition. The *then* part of an *if–then* proposition is called the *consequent*. In the first reason of Example 6:6, *Ben is an animal* is the consequent.

Before going on to look at other forms of reasoning, let us pause to identify antecedents and consequents. The antecedent often comes first, but it does not always do so. Sometimes the antecedent comes second and the consequent comes first (Example 6:7*a*), and sometimes the antecedent is inserted between parts of the consequent (Example 6:7*b*):

Example 6:7

    a. Ben is an animal if Ben is a cat.
    b. Sybil, if parking is prohibited on this street, is in trouble.

Examples 6:6*a* and 6:7*a* mean the same thing, even though the order is reversed. This is because the word *if* is attached to the same proposition (*Ben is a cat*) in both cases. The total *if–then* proposition, whatever the order (as long as *if* stays with *Ben is a cat*), tells us that Ben's being a cat is sufficient to establish that Ben is an animal.

Note that the word *if* is not part of the antecedent; rather it is an indicator of the antecedent. The antecedent is the proposition coming right after the word *if*. The consequent is the other unit of the complex proposition. The word *then,* if it is used, is *not* part of the consequent. When it appears, it is an *indicator* of the consequent. In Example 6:7, the word *then* was omitted, as it always is when the consequent comes first. Sometimes it is omitted even when the consequent comes second, as in *If Ben is a cat, Ben is an animal.* The word *then* is not really needed in front of the consequent (*Ben is an animal*) to make the complex proposition read smoothly. However, it can be there, as in reason *a* in Example 6:6.

Another difference that we can usually ignore comes from the substituting of a pronoun or some similar term to refer to something already named. Hence (assuming that Ben is male) the *if–then* propositions in Example 6:8 are essentially the same in meaning for our purposes:

Example 6:8

    a. If Ben is a cat, then Ben is an animal.
    b. If Ben is a cat, then he is an animal.

Summary

Propositions can stand alone and make sense when asserted. When two propositions are appropriately joined together by the words *if* and *then* (although *then* is not always needed), the result is a more complex *if–then* proposition). The *if* part is the *antecedent*. The *then* part is the *consequent*. Although the antecedent usually comes first, the consequent sometimes comes first, and sometimes the antecedent comes between parts of the consequent. The substitution of a pronoun, when referring to something already named, generally does not change the meaning of an *if–then* proposition. When an argument consists of an *if–then* proposition as one reason, the affirmed antecedent as the other reason, and the consequent by itself as the conclusion, this argument is of the form, *affirming the antecedent,* a deductively valid form of argument.

Check-Up 6A

True or False?
If a statement is false, change a crucial word or words to make it true.

6:1 The *if* proposition in an *if–then* proposition is called the *antecedent.*

6:2 The *then* proposition in an *if–then* proposition is called the *consequent,* but only when the word *then* is actually there.

6:3 The following two complex propositions mean the same thing:

   a. If John is in school, then Mary is happy.
   b. Mary is happy, if John is in school.

6:4 In the following two complex propositions, the antecedent is the same:

   a. Karl was depressed, if he lost the election.
   b. Karl lost the election, if he was depressed.

6:5 Propositions can stand alone, and do make sense if asserted.

6:6 *Tom is a turtle* is a proposition.

6:7 The proposition that comes first in an *if–then* proposition is called the *antecedent.*

6:8 The following argument is of the form, affirming the antecedent, and is deductively valid:

   a. Tom is slow, if Tom is a turtle.
   b. Tom is slow.
   c. Therefore, Tom is a turtle.

Short Answer
For each of the following items, (a) underline the antecedent once and (b) underline the consequent twice, but do not underline *if* and *then* because they are not in these examples part of the antecedent and consequent. The first two are done as examples. If your instructor has not made another suggestion, either photocopy these pages or copy the items.

6:9 If Tom is a turtle, *then Tom is slow.*

6:10 Tom is slow, *if Tom is a turtle.*

6:11 If junipers are poisonous, then the cattle are in danger.

6:12 The cattle are in danger, if junipers are poisonous.

6:13 If the supervisor forgot about us, then there is a shortage of concrete.

6:14 If Terry got into the Blue Room, then she lied about her age.

6:15 If Terry lied about her age, then she got into the Blue Room.

6:16 If Joanna is a liberal, then she supported the prime minister.

6:17 Joanna, if she supported the prime minister, is a liberal.

6:18 If Arlene admitted that she did it, then she did it.

6:19 Martin thinks, if he is wearing a red hat, that hunters might be around.

6:20 Arlene, if she admitted that she did it, did it.

6:21 If she killed him, then she performed the act that caused his death.

6:22 She killed him, if she performed the act that caused his death.

6:23 If the blood is Al's blood, then it is type A.

6:24 The blood, if it is type A, is Al's blood.

6:25 Tom Jeffers, if he was seen in the hospital waiting room between 10 P.M. and midnight, did not do it.

6:26 If Tom Jeffers was seen in the hospital waiting room between 10 P.M. and midnight, then he did not do it.

Affirming and Denying the Antecedent and Consequent

In addition to affirming the antecedent, there are three other basic moves one can make from an *if–then* proposition. Two are deductively invalid, and one is deductively valid. Example 6:9 is an illustration of the move called *denying the antecedent,* so called because one of the reasons denies the antecedent of the other reason.

Example 6:9

    a. If Ben is a cat, then Ben is an animal.
    b. <u>Ben is not a cat.</u>
    c. Therefore, Ben is not an animal.

Reason *b* denies the antecedent of reason *a* and the conclusion does not necessarily follow. Even if the reasons are true, it would still be possible for Ben to be an animal. He might be a goat, for example. Denying the antecedent is a deductively invalid form.

Another deductively invalid form is *affirming the consequent,* so called because one reason affirms the consequent of the other reason, as in Example 6:10:

Example 6:10

    a. If Ben is a cat, then Ben is an animal.
    b. <u>Ben is an animal.</u>
    c. Therefore, Ben is a cat.

Reason *b* affirms the consequent of reason *a*. Again, the conclusion does not necessarily follow. The reasons allow that Ben could be some other kind of animal than a cat, even though his being a cat would ensure his being an animal. Affirming the consequent is a deductively invalid form.

The last basic form in this series is called *denying the consequent* because one reason denies the consequent of the other reason, as in Example 6:11:

Example 6:11

    a. If Ben is a cat, then Ben is an animal.
    b. Ben is not an animal.
    c. Therefore, Ben is not a cat.

Reason *b* denies the consequent of reason *a*. This time, the conclusion necessarily follows. If you do not see this, consider: Assuming that the reasons are true, suppose, contrary to the conclusion, that Ben *were* a cat. Then according to reason *a*, Ben would have to be an animal. But reason *b* says that he is not an animal. So, he cannot be a cat. Denying the consequent is a deductively valid form.

Summary So Far

This chapter so far has further explored the *I* in *FRISCO* by elaborating some basic features of propositional logic, a kind of deductive logic that is in some ways similar to class logic. In propositional logic, the basic building block is the proposition, which consists of a subject and predicate, and can stand alone and meaningfully be asserted.

The most important propositional-logic relationship is implication, as found in *if–then* propositions that connect an antecedent (the *if* part) with a consequent (the *then* part). Each of these is itself a proposition.

An *if–then* proposition says that the truth of the antecedent proposition is enough to establish the truth of the consequent proposition. It says that the consequent must be true in order that the antecedent be true. That is, unless the consequent is true, the antecedent cannot be true. But a standard *if–then* proposition does *not* say that the truth of the consequent is enough to establish the truth of the antecedent, nor does it say that the antecedent must be true in order that the consequent be true. It is a common deductive error to think that an *if–then* proposition says these things.

Affirming the antecedent and *denying the consequent* are deductively valid moves. *Affirming the consequent* and *denying the antecedent* are deductively invalid moves.

Table 6.1 summarizes the relationships among affirming and denying antecedents and consequents. Do not memorize it. Just think about its parts until you are sure that you feel comfortable with what it says in terms of your own examples.

TABLE 6.1 Deductive validity of the Four Basic Forms of "If–Then" Reasoning

	Antecedent	*Consequent*
Affirming	Deductively Valid	Deductively Invalid
Denying	Deductively Invalid	Deductively Valid

Check-Up 6B

True or False?
If a statement is false, change a crucial word or words to make it true.

6:27 *Affirming the antecedent* is a deductively valid form.
6:28 *Denying the antecedent* is a deductively invalid form.
6:29 The following is a case of denying the consequent:

    a. If Marguerite is here, then Estelle is happy.
    b. Estelle is not happy.
    c. Therefore, Marguerite is not here.

6:30 *Denying the consequent* is a deductively invalid form.
6:31 *Affirming the consequent* is a deductively invalid form.

Short Answer
For each of the following items, indicate the form of the argument, using the following abbreviations: For *affirming the antecedent,* use *AA*; for *denying the antecedent,* use *DA;* for *affirming the consequent,* use *AC;* and for *denying the consequent,* use *DC.* Also indicate whether the argument is deductively valid (DV) or deductively invalid (DI). The first one is done as an example.

6:32 **a.** If Marguerite is here, then Estelle is happy.
    b. Estelle is happy.
    c. Therefore, Marguerite is here.   AC, DI

6:33 **a.** If Joanna supported the prime minister, then she is a liberal.
    b. Joanna is not a liberal.
    c. Therefore, Joanna did not support the prime minister.

6:34 **a.** If Joanna supported the prime minister, then she is a liberal.
    b. Joanna is a liberal.
    c. Therefore, Joanna supported the prime minister.

6:35 **a.** If Joanna is a liberal, then she supported the prime minister.
    b. Joanna did not support the prime minister.
    c. Therefore, Joanna is not a liberal.

6:36 **a.** Terry, if she lied about her age, got into the Blue Room.
    b. Terry got into the Blue Room.
    c. Therefore, Terry lied about her age.

6:37 **a.** Terry lied about her age, if she got into the Blue Room.
    b. Terry did not get into the Blue Room.
    c. Therefore, she did not lie about her age.

6:38 **a.** The blood is type A.
    b. The blood is type A, if it is Al's.
    c. Therefore, the blood is Al's.

6:39 **a.** If junipers are poisonous, then the cattle are in danger.
    b. The cattle are in danger.
    c. Therefore, junipers are poisonous.

6:40 **a.** Arlene, if she admitted that she did it, did it.
    b. Arlene did not do it.
    c. Therefore, Arlene did not admit that she did it.

6:41 **a.** Arlene admitted that she did it.
    b. If Arlene admitted that she did it, then she did it.
    c. Therefore, Arlene did it.

Conversion

Exchanging the antecedent and consequent is a significant change. That is, the two statements in Example 6:12 (*a* and *b*) are very different from each other.

Example 6:12

    a. If Ben is a cat, then Ben is an animal.
    b. If Ben is an animal, then Ben is a cat.

In Example 6:12*b*, the word *if* is attached to (that is, it comes just before) the proposition *Ben is an animal*. That makes *Ben is an animal* the antecedent, instead of *Ben is a cat*, and radically changes the meaning of the whole *if–then* proposition. The new *if–then* proposition (Example 6:12*b*) asserts that Ben's being an animal is sufficient to establish that Ben is a cat. This clearly is not what the original asserted. The original asserted that Ben's being a cat was sufficient to establish that Ben is an animal.

The distinction between the antecedent and the consequent is the most important distinction in *if–then* propositional logic. Many of the mistakes people make in propositional logic can be roughly characterized as getting this distinction confused, although usually in more complex circumstances.

Exchanging these two different ways of joining the elementary propositions in *if–then* propositions is common enough to have a name: *conversion*. To *convert* an *if–then* proposition is to exchange the antecedent and the consequent. Example 6:12*b* is the converse of Example 6:12*a* and Example 6:12*a* is the converse of 6:12*b*.

The location of the antecedent and consequent with respect to each other has no bearing on whether they have been exchanged. All that matters is the location of the word *if.* Hence, the two propositions in Example 6:13 are also converses of each other:

Example 6:13

    a. Ben is an animal if Ben is a cat.
    b. If Ben is an animal, Ben is a cat.

    Conversion is a deductively invalid form. It is also usually a mistake (that is, invalid in the everyday meaning of *invalid*).

Contraposition

A *contrapositive* of a proposition is the proposition with the antecedent and consequent exchanged and each denied. In Example 6:14, *b* is the contrapositive of *a*.

Example 6:14

    a. If Ben is a cat, then Ben is an animal.
    b. Therefore, if Ben is not an animal, then Ben is not a cat.

    Ordinarily, contrapositives can be substituted for each other in arguments.
    The move from *a* to *b* in Example 6:14 is called *contraposition:* The antecedent and consequent were exchanged and each was denied (or negated). More precisely, the exchange calls for shifting the *if* from one proposition to the other, accompanied by the denial of each. The conclusion (*b*) follows from the reason (*a*) by the same kind of thinking that shows denying the consequent to be deductively valid: Example 6:14*a* tells us that if Ben is a cat, then Ben is an animal. Granting that, let us suppose that Ben is not an animal. Then we would have to conclude that Ben is not a cat. Otherwise, he would be an animal (from *a*). So, if Ben is not an animal, then Ben is not a cat. This *if–then* proposition is our conclusion (6:14*b*). Contraposition is a deductively valid form.[3]

Negation

To negate the proposition *Ben is a cat* is to assert that Ben is not a cat. Generally speaking, one negates by introducing such words or prefixes as *not, non-, no, un-,* and *it is not the case that.* The three propositions in Example 6:15 are negations (or denials) of the proposition *Ben is a cat* and are propositions themselves. For present purposes, they are essentially equivalent to each other:

Example 6:15

    a. Ben is not a cat.
    b. It is not true that Ben is a cat.
    c. Ben is a non-cat.

---

3. Beware of contraposing *if–then* propositions that express causal connections. Make sure that the contrapositive is stated so that it makes sense in the situation.

Example 6:15*a* is the more convenient way to express the thought.

Double Negation

The standard double negation rule is this: *Two negatives make a positive.* That is, two negatives cancel each other out. Following this rule, the propositions in Example 6:16 are basically equivalent to each other:

Example 6:16

a. Ben is a cat.
b. It is false that Ben is not a cat.
c. It is not true that Ben is not a cat.
d. It is not the case that Ben is a non-cat.

The last three (*b, c,* and *d*) contain double negations. The double negations cancel each other out to make the positive proposition *Ben is a cat.* Think about the meaning of each of these to make sure you understand why each of the last three contains a double negation, and why each means the same as the first.

But a problem can arise when handling some double negations. Suppose, for example, someone says that it has not been proved that the apple trees are not productive. The person who says this might be holding that the trees are midway between being unproductive and productive, or that even though they might well be unproductive, it simply has not been proved. In such a case, it would be misleading simply to eliminate the double negative and conclude that it has been proved that the apple trees are productive. Therefore, you should keep an amendment to the rule in the back of your mind: *Two negatives make a positive, unless some middle ground is possible.*

The double-negation rule is more difficult to use with this amendment, but that is the way things are. The language and its users are sometimes very subtle and sometimes very plain. You must judge a situation for what it is.

Double Negation and Contraposition

Sometimes when you make the contrapositive of a proposition you produce a double negation, which usually can then be eliminated.

Example 6:17

a. If Ben is a cat, then Ben is not a dog.
b. If it is false that Ben is not a dog, then Ben is not a cat.
c. If Ben is a dog, then Ben is not a cat.

In Example 6:17, the move from *a* to *b* is contraposition. The move from *b* to *c* is the elimination of a double negative in the antecedent of *b*.

Eliminating double negatives makes things easier to understand, but it must be done with caution, and sometimes must not be done (as you saw in the previous section).

Summary

The converse of an *if–then* proposition is formed by exchanging the antecedent and the consequent so that the antecedent becomes the consequent, and vice versa. Conversion is a deductively invalid move.

The contrapositive of an *if–then* proposition is formed by exchanging and negating the antecedent and the consequent. Contraposition is a deductively valid move.

Double negatives can be dropped, unless there is a middle ground. Beware.

Check-Up 6C

True or False?
If a statement is false, change a crucial word or words to make it true.

6:42 Conversion is deductively invalid.

6:43 *We are short of concrete if the supervisor forgot about us* is the converse of *If the supervisor forgot about us, we are short of concrete.*

6:44 *If we are short of concrete, then the supervisor forgot about us* is the converse of *We are short of concrete if the supervisor forgot about us.*

6:45 Exchanging the antecedent and consequent, while moving the word *if* to the other clause, is called *conversion* and is generally a mistake.

6:46 To make a contrapositive, you exchange the antecedent and consequent so that the antecedent becomes the consequent and the consequent becomes the antecedent, and then you separately deny each.

6:47 Contraposition is deductively valid.

6:48 Two negatives always make a positive, enabling us to drop every pair of negatives in a proposition.

6:49 The following two *if–then* propositions are contrapositives of each other and therefore imply each other:

   a. If Tom is a turtle, then Tom is slow.
   b. If Tom is not slow, then Tom is not a turtle.

6:50 The following two *if–then* propositions are contrapositives of each other and therefore imply each other:

   a. It is type A, if it is Al's blood.
   b. If it is not type A, then it is not Al's blood.

6:51 The following two *if–then* propositions are contrapositives of each other and therefore imply each other:

   a. Tom Jeffers did not do it, if he was seen in the hospital waiting room between 10 P.M. and midnight.
   b. If Tom Jeffers was not seen in the hospital waiting room between 10 P.M. and midnight, then he did it.

6:52 The second of these two *if–then* propositions is a useful simplification of the first:

    a. Joanna is not a liberal, if it is not true that she did not support the prime minister.

    b. If Joanna supported the prime minister, then she is not a liberal.

Short Answer

For each of the following, on a separate sheet of paper, fill in an appropriate word or words in the second proposition so that it means the same as the first (or write only the words *if* and *then* in the proper order). Capitalize a letter if necessary. Avoid conversion. The first is done as an example.

6:53 **a.** Our cattle are in danger, if junipers are poisonous.

      b. If *junipers are poisonous, then* our cattle are in danger.

6:54 **a.** If Joanna supported the prime minister, then she is a liberal.

      b. _____ Joanna is a liberal, _____ she supported the prime minister.

6:55 **a.** Arlene did it, if she admitted that she did it.

      b. _____ Arlene admitted that she did it, _____ Arlene did it.

6:56 **a.** The blood, if it is Al's blood, is type A.

      b. _____ the blood is Al's blood, _____ it is type A.

6:57 **a.** This vehicle, if it has a motor, is prohibited.

      b. _____ this vehicle has a motor, _____ the vehicle is prohibited.

More Short Answer

Simplify the following by eliminating the double negatives. If you do not think that the double negative can be eliminated because the simple rule ("Two negatives make a positive") does not apply, then say that the double negative may not be eliminated. The first is done as an example. Use a separate sheet of paper.

6:58 It is not true that John is not here. *Result:* John is here.

6:59 It is false that motorcycles are not permitted.

6:60 It is not true that the diamond is not in the queen's crown.

6:61 There is no doubt that she is not guilty.

6:62 If Arlene did it, then it is not true that she did not admit that she did it.

6:63 It is not true that our cattle are not healthy, if they did not eat the junipers.

6:64 If the pork we had tonight was not inexpensive, then our budget will be exceeded.

6:65 If a majority approved the resolution, then the society will not meet in a state that has not passed the proposed constitutional amendment.

6:66 If Arlene did not do it, then she did not admit doing it.

More Short Answer

Write a contrapositive of each of the following propositions. Simplify, if a double negative can be eliminated without changing the meaning.

6:67 If Arlene admitted it, then she did it.

6:68 If junipers are poisonous, then our cattle are ill.

6:69 The blood is type A, if it is Al's blood.

6:70 If a vehicle has a motor, then the vehicle is prohibited.

6:71 If Sara Lee did not lie about her age, then she was not admitted to the Panama Club.

6:72 If the supervisor did not forget about us, then we have enough concrete.

6:73 Martin, if he is wearing a red hat, thinks that hunters might be around.

6:74 If the gift is inexpensive, then Shiboen bought it.

6:75 If she was convicted, then the jury was convinced beyond a reasonable doubt that the three conditions for murder were satisfied.

6:76 The battery is in bad condition, if you left the lights on all night.

6:77 If a majority approved the resolution, then the society did not meet in a state that has not passed the proposed constitutional amendment.

More Short Answer

For each of the following arguments, state the final conclusion. Then decide whether each is deductively valid, indicating your reasons in abbreviated form. For these items, choose your reasons from the following list:

TABLE 6.2

Justifications of a judgment of deductive validity (DV):	Justifications of a judgment of deductive invalidity (DI):
Affirming the Antecedent (AA)	Denying the Antecedent (DA)
Denying the Consequent (DC)	Affirming the Consequent (AC)
Contraposition (CONTR)	Conversion (CONV)
Eliminable Double Negation (EDN)	Noneliminable Double Negation (NDN)

For some items, you will need to break the argument into parts and deal with each part separately, giving more than one justification. If any part of the argument is deductively invalid, the whole argument is deductively invalid. The first two items are done as examples. If your answer needs a special explanation, then give it.

6:78 Suziko lost the election. I conclude this because I know that if she lost the election, she is depressed. And clearly she is depressed.

Final conclusion: Suziko lost the election. AC; DI

6:79 If John is at work today, then Juanita is happy. If Juanita is happy, then she is smiling. I just saw Juanita and noticed that she was not smiling. Hence, John is not at work today.

Final conclusion: John is not at work today.   DC, DC; DV

6:80 Karl did not lose the election. I conclude this because I know that if he lost the election, he would be depressed. And he obviously is not depressed.

6:81 If Mary went out last night, then Pedro is angry today. I have just seen Pedro and he is not angry today. Therefore, Mary did not go out last night.

6:82 Terry is in trouble, if she lied about her age. Therefore, if Terry is in trouble, then she lied about her age.

6:83 Terry lied about her age, if she managed to get into the Blue Room. But Terry did not manage to get into the Blue Room. We saw her at Shack's Fish & Chips. From all this, it follows that she did not lie about her age.

6:84 If John is in school, then Mary is happy. Hence, if Mary is unhappy, then John is not in school.

6:85 There is not a shortage of concrete. I conclude this from the fact that if the supervisor forgot us, there would be a shortage of concrete. But the supervisor never forgets us and she has not done so this time.

6:86 This blood on the porch is type A. If the blood is Al's blood, then it is type A, according to the blood analyst. Hence, the blood on the porch is Al's.

6:87 Tom Jeffers, if he was seen in the hospital waiting room at 10 P.M. and at midnight, did not do it. Someone claimed to see him, but the identification was a mistake. Because he really was not seen in the hospital waiting room at 10 P.M. and at midnight, he did it.

6:88 If it has not been proven beyond a reasonable doubt that she knew that at least there was a strong probability that she would do him serious harm, then she is not guilty. However, it has been proven beyond a reasonable doubt that she knew that there was a strong probability that she would do him serious harm. Therefore, she is guilty. (Suggestion: Use *PBRD* to stand for *proven beyond a reasonable doubt*.)

6:89 Arlene did not admit that she did it, if she did not do it. But she did admit that she did it. Clearly then, she did it.

6:90 Joanna is not a liberal, if she did not support the prime minister. Therefore, if she supported the prime minister, she is a liberal.

6:91 If the hogs are not behaving strangely, then they did not eat thistles recently. But they are behaving strangely. From all this, I conclude that they ate thistles recently.

6:92 If Michael has a conflict of interest, then his testimony is not to be trusted. If Michael's brother is a suspect, then Michael has a conflict of interest. Michael's brother is a suspect. Therefore, Michael's testimony is not to be trusted.

6:93 If Shakespeare had intended Polonius to be a comic figure, then he would not have made Polonius the father of two tragic characters. But Polonius was made the father of two tragic characters, Laertes and Ophelia. Hence, Polonius was not intended by Shakespeare to be a comic figure.

6:94 No photosynthesis can be occurring in this plant. That this is so can be seen from the fact that it is not getting any light whatsoever. Furthermore, photosynthesis cannot occur in this plant, if there is no light reaching it.

6:95 If the Board of Education suspends young Brown from school, then it will be punishing him for refusing on religious grounds to salute the flag. And if it does that, it will be acting unconstitutionally. Because the board, we can be sure, will not act unconstitutionally, we can be sure that the board will not suspend young Brown.

6:96 If Arlene did not intentionally perform the act that caused Al's death, then she is not guilty. But the prosecutor has proven beyond a reasonable doubt that Arlene did intentionally perform the act that caused Al's death. Therefore, she is guilty.

6:97 Martin is wearing a red hat, if he thinks that hunters might be around. We just saw him and noticed that he is wearing a red hat. Therefore, he thinks that hunters might be around.

6:98 It has not been proven beyond a reasonable doubt that she believed that she was not safe. Therefore, it has been proven beyond a reasonable doubt that she believed that she was safe.

6:99 If she believed that he wanted to hurt her, then it has not been proven beyond a reasonable doubt that she was not justified in using the force that she used. It is clear that she really did believe that he wanted to hurt her. Therefore, it has been proven beyond a reasonable doubt that she was justified in using the force that she used.

More Short Answer

For the following sets of reasons, if a conclusion that is different from the reasons follows necessarily, write it in. Otherwise write *Nothing,* by which you should mean that the conclusion that is probably intended does not follow necessarily. In any case, label the form of the probably intended argument. The first is done as an example.

6:100 If Anita stands to make a profit from your believing what she says, then you should be careful about believing what she says. It is clear that you should be careful about believing what she says. Therefore?

Nothing; AC

6:101 The spectator was lying, if the motorist told the truth about the accident. The spectator was certainly lying. Therefore?

6:102 If Amandita believes John, then she is a fool. However, Amandita is no fool. Therefore?

6:103 If our leader tells you to commit suicide, then he is not worthy of being our leader. By ordering you to drink the poison, our leader has in effect told you to commit suicide. Therefore?

6:104 Mr. Davis, if he was suspected to have a friendship with someone involved in the trial, was excused from the jury by the judge. Mr. Davis was excused from the jury by the judge. Therefore?

6:105 If Frankie did not step out of bounds, then the basket counts. But see, the referee is declaring that the basket does not count. Therefore?

6:106 John, if Jane said "No," went to the movies alone. John did not go to the movies alone. Therefore?

6:107 If the state has not proven beyond a reasonable doubt that she was not justified in using the force that she used, then she is not guilty. However, the state has proven beyond reasonable doubt that she was not justified in using the force that she used. Therefore?

6:108 If Arlene did not believe that circumstances existed that would justify the killing of Al, then she is not guilty of voluntary manslaughter. However, Arlene did believe that such circumstances existed. She was very jealous and believed that he was disloyal to her. Therefore?

Saving Time with Letters

In propositional logic, we can save time in organizing arguments by using letters to represent each significant proposition in an argument. An arrow is used to show the *if–then* relationship. This system helps us show not only the overall picture, but also the way the parts are put together in complex propositions. This in turn helps us to decide whether the argument is deductively valid.

For propositional assignments, it is fairly traditional to use small letters, starting with *p*, then *q*, then *r*, etc. We assign a different letter to each basic proposition, generally using *p* to represent the antecedent. For our standard Ben example:

Let *p* = *Ben is a cat.*
Let *q* = *Ben is an animal.*

If you prefer, you can instead assign letters that have some connection with the proposition. For example, the assignment could be as follows:

Let *bc* = *Ben is a cat* (*b* for *Ben*; *c* for *cat*).
Let *ba* = *Ben is an animal.*

With these assignments, our standard *affirming-the-antecedent* example looks like this:

Example 6:18

a. If Ben is a cat, Ben is an animal.	$p \to q$		$md \to ma$
b. Ben is a cat.	p	**OR**	bc
c. Therefore, Ben is an animal.	Therefore, q		Therefore, ba

The fact that *p* (or *bc*) is to the left of the arrow shows it to be the antecedent in *a*. It is this same thing that is affirmed in *b*, so the argument is a case of affirming the antecedent. You knew this all along, but the example is helpful in showing how to use letters and arrows.

Henceforth, I shall use the traditional letter assignments (*p, q, r,* etc.). You should use whatever letter system you prefer.

The negation of the proposition *p* is represented by *not p,* meaning *It is not the case that* p. Here is a symbolization of an argument of the form, denying the consequent, using the same assignment of *p* and *q* as was used previously:

Example 6:19

a.	If Ben is a cat, then Ben is an animal.	**a.**	$p \rightarrow q$
b.	Ben is not an animal.	**b.**	*not* q
c.	Therefore, Ben is not a cat.	**c.**	Therefore, not *p*

Sometimes it is convenient to assign a letter to a proposition containing a negation, instead of showing the negation of a proposition. Consider the argument in Example 6:20:

Example 6:20

a. Tom Jeffers did not do it, if he was seen in the hospital waiting room between 10 P.M. and midnight.

b. He was seen in the hospital waiting room between 10 P.M. and midnight.

c. Therefore, he did not do it.

Let *p = He was seen in the hospital waiting room between 10 P.M. and midnight.* Let *q = Tom Jeffers did not do it.* (The negation, *not,* is here treated as part of *q.*)

The argument can be represented as in Example 6:21:

Example 6:21

a. $p \rightarrow q$
b. p
c. Therefore, *q*

Here is an assignment of letters that changes the assignment for *q,* although it makes the same assignment for *p.*

Let *p = He was seen in the hospital waiting room between 10 P.M. and midnight.* Let *q = Tom Jeffers did it.* (The negation here is not treated as part of *q.*)

In this new assignment for *q,* the *not* has been omitted from the proposition to which *q* is assigned. So, we must take care of this fact in representing the argument:

Example 6:22

a. $p \rightarrow$ not *q*
b. p
c. Therefore, not *q*

Examples 6:21 and 6:22 are two different ways of representing the same argument. I find the first way more convenient; you might prefer the second. Either way is all right, as long as you stay with your original assignment throughout your analysis of the argument. Be consistent.

Summary

In evaluating complicated deductive arguments, it is often helpful to assign individual letters to propositions and to represent the argument in terms of these letters. Use arrows to represent *if–then* relationships, and the word *not* to represent negation. In so doing, make sure that the same letter represents the same proposition throughout the argument.

Check-Up 6D

True or False?
If a statement is false, change a crucial word or words to make it true.

6:109 Small letters are generally used to represent propositions.
6:110 The *q if p* relationship is represented by $p \rightarrow q$.
6:111 In the symbolization, $q \rightarrow r$, the antecedent is q.
6:112 In the symbolization, $r \rightarrow p$, the consequent is p.
6:113 The following symbolized lines of reasoning are deductively valid:

    1. a. $p \rightarrow q$
       b. <u>not q</u>
       c. Therefore, not p

    2. a. $p \rightarrow$ not q
       b. <u>p</u>
       c. Therefore, not q

6:114 The following symbolized lines of reasoning are deductively invalid:

    1. a. $p \rightarrow$ not q
       b. <u>not q</u>
       c. Therefore, p

    2. a. $p \rightarrow$ not q
       b. <u>q</u>
       c. Therefore, not p

6:115 The form of example #1 in 6:113 is *denying the consequent*.
6:116 The form of example #2 in 6:113 is *affirming the antecedent*.
6:117 The form of example #1 in 6:114 is *denying the consequent*.
6:118 The form of example #2 in 6:114 is *affirming the consequent*.

Short Answer

For the next items, assign letters to the propositions, and represent the total statement in symbols. The first is done as an example.

6:119 If John is in school, then Mary is happy.

Let *p* = *John is in school.*
Let *q* = *Mary is happy.*   *p → q*

6:120 If Karl lost the election, then he was depressed.
6:121 Estelle is happy if Marguerite is here.
6:122 Karl lost the election if he was depressed.
6:123 The supervisor forgot about us if there is a shortage of concrete.
6:124 The cattle, if junipers are poisonous, are in danger.

For the next set of items, state the final conclusion, assign letters, represent the argument symbolically, label the type of logical move, and judge the validity. Show your judgment as before, using *AA, DA, AC, DC, CONTR, CONV, EDN,* or *NDN,* and *DV* or *DI.* You have seen these items before. They are presented here again for practice in using symbols. By doing the same items both ways, you can see whether symbols make things like this easier for you. The first is done as an example.

6:125 If John is at work today, then Juanita is happy. I just saw Juanita and noticed that she is happy. Therefore, John is at work today.

Final conclusion: John is at work today.

Let *p* = *John is at work today.*
Let *q* = *Juanita is happy.*
p → q
q
Therefore, *p*   AC, DI

6:126 If Pedro went out last night, then Mary is angry today. I have just seen Mary and she is not angry today. Therefore, Pedro did not go out last night.
6:127 Suziko lost the election. I conclude this because I know that if she lost the election, she is depressed. And clearly she is depressed.
6:128 Terry, if she lied about her age, is in trouble. But she is not in trouble, so she did not lie about her age.
6:129 Terry lied about her age, if she managed to get into the Blue Room. But Terry did not manage to get into the Blue Room. We saw her at Shack's Fish & Chips. From all this, it follows that she did not lie about her age.
6:130 This blood on the porch is type A. If the blood is Al's blood, then it is type A, according to the blood analyst. Hence, the blood on the porch is Al's.
6:131 Joanna is not a liberal, if she did not support the prime minister. Therefore, if she supported the prime minister, she is a liberal.

6:132 If it has not been proven beyond a reasonable doubt that she knew that at least there was a strong probability that she would do him serious harm, she is not guilty. However, it has been proven beyond a reasonable doubt that she knew that at least there was a strong probability that she would do him serious harm. Therefore, she is guilty.

6:133 If the Board of Education suspends young Brown from school, then it will be punishing him for refusing on religious grounds to salute the flag. And if it does that, it will be acting unconstitutionally. Because the board, we can be sure, will not act unconstitutionally, we can be sure that the board will not suspend young Brown.

6:134 If Michael has a conflict of interest, then his testimony is not to be trusted. If Michael's brother is a suspect, then Michael has a conflict of interest. Michael's brother is a suspect. Therefore, Michael's testimony is not to be trusted.

Conjunction, Alternation, and Embedded Complex Propositions

In the following argument (which you saw at the beginning of this chapter), two propositions are conjoined (connected by the word *and*). The two are then treated as one unit and become the antecedent for the overall implication. Can you assign letters and judge the deductive validity? The basic propositions are italicized:

Example 6:23

If *parking is prohibited on this street* and *Sybil parked there last night*, then *Sybil is in trouble*. However, I know that *Sybil is not in trouble*, and that *parking is prohibited on this street*. Therefore, *she did not park there last night*.

Try it before I discuss it in the next section.

Conjunction and Embedded Complex Propositions

The propositions in Example 6:23 can be assigned letters as follows:

Let p = *Parking is prohibited on this street.*
Let q = *Sybil parked there last night.*
Let r = *Sybil is in trouble.*

The first two propositions are joined together by the word *and*, as in p *and* q. The way to show that they jointly form the antecedent is to put parentheses around them before adding the arrow to show implication, as in Example 6:24:

Example 6:24

$(p$ and $q) \rightarrow r$

Thus, p and q are conjoined and the conjunction is *embedded* in the whole implication.

The first step in the argument is the denial of the consequent, r, resulting in the denial of the conjunction:

Example 6:25

$(p$ and $q) \rightarrow r$

not r

Therefore, not $(p$ and $q)$

It is important to retain the parentheses in the conclusion of Example 6:25 because it is the whole conjoined unit that is being denied, not any individual part. This conclusion can be read, "Not both p and q." The conclusion does not tell us which of the parts is denied. It only tells us that at least one is to be denied (or perhaps both). The next step in the argument clarifies this because the original argument asserts p. The next step is reasoning from a denied conjunction, one part of which is affirmed:

Example 6:26

not $(p$ and $q)$ (This is the conclusion of Example 6:25. We use it in this next step.)

p

Therefore, not q

If one part of a denied conjunction is affirmed, the other must be denied. They cannot both be accepted, so the argument is deductively valid. The conclusion of Example 6:23, "She did not park there last night," follows necessarily from the reasons given.

This type of argument will appear again in Chapters 8 and 9 in connection with the refutation of hypotheses. It is a combination of *denial of the consequent* and *affirmation of one part of a negated conjunction*. This last label is long and awkward, but at least it describes what happens. There is no good label for it without inventing another technical term.[4]

When a conjunction of propositions appears by itself, and is affirmed, then it is implied that each conjunct can be affirmed separately. For example, if someone said, "Parking is prohibited on this street and Sybil parked there yesterday," it would deductively follow from the conjunction that parking is prohibited on this street. But if the conjunction is denied, and there is no other information, then the denial of each or either does not follow deductively. All that we know then is that at least one is to be denied, but we do not yet know which one.

---

4. This is a controversial point, again beyond the scope of this book. See the Lewis, Strawson, and Grice references mentioned at the beginning of Chapter 5 if you want to pursue it.

Alternation

An alternation consists of two propositions (alternants) connected by the word *or,* as in *Myrna is going back to California, or she is foolish.* The denial of either alternant then implies the assertion of the other. Suppose that Myrna is not going back to California. It follows that she is foolish. Suppose that she is not foolish. It follows that she is going back to California. Example 6:27 illustrates the first of these two deductively valid arguments.

Example 6:27

Let p = *Myrna is going back to California.*
Let q = *She is foolish.*

a.	Myrna is going back to California, or she is foolish.	p or q
b.	Myrna is not going back to California.	not p
c.	Therefore, she is foolish.	Therefore, q
	Denial of an alternant; DV	

Example 6:28 illustrates the denial of the other alternant:

Example 6:28

a.	Myrna is going back to California, or she is foolish.	p or q
b.	Myrna is not foolish.	not q
c.	Therefore, Myrna is going back to California.	Therefore, p
	Denial of an alternant: DV	

On the other hand, the affirmation of either of these alternants does not imply the denial of the other. For example, suppose that Myrna *is* foolish. That does not imply that she is not going back to California. Her going is not precluded by the alternation and her being foolish. She might go for some foolish reason. Similarly, suppose that she *is* going back to California. That, together with the alternation, does not imply that she is not foolish. Again, she might be going back for some foolish reason. Example 6:29 presents this latter case.

Example 6:29

a.	Myrna is going back to California, or she is foolish.	p or q
b.	Myrna is going back to California.	p
c.	Therefore, she is not foolish.	Therefore, not q
	Affirmation of weak alternant; DI	

+ However, in a strong sense of the word *or,* the affirmation of either alternant does imply the denial of the other, as in **Either Marguerite is at the movies or she is with Estelle.** Example 6:30 illustrates the use of the strong *or.*

Example 6:30

Let p = *Marguerite is at the movies.*
Let q = *She is with Estelle.*

   a. *Either* Marguerite is at the movies *or* she is with Estelle. p **or** q
   b. Marguerite is at the movies. p
   c. Therefore, she is not with Estelle.   Therefore, not q
      Affirmation of strong alternant; DV

+ You must decide from the situation which sense of *or* is in use, the weak sense (as in Examples 6:27, 6:28, and 6:29), or the strong sense (as in Example 6:30). But remember, there is no free ride. If the strong sense is in use, the alternation reason (a) is harder to establish, so the total argument might be in trouble if the strong sense is in use. If in doubt, I suggest the weak interpretation.

Summary

When two propositions are *conjoined* by the word *and,* they form a unit. If the whole unit is asserted, that implies that each *conjunct* can be asserted separately. If the unit is denied (or negated), then at least one conjunct must be denied. Without further information, it is not clear which one is the one to be denied. Furthermore, the unit can itself be a proposition in an argument (as can any complex proposition). This is shown by the use of parentheses around the unit when it is represented symbolically.

When two propositions are connected by the word *or,* they are *alternants.* The denial of one alternant implies the assertion of the other, if the total alternation is asserted.

+ However, unless the alternation is a *strong* alternation, the assertion of one alternant does not imply the denial of the other. You must determine from the situation whether the *or* is strong or weak. If in doubt, I suggest that you choose the weak interpretation.

Check-Up 6E

True or False?
If the statement is false, change a crucial word or words to make it true.

   6:135 The affirmation of one conjunct implies the denial of the other.
   6:136 The denial of one weak alternant implies the affirmation of the other.
   6:137 Affirming a conjunct in a negated conjunction is a deductively valid move.
   6:138 Denying a conjunct in a negated conjunction is a deductively valid move.
   6:139 There is little practical difference between these two complex propositions: (1) *not* (p *and* q) and (2) *not* p *and* q.
+ **6:140** The affirmation of one strong alternant implies the denial of the other.
+ **6:141** The affirmation of one weak alternant implies nothing about the other.

Short Answer

State the conclusion, assign letters, symbolize the argument, judge the deductive validity, and give your reason.

6:142 This piece of cloth is warm and it is 50 percent wool. If the dog is shivering from cold, then the cloth is not warm. Therefore, the dog is not shivering from cold.

6:143 If the label on this piece of cloth reads "50 percent wool," then it is 50 percent wool. This morning John, who knows about such things, said that the piece of cloth is warm, but it is only 25 percent wool. Therefore, the label certainly does not read "50 percent wool."

6:144 Thomas Jefferson did not make the mistake of which you are accusing him. If he had, then he would not have been an astute politician. But he was a scholar; he was a gentleman; and he was an astute politician.

6:145 Either there will be rain within the week, or the crops will be ruined. We can be sure that it will not rain within the week. Hence, we can be sure that the crops will be ruined.

+ 6:146 The two colors that you select will match or the room will be ugly. If I help you select the colors, then they will match. I am going to help you select the colors. Therefore, the room will not be ugly.

6:147 Abraham Lincoln must have thought that his Gettysburg Address was a failure. The following reasons make this apparent: Either he thought that it was reverently received, or he thought that it was a failure. From his remarks made immediately afterward, we can be sure that he did not think that it was reverently received.

6:148 If Dick took a driver training course and passed it with a grade of B or higher, then he is entitled to a lower rate on automobile insurance. Dick did take a driver training course. Therefore, he is entitled to a lower rate on automobile insurance.

6:149 I believe that Tom Jeffers did not stab Al. Here's why: Either Tom was in the hospital when the stabbing took place five miles away or, during the ten minutes when he was not under observation, he managed to travel to the site, spend some time, and return. If he did all that, then he is superman—and we all know he is not anything like superman. Not Tom Jeffers. If he was in the hospital when the stabbing took place, then he did not stab Al. I rest my case.

6:150 If Pedro has lived in his election district for over thirty days, and is over eighteen, he is entitled to vote. Pedro has lived in his election district for over a year, and he turned nineteen last month. Therefore, he is entitled to vote.

6:151 Hamlet must not have been in doubt of the guilt of his uncle. Consider: He certainly was not both in doubt of the guilt of his uncle and convinced that he had actually spoken to his father's ghost. He was convinced that he had actually spoken to his father's ghost. Hence, in his mind there was no doubt of the guilt of his uncle.

6:152 You have seen rainbows when it was raining, and you have seen rainbows when it is sunny. But one thing is certain: It is not the case both that there is a rainbow now and that the sky is completely overcast now. You will note that there is no rainbow now. From this, it follows that the sky is completely overcast now. There is no way around it.

6:153 It is not true both that Sheila is in love with Jim and at the same time in love with John. Nobody can be in love with two different people at the same time. From all we can see, it is clear that Sheila is in love with Jim. Therefore, Sheila is not in love with John.

6:154 I do not agree that it is not possible to be in love with two people at the same time. But be that as it may, I still think that we can conclude that Sheila is not in love with John. Here's why: If Sheila is in love with John, then she will have secured John's signature in her yearbook. Now she did not both secure John's signature in her yearbook and go to the dance with Jim. If she did not go to the dance with Jim, then she is at home right now. I just checked, and she is not at home, so you can see why I think that she is not in love with John. It follows.

6:155 Arlene is not both guilty of murder and innocent of voluntary manslaughter. If she might have been justified in using the amount of force she used, then she is innocent of voluntary manslaughter. Therefore, she is not guilty of murder because she might have been justified in using the amount of force she used.

Suggested Answers for Chapter 6

Check-Up 6A

6:1 T	**6:2** F	**6:3** T	**6:4** F	**6:5** T	**6:6** T
6:7 F	**6:8** F				

6:2 Omit clause starting with *but*.

6:4 Replace *is the same* with *in one is the consequent in the other*.

6:7 Change *first* to *after the if*.

6:8 Move the *if* to the beginning of the first clause in *a*.

6:9–6:10 These were done as examples.

6:11–6:28 The antecedent is *a* and the consequent is *b*:

6:11 **a.** junipers . . . poisonous
     b. the cattle . . . in danger

6:12 **a.** junipers . . . poisonous
     b. The cattle . . . in danger

6:13 **a.** the supervisor . . . us
     b. there . . . concrete

6:14 **a.** Terry . . . Room
     b. she . . . age

6:15 **a.** Terry . . . age
     b. she . . . Room

6:16 **a.** Joanna . . . liberal
     b. she . . . minister

6:17 **a.** she . . . minister
      b. Joanna . . . liberal

6:18 **a.** Arlene admitted . . . it
      b. she did it

Note: Henceforth in this set, odd-numbered answers will be omitted.

6:20 **a.** she admitted . . . it
      b. Arlene did it

6:22 **a.** she . . . death
      b. she . . . him

6:24 **a.** it . . . A
      b. The blood . . . blood

6:26 **a.** Tom . . . midnight
      b. he did not do it

Check-Up 6B
6:27 T   6:28 T   6:29 T   6:30 F   6:31 T
6:30 Change *valid* to *invalid*.
6:32 Done as an example.
6:33 DC, DV   6:34 AC, DI   6:35 DC, DV   6:36 AC, DI
6:37 DA, DI   6:38 AC, DI   6:39 Deliberately omitted.
6:40 DC, DV   6:41 Deliberately omitted.

Check-Up 6C
6:42 T   6:43 F   6:44 T   6:45 T   6:46 T   6:47 T
6:48 F   6:49 T   6:50 T   6:51 F   6:52 T
6:43 Change *the converse of* to *the same as*.
6:48 Two negatives usually make a positive.
6:51 One way: Exchange the antecedent and the consequent in the second
     reason.
6:53 Done as an example.
6:54 [Blank] . . . if
6:55 If . . . then
6:56 If . . . then
6:57 Deliberately omitted.
6:58 Done as an example.
6:59 Motorcycles are permitted.
6:60 The diamond is in the queen's crown.
6:61 Not eliminable.
6:62 If Arlene did it, then she admitted that she did it.
6:63 Deliberately omitted.
6:64 Not eliminable.
6:65 Deliberately omitted.
6:66 Not eliminable because one negation is in an antecedent and the other
     in a consequent.
6:67 If Arlene did not do it, then she did not admit doing it.

6:68 If our cattle are not ill, then junipers are not poisonous.

6:69 If the blood is not type A, then it is not Al's blood.

6:70 If the vehicle is not prohibited, then it does not have a motor.

6:71 If Sara Lee was admitted to the Panama Club, she lied about her age.

6:72 If we do not have enough concrete, the supervisor forgot about us.

6:73 If Martin does not think that hunters might be around, then he is not wearing a red hat.

6:74 If Shiboen did not buy it, then the gift is not inexpensive.

6:75 Deliberately omitted.

6:76 If the battery is not in bad condition, then you did not leave the lights on all night.

6:77 Deliberately omitted.

6:78–6:79 These were done as examples.

6:80 Karl did not lose the election. DC; DV

6:81 Mary did not go out last night. DC; DV

6:82 If Terry is in trouble, then she lied about her age. CONV; DI

6:83 She did not lie about her age. DA; DI

6:84 If Mary . . . school. CONTR; DV

6:85 There is not a shortage of concrete. DA; DI

6:86 The blood on the porch is Al's. AC; DI

6:87 He did it. DA; DI

6:88 She is guilty. DA; DI

6:89 She did it. DC; DV

6:90 If she supported the prime minister, she is a liberal. CONV of CONTR; DI.

Note: This last item is more complicated than the previous ones in that the conclusion is neither simple conversion nor contraposition. Rather, it can be viewed as the conversion of the contrapositive (or the contraposition of the converse). The contrapositive of the original assertion is *If she is a liberal, then she supported the prime minister.* This would follow necessarily, but the proposed conclusion is the converse of this.

Henceforth in this set and the next, odd-numbered answers are omitted.

6:92 Michael's testimony is not to be trusted. AA, AA; DV

6:94 No photosynthesis can be occurring in this plant. AA; DV

6:96 She is guilty. DA; DI

6:98 It has been PBRD that she believed she was safe. NDN DI

6:100 Done as an example.

6:102 Amandita does not believe John. DC

6:104 Nothing. AC

6:106 Jane did not say "No." DC

6:108 Nothing. DA

Check-Up 6D

6:109 T	**6:110** T	**6:111** T	**6:112** T	**6:113** T
6:114 F	**6:115** T	**6:116** T	**6:117** F	**6:118** F

6:114 #1 is deductively invalid, but not #2.

6:117 Replace *denying* with *affirming*.

6:118 Replace *affirming* with *denying*.

6:119 Done as an example.

6:120 Let *p* = *Karl lost the election.*
Let *q* = *he was depressed.*
p → *q*

6:121 Let *p* = *Marguerite is here.*
Let *q* = *Estelle is happy.*
p → *q*

6:122 Let *p* = *he was depressed.*
Let *q* = *Karl lost the election.*
p → *q*

6:123 Deliberately omitted.

6:124 Let *p* = *junipers are poisonous.*
Let *q* = *The cattle are in danger.*
p → *q*

6:125 Done as an example.

6:126 Final conclusion: Pedro did not go out last night.

Let *p* = *Pedro went out last night.*
Let *q* = *Mary is angry today.*

p → *q*
not *q*
Therefore, not *p*   DC; DV

6:127 Final conclusion: Suziko lost the election.

Let *p* = *Suziko lost the election.*
Let *q* = *she is depressed.*

p → *q*
q
Therefore, *p*   AC; DI

6:128 Final conclusion: She did not lie about her age.

Let *p* = *she lied about her age.*
Let *q* = *Terry is in trouble.*

p → *q*
not *q*
Therefore, not *p*   DC; DV

6:129 Final conclusion: She did not lie about her age.

Let *p* = *she managed to get into the Blue Room.*
Let *q* = *Terry lied about her age.*

p → *q*
Not *p*
Therefore, not *q*   DA; DI

6:130 Final conclusion: The blood on the porch is Al's.

Let p = *the blood is Al's.*
Let q = *the blood is type A.*

$p \rightarrow q$
q
Therefore, p AC; DI

Henceforth in this set, odd-numbered answers are omitted.

6:132 Final conclusion: She is guilty.

Let p = *it has not been PBRD . . . harm.*
Let q = *she is not guilty.*

$p \rightarrow q$
not p
Therefore, not q DA; DI

6:134 Final conclusion: Michael's testimony is not to be trusted.

Let p = *Michael has a conflict of interest.*
Let q = *his testimony is not to be trusted.*
Let r = *Michael's brother is a suspect.*

$r \rightarrow p$
$p \rightarrow q$
r
Therefore, q AA, AA; DV

Check-Up 6E
6:135 F   **6:136** T   **6:137** T   **6:138** F   **6:139** F
6:140 T   **6:141** T
6:135 Replace *the denial of* with *nothing about.*
6:138 Change *valid* to *invalid.*
6:139 Change *little practical* to *a great.*
6:142 Conclusion: The dog is not shivering from the cold.

Let p = *this piece of cloth is warm.*
Let q = *it is 50 percent wool.*
Let r = *the dog is shivering from cold.*

p and q
$r \rightarrow$ not p
Therefore, not r DC; DV

6:143 Conclusion: The label does not read "50 percent wool."

Let p = *the label reads "50 percent wool."*
Let q = *it is 50 percent wool.*
Let r = *the piece of cloth is warm.*

$p \rightarrow q$
r and not q
Therefore, not p DC; DV

6:144 Conclusion: Thomas Jefferson did not make . . . him.

Let p = *Thomas Jefferson made . . . him.*
Let r = *he was an astute politician.*
Let s = *he was a scholar.*
Let t = *he was a gentleman.*

$p \rightarrow$ not r
s and t and r
Therefore, not p DC; DV

Henceforth in this set, odd-numbered answers are omitted.

+ **6:146** Conclusion: The room will not be ugly.

Let p = *the two colors you select will match.*
Let q = *the room will be ugly.*
Let r = *I help you select the colors.*

Argument in steps:

Step 1:
$r \rightarrow p$
r
So, p (AA; DV)

Step 2
p or q
p
Therefore, not q (affirmation of weak alternant; DI)

Total argument:
p or q
$r \rightarrow p$
r
Therefore, not q
AA, Affirmation of weak alternant (AWA); DI

Note: If you interpreted the *or* as strong, the argument would have been deductively valid, but then it would have been more difficult to establish the alternation p *or* q.

6:148 Conclusion: He is entitled . . . insurance.

Let p = *Dick took a driver training course.*
Let q = *he passed it with a grade of B or higher.*
Let r = *he is entitled . . . insurance.*

$(p$ and $q) \rightarrow r$
p
Therefore, r
Only one conjunct in the antecedent was affirmed; DI

6:150 Conclusion: He is entitled to vote.

Let p = *Pedro has . . . over thirty days.*
Let q = *he is over eighteen.*
Let r = *he is entitled to vote.*

(p and q) → r
p and q
Therefore, r AA; DV

6:152 Conclusion: The sky is completely overcast now.

Let p = *there is a rainbow now.*
Let q = *the sky is completely overcast now.*

not (p and q)
not p
Therefore, q
Denial of part of a negated conjunction; DI

6:154 Conclusion: Sheila is not in love with John.

Let p = *Sheila is in love with John.*
Let q = *Sheila has John's signature in her yearbook.*
Let r = *Sheila went to the dance with Jim.*
Let s = *Sheila is at home right now.*

Argument in steps:

Step 1:
not r → s
not s
Therefore, r (DC, DV)

Step 2:
not (q and r)
r
Therefore, not q (Affirm part of negated conj.; DV)

Step 3:
p → q
not q
Therefore, not p (DC, DV)

Overall argument:
not r → s
not (q and r)
p → q
not s
Therefore, not p (DC, Affirm part of negated conj., DC; DV)

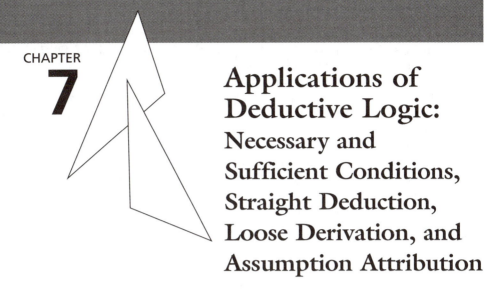

7

Applications of Deductive Logic: Necessary and Sufficient Conditions, Straight Deduction, Loose Derivation, and Assumption Attribution

This chapter presents a discussion of some applications of deductive logic. Although deductive ideas are useful in directly developing and judging some arguments, they are more often useful in other ways. In this chapter, you will see examples of direct and indirect use: necessary and sufficient condition language, straight deduction from acceptable reasons, loose derivation, assumption attribution, and evaluation of deduction's role in hypotheses. Elaboration of evaluation of generalizations and hypotheses, and its applications in one type of explanation and in value judging, appear in Chapters 8–11.

Necessary and Sufficient Conditions

Sometimes it is convenient to discuss class logic relationships in terms of necessary conditions, sufficient conditions, or both. For example, "Being a dog is a sufficient condition for being an animal" is, roughly speaking, another way to say that all dogs are animals. To say that one condition is sufficient for another is to say that establishing that the first holds is enough to establish that the second holds.

Similarly, "Being an animal is a necessary condition for being a dog" is, roughly speaking, another way to say that showing something not to be an animal establishes that it is not a dog. To say that one thing is a necessary condition for another is to say that if the first does not hold, the second cannot hold either—that the first must hold in order that the second hold. This is the sort of thing we have in mind when we say that being a citizen is a necessary condition for being eligible to vote. Being a necessary condition does not imply that something is a sufficient condition, and vice versa. Being a citizen is not a sufficient condition for being eligible to vote.

The language of necessary and sufficient conditions also can be used in propositional logic, as in "The truth of *Mike is a dog* is a sufficient condition for the truth of *Mike is an animal*." This can be conveniently translated into talk using gerunds, as in "Mike's being a dog is a sufficient condition for Mike's being an animal."

Similarly, given our standard example in Chapter 6, the truth of "Mike is an animal" is a necessary condition for the truth of "Mike is a dog." Or, Mike's being an animal is a necessary condition for Mike's being a dog.

This brief treatment of necessary and sufficient conditions should enable you to follow the use of these terms as we proceed. Unfortunately, there are some tricky features about these terms in causal contexts. Let me elaborate a bit. The consequent's holding is a logically necessary condition, as you just saw in the Mike example. But consider this if–then proposition: "If Mike is frightened, he barks." It could be confusing to say that his barking is a necessary condition for his being frightened. Always make sure that your use of the language of necessary and sufficient conditions makes sense in the given situation.[1]

Soundness in Deductive Logic

When an argument has true reasons and is deductively valid, then we are required to accept its conclusion. Such an argument is called *sound* by deductive logicians. Because this precise use of the word *sound* is not widely accepted (by other than logicians and some philosophers), you can expect most people with whom you have discussions not to use the term *sound* this way. For most people, a sound argument is a good argument, whether or not it is deductively valid.

Not all good arguments are deductively valid, although in some fields (such as mathematics) most arguments must be deductively valid in order to be good arguments. An example of a good argument that is not deductively valid is the prosecutor's argument in Chapter 2 that has as its conclusion "Arlene performed the act that caused Al's death." That argument is sound in the ordinary sense of *sound,* but not in the logician's sense. In the logician's sense, it is an unsound argument. Beware of thinking that it is necessarily a bad or weak argument.

In view of the ambiguity of the word *sound,* make sure that your audience (that is, those with whom you are communicating) is not confused by your use of this term. If you are confident that no one in your audience has studied deductive logic, then use it in the everyday sense. (You are less likely to mislead people.) Otherwise, in real situations, make sure that it is clear how you are using the term, if you use it at all. Also make sure that no one else is shifting in their meaning of the term (which, of course, *you* would not do). For example, make sure that no one is judging an argument unsound on the ground that it is not deductively valid, and then concluding that it is not a good argument on that basis alone. As the prosecutor's argument in Chapter 2 shows, some unsound arguments in the logician's sense of the term are quite sound (using the term in its everyday sense).

Three Cases of Deduction in Context

Read these illustrative cases closely several times and make sure that you understand each step. If you have trouble with class logic, you should review Chapter 5 for

---

1. See my *Natural Language Logic* (forthcoming) for further discussion of this topic.

detailed instruction and extensive practice. If you have trouble with propositional logic, review Chapter 6.

Chapters 5 and 6 gave you the opportunity to see and use deductive standards. Not all of the exercises there are realistic, although those from the context of the jury trial are realistic. Next, from that same context, we will examine the deductive application of the jury's instructions about voluntary manslaughter. Subsequently, you will see two cases from a discussion of Shakespeare's play *Othello*, in which parts of the total argument conform to the standards of deductive validity. The jury's instructions regarding the charge of murder appear in the first Check-Up and provide another example of deduction in context.

Applying Detailed Instructions About the Charge of Voluntary Manslaughter

After the prosecution and defense attorneys had finished presenting their cases, the judge provided the jury with a copy of the conditions to be established for voluntary manslaughter and for murder. You will see the conditions for murder in a Check-Up. Here are the conditions for voluntary manslaughter:

Example 7:1

To sustain the charge of voluntary manslaughter, the state must prove the following propositions:

First: That the defendant intentionally or knowingly performed the acts that caused the death of the victim.
Second: That when the defendant did so, she believed that circumstances existed that would have justified killing the victim.
Third: That the defendant's belief that such circumstances existed was unreasonable.
Fourth: That the defendant was not justified in using the force she used.

1. If you find from your consideration of all the evidence that each of these propositions has been proved beyond a reasonable doubt, then you should find the defendant guilty.
2. If you find from your consideration of all the evidence that any of these propositions has not been proved beyond a reasonable doubt, then you should find the defendant not guilty.

What does it all mean? One way to help grasp this detailed specification is to think in terms of necessary and sufficient conditions. Try to do so before you read further.

Here is one possible rough summary statement in terms of necessary and sufficient conditions: According to the first if–then proposition, the conjunction of the first four conditions (each proven beyond a reasonable doubt) is sufficient for a guilty verdict. According to the second if–then proposition, proof beyond a reasonable doubt of each one of the four conditions is a necessary condition for a guilty verdict. More compactly, the four conditions (each proven beyond a reasonable doubt) are jointly sufficient and each necessary for a guilty verdict. Looking at it in these terms was helpful to me, as it should be to you, now that you are familiar with the language of necessary and sufficient conditions.

But my associates on the jury were not all familiar with this language. When I tried to make overall sense of it for them, I did not use the words *necessary* and *sufficient*. Instead, I said something like the following: "If every one of those four conditions has been proven beyond a reasonable doubt, then that is enough for a verdict of guilty and we should vote for a guilty verdict. But each of them is needed. Without any one of them, we must declare her not guilty." This is an example of what I hope you can do: Think in terms of necessary and sufficient conditions and use that language with people who understand it. But when you are with people who might be confused or intimidated by this language, express necessary and sufficient relationships in simpler, though usually lengthier, terms.

It might also help you to symbolize the relationships, although it would probably not help those unfamiliar with the basic symbolization strategies presented in Chapter 6. Doing this symbolization helped me, partly because of the precision it required of me. Before reading further, stop and try to symbolize the statement of conditions for a verdict of voluntary manslaughter.

Here is my thinking in developing this symbolization: Each condition must be proven beyond a reasonable doubt. In order to save time and space, I shall use the letters *PBRD* (read *proven beyond a reasonable doubt*) to mean "You find from your consideration of all the evidence that it has been proven beyond a reasonable doubt." I do that because this idea is part of each of the four listed conditions. Assuming this use of *PBRD*, Example 7:2 provides my symbolization of the voluntary manslaughter charge.

Example 7:2

Let p = "PBRD that the defendant intentionally or knowingly performed the acts that caused the death of the victim."
Let q = "PBRD that when the defendant did so, she believed that circumstances existed that would have justified killing the victim."
Let r = "PBRD that the defendant's belief that such circumstances existed was unreasonable."
Let s = "PBRD that the defendant was not justified in using the force she used."
Let t = "You should find the defendant guilty."
Let u = "You should find the defendant not guilty."

The symbolized charge is as follows:

1. $(p$ and q and r and $s) \rightarrow t$.
2. not $(p$ and q and r and $s) \rightarrow u$.

Our argument for our guilty verdict for voluntary manslaughter went as follows:

Example 7:3

$(p$ and q and r and $s) \rightarrow t.$
p
q
r
$\underline{s}$
Therefore, t AA; DV

We jurors believed Example 7:3 to be a sound argument in both meanings of *sound*.

Example 7:3 summarizes and masks the long discussions that we had, especially for condition *s*. But Example 7:3 exhibits the overall structure of the situation within which we were working. It helped me to keep in mind the relevance of what was going on.

The structure of the conditions for murder in this situation was more complicated than that for voluntary manslaughter. These conditions for murder appear in the next Check-Up, together with our argument leading to a verdict of not guilty of murder.

In this case, all the parts of the deductive argument are explicitly stated, probably because in the courtroom, these sort of things must be totally in the open. Often, however, in situations where deductively valid reasoning is used, the speaker does not explicitly state all the reasons, leaving it up to us to fill in what is obviously intended. Furthermore, the deductive reasoning is often only part of the entire argument. The passage in Example 7:4 about the interpretation of *Othello* is from A. C. Bradley's *Shakespearean Tragedy* and serves as an example:

Example 7:4

Nothing could be less like Iago than the melodramatic villain so often substituted for him on the stage, a person whom everyone in the theatre knows for a scoundrel at the first glance. . . . [His wife Emilia] never dreamed he was a villain. No doubt she knew rather more of him than others.[2]

In this argument, the hypothesis that Iago is a melodramatic villain is argued against. Restated with the probably intended assumption added at the beginning in brackets (a step discussed later in this chapter), the argument goes as in Example 7:5, and is a case of denial of the consequent (plus the affirmation of one part of a negated conjunction):

Example 7:5

[If Emilia knew her husband rather more than others did and he was a melo-

---

2. A. C. Bradley, *Shakespearean Tragedy* (London: Macmillan and Co., Ltd, 1937), p. 213.

dramatic villain, then she suspected him of villainy.] Emilia did not suspect him of villainy and she knew rather more of him than others. So Iago was not a melodramatic villain.

Let p = "she knew her husband rather more than others."
Let q = "he was a melodramatic villain."
Let r = "she suspected him of villainy."

Using letters, the argument looks like this, with each line explained on the right side:

Part 1:

$(p$ and $q) \rightarrow r$	Unstated assumption
not r	Stated reason
Therefore, not $(p$ and $q)$	DC; DV

Reminder: This conclusion means "not both p and q."

Part 2:

not $(p$ and $q)$	Conclusion of Part 1
p	Stated reason
Therefore, not q	Affirmation of one member of a negated conjunction; DV

The argument in Example 7:5 is deductively valid. I broke the argument into two parts so you could see how an intermediate conclusion was derived (in Part 1) and then used (in Part 2) as a reason in deriving the final conclusion. In Part 1, the conjoined propositions, p and q, form the antecedent. The denial of this antecedent is the conclusion of Part 1, "not $(p$ and $q)$." In Part 2, this negated conjunction becomes the first reason. Because one part (p) of this negated conjunction is true, the other part must be false because they cannot both be true. Thus, we get the conclusion, "not q." If both parts of such an argument are deductively valid, then the whole thing is deductively valid.

Example 7:6 is another argument from Bradley's book:

Example 7:6

It is false that Iago was . . . chiefly incited by two things, the desire of advancement, and a hatred of Othello due principally to the affair of the lieutenancy. A man moved by simple passions due to simple causes does not stand fingering his feelings, industriously enumerating their sources, and groping about for new ones. But this is what Iago does.[3]

I added the apparent assumption that the desire of advancement and the hatred of Othello due principally to the affair of the lieutenancy are simple passions due to simple causes. Then the argument can be seen to be deductively valid by the following diagram:

---

3. A. C. Bradley, *Shakespearean Tragedy* (London: Macmillan and Co., Ltd, 1937), p. 220.

Diagram 7:1

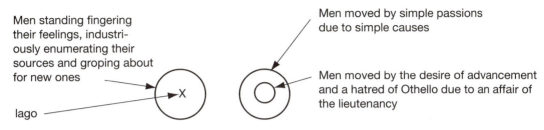

Men standing fingering their feelings, industriously enumerating their sources and groping about for new ones

Iago

Men moved by simple passions due to simple causes

Men moved by the desire of advancement and a hatred of Othello due to an affair of the lieutenancy

Therefore, the argument is deductively valid. Diagramming the reasons *forces* us to diagram the conclusion. The reasons force the *X* for Iago to be outside the inner circle on the right-hand side.

Cases like this of the direct use of deduction abound, but they are usually only part of a larger argument. In Example 7:6, the conclusion of the larger argument is that Iago is not a melodramatic villain. In Example 7:4, the conclusion of the larger argument is the same, but there is a significant prior inductive argument to try to establish the reason "Emilia never dreamed he was a villain."

Furthermore, real occurrences of deductive reasoning generally require supplementation and interpretation, which I have done here. This supplementation and interpretation is often difficult. It requires attention to the context and the nuances of language. In adding the assumptions I added, I was looking for propositions that probably needed to be true if the arguments are to be good arguments. Attributing assumptions to arguments is a difficult thing to do well. More about this later in this chapter.

Loose Derivation

Does the conclusion follow in Example 7:7?

Example 7:7

    a. Generally, defendants who admit to a stabbing have done it.
    b. Arlene, the defendant, admitted that she stabbed him.
    c. Therefore, she probably did stab him.

In this example, there are qualifying words: *probably* (in the conclusion) and *generally* (in the first reason). The conclusion does not necessarily follow. It might be true that defendants have *generally* done those acts to which they have confessed, yet also true that Arlene probably did not stab him, although she admitted doing so. That is, this is logically possible. What strategy should one follow?

I recommend that you first strip the qualifying words from the argument and make a judgment about the deductive validity of the resulting argument. Then put the qualifying words back in and, based on your understanding of the situation, make a judgment about the original argument, taking into account your judgment about the deductive validity of the stripped argument. Given all the other circumstances revealed in the trial, I felt that the reasons were sufficient to show that it was probable that Arlene did it. (But I am not saying that by this argument alone it was proved beyond a reasonable doubt that she did it.)

An argument that appears to require something close to deductive validity might well be judged unsatisfactory if the stripped argument is deductively invalid.

Example 7:8

    a. Generally, Communists were opposed to United States policy in El Salvador.
    b. Ambassador White was opposed to United States policy in El Salvador.
    c. Therefore, Ambassador White was probably a Communist.

The argument in Example 7:8 is deductively invalid even when the qualifying words, *generally* and *probably,* are stripped from it. In the context in which I heard this argument, there were no other plausible background assumptions to support the inference from the reasons to the conclusion, so I judged the argument defective. The argument seemed to require something close to deductive validity in that situation, but deductive validity was not there, as shown in Diagram 7:2.

Diagram 7:2

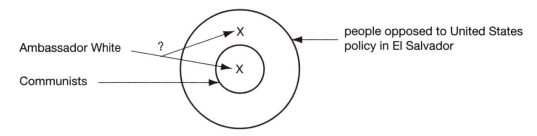

Summary So Far

The language of necessary and sufficient conditions is often useful in discussing relationships among things and in appraising deductive arguments. A *sufficient* condition is one that is enough to establish that something else holds. A *necessary* condition is one that must hold if another is to hold. A sufficient condition is enough, but it might not be necessary; a necessary condition is needed, but often is not enough. Although the language of necessary and sufficient conditions is also used in causal propositions, be careful about causal interpretations of logically necessary and sufficient condition relationships. Make sure that what you are saying makes sense.

In the language of deductive logic, a sound argument is a deductively valid one with true reasons. In everyday language, a sound argument is a good argument.

Direct cases of deductive validity are common in our everyday reasoning, but they usually are part of a larger argument, and they usually require some supplementation and interpretation in order to be judged. This supplementation and interpretation is often difficult to do. It requires sensitivity to the context and the language.

Often we see and use arguments that would be deductively valid if they did not include qualifying terms such as *probably, usually, in all probability,* and *likely.* There are no formulas that yield a judgment about such arguments, which are here called *loose derivations;* the best one can do with them is to strip the qualifiers, make a judgment about the deductive validity of the result, and then make a final judgment of the argument with the qualifiers reinserted (taking into account the judgment made about the deductive validity of the stripped argument).

This final judgment requires sensitivity to the situation, background information in the field or area of knowledge, experience, and wisdom. Because we have to make such decisions often, there is no point in hiding from this fact. But we must admit that these decisions are matters of judgment, and not fully determined by rules.

If you feel that you need more practice with deduction, go back and do more items from Chapters 5 and 6.

Check-Up 7A

True or False?

If false, change it to make it true. Try to do so in a way that shows that you understand.

7:1 A deductively valid argument is one in which the conclusion follows necessarily from the reasons.

7:2 The following argument is deductively valid when stripped: "Because totalitarian systems of government generally fail and the government of Ladia is about to fail, it is probably a totalitarian government."

7:3 A sufficient condition is one that is enough and that is needed in order for another to hold.

7:4 A necessary condition is one that must hold in order that another hold.

7:5 A good formula for dealing with deductive-appearing arguments containing qualifiers is to strip the qualifiers, make a deductive validity judgment, and apply exactly that judgment to the total argument.

7:6 Many real arguments omit one or the other of the reasons that would make them into deductively valid arguments.

Medium Answer

7:7 In the jury room one of the jurors argued as follows:

"She probably would not have taken Al's keys and zipped them in her purse if she wanted him to leave her alone. The detective testified that Al's keys were found in a zipped-up pocket of her purse. Because they could not have been there if she did not both take them and put them there, she probably did not want him to leave her alone."

Judge this argument using the FRISCO outline. Assume that the juror was ultimately trying to discredit Arlene's contention that she was defending herself against attack.

7:8 The following instructions to the jury specified the conditions for murder:

To sustain the charge of murder, the state must prove the following propositions:

First: That the defendant performed the acts that caused the death of the victim.
Second: That when the defendant did so, she intended to kill or do great bodily harm to the victim, or she knew that her act would cause death or great bodily harm to the victim, or she knew that her acts created a strong probability of death or great bodily harm to the victim.
Third: That the defendant was not justified in using the force she used.

> 1. If you find from your consideration of all the evidence that each of these propositions has been proven beyond a reasonable doubt, then you should find the defendant guilty.
>
> 2. If you find from your consideration of all the evidence that any of these propositions has not been proven beyond a reasonable doubt, then you should find the defendant not guilty.

Simplify by treating the second condition as a single proposition to be represented by a single letter.

> a. Interpret this set of specifications in the language of necessary and sufficient conditions.
> b. Interpret this set of specifications in less technical language (using words such as *enough* and *needed*), as you might for a group of people who might be intimidated by the language of necessary and sufficient conditions.
> c. Assign letters to the propositions in this set of specifications.
> d. Assuming that the second condition has not been proven beyond a reasonable doubt, symbolize an argument based on this assumption and concluding that the defendant is to be found not guilty.

+ 7:9 Do the same things as in 7:8, but do not simplify the second condition. Instead elaborate its constituent propositions. For example, *she intended to kill the victim* is one possible constituent proposition, assuming one way of analyzing the instructions.

7:10 Find an argument in print, broadcast, or conversation in which the conclusion appears to be loosely derived. Judge the argument and defend your judgment following the FRISCO outline.

Assumption Attribution and Identification

Usually, arguments that we offer and see have gaps in them. Consider Example 7:9. As it stands, the argument has a gap. The conclusion that Mollie is not on the team does not reasonably follow, unless some assumption is added to the argument. The most obvious candidate is that Mollie is not tall. This proposition, if added to the argument, makes it deductively valid.

Example 7:9

> You ask me whether Mollie is on the volleyball team? Definitely not. She couldn't be. Everyone on the volleyball team is tall. That's why I think that Mollie is not on the team.
> Probable assumption: Mollie is not tall.

Adding a proposition that would strengthen the inference part of an argument— often by making the argument deductively valid (or loosely so)—is a standard procedure for attributing assumptions to arguments. But there are pitfalls and qualifications, which I shall discuss after looking at some uses of the word *assumption* and considering several reasons for attributing assumptions to arguments or explanations.

Two Senses of the Word Assumption

Pejorative Sense

In one standard sense of the word *assumption,* to call something an *assumption* is to claim that it is more or less dubious. This is the pejorative sense of the word *assumption.* (A *pejorative* term is one that is used to condemn or deprecate in some way.) In the trial, one juror said, "That's an assumption," referring to the defense attorney's claim that Arlene was defending herself against attack. The juror was saying that the defense attorney's claim was dubious.

Even a conclusion can be a pejorative type of assumption, as in "Because you are wearing your hat, I assume that you are going out." Here, the conclusion "You are going out" is an assumption, but it is offered with some hesitancy. The word *assume* indicates this hesitancy, and shows that the speaker regards the conclusion to be at least somewhat dubious.

Undefended Basis

In a second standard sense of the word *assumption,* an *assumption* is an undefended (in the context) starting point in an argument. It might be explicit, it might be implicit, but it is undefended in the context, and other parts of the argument are supported by it. This is the undefended-basis sense of the word *assumption.* In Example 7:9, the proposition that Mollie is not tall is an *implicit* undefended-basis assumption. The proposition "Everyone on the volleyball team is tall" is an *explicit* undefended-basis assumption. When engaged in attributing and identifying assumptions, we usually are looking for the implicit ones. They are usually less obvious, and thus more likely to slip by unnoticed.

The undefended-basis sense of the word *assumption* is not necessarily associated with the pejorative sense. We can call a proposition an undefended basis without implying that it is dubious. This is often done in mathematics. However, in everyday situations, the two senses of the word *assumption* often overlap. That is, often things called assumptions are held to be both undefended and dubious. In order to avoid confusion and to concentrate on the techniques and criteria for undefended-basis assumptions, I shall in the rest of this chapter focus on the undefended-basis sense of the word *assumption,* not the pejorative sense.

Reasons for Attributing Assumptions to Arguments

Evaluation of Arguments

A common reason for attributing assumptions to arguments is to evaluate the argument. If an assumption in an argument is false, then the argument does not establish its conclusion, even if the stated reasons are true and the argument is deductively valid (when the assumption is added). Example 7:10 provides a sample conversation.

Example 7:10

SUE: Is Mollie on the volleyball team?
MIKE: Definitely not.
SUE: How do you know?
MIKE: Because everyone on the volleyball team is tall.
SUE: You're assuming that Mollie is not tall, but you're wrong. I guess you haven't seen her lately. You can't be sure from what you said that she is not on the team.

In Example 7:10, Sue attributed the assumption "Mollie is not tall" to Mike's argument (which is basically the argument presented in Example 7:9). Sue then found Mike's argument defective because it made a false assumption. So Sue judged that Mike's conclusion had not been established.

On the other hand, if the assumptions and the reasons in an argument are true, and together they give very strong support for the conclusion, then the argument should probably be judged to be acceptable and the conclusion accepted.

Figuring Out What Another Person Is Thinking

Often we attribute assumptions to arguments in order to get clear about the thinking of the arguer so that we know what to expect of that person in the future or so that we can judge that person.

Example 7:11

TEACHER: Sam should receive an A because he did well on the test.

After hearing a teacher make the comment in Example 7:11, a student might attribute to the teacher the assumption that people who did well on the test should get A's or, more generally, that people who do well on tests get A's. The student's purpose here is not to evaluate the teacher's argument. The purpose is to figure out the teacher. More evidence is needed to be sure that this is the right assumption to attribute to the teacher, but my point here is to exhibit this second purpose that people have for attributing assumptions: figuring out what other people are thinking (their motives, values, beliefs, etc.). We do this sort of thing with arguments by political candidates, as well as the arguments of close friends. However, because people know we do this, they sometimes deliberately mislead us about their true motives and beliefs. So be wary.

Showing What Someone's Real Commitments Are

A third, much less frequently pursued purpose for attributing assumptions to someone is to try to show the real commitments of a person. We might do this in order to show that the person is really on our side, or really against us, or really lined up with some view that the person claims to oppose or have doubts about, etc. For example, in a debate with Bertrand Russell, F. C. Copleston once urged that scientists in their investigations assume that nature is uniform—that there is a universal regularity in the nature of things.[4] He did this in order to show that scientists are really on his side in support of the proposition that nature is uniform. Russell did not think that nature is necessarily uniform.

A Basic Deductive Gap-Filling Move in Assumption Attribution

As you will see, there are usually various possible assumptions that can be attributed in a situation, but a good first guess is the simplest, most plausible proposition that transforms an argument into a deductively valid one. Consider Examples 7:12, 7:13, and 7:14, drawing on situations used in the chapters on deduction.

Example 7:12

Argument: All of Thomas Mann's books are good, so *Magic Mountain* must be a good book.
Assumption: *Magic Mountain* is by Thomas Mann.

Example 7:13

Argument: Those wheat plants must be weeds because all unwanted plants are weeds.
Assumption: Those wheat plants are unwanted.

Example 7:14

Argument: If the blood is Al's, it is type A. So it is not Al's blood.
Assumption: It is not type A.

Sometimes there are two or more appealing assumptions, any of which would fill the gap to make the sequence deductively valid, as in Example 7:15.

4. Bertrand Russell and F. C. Copleston, "A Discussion on the Existence of God" (first broadcast on the *Third Programme of the British Broadcasting Corporation,* January 28, 1948).

Example 7:15

Argument: Because John continually puts people down, he must feel insecure. Two Possible Assumptions: 1. Males who continually put people down feel insecure. 2. People who continually put others down feel insecure.

Ordinarily, when choosing one from among several candidates, we should try to be as charitable as we can to the arguer. It is not fair to the arguer to claim that his or her argument needs something stronger than it really needs.

Presuppositions

Another type of assumption attribution depends not on filling gaps in arguments, but on the meaning of the words in statements. Often, individual statements assume things without explicitly asserting them. Such assumptions are sometimes dangerous because they can slip things by us without our noticing them, as might happen in Examples 7:16 and 7:17.

Example 7:16

The students' bias is the fault of the parents, not the teachers.

Example 7:17

The great strength of our economy is attributable to our system of free enterprise.

These examples appear to be attempting to allocate responsibility, but they assume (that is, presuppose) that the students are biased and that our economy has great strength. If you straightforwardly affirm or deny either statement in Examples 7:16 and 7:17, you are accepting the presupposition. That is, if you deny Example 7:16 by saying that it is not the parents' fault, you are still committed to the students' being biased. If you deny Example 7:17 by saying that it is not attributable to our system of free enterprise, you are still committed to the belief that our economy has great strength. These statements are like the question "Have you stopped beating your child?" Either a *Yes* or *No* answer commits you to having beaten your child (the presupposition of that question).

Presuppositions are easy to identify if you are sensitive to their presence. That is, the presuppositions "They are biased," "This economy has great strength," and "You have beaten your child at some time" are clearly there. No one would question their being presupposed once their presence is noticed. The important (and sometimes difficult) thing is to *notice* them, and be ready to challenge them, if they are dubious.

Summary and Comment

Although one of the senses of the word *assumption* is pejorative, for our purposes here, I shall avoid that sense. But keep it in mind when communicating with others.

You will often use and encounter the pejorative sense of *assumption* and will need to attend to the pejorative claim involved.

There are at least three reasons for identifying or attributing undefended-basis assumptions: To flesh out an argument or explanation so that it can be evaluated for its strength, to figure out the thinking of someone who has offered an argument or explanation, and (less often) to show that someone is committed for or against some position.

A common first step in attributing an assumption to a position is to add a simple proposition that makes the stated material into a deductively valid argument, and that is charitable to the arguer. This added proposition is likely to be an assumption that can be attributed to the position.

A presupposition is a proposition that is embodied in a statement and assumed by it. It is also assumed by the denial of the statement, so it might slip by unnoticed.

Because there is more than one way to convert an argument or explanation into a deductively valid sequence, you have to be cautious in attributing assumptions. You might be wrong even though the proposition does convert the sequence into a valid deductive sequence. It is usually best to check with the person making the assumption, if you can, by asking, "Are you assuming that. . .?" or "Are you basing your decision on this idea: . . . ?" or some such question.

One difficulty with the first question, "Are you assuming that. . . ?," is that the word *assuming* might be taken pejoratively. That is, you might be taken to be suggesting that the assumption is dubious or false (which it might well be); in response, the speaker might resist admitting it as an assumption because he or she thinks that such an admission implies the admission of dubiousness or falsity. Therefore, you must be sensitive to how such an inquiry will be taken.

Check-Up 7B

True or False?
If false, change it to make it true. Try to do so in a way that shows that you understand.

> **7:11** Assumptions cannot be conclusions.
>
> **7:12** The word *assumption* is often used pejoratively.
>
> **7:13** There is one and only one possible proposition that can convert an argument with a deductive gap into a deductively valid one.
>
> **7:14** In the following sequence, the proposition labeled "A" is a possible candidate for being the assumption of the argument.
>
> > Argument: Mike is not a dog because all dogs are animals.
> > A: Mike is not an animal.
>
> **7:15** The proposition labeled "A," if added to the argument, would make it deductively valid.
>
> > Argument: Nothing written by that bureaucrat makes any sense, so Regulation EZTHINK was not written by that bureaucrat.
> > A: Regulation EZTHINK does not make any sense.

Short Answer

For each of the following, add a proposition that would make the sequence deductively valid. If there is a choice among candidates of different amounts of complexity and plausibility, pick the simplest and most plausible one. Do this on a separate piece of paper. (Note: For the arguments that refer to the trial, it might be helpful to refer to the statement of conditions for voluntary manslaughter and murder in Example 7:1 and Check-Up item 7:8.)

7:16 If Karl lost the election, then he is a fool. Therefore, Karl is a fool.

7:17 If Karl lost the election, then he is a fool. Therefore, Karl did not lose the election.

7:18 If Cecille won the tennis tournament, then Mirabelle is dejected. Therefore, Cecille must have lost.

7:19 Motorcycles are legally classified as motor vehicles, so Sarah's motorscooter is legally classified as a motor vehicle.

7:20 Mary is in good spirits today. Therefore, she must have gone out with Pedro last night.

7:21 Pedro must be in good spirits today. I know this because he went out with Mary last night.

7:22 If Arlene did it, then she admitted it. Therefore, she did not do it.

7:23 If Shakespeare had intended Polonius to be a comic figure, then he would not have made Polonius the father of two tragic characters. Therefore, Shakespeare did not intend Polonius to be a comic figure.

7:24 The strawberries in the cabbage patch are weeds because we do not want them there.

7:25 Raoul is in good physical shape because he plays soccer.

7:26 Zoning is unjust because it interferes with the desires of honest people.

7:27 Fights should be avoided because they hurt people.

7:28 Contemporary pop music is repetitive, uninteresting, and a threat to the peace, so it should be banned.

7:29 Everyone on the team is tall, so John is tall.

7:30 Everyone on the team is tall, so Enrico is not on the team.

7:31 Good chess players are critical thinkers, so Sally is a critical thinker.

7:32 Texas Jane will certainly lash out at the world because she has been treated unfairly for her entire life.

7:33 The new mayor made mistakes in her first speech because she is inexperienced.

7:34 Our students are not permitted in this joint because nobody under eighteen is permitted.

7:35 Because all genuine foods contain carbon, hydrogen, and oxygen, all genuine foods are carbohydrates.

7:36 If she killed him, then she performed the act that caused his death. Therefore, the first condition for murder is satisfied. (Hint: Fill two gaps here. Reminder: The statement of conditions given us for the charge of murder is in Check-Up item 7:8. Use it.)

7:37 Because June's Honda is a motorcycle and motor vehicles are not permitted on Rock Island, June's Honda is not permitted on Rock Island.

7:38 Nothing written by that bureaucrat makes any sense. Because Regulation EZTHINK was written by that bureaucrat, I refuse to publish it.

7:39 Nobody under thirty-five can be president. Because Tina is under thirty-five, we should not nominate her to be president.

7:40 If the Board of Education suspends Tammy from school, then it will be punishing her for expressing her opinions. If it does that, it will be acting unconstitutionally, so we can be sure that the Board of Education will not suspend Tammy.

7:41 If the blow was only moderate in force, then it has not been proven beyond a reasonable doubt that she knew that there was a strong probability of great bodily harm. Because the blow was only of moderate force, she is not guilty. (Reminder: See Check-Up item 7:8 for the conditions for the charge of murder.)

7:42 Samantha, if she is in town, is at the cinema. Because Samantha is not at the cinema, she must be in the country.

7:43 If our leader told you to commit suicide, then he is not worthy of being our leader. If our leader told you to drink poison, then he has told you to commit suicide. Because our leader did tell you to drink poison, I should be leader.

7:44 Whoever misses band practice is in trouble with the director. Whoever goes to the meeting will miss band practice. Marla is going to the meeting. Therefore, Marla will be kicked out of the band.

7:45 She was not justified in using the force she used because she could have run away to her parents' room. Therefore, she is guilty of voluntary manslaughter. (Hint: Fill two gaps here. Reminder: The conditions given us to establish the charge of voluntary manslaughter are in Check-Up item 7:1. Use them.)

Medium Answer

7:46 Select a sentence from a newspaper or magazine that contains a presupposition with which you agree and a sentence containing one with which you disagree. Identify them, indicating which is which.

Applications of Deductive Logic in Writing Position Papers

In position papers, as well as any other writing in which you take positions (that is, make points and give reasons), deductive logic, loose derivation, and assumption identification play an important role. Usually, this role is part of a larger argument.

Deductive Logic and Loose Derivation

Sometimes, you use (or find) straightforward deduction, as in Example 7:18, which is adapted from a recent newspaper editorial and exemplifies denying-the-consequent reasoning.

Example 7:18

> The president was unaware that these things would have such an impact. If she had known, she would not have done them. [Unstated assumption: She did them]

Example 7:18 is a strong argument if the reasons are true. In the selection from which I have taken this argument, a larger point was being made—that the president is naïve. The president's not being aware was supposedly explained by the president's naïveté, and thus was evidence for this alleged naïveté. So this is a case in practical writing in which deduction played an important role, although it was only part of the total argument.

Similarly, you will often find it convenient to incorporate deductively valid arguments or loose derivations in your larger arguments. When you do so, make sure that the deductive parts are deductively valid.

Straightforward Assumption Identification

You will note that I did some assumption identification in presenting the argument of Example 7:18. This sort of assumption identification is usually necessary in responding in writing (or orally) to the writing of others. People usually do not state their full arguments, often because doing so seems to be a waste of time. In Example 7:18, it probably would have been a waste of time for the writer to state explicitly that the president did these things. It is obvious that this proposition is part of the argument. Identifying this assumption is so easy that the author did not bother to state it.

Incidentally, in this case, the assumption identification is made easier by the fact that the one identified in Example 7:18 is not only a gap-filling assumption, but also a presupposition, given the way the argument is stated. The phrase "she would not have done them" presupposes that she did them. In that context, the use of that phrase involves a commitment to the assumption, regardless of the argument, making it a presupposition as well.

But although its being an assumption is obvious, bringing such an assumption out in the open is often helpful. Suppose that you believe that the president actually did not do the things to which reference is made, or that it is uncertain whether or not she did them, or that she only did some of them and those that she did had little impact. Bringing the assumption out in the open is then a necessary step in writing a reply to the argument in Example 7:18. The argument is no stronger than its reasons, including its assumptions. In writing a reply, if the assumption is dubious, it should be made explicit and then discussed.

Identifying Your Own Assumptions

Similarly, it is wise to check your own assumptions when you write. Are you committing yourself to something you do not want to include in your commitments? Are you committing yourself to something you cannot defend? If so, it is a good idea to be aware of it. I am not saying that you must be able to defend every assumption. That would be impossible if you keep going back, and back, and back. But identifying your basic assumptions helps you to understand yourself and your disagreements with others. Furthermore, your basic assumptions should be defensible.

Though not a writing example, the jury's judgment that Arlene was not justified in using the force she used employed an argument (Item 7:45, repeated as Example 7:19) using an unstated assumption that has since been identified and questioned by some associates.[5]

Example 7:19

She was not justified in using the force she used because she could have run away to her parents' room. (Reminder: Establishing that she was not justified in using the force she used was a necessary condition in both the murder and voluntary manslaughter charges. See Example 7:1 and Check-Up item 7:8.)

Although more assumptions are needed to completely fill the gap in the reasoning, the key controversial assumption that has been attributed to the jury's argument was that *in responding to a death threat, women are not justified in using deadly force when escape from the situation is available.*

The members of the jury did not stop to consider the assumptions behind the reasoning in Example 7:19. If they had, the decision could possibly have been different. It might have been the same though, on the ground that both men and women are not justified in using deadly force in responding to threats of death when escape from the situation is available. How would you have decided in this matter?

Regardless of how you would have decided, I hope that you see the importance of bringing forward unstated assumptions of your own arguments, in writing as well as verbal exchanges. The critical thinking disposition to try to be reflectively aware of one's own basic beliefs, mentioned in Chapter 1, applies here.

Slippery Assumption Identification

A significant danger in identifying someone else's assumptions is attributing assumptions that are more broad than the person needs, so broad that the assumption is easy to refute. You saw the potential for this before in the Texas Jane case (Item 7:32). One possible gap-filler in that argument is that all creatures throughout time that are treated unfairly for their entire lives will lash out at the world. This assumption is easy to refute for two reasons. First, it is a universal statement, and there are usually counterexamples to universal statements. Second, it is about all creatures throughout time, including horses and slaves, and we know of some who were treated unfairly throughout their lives, but did not lash out.

A more modest assumption would be that contemporary Texans *tend to* lash out at the world, if they have been treated unfairly for their entire lives. It is more modest in part because it refers to a much smaller group, a group many of whose members advertise their dislike for being messed with. It is also more modest because of the inclusion of the words *tend to,* which, even though the conclusion no longer follows necessarily, still provide gap-filling potential through the process of loose derivation. This more modest assumption might be false, but it is more defensible than the universal timeless one about creatures. To attribute this modest assumption to the position could well be more fair to the position.

---

5. Including my astute associate, Professor Anita Silvers of San Francisco State University.

When you are writing about a position and identifying its assumptions, try to be as fair as you can. Give the position its best chance to succeed. After all, you would not want to reject a conclusion that is actually correct.

Furthermore, when you are responding to someone's analysis of your position, be very wary of assumptions that the person attributes to you. People are often careless when identifying assumptions, attributing much broader assumptions than the position needs and then trying to refute the position on the ground that the position rests on a false assumption. This is one example of the *straw person fallacy* (setting up a "straw person" instead of the real position and refuting the set-up position). If someone does that to you, appropriate responses include asking why that assumption has been attributed to you and showing that your argument is a good one with a much less ambitious, and more plausible, assumption. Perhaps even more important, when someone attributes an assumption to you, ask yourself whether this attribution is a fair one. Can your argument stand with a less ambitious assumption?

+ The Distinction Between Needed and Used Implicit Assumptions in Real Situations

As you saw earlier, in attributing assumptions, you should try to be fair to the position. In actually deciding what to attribute, it helps to be clear about why you are attributing an assumption to the person or position. Are you trying to evaluate the argument to see whether you should believe the conclusion? Are you trying to show that the assumer is committed to something? Or are you trying to find out something about the way the person thinks? If you are trying to do the first two things, you are looking for *needed assumptions*. If the third, you are looking for a *used assumption*.[6]

Needed Assumptions

Evaluating a Position

Needed assumptions are those that the argument, position, or explanation needs in order to be at its best. Suppose you are trying to evaluate a position in order to decide whether to accept the conclusion. Then you want to find out what is needed, but you want to give the argument its best chance to succeed; otherwise you might miss a good argument and fail to accept a conclusion that is justified. So you should be charitable in attributing assumptions to the position. In argument evaluation aimed at deciding the acceptability of the conclusion, you do not give an argument with an obviously false assumption when there is a better one available. This point was illustrated earlier with the Texas Jane example, Example 7:19.

Ascertaining the Commitments of a Person or Position

Similarly, when we are ascertaining the commitments of a person or a position, we look for needed assumptions and again should be charitable. We do not want to say

---

6. For an extended discussion of these distinctions, see my "Identifying Implicit Assumptions," *Synthese, 51,* 1982, pp. 61–86. David Hitchcock (personal communication) has labeled these two types as *assumptions of the argument* and *assumptions of the arguer,* respectively.

a position needs something implausible when it could get along with a more restricted and thus more plausible basis.

Used Assumptions

When we are trying to figure out the thoughts or beliefs of someone, we do not try to be either charitable or uncharitable. Instead, we try to get it right. That is, we try to determine what is actually going on in the person's head because that is what will influence the other decisions the person makes. Here we are looking for a proposition that was actually *used* by the person in reaching the conclusion or offering the explanation. Therefore, these assumptions can be called *used assumptions*.

When identifying used assumptions, we pick from among the candidates the one that the person most probably used. In fact, here we might even pick one that does not make the argument deductively valid because the person might actually have been reasoning deductively invalidly. But unless we have reason to think otherwise, it is usually best to work from the candidates that produce deductive validity.

When I heard a teacher say, "Sam should receive an A because he did well on the test," I attributed to the teacher the used assumption, "People who do well on my tests should receive an A." I believed that that proposition was in the teacher's mind and was used to defend the decision. Incidentally, as this example shows, an assumption can be both used and needed.

The process of identifying the one that the person most probably used is an inductive inference-to-best-explanation process, the topic of the next two chapters, so I shall only hint at it here. But the idea is to pick a proposition that best explains what the person does and says. Attributing this belief to the person should fit in with whatever else you know about the person.

Summary

In this chapter, you have seen a brief review of some basic elements of deductive logic and an attempt to show the applications of deductive logic in straight deduction from acceptable reasons, loose derivation, assumption attribution, and the evaluation of hypotheses. This latter area of application, as well as the role of deductive logic in the evaluation of generalizations, in one type of explanation, and in value judging, are further considered in Chapters 8–11.

Straight deduction is the direct application of deductive validity to arguments. In loose derivation, you drop the qualifying words from an argument and judge the deductive validity of the stripped argument. Then you put the words back in and, taking into account the validity judgment just made, make an overall judgment about whether to accept the conclusion, taking the situation into account. There are no precise rules for this judgment, but FRISCO is a guide to keep in mind.

The word *assumption* is either used pejoratively or used to refer to an undefended basis, or both. Be sensitive to the possible pejorative interpretation when you are attributing assumptions or having assumptions attributed to you.

In attributing assumptions, a good first step is to find a proposition that would convert the argument or explanation into a deductively valid argument. The results are good candidates for the assumption, though not the only possible ones. If you are interested in judging the conclusion, a good next step is to pick the most plausible of the candidates.

A special type of assumption, a presupposition, is a proposition implicit in a statement, but not explicitly asserted by a statement. Either agreeing with or denying the statement commits you to the presupposition. Identification of presuppositions is easy, once a question has been raised about them. The problem with them is that they easily slip by unexamined.

In your writing, it is well to be aware of your own assumptions so that you can better understand and evaluate your own position. Similarly, in writing about the positions of other people, identifying their assumptions is helpful, again because it helps you understand and evaluate their positions.

A principal danger in assumption identification is attributing an assumption to a position that is broader and more ambitious than the position needs, often resulting in the straw-person fallacy. Be careful not to do this yourself, and be wary when others attribute assumptions to you. Ask yourself whether your position really needs something that broad and ambitious. On the other hand, give serious consideration to assumptions attributed to you. The attributor might have unearthed an assumption to which you are committed and that requires further examination. Be open-minded about it.

+ When evaluating arguments in order to decide whether to accept the conclusion, you attribute needed assumptions to the argument. You also attribute needed assumptions when deciding what is an implicit proposition to which the argument, explanation, or person is committed. In so doing, you usually select from candidates the one that is most plausible.

+ When figuring out what a person believes, you identify used assumptions. To do this, you pick the one that is most likely to have been actually consciously (or unconsciously) used by the person. To decide this, you select the one that best explains what the person did and said. The result should fit with other knowledge about the person. Best-explanation inference is the topic of subsequent chapters.

Check-Up 7C

True or False?
If false, change it to make it true. Try to do so in a way that shows that you understand.

> **7:47** If a proposition fills a gap in your argument, then that proposition is an assumption of your argument.
>
> **7:48** The straw-person fallacy can be defined as attributing to a person a view the person does not hold (or does not need to hold, if an assumption), refuting that view, and then acting as if the person's real view has been refuted.
>
> **7:49** If a presupposition is shown to be false, then the truth or falsity of the statement of which it is a presupposition cannot be settled.
>
> + **7:50** In attributing a needed assumption, one should try to be charitable, doing the best one can to help the argument.

Medium Answer

Consider the following passages. From the point of view of fairness in assumption attribution, tell whether you think the assumption attributions are justified and why. Add comments, if you like.

7:51 Argument: You accuse me of being selfish, but there's nothing wrong with being selfish. Everybody is selfish all the time. They can't avoid it. After all, everyone is acting in accord with their own desires all the time, even though they might fool themselves into thinking otherwise. Even the condemned murderer marching to his execution is acting in accord with his desires. He desires to march to his execution rather than be dragged there.

Response: You're *assuming* that to be selfish is to act in accord with one's desires. But that's not what *selfish* means. According to the dictionary, to be selfish is to act in one's own interests in disregard of the interests of others. So it's not true that people are always selfish.

7:52 I see that you are trying to interfere with parents' rights to raise their children as they see fit, including punishing them when needed. We all realize that punishment sometime results in injury, but that is for the best if it cures the bad behavior. You are *assuming* that no living thing should be injured without its consent. But that is a foolish position. We all (including you) injure living things every day. We kill animals and cut vegetable plants for food, cut trees for paper, trap mice that we feel are pests, and put painful handcuffs on criminals.

7:53 We have proposed a set of zoning laws to protect property values. In particular, the proposed laws would prohibit the raising of chickens and hogs in our neighborhood. Your condemnation of our zoning laws *assumes* that everybody should be totally free all the time. But that is impossible. If I am totally free, then I am not restrained from punching you in the nose, but then you would not be free to live your life the way you want to live it.

7:54 You have said that the defense attorney should not be believed because he has a raspy voice and a limp. Aren't you assuming that having a raspy voice and a limp are indicators of lack of credibility? If so, then tell us why such things indicate lack of credibility.

7:55 Argument: You demand equality on the ground (as asserted in the Declaration of Independence) that all people are created equal. But people are not equal. People are different. Some people are taller than others. They have different eye colors. Males and females are obviously different from each other in appearance from birth onward. So not all people are created equal.

Response: You are *assuming* that I define equality as equality in traits. But that's not what I mean. I am talking about equality in basic rights. We have equal rights to life, liberty, and the pursuit of happiness, among other things.

More Medium Answer

7:56 In your own writing, identify an unstated assumption that you have made, justify your claim that your passage did actually assume this proposition, and tell whether your assumption is justified. Supply a copy of the passage.

7:57 Find a passage in which someone attributes an assumption to another person's argument and then challenges the argument on the ground that the assumption is false or, at best, dubious. Do you think that the assumption attributor is committing the straw-person fallacy? Why?

+ 7:58 In our deliberations about voluntary manslaughter, we decided that she was not justified in using the force she used because she could have run away to her parents' room. (Reminder: The conditions provided to the jury for voluntary manslaughter are in Example 7:1.)

    a. Assuming that the question at issue is whether she is guilty, what kind of assumption would you attribute to us: a needed assumption or a used assumption? Defend your answer.

    b. Attribute to us an assumption of the type you just decided on (needed or used) and explain why you attribute that assumption to us.

+ 7:59 Suppose that you are investigating the thought processes of juries in order to see whether there is bias against women in their thinking.

    a. What kind of assumption would you attribute to the members of my jury: a needed assumption or a used assumption? Defend your answer.

    b. Attribute to us an assumption of the type you just decided on (needed or used) and explain why you attribute that assumption to us.

+ 7:60 From a book, article, hearing, or conversation, present a passage containing an argument or an explanation that is intended to account for certain facts.

    a. Decide on your approach to it. Do you want to attribute a used or needed assumption? Why?

    b. State an assumption of the sort you just chose. Defend your decision to attribute that assumption to the passage.

Suggested Answers for Chapter 7

Check-Up 7A

    7:1 T   **7:2** F   **7:3** F   **7:4** T   **7:5** F   **7:6** T

    7:2 Change *valid* to *invalid*.

    7:3 Omit *and that is needed in order*.

7:5 Change *apply exactly that judgment to the total argument* to *put the qualifiers in and make an informed judgment about the result.*

7:7 This is up to you.

7:8 a. Here is one possibility: Each of the three conditions is necessary for guilt; they are jointly sufficient.

   b. Here is one possibility: In order to find her guilty, we have to decide that each of the three conditions is true, namely that each thing mentioned has been proven beyond a reasonable doubt. Each is needed. If any one has not been proven beyond a reasonable doubt, then we must find her innocent. If all three have been proven beyond a reasonable doubt, that is enough for a verdict of guilty. That is, if all three have been proven beyond a reasonable doubt, we must find her guilty.

   c. Let p = "PBRD that the defendant performed the acts that caused the death of the victim."

   Let q = "PBRD that when the defendant did so, she intended to kill or do great bodily harm to the victim, or she knew that her act would cause death or great bodily harm to the victim, or she knew that her acts created a strong probability of death or great bodily harm to the victim."

   Let r = "PBRD that the defendant was not justified in using the force she used."

   Let s = "You should find the defendant not guilty."

   d. Part 1:

   (not $p \rightarrow s$) and (not $q \rightarrow s$) and (not $r \rightarrow s$)
   Therefore, (not $q \rightarrow s$)

   Justification:
   This is the second if–then.[7]
   Separating off one conjunct

   Part 2:
   not $q \rightarrow s$
   not q
   Therefore, s

   Conclusion of Part 1
   Assumed reason
   AA, DV

7:9 Deliberately omitted.

---

7. + Note: There is a more elegant way to do *d,* using an interpretation of *or* not discussed in this book, the disjunctive sense. In this sense, an either–or proposition means that at least one of its members (or disjuncts) holds. See any deductive logic text for an elaboration. A full discussion of the issues involved would take up too much space in this book. See the items by Lewis, Strawson, and Grice cited at the beginning of Chapter 5 for an introduction to the issues, and my *Natural Language Logic,* forthcoming, for a more complete elaboration of meanings, though not an exploration of the issues.

7:10 This is up to you.

7:11 F   **7:12** T   **7:13** F   **7:14** T   **7:15** F

7:11 Assumptions are sometimes conclusions.

7:13 There are usually many propositions that can convert an argument with a deductive gap into a deductively valid one.

7:15 Change A to read *Regulation EZTHINK makes sense.*

7:16 Karl lost the election.

7:17 Karl is not a fool.

7:18 Mirabelle is not dejected.

7:19 Sarah's motorscooter is a motorcycle.

7:20 Whenever Mary is in good spirits, she has gone out with Pedro the night before.

7:21 Whenever Pedro goes out with Mary, he is in good spirits the next day.

7:22 Arlene did not admit it.

7:23 Shakespeare made Polonius the father of two tragic characters.

7:24 Whatever we do not want in the cabbage patch is a weed.

7:25 All soccer players are in good physical shape.

7:26 Whatever interferes with the desires of honest people is unjust.

Note: Henceforth in this set, answers to the odd-numbered items are omitted.

7:28 Whatever is repetitive, uninteresting, and a threat to the peace should be banned.

7:30 Enrico is not tall.

7:32 Anyone who has been treated unfairly for her entire life will certainly lash out at the world.

7:34 Our students are under eighteen.

7:36 (a) She killed him. (b) If she performed the act that caused his death, then the first condition for murder is satisfied.

7:38 I refuse to publish anything that does not make any sense.

7:40 The Board of Education will not act unconstitutionally.

7:42 If Samantha is not in town, then she is in the country.

7:44 Whoever is in trouble with the director will be kicked out of the band.

7:46 This is up to you.

Check-Up 7C

7:47 F   **7:48** T   **7:49** T   **7:50** T

7:47 Change *is* to *might be.*

7:51 Yes, the assumption attribution seems justified. There seems to be no other more plausible gap filler than that the given definition of *selfish* is being assumed.

7:52 This assumption attribution goes too far. The objector to punishment might only be assuming that the consent of human beings is ordinarily needed before they are deliberately injured. Whether this position is reasonable or not is another issue, but the assumption attributor assigned to the position a much too ambitious proposition.

Note: Henceforth in this set, odd-numbered answers are omitted.

7:54 This is a reasonable job of assumption attribution. It fills a gap in the argument in a quite plausible way. However, there is more to the issue: The definition of *credibility* is possibly in contention. The assumption attributor probably interpreted credibility as the degree to which a source ought to be believed; the other probably defined it as the degree to which a source is likely to be believed. In the context of the jury trial, the first definition expresses the concept of concern. We were trying to decide whether we should believe him, not whether people are likely to believe him.

7:56 and 7:57 These are up to you.

7:58 a. A needed assumption, because the concern is about the truth of the conclusion "She is guilty."

b. I would attribute these assumptions: 1. If she could have run away to her parents' room, then she had a safe alternative to responding with violence. 2. If she had a safe alternative to responding with violence, then she was not justified in using the force she used.

These propositions do fill the gap, and seem more plausible than alternative gap-fillers. Proposition 2 is more defensible than a broad claim to the effect that anyone who has a safe alternative to responding with violence should pursue it. However, I might, as an alternative to Proposition 2, attribute this somewhat broader (than Proposition 2) set of propositions: "If someone can easily escape a threatened attack and there is no other reason to do violence to the attacker, then one should escape rather than respond with violence. There was no other reason to do violence to the attacker. If she should have escaped rather than responded with violence, then she was not justified in using the force she used." I might use this broader set because a defense of the narrow Proposition 2 would probably drive us back to this set, and the set seems fairly plausible. However, it is still open to a challenge of a crucial part, "There is no other reason to do violence to the attacker."

7:59 Deliberately omitted.

7:60 This is up to you.

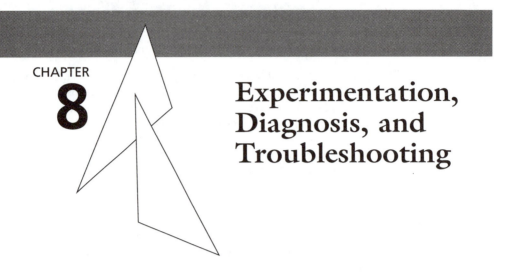

CHAPTER

8

Experimentation, Diagnosis, and Troubleshooting

We all do experiments, sometimes good ones, sometimes bad ones, and sometimes in between. The results of an experiment are often offered as reasons in support of a conclusion. This chapter is concerned with experimenting and deciding whether experimental results provide enough support for a conclusion. It is also concerned with diagnosis of a problem situation, sometimes called troubleshooting, sometimes diagnosing, both of which have similarities to experimenting but are focused on what is wrong in some situation. Experimenting, on the other hand, is focused on generalizing, even though the result of an experiment is sometimes very specific.

More precisely, *experimenting* is the deliberate changing of something in a situation in order to see what happens. We do this in order to get ideas for a conclusion or to test a proposed conclusion, called a *hypothesis*. The testing and judging of a hypothesis can be done by ways other than experimenting. But for now, our focus will be on experimenting.

In terms of the FRISCO approach, we shall be examining whether reasons (R) support (I) the conclusion (F), when inferring (I) from experimental results and information (R) that is methodically gathered. We will also be concerned with writing, particularly of reports of the type of investigations discussed here.

Control Group Experimentation

A friend has a patch of grass. For many years, a number of dandelions have been growing in this patch. Last year the friend decided to try a chemical on the patch in the hope that it would kill the dandelions, but not the grass. At the time of writing, the end of April, there are no dandelions in the patch, although there were many at this time last year. "She tried it and it worked!"

She had varied one thing, and only one thing. But with the passage of time, other things occurred as well. There was a fierce winter, for one thing; there has been talk of acid rain; and there is a variety of bug around that was not noticed before. Can my friend conclude that the chemical killed the dandelions? She has insufficient evidence to rule out other possible explanations of the disappearance of the dandelions. The report "I tried it and it worked" must often be regarded with suspicion.

Because the mistake I have just described is so common, it has a special name, the *post hoc* fallacy. To commit this fallacy is to conclude that one thing caused another just because the second occurred after the first. I mention this name to you, not in the hope that you will use it, but so that when others use it, you will not be confused or intimidated. Such Latin words are often confusing and intimidating to others. Of course, you should feel free to use it if the people you are talking to know what it means. Then its use is a quick way to state an important idea.

Here is one way to have improved the experiment and avoided the *post hoc* fallacy: Observe another area of grass and dandelions, similar to the first, that did not receive the chemical treatment. Then compare the two areas. If there were no dandelions in the second area, then we might well suspect that something other than the chemical had eliminated the dandelions in the first area. On the other hand, if there were dandelions in the second, but not the first, then we have fair support for the conclusion that the chemical somehow eliminated the dandelions. This support is strengthened by the other conditions' having been the same.

One simple kind of experiment (which I have just illustrated) is one in which the experimenter sets up two similar groups, introduces a special condition called the *experimental condition* in one group, but tries to keep the two groups otherwise the same. The group that undergoes the experimental condition is called the *experimental group*. The other group, called the *control group,* experiences standard conditions. The purpose is to see the difference, if any, in the results of the experimental and standard conditions. If there is only this one difference in conditions, a difference in the results is explained by the experimental condition, so the thinking goes. If other factors were also allowed to vary, then their variations might also explain the results. The point of a control-group experiment is to rule out possible competing hypotheses. You can see this in greater detail in two examples I shall describe. One is a classic control-group experiment about the origin of maggots and the other is an experiment that is like one I have conducted.

Redi's Experiment with Meat

In the seventeenth century, it was widely believed that the "worms" one finds in decaying organic matter were spontaneously generated there. Spontaneous generation is the development of some form of life by itself without being parented. Francesco Redi (1626–1697), after making a variety of observations, developed the hypothesis that the "worms" developed from eggs that were laid by flies. In reading his report and in deciding whether to accept this evidence, be aware of the importance of Redi's credibility and of his having satisfied observation criteria:

> Belief would be vain without the confirmation of experiment, hence in the middle of July, I put a snake, some fish, some eels of the Arno, and a slice of milk-fed veal in four large, wide-mouthed flasks; having closed and sealed them, I then filled the same number of flasks in the same way, only leaving these open. It was not long before the meat and the fish, in these second vessels, became

wormy and flies were seen entering and leaving at will; but in the closed flasks, I did not see a worm, though many days had passed since the dead flesh had been put in them.

The unsealed flasks were Redi's control group. He introduced a special factor, the sealing of the flasks, to create an experimental group. But if he had not provided the set of unsealed flasks (the control group), then he would not have known to what to attribute his results. For example, the temperature or the flask material might have prevented the development of the maggots, and might have been offered as alternative explanations of the failure of the maggots to develop. The position of the moon might have prevented the development, for all he knew, or something else might have done so. But the second group of flasks, the open ones, had the same temperature conditions, the same flask material, the same relationship to the moon, and so on. He assumed that if the temperature, the flask material, the position of the moon, or some other factor had prevented the growth of the maggots in the first set, then it should have done the same thing in the second set. But it did not. Using denial-of-the-consequent reasoning (do you see how?), he was in a position to reject the hypotheses that the temperature and the material of the experimental group flasks caused the lack of growth of maggots. Similarly, he was in a position to reject the hypothesis that the position of the moon caused the lack of growth of maggots. The presence of the control group enabled him to reject many possible explanations of the lack of growth of maggots in the sealed flasks. The use of a control group, thus, is a powerful way to eliminate alternative hypotheses.

The results for the control group made the experimental hypothesis more credible. The experimental hypothesis is that the sealing of the flasks prevented maggots from developing in the meat. This hypothesis was made credible by the elimination of alternative hypotheses. It was the control group results that justified the elimination of these alternatives.

Note that there are other possible explanations that a creative person can imagine. For example, another possible explanation is that the material used in covering the flasks was poisonous to maggots. Another is that the material frightened the little maggots, so that they did not develop. There are always other possible explanations resulting from the introduction of the experimental factor. One strategy in experimentation is to design the experiment so that the plausible ones can be eliminated on the basis of the results, or to design other experiments to test these other possible explanations. For example, Redi might have designed an experiment to test the compatibility of the covering with the maggots, perhaps by leaving a hole in the covering for one group of flasks to see whether the covering is poisonous or frightens little maggots. But there would still be other possibilities, perhaps even less plausible than the ones I suggested. Can you think of any?

A Critical Thinking Experiment

My other example bears on a general hypothesis of mine. It is that taking a course in critical thinking, using this book, tends to improve the critical thinking ability of students. I have designed an experiment to test this hypothesis. It goes as follows. I pick an experimental group and a comparable control group and give the students in each group a critical thinking pretest such as the *Cornell Critical Thinking Test, Level Z*.[1] Then I teach this course to the experimental group and make sure that the control group is not exposed to this course or any like it. Let us suppose that the other experiences of the two groups (for example, their other courses) are essentially the same. Then, at the end of the course, I give the test over again. Suppose that the experimental group's average improvement turns out to be significantly more than the average improvement of the control group. I might well conclude that the critical thinking course brought about the greater experimental-group improvement in critical thinking ability revealed by the testing. Note that this is a specific conclusion about this one experiment. It is loosely implied by the general hypothesis mentioned at the beginning of this paragraph, but is different.

My reasoning in drawing the specific conclusion would be as follows: The greater experimental-group improvement is best explained by the fact that the course was given to the experimental group and not to the control group. What other explanation could there be, since all other things were essentially the same for the two groups?

Actually there would be other possible explanations, some arising from the conditions that could have accompanied the introduction of the experimental condition. One might be that there were thought-provoking posters in the room where the instruction occurred and that these were responsible. Another might be that my dour personality was the cause. Another might be that because the experimental group was picked out for special treatment, its members were motivated to become better critical thinkers or to try harder on the posttest. A fourth could arise from the grading situation: If the members of the experimental group get a score on the test that counts in the course grade, but the members of the control group get no grade for critical thinking ability, then the difference in grade motivation might account for the difference. Yet it would not seem fair to give the control group members a grade on something they had not studied; and it would probably be a mistake in a grade-oriented system, as ours often is, to fail to use the critical thinking test final score in calculating a grade for the experimental group students. Each of these four problems might be avoided by a careful design and implementation of the experiment, but I cannot take steps to defeat all possible alternative hypotheses. The best I can do in one experiment is to try to design it so that the plausible alternative hypotheses that occur to me could be shown to be false, and to watch the progress of the experiment very closely to see whether other plausible alternative explanations appear.

The imagined results also support the general hypothesis that taking a course in critical thinking, using this book, tends to improve the critical thinking ability of students. The original conclusion was not a generalization. It was only about the one particular situation. The generalization would be supported because it would be a broader explanation of the results of the experiment. However, the generalization would not be established by the one experiment because (among other reasons) the representativeness of the student population has not been established. It might be that such a course is effective in this decade for a certain kind of student from a certain part of the world, but not otherwise effective. From this one experiment, I

---

1. Ennis, Robert H., and Millman, Jason, *Cornell Critical Thinking Test, Level Z* (Pacific Grove, CA: Midwest Publications, 1985).

should not generalize unless the situation and people involved are representative of the population covered by the generalization. I shall say more about generalizing later, but at least want to point out that the generalization might well receive some support from the results I imagined. The amount of support can vary with the specific situation and details.

Summary and Comment

In the maggot example and the critical thinking example, I have indicated the value of a control group when checking a hypothesis about a causal relationship. There are many complicated variations of control-group experimentation, but all are governed by the goal of avoiding possible alternative explanations of the result. As with all experiment-based conclusions, the details in these two cases are very important and more complex than I have been able to represent. I have only tried to convey the flavor of the thinking.

Because it is difficult to obtain representative samples of students, I emphasized the distinction between a specific hypothesis that applies only to the experiment in question and a general hypothesis. I did not emphasize this distinction in the Redi experiment because I wanted to minimize the complexity of the first experiment I considered, and because I was willing to assume that Redi's samples of organic matter were fairly representative of maggot havens.

Check-Up 8A

True or False?
If false, change it to make it true. Try to do so in a way that shows that you understand.

8:1 In an experiment the control group is the group that is controlled.

8:2 The purpose of a control group is to eliminate other possible explanations of the result.

8:3 Although it is possible to reduce the list of other possible explanations, it is never possible with a control group to eliminate all other possible explanations.

8:4 One should not generalize experimental results to a broader population if the members of the experimental and control groups are not representative of the broader population.

Medium Answer

8:5 A student was interested in what brings about germination of seeds. He was considering the hypothesis that it is contact with soil that causes germination. He took four pole-bean seeds randomly from a recently purchased package and placed them in an empty open jar. At the same time, he took another four randomly selected bean seeds from the same package and placed them in some freshly dug soil in a similar open jar. He put both jars in the window sill on the first day of spring. He observed them every day and took out the results for close observation seven days later. All four seeds in the jar containing soil had germinated. None of the seeds in the empty jar had germinated. From this, he concluded that the soil was the cause of the germination of the seeds.

    a. Assuming that the experimental condition was contact with soil, what was the control group?

    b. Was this a good experiment? Why?

8:6 Another student set about testing the hypothesis that it is moisture that causes germination of seeds. For her experimental group, she placed four randomly selected seeds (from the same package as in 8:5) in an open small-mouth jar containing wet soil. For her control group, she used four randomly selected seeds from the same package and placed them in a similar jar containing dry soil. The two samples of soil were from the same source. The original soil was put in a large jar, was thoroughly mixed, and then was divided in half. One half (with enough tap water added to make it feel wet, but not muddy) was used for the experimental seeds. The other half was heated to make it thoroughly dry and crumbly, allowed to cool to room temperature, and then used for the control seeds. The rest of the method was the same as in 8:5. At the end of the seventh day, she noticed that the four seeds from the wet-soil group had sprouts ranging in length from one to two inches, and that the seeds from the dry-soil group had not sprouted at all. She concluded that the moisture caused the experimental seeds to germinate.

    a. State an alternative hypothesis not ruled out in this experiment.

    b. Was this a good experiment? Why?

    c. Design and describe an experiment to test the hypothesis you suggested in *a*.

8:7 A new method of examining teeth, called Ultralight, was suspected of causing cancer. A group of twenty white rats was randomly split in half into experimental and control groups. Each member of the experimental group was given one Ultralight treatment of three hundredths of the strength of that used for a standard human tooth examination. The members of the experimental and control groups were assigned each to separate alternate cages and given the same food, water, and living conditions for a period of three months. Then each rat was examined. All of the treated rats had cancer. None of the control group had cancer. Assume for the present purposes that rats and humans are identical in cancer receptivity. It was concluded that Ultralight treatments cause cancer in the rats.

    a. Can you think of an advantage of randomly assigning rats to experimental and control group (as opposed to assigning the first ten you catch to the experimental group and the other ten to the control group)? State the advantage.

b. State an alternative possible explanation that is not ruled out by the control group results.

c. State the advantage of using twenty rats instead of two (one as experimental, one as control).

d. State an advantage, in terms of this experiment, of using a control group (as opposed to having all twenty rats as an experimental group).

e. Is this a good experiment? Why?

8:8 A social studies teacher at Renfrew High was also the volleyball coach, and was very concerned about lack of community interest in the volleyball team. Applying an idea from sociology, she wondered whether familiarity with the story of the team and its accomplishments would increase interest. So she tried an experiment.

In one of her civics classes, she passed out a well-written story about how the team was started and how tryouts were conducted. After each game, she wrote an account of the game, passed it out in class, and asked her students to take it home to their parents.

In her other civics class, there was no mention made of the volleyball team, and no written material about the team was distributed.

The last game of the season was at night. On the next day, she asked the students in each class how many of their parents went to the game. In the class that received information about the team, twenty out of twenty-five raised their hands. In the other class, four out of twenty-eight raised their hands. She concluded that familiarity with the team had resulted in increased parental interest in the volleyball team.

a. Can you think of any other possible explanation of the result? If so, state one.

b. Was this a good experiment? Why?

c. Could the experiment have been improved? If so, state two ways of improving it.

Longer Answer

8:9 It is widely believed in some areas that planting root crops by the dark of the moon makes it much more likely that the crop will be a good crop. The dark-of-the-moon period of the month is that of the new moon (the opposite of a full moon).

A resident of East Central Illinois devised an experiment to test this hypothesis. He planted a row of seed potatoes on the tenth of April (which was the dark of the moon that year) and an equal amount in an adjoining row two weeks later in the full moon period. For each planting, he used white seed potatoes bought from the local seed store, planted in accord with the recommendations of the store manager. All the seed potatoes were bought at the same time and came from the same bag. They were bought just before the first planting, were randomly assigned to the two groups; the ones not immediately planted were stored in a cool, dark root cellar until time for planting.

Each row was ten feet long. They were two feet apart and were two feet from adjoining plants, which were also potatoes. No fertilizer was used in this rich Illinois soil, which had been planted in grass for the previous ten years.

All potatoes were dug on September 30, by which time all the vines had stopped growing and had died (a normal occurrence). The potatoes from each row were weighed. The total weight from the dark-of-the-moon row was 17.5 pounds; from the full moon row, 16.8 pounds.

a. Can you think of any plausible explanations of the result other than the widely held belief? If so, state one.
b. Was this a good experiment? Why?
c. What, if anything, would you conclude from this experiment? Why?
d. How would you redesign this experiment? Explain why you make the changes you make.

8:10 Design an experiment that uses a control group to test a hypothesis that interests you. Describe your experiment and tell why you plan it the way you do.

Systematic Control of the Variables in an Experiment—Without Using a Separate Control Group

In some experiments, it does not seem reasonable to set up a separate control group, but we still want to be able to limit the possible alternative explanations of the results. Suppose, for example, that we are trying to find out what influences the period of a pendulum, as found in a playground swing, or a grandfather clock. (The period is the time it takes for one swing back and forth). A separate control group does not seem necessary here. That is, it seems unnecessary to set up two groups of pendulums that are comparable to each other and to make a change in some factor in one group, leaving the other group as is, and watch them both at the same time. It seems that we need only a representative group of pendulums. A basis for comparison can be the pendulums before we make the change. We might even do our work with only one pendulum and then see whether we get the same results with other pendulums and in other situations. But we would vary only one thing at a time to locate the factor or factors that influence the period.

One fruitful beginning seems to be to make some intelligent guesses about what might influence the period, and experiment by varying them one at a time. First, we might change the amount of weight and see whether that affects the period, holding everything else constant. Then we might change the length (from the pivot point to the weight) and see whether that affects the period, again holding everything else (including the weight) constant. If we vary two factors at the same time, then we would not know which was responsible for the result, if any. That is, we would have two alternative possible explanations of a change in the period. For example, if we doubled the weight and doubled the length of the pendulum, and discovered that the period increased, we would have three alternative possible explanations of the result: the change in weight, the change in length, and perhaps a combination of the two. Furthermore, if each really did have an effect, and if the effects were in opposite directions, then we might get no observed change because each change we introduced canceled the other. Then we might be tempted to conclude mistakenly that neither type of change has an effect.

But if we vary just the weight, and there is no change in the period, then we can probably rule out weight as a factor that has independent influence. The hypothesis that weight influences the period would be inconsistent with the facts. Then, if we vary the length but hold everything else constant, and find that the period is significantly different, we could probably conclude that length is a factor. This hypothesis would seem to be the only explanation of the change in period that we find. Thus, varying only one thing at a time can be a useful way to test hypotheses experimentally.

Dependent and Independent Variables

We use the word *variable* to refer to the things that change or might change in an experiment. In the investigation of factors that affect the period of a pendulum, the length of the pendulum is a variable. So is the weight. The period of the pendulum is also a variable. The period is called a *dependent variable* because, according to the hypothesis, its variation, if any, would *depend* on the variation of the others, which are called *independent variables*. They are called *independent* because variation in them is presumed not to be dependent on the variation of the other variables. For example, variation in the length is presumed for the sake of the investigation not to be dependent on the period. Independent variables, then, are those that are manipulated to see whether they affect a dependent variable. In the pendulum experiment, as I described it, the length and the weight are independent variables; the period is a dependent variable.

Beware: There are technical uses of these terms that supposedly do not imply the causal relationships that I have just assumed. They occur in fields where some people are reluctant to assume or conclude that there are causal relationships. In these fields, the independent variable is that which is somehow prior. I find such uses misleading where I have encountered them, and do not recommend them to you.

Difficulty in Controlling the Possible Independent Variables

In the pendulum experiment, it is fairly easy to vary the length while holding the weight constant, and to vary the weight while holding the length constant. But the independent variable, *time,* is not held constant. (The observations before and after the variation occur at different times.) Neither are all the things that vary with the time, such as weather conditions, phases of the moon, position of the sun, interest rates, the price of gasoline, the mood of the experimenter, and the number of bicycles in the bicycle rack. For the pendulum experiment, I would be willing to assume that these things do not matter. But for other experiments in which one tries to vary one thing at a time, things that change with time can matter. For example, in the dandelion experiment I described at the beginning of this chapter, the other things that occurred during the passage of time from one year to the next could have explained the absence of dandelions in my friend's patch of grass.

Consider next an example that falls somewhere in between the pendulum experiment and the original dandelion experiment, given our concern with the strategy of varying one thing at a time.

My associates and I did a critical thinking teaching experiment with only one group. We gave a critical thinking pretest to a class and waited for one semester. Then we gave the class the same test again, and then instructed the class in critical thinking for one semester, after which we gave the test a third time. We tried to vary only one thing: critical thinking instruction. The independent variable was critical thinking instruction. The dependent variable was critical thinking ability, as indicated by the test. We compared their improvement in the first semester with that in the second semester. Although we tried to vary only the independent variable (the instruction), other variables in the students' lives besides critical thinking instruction must have changed during the experiment. The students were out in the world and had many varied experiences. They became older and wiser, and might have passed through a phase of rapid natural growth in wisdom during the critical thinking semester. They took other courses during that semester, in some of which they were learning things that might well have improved their thinking ability. National and international events occurred during the critical thinking semester. These might have provoked them to think more critically and practice their skills, and thus might have explained the results.

These are all exterior possibilities that were not introduced by us in the experiment. There were some that we introduced as well. For example, by giving the test two times and by telling them they would receive critical thinking instruction, we might then have provoked the students to improve their thinking on their own. Or the tests might have so familiarized them with critical-thinking questions that they developed skills on their own, without the course. These all provide other possible explanations of the results.

The test score difference from the second to third administration was significantly greater than the difference from the first to the second. Could we conclude *from only what I have told you* that the critical thinking course improved the students' critical thinking ability? I think not. Not only are there some possible alternative explanations introduced by what we did, but a number of things could have occurred as *time* passed that could explain the results, as I have indicated.

Importance of Knowledge in the Area of Investigation

From these three examples, we can see that the idea of isolating and varying the independent variables one at a time (for a single group or thing) can be a good one, but there are limitations. One must be familiar with the area of investigation to decide this. We had to know about weights, lengths, and pendulums to decide on a good strategy for pendulums. Our knowledge of plants and things that influence them enabled us to realize that, even though the use of the chemical was followed by the nonappearance of dandelions at the regular time, this fact does not establish the effectiveness of the chemical. Instead, it provided a slim amount of support: The hypothesis that the chemical is effective could explain the results in my patch, but so could many alternative hypotheses.

It is important to have general knowledge about the sort of situation being investigated, but knowledge of the particular experimental situation was also very important to the critical thinking case. We watched the situation very closely, keeping track of what else the students were doing, and talking with them to see what was influencing their thinking. We watched them catch onto things and heard them talk about what it was in the teaching and the materials that helped them learn.

We tentatively concluded that the critical thinking instruction did help improve their critical thinking ability. We felt that the instruction was part of the explanation of their improvement. But we would not have been justified in drawing this conclusion if we had not followed the students closely. We found no plausible alternative explanations of their improvement, even though we looked for them.

When there are other plausible explanations of the results, the best we can say about a vary-one-thing-at-a-time experiment with a single group of subjects is that the hypothesis could explain the data and is consistent with it. We must undertake further investigation and experimentation to try to rule out the other plausible and even-slightly-plausible explanations, if we want to say something stronger.

Greater Complexity: Multiple Variables

In one well-known chemical puzzle, five colorless liquids, when mixed together, become yellow. Suppose the problem is to find out what minimal combination produces the color. What would you do? Think about this before reading further. (Incidentally, this problem—and the next one—show that there is not a sharp line between experimentation and diagnosis and troubleshooting. Their solutions seem to involve both experimentation and diagnosis.)

My strategy would be first to label the liquids A, B, C, D, and E. Then I would vary one thing at a time, looking for a liquid that can be omitted from the mixture. Given the way things are in this puzzle, two of the liquids would turn out not to be part of the explanation of the yellow color. That is, for two of them, say A and E, I would find that the color appears even when these two are omitted from the mixture, even though the hypothesis for each of them is that it is necessary for the color. For the other three, B, C, and D, I would find that their omission would be accompanied by colorlessness. Then, to check myself, I would make a mixture of the three, B, C, and D, and would find the yellow color. My final conclusion is that each of the three, B, C, and D, is a necessary condition for the color, and that jointly the three are sufficient for the color. This double hypothesis explains the data and is consistent with it. The competing hypotheses that give each of the other two liquids a role would be inconsistent with the data. Both of these competitor hypotheses would be inconsistent with my finding the yellow color from the three. Furthermore, each competing hypothesis is inconsistent with our finding the yellow color from the other four.

Things can get more complicated than this. Suppose that you have five color-less liquids, A, B, C, D, and E, but that A and B are in fact the same kind of liquid. Suppose that the combination of C, D, and either A or B is necessary and sufficient to get the color, and that E makes no difference. But all you know at the beginning is that all five together make the color, and you are asked to find out which ones matter. You might find it interesting to try to design an investigation that will enable you to discover the factors that matter, doing at most, nine tests. Remember that your hypothesis must explain the data and that alternative hypotheses must be ruled out by the data.

Check-Up 8B

True or False?
If false, change it to make it true. Try to do so in a way that shows that you understand.

8:11 The independent variable is the one the investigator observes to see the effect, if any, of varying the dependent variable(s).

8:12 If we have identified all the relevant variables, then varying them one at a time, holding the others constant, is a strategy that is certain to identify a variable that explains the changes in the dependent variable.

8:13 A major goal in isolation and methodical variation of the independent variables is the elimination of alternative possible explanatory hypotheses.

8:14 One disadvantage of control-group experimentation is that it generally does not try to rule out time-related explanatory factors.

8:15 Knowledge about the facts and generalizations surrounding an experiment is not very important if you carefully vary each of the identified variables one at a time.

Medium Answer

8:16 Criticize the following argument using the FRISCO approach:

I had been getting about 30 miles to the gallon in my car ever since I bought it six months ago. I have checked this at least five times. Then I added one ounce of Triple-X Fuel Miser. I found at my next fill-up that I got 38 miles to the gallon. Triple-X Fuel Miser obviously saves fuel. I tried it and it worked.

8:17 Do the same for the following argument adapted from an advertisement:

I have been twenty pounds overweight for as long as I can remember. Then, on the recommendation of a friend, I started taking Frank's Minimizer Tablets, one each day. Since then, I lost about two pounds a week for the next ten weeks. When I got down to the right weight, I kept taking the tablets. My weight stayed there and has been there ever since. These tablets, as you can see, are quite effective in weight control. You should try them.

8:18 Do the same for a control-group experiment you find described in a newspaper, magazine, or report. Include a copy. Remember under *R* to evaluate the reasons from the point of view of their acceptability, as well as (under *I*) the degree of support that they would provide, if true.

8:19 Do the same for an experiment that you find described in a newspaper, magazine, or report, and that involves variation without a control group. Include a copy.

Longer Answer

8:20 Plan an experiment that is addressed to a concern of yours. Here are some concerns of mine, which might suggest some concerns that you have: How can you make a good omelette, using a stove to which you have access? Another: What bicycle helmet materials best resist impact? Still another: Which of two or more engine oils best retains its viscosity, given a certain kind of usage? Do not use a control group, but do plan to vary one or more variables.

    a. State your concern.
    b. State a hypothesis.
    c. Describe your experimental plan for testing the hypothesis. Be sure to identify your independent and dependent variables.
    d. Imagine and describe a set of possible results (or do the experiment and describe your results).
    e. State an alternative hypothesis that is ruled out by these results, and explain why it is ruled out.
    f. Tell whether the results are reason enough to accept your hypothesis, and tell why.

8:21 Puzzle: There are five colorless liquids, A, B, C, D, and E. A and B are the same kind. The combination of C, D, and either A or B is necessary and sufficient for any mixture of them to be colored. E makes no difference. Describe an investigation in which you could discover these facts without knowing them in advance. Your investigation should employ at most nine tests, given that you already know that all five together make a yellow liquid.

Comparability

In a well-conducted experiment, the things compared and the treatments they receive must be sufficiently similar. Without similarity, there would be another possible explanation of the results: the dissimilarity.

In my experimental-control-group critical-thinking experiment, for example, if the two groups are different at the beginning, then that difference might account for the experimental results. If the groups are treated differently (in addition to the critical-thinking-instruction difference), then that difference might account for the differences in results.

Random Assignment to Experimental and Control Groups

One commonly recommended way to secure comparability of experimental and control groups is to start with one pool of objects (seeds, people, etc.) and assign them at random to the experimental and control groups. *Random assignment* is an assignment in which each object has an equal chance of being in either group. Random assignment does not guarantee that the groups will be the same because by chance one group could contain, for example, more tall students or more mathematics majors. But random assignment is held by many authorities to be the best way to secure similar groups.

Although random assignment to experimental and control groups is easy to achieve for many types of objects (such as bean seeds and white rats), it is usually difficult to achieve in practical *and* representative situations involving human beings. For example, I have never succeeded in getting such random assignment in studies of critical thinking, nor do I know of any significant critical thinking study in which such random assignment was achieved. There have always been a number of practical problems that interfered. Random assignment is not impossible for human beings in practical situations; rather, it is difficult. Sometimes this difficulty leads people to select hypotheses that deal with artificial or nonhuman situations, for which random assignment is easier. Sometimes the difficulty leads people to test a hypothesis that they are really interested in, but in situations that are not at all representative of those we care about. Sometimes, the result is the neglect of experimental study of such important areas as critical thinking instruction.

Alternative Ways of Securing Comparability of Groups

People sometimes use other ways to achieve comparability of experimental and control groups. One is to try to match individuals, neglecting the individuals who were not matched. For example, for each individual in the experimental group, we might seek an individual outside of it who matches on IQ, sex, age, and socioeconomic status. The group of individuals who match up with the members of the experimental group would then be the control group. The unmatched members of the experimental group, if any, would then be neglected in compiling experimental results. But matching is very difficult to do, and the design is open to the charge that there might well be some other significant variable that could influence the results (for example, the one that accounts for the inability to find a matchee) and that is more heavily weighted in one of the groups. There is another common difficulty called *regression to the mean*, but it is beyond the scope of this book.

A commonly used way to achieve similarity is to find a total group that seems roughly the same as the experimental group in important respects (such as the same school or college, or the same level). This method has dangers because there are usually significant differences between the groups.

There are also statistical ways of attempting to equate experimental and control groups. I will not go into them here, nor into their difficulties. Consult a statistics text if you want to know about them.

Experiments Without a Separate Control Group

The comparability problems exist not only for separate control-group experiments, but also for experiments in which the variables are controlled without using a separate control group. In the two-semester critical thinking instruction experiment described earlier (done without a separate control group), it was important that the group not have significantly changed from the fall semester to the spring semester. Otherwise, there would have been another possible explanation of the results. We had to monitor the situation closely, and even then we could not be certain that the group had not changed, thus inviting another plausible explanation.

Summary So Far

Control-group experimentation and systematic variation without a control group can both be very helpful in eliminating possible alternative hypotheses. The simplest control-group experiment requires comparable experimental and control groups and the addition of one special factor to the experimental group situation; furthermore, all other factors should be the same for the experimental and control groups. The simplest systematic variation without a control group is to vary one thing at a time, holding the others constant. An advantage of control-group investigation is its control of factors that change with time.

Neither procedure completely eliminates the possibility of alternative hypotheses. They are simply effective ways of reducing the number. An investigator must be aware of the facts and general characteristics of the situation in order to be a good judge of the extent to which possible alternative hypotheses have been eliminated.

There are no perfect ways of equating experimental and control groups and situations. You must know the field of study, be aware of types of problems that can develop, and do the best you can. When using a control group to study individuals who vary significantly from one to the next, random assignment to experimental and control groups is a good procedure, though often difficult to achieve. The degree to which you need a separate control group, as well as strategies for handling comparability of subjects and treatments, depends on the nature of the subjects. People, bean seeds, and pendulums are significantly different from each other. But in all cases, skillful planning, familiarity with the subjects and the field of study, careful work, and close monitoring of the situation are helpful in achieving comparability of subjects, treatments, and conditions.

You encountered a Latin term in this chapter, *post hoc*. The *post hoc fallacy* is the mistake of concluding simply on the basis of one thing's coming after another that the first caused the second. The mistake is a common one; you should recognize it when it occurs and avoid making it yourself. Furthermore it is important for you to know the meaning of the term *post hoc* so that you will not be puzzled or intimidated when you hear or see it.

Experimental investigations must be accompanied by a good understanding of the situation and some good judgment as well. You have encountered the main ideas in experimental investigations, but there are many refinements. The main things to remember are to be alert for alternative possible explanations and keep asking yourself whether it all makes sense.

Check-Up 8C

True or False?
If false, change it to make it true. Try to do so in a way that shows that you understand.

8:22 Random assignment of subjects is any assignment that proceeds without a definite plan.

8:23 Random assignment of subjects might result in two groups that are different in significant respects.

8:24 Separate experimental and control groups are never identical in all respects.

8:25 Separate experimental and control groups never have identical sets of experiences, even when the independent variable is neglected.

8:26 The lack of a separate control group is never acceptable in an experiment.

8:27 When using a separate control group, assignment to experimental and control groups should always be done at random, even though it is sometimes difficult.

8:28 The main reason for achieving comparability in subjects and treatment is to reduce the number of possible alternative explanations of the results.

Medium Answer
Consider these experiments and answer the questions that follow.

8:29 What happens when sugar is eliminated from the diet? Alan and Rose said they wanted to find out. They secured the cooperation of their twenty-five classmates. In the beginning of April, they explained to the class some of the suspicions they had about sugar and persuaded them to agree not to put sugar on any of their foods for a two-month period. During the period, Alan and Rose continually encouraged their classmates to stay with the plan, telling them how much better they would feel if they ate no sugar. The classmates all said that they had not and would not add sugar to their food during the two-month period. At the end of the period, Alan and Rose asked their classmates to fill out a questionnaire dealing with how they felt about life.

Twenty said they felt better about life than at the beginning of the study, and eighteen of these said that they believed that it was because they had stopped adding sugar to things. The other five said that they did not feel good about life, but did not think that this had anything to do with the sugar. On the basis of this experiment, Alan and Rose concluded that the elimination of sugar from the diet promoted a good attitude toward life for most of their classmates.

   a. Was there a control group in the study? If so, identify it.
   b. What steps were taken to ensure the comparability of the situations before and during the treatment?
   c. Were the situations before and during the treatment similar enough? Why?
   d. State another plausible explanation of the results. Make it as plausible as you can.
   e. Were they justified in drawing the conclusion they did? Why?

8:30 Millie and Arturo were curious to see whether a particular cream is helpful in reducing painful sunburn. They marked out ten equal (1″ × 1″) sections across each of their shoulders (making twenty areas in all) and numbered the sections on each back from 1 to 10, going from left to right. For each pair of sections (for example, Millie's #1 and Arturo's #1), they flipped a coin to decide which would receive the cream treatment. It turned out that four sections from Millie's and six sections from Arturo's shoulder were selected to receive cream. They applied the cream to the selected sections and lay in the midday sun face down for one hour with their shoulders uncovered. That night, the cream was washed off. The next day, they examined the twenty sections and found that in all cases the ones that were not creamed were painful and the ones that had been creamed were not painful. They concluded that the cream prevented painful sunburn on the sections to which it had been applied.

   a. What was the experimental group? The control group?
   b. Did they achieve random assignment to the experimental and control groups?
   c. Were the experimental and control groups similar enough? Why?
   d. State another possible explanation of the results. Make it as plausible as you can.
   e. Were Millie and Arturo justified in drawing the conclusion that they did? Why?

Experimental Reasoning Assumptions

When we reason about experiments, we make assumptions. That is, we take certain things for granted. Because of these assumptions, our results never give us the absolute certainty of a conclusion's following necessarily from the data. The most we can ever hope for is proof beyond a reasonable doubt, and often we have less than this.

The type of assumptions I shall be discussing here come under the *I* in the FRISCO approach. This is the type of assumption that is needed to justify an inference.

The Assumption that the Experiment Was Carefully and Properly Done

Consider again the Redi experiment. One possible alternative explanation of the absence of maggots in the sealed flasks is that the meat was poisoned. That alternative hypothesis would explain why no maggots were observed by Redi in the sealed flasks. But if the experiment had been conducted properly, Redi would have taken steps to see to it that the meat was normal meat. In reasoning about the experiment, he assumed that the steps had been effective and that the meat was normal meat. This is one part of his broader assumption that the experiment had been conducted properly.

The control group (consisting of the pieces of meat in the open flasks) was supposed to provide a check on the possibility of such things as poisoned meat. The alternative hypothesis that the meat was poisoned seems to be ruled out by what happened to the control group. From the poisoned-meat hypothesis, we would have predicted that maggots would not grow in the control flasks, but maggots did grow in the control flasks. By denial-of-the-consequent reasoning, it seemed to follow that the poisoned-meat hypothesis was false.

However, comparability of experimental and control groups was assumed in deriving this prediction from the poisoned-meat hypothesis. The two selections of meat were supposed to have been the same at the outset, so that they could be compared at the end of the experiment. But suppose that the meat in the covered flasks had been poisoned, through carelessness, but the meat in the open flasks had not been poisoned. Then the explanation that the meat (in the covered flasks) was poisoned would not have been ruled out by the results for the open flasks.

In order that the control group results rule out the poisoned-meat hypothesis, Redi assumed that the experimental and control groups were similar at the outset. This assumption is part of the broader assumption that the experiment was properly conducted.

Assumptions About the Way Things Happen

A second kind of assumption we generally make is about the way things generally happen. For example, as I suggested earlier, it was logically possible that maggots developed in the experimental group meat but saw the covering, were frightened by it, and became immobile, like a baby rabbit when frightened. Perhaps they then stopped growing because they did not eat, but went into a state of suspended animation, like hibernating bears. We might think that this is all wildly implausible, based on what we know about maggots, but if it had happened, it would have been an alternative explanation of Redi's failure to observe maggots around the meat in the covered flasks. In drawing his conclusion, Redi assumed that the maggots, if any were produced, would be detectable. This seems to be a plausible assumption about the way things happen, but Redi's reasoning did depend on it. It was one of many assumptions he made about the way things generally happen.

Summary and Comment

At least two general types of assumptions are generally needed in reasoning about experiments: assumptions about the degree to which the experiment was well-conducted, and assumptions about the way things generally happen. There is not always a sharp line between these types, because in deciding whether the experiment was conducted well, we make assumptions about the way things happen. For example, in deciding that the possible poisoning of the meat was a relevant condition, we made the assumption that poisoning of the meat would have prevented the growth of maggots. This last is an assumption about the way things happen. The need for these assumptions to be true makes thinking about the following two questions useful:

1. Was the experiment *conducted well?*
2. Is the reasoning supported by what it is plausible to believe about *the way things happen?*

The importance of the assumptions about the way things happen shows the importance of knowing the field of study when doing or judging an experiment. This is part of knowing the situation, the *S* in *FRISCO*.

The Reasoning Pattern in Rejecting Hypotheses

When we reason from a denied prediction back to a denial of a hypothesis, the form of the reasoning follows deductive patterns you have seen earlier (in Chapters 5, 6, and 7). In Example 8:1, this rejection-of-the-hypothesis-reasoning is presented as a two-step process in order to emphasize the role of the assumptions.

Example 8:1

First Step:

1. If the hypothesis is true and the assumptions are true, then the prediction will be true.
2. The prediction is not true.
3. Therefore, not both the hypothesis and the assumptions are true.

1. If *h* and *a*, then *p*.

2. *Not* p.
3. Therefore, not (*h* and *a*) (not both *h* and *a*).

Second Step:

4. Not both the hypothesis and assumptions are true
5. The assumptions are true.
6. Therefore, the hypothesis is not true.

4. Not (*h* and *a*) (using the conclusion of the first step as a reason in the second).
5. a.
6. Therefore, not *h*.

In this two-step process, the conclusion of the first step (line #3) is used as a reason (line #4) in the second step. The first step is deductively valid because it consists of the denial of the consequent. The second step is deductively valid because it consists of the affirmation of one part of a denied conjunction. If you affirm one part, you have to deny the other. Therefore, the whole argument is deductively valid.

Note that the falsity of the prediction does not by itself require us to deny the hypothesis. An alternative would be to deny one of the assumptions. The falsity of the prediction requires us only to deny *either* the hypothesis or at least one of the assumptions.

One key point here is that such reasoning is not simple denial-of-the-consequent reasoning that leads from a false prediction to the denial of the hypothesis. There is a logical way out for a defender of the hypothesis: to claim that one or more of the assumptions is false.

Consider the poisoned meat hypothesis (*PMH* for short), which is offered to explain why the maggots did not grow in the experimental (covered) flasks:

PMH: The meat in the covered flasks was poisoned.

One of the assumptions in reasoning to a rejection of this hypothesis is that the experiment was otherwise done well, which includes the assumption that the experimental group and control group were similar. There were many other assumptions as well. (For simplicity, let us group them all together under the label *EODW* for *experiment otherwise done well*.) If this broad assumption and the alternative hypothesis, *PMH*, are true, then we would have predicted that there would be no maggots in the control group pieces of meat. (Call this prediction *NMC*.) But there were maggots in those pieces of meat. Therefore, (by denial-of-the-consequent reasoning) not both the assumption and the hypothesis, *PMH*, are true. Example 8:2 presents this first step, using intuitive abbreviations on the left and generic abbreviations on the right.

Example 8:2

1. If *PMH* and *EODW*, then *NMC*.	**(or)** **1.** If *h* and *a*, then *p*.
2. Not *NMC*.	**2.** *Not* p.
3. Therefore, not both *PMH* and *EODW*.	**3.** Therefore, not (*h* and *a*).

Suppose further that the assumption, *EODW*, is true. Then (by deductively valid reasoning using the assertion of one part of a negated conjunction), the hypothesis, *PMH*, must be false. Example 8:3 presents this second step.

Example 8:3

4. Not both *PMH* and *EODW*.	**(or)** **4.** Not (*h* and *a*).
5. *EODW*.	**5.** a
6. Therefore, not *PMH*.	**6.** Therefore, not *h*.

Thus, establishing the falsity of *PMH* depends not only on the results in the control group, but also on the assumption that the experimental and control groups were similar, together with many other assumptions. If one of these assumptions is false, then the control group results do not refute the hypothesis, *PMH*.

Can you develop an argument against the spontaneous-generation hypothesis, using the two-step procedure and a broad assumption? Try it.

Accepting Hypotheses: Four Criteria

Although rejection of hypotheses follows a deductive pattern, the acceptance of hypotheses instead depends on the satisfaction of these four criteria:

1. The hypothesis should explain some facts, given reasonable assumptions.
2. Other possible explanations should be inconsistent with some other facts, given reasonable assumptions.
3. The hypothesis itself should not be inconsistent with any facts, given reasonable assumptions.
4. The hypothesis and the mechanism of operation should be plausible.

The first three criteria give necessary conditions, and the fourth a desirable condition.

Let us see how these criteria apply to the Redi hypothesis about the source of the maggots. In this discussion of these criteria, I leave out a number of qualifying words in order to convey the total picture. The application of these criteria is not as neat as it may appear, and requires good well-informed judgment.

1. The hypothesis would explain some facts.

If true, the hypothesis that the maggots were introduced by flies would explain how the maggots got to be on the meat: The flies had access to the meat and brought the maggots (by laying eggs that developed into maggots). In applying this criterion, we do not require that the hypothesis explain all facts, only some facts. It does this.

2. All other explanations of these facts are inconsistent with some other facts, given reasonable assumptions.

This is the elimination criterion. Roughly speaking, if all other hypotheses are ruled out, given reasonable assumptions, then the remaining one is probably acceptable, provided the other criteria are satisfied. If the hypothesis that the meat was poisoned, the hypothesis that the maggots generated spontaneously, and the hypothesis that the maggots were there but not observed, were all shown to be inconsistent with some facts, given reasonable assumptions, and these are the only hypotheses that have any plausibility, then Redi's hypothesis was strongly supported. It would satisfy this elimination-of-other-explanations criterion.

An implication of this criterion is that if there is a plausible alternative hypothesis, then we must not endorse the original hypothesis. Furthermore, we must have made a legitimate effort to uncover plausible alternative hypotheses.

3.   The hypothesis is not inconsistent with any facts.

The accepted hypothesis should not be inconsistent with any facts. Imagine it to be a fact that flies lay eggs that hatch out as flies (in a way similar to chickens). Then Redi's hypothesis would have been unacceptable because the hypothesis is inconsistent with this imagined fact. However, this imagined fact was never established, so it did not refute the hypothesis. Ideally, the absence of facts that appear to be inconsistent with the hypothesis is a necessary condition for the acceptability of a hypothesis.

However, we must not be too hasty. Apparently inconsistent facts or information can sometimes be explained away. For example, the fact that no eggs were observable in the meat that was open to the air seemed inconsistent with the Redi hypothesis, if the intermediary between the flies and the maggots was assumed to be eggs laid by the flies. This apparent inconsistency could be explained away by the assumption that the eggs were too small to be observed. This assumption turned out to be true when magnification techniques were used. There is often an uncertain area between inconsistency and the possibility that something can be explained away. Judgment is required and we often cannot be sure.

4.   The hypothesis is plausible.

Satisfaction of the plausibility criterion is not a strict requirement. It just helps. Sometimes the hypothesis is a radical departure from what seems plausible. At one time, for example, it seemed implausible that flies laid eggs that turn into maggots. At one time, it seemed implausible that the earth was round, and at one time, Einstein's relativity hypothesis seemed implausible (and still does to many people).

But the more implausible the hypothesis, the stronger must be the satisfaction of the other criteria, especially the elimination-of-alternatives criterion. If we accept a hypothesis that seems implausible at first sight, then the alternatives that have occurred to us must be that much more implausible. And we must be that much more certain that there are no other alternatives.

The reasoning for hypothesis acceptance is not as neat as that in which hypotheses are rejected. In hypothesis rejection, given the assumptions and the results, it could follow necessarily that the hypothesis is false. In hypothesis acceptance, satisfaction of the criteria can make it very probable that the hypothesis is true, but it is still possible that the hypothesis is not true: There might be another possible explanation of the facts that has not occurred to us. For example, most people living in the fifteenth century believed that the world is flat. From their everyday experiences, they had no reason to think otherwise. The hypothesis that the world is flat explained why it looked roughly flat and explained, they thought, why people do not fall off the world: The world is always under them. It explained why people who traveled very far away sometimes did not return: They fell off, according to the view. But there was another explanation of those facts. Suppose you had lived then. What would you have thought?

Roughly speaking, the reasoning pattern in accepting a hypothesis is a process of elimination. We try to eliminate all the hypotheses; if just one remains and explains certain facts, we probably should accept it, at least provisionally. This pattern fits experimental reasoning. It also fits diagnosis, troubleshooting, and many other areas of reasoning, as we shall see.

Actually, this account and the examples of hypothesis acceptance and rejection are simplified for purposes of explaining the patterns. When people are deeply involved in an investigation, things tend to get much more complex. Word meanings change, and auxiliary assumptions are invented to save hypotheses. Sometimes, even when there is conflicting evidence, hypotheses are kept because they work for many situations, and there is no better hypothesis. You must use your judgment, try to be well-informed, and be patient.

Summary So Far—And Comment

The criteria for accepting a hypothesis are as follows:

1. The hypothesis should explain some facts, given reasonable assumptions.
2. Other possible explanations should be inconsistent with some other facts, given reasonable assumptions.
3. The hypothesis should not be inconsistent with any facts, given reasonable assumptions.
4. The hypothesis should be plausible.

The first three criteria are ideal necessary conditions; the fourth is a desirable condition. The second criterion requires that we not accept a hypothesis, if there is a plausible alternative—and we must have made a legitimate effort to uncover alternative hypotheses.

The third criterion requires that we not accept a hypothesis, if it is inconsistent with known facts. But in complex cases, it is often difficult to be sure of this inconsistency. The third criterion expresses an ideal.

These criteria are broad and general. Different fields of study emphasize different ones of the four, and add refinements and rules that are specific to the field. But these four provide a good basis for understanding the basic thinking in any experimentation.

The criteria we use in judging hypotheses of experiments do not give us a guarantee of success in selecting correct conclusions. These criteria must be applied with care and thought, and must be applied by someone who knows something about the topic. There are assumptions involved in deciding that the competing hypotheses are inconsistent with some set of facts, in deciding that the selected hypothesis is consistent with the facts, and in deciding about the plausibility and explanatory ability of the hypothesis. Good judgment and background knowledge are required in deciding about the assumptions.

I am not saying that we can never know anything. We do know that maggots do not spontaneously generate in meat. We do know that flies often lay eggs on meat, if they get the chance, and that these eggs often develop into maggots. We do know that the defendant in the jury trial I discussed performed the act that caused the death of the victim. To use the language of the courts, these things have been proven beyond a reasonable doubt.

Actually, these four criteria for hypotheses are appropriate to apply in many elements in the FRISCO approach. As shown in the Redi example, the hypothesis-acceptance criteria apply to the inference (*I*) step in *FRISCO*. But they apply to more than inferences to hypotheses in experiments. As you will see, they also apply to inferences to hypotheses about what someone is thinking, about what actually happened in the past (including the claim that Arlene killed Al, as well as all of history), and about what someone meant in saying or writing something.

Furthermore, in complex cases, the identification of many elements within FRISCO constitutes hypothesis formulation and judgment. For example, identification of the conclusion in some arguments, is difficult and engenders the hypothesis that a given proposition is the conclusion. It is similar with the identification of reasons, with the determination of the situation, with the identification of some assumptions, and with judgments about clarity (which often require judgments about what someone meant). There will be more about this broader applicability of these criteria for hypotheses in the next chapter.

Check-Up 8D

True or False?
If false, change it to make it true. Try to do so in a way that shows that you understand.

8:31 In concluding that the "worms" were introduced by flies, Redi assumed that the experiment was conducted properly.

8:32 One criterion for judging hypotheses of experiments is that there are no more than two other plausible explanations of the facts.

8:33 If the results turn out other than predicted, then the hypothesis must be false, regardless of the truth of the assumptions.

8:34 In a good control-group experiment, the only significant difference in the treatments of the experimental and control groups is the difference in the independent variable.

8:35 Judging hypotheses involves all elements of *FRISCO*.

Medium Answer
8:36 Two English teachers were interested in the view that reading about violence tends to make adolescents more violence-prone. They decided to check one implication of this view: that reading *Hamlet* would tend to make their adolescent students more violence-prone. At the beginning of the school year the teachers took their alphabetized literature class lists (each teacher had one class of twenty-five students) and assigned every other student to an experimental group. The others were assigned to a control group. There were twenty-five twelfth-grade students in each group, with an average age of about seventeen years. Because the classes met concurrently, one teacher, who specialized in *Hamlet*, taught all the experimental students a unit on *Hamlet* that lasted three weeks. The other teacher taught the control students a unit on Romantic poetry.

At the end of the three-week period, each student was asked to rate the following statement on a scale ranging from a "Strongly disagree" through "Strongly agree": "The use of force and violence is often justified in our daily lives."

Suppose that the experimental group's average score was significantly more toward the "Strongly Agree" end of the scale than the
control group's average score. Suppose also that the teachers concluded that reading about violence in *Hamlet* did tend to make the
experimental group students violence-prone.

    a. Name a variable (other than the independent variable) that might
have accounted for such results.

    b. State an assumption that the teachers would have made in draw-
ing such a conclusion.

    c. If the assumption you just stated were false, would the teachers
have been justified in drawing the conclusion? Why?

8:37 Now suppose that, in the experiment described in 8:36, there was no
significant difference between the two groups in their answer to the
question. Also suppose that the teachers concluded that reading about
violence in *Hamlet* did not tend to make the experimental-group students violence-prone.

    a. State an assumption that the teachers would have made in draw-
ing that conclusion.

    b. If the assumption you just stated were false, would the teachers
have been justified in drawing their conclusion? Why?

    c. State one weak feature in this experimental plan. Tell why you
think it is a weak feature.

    d. State one good feature in this experimental plan. Tell why you
think it is a good feature.

    e. Describe at least one change you would have made in the experi-
mental plan and defend your suggestion.

    f. Given the specified results (no significant difference), tell whether
you think the teachers would be justified in drawing the conclusion given. Defend your judgment.

8:38 Using Redi's evidence, develop and write out an argument against the
spontaneous generation hypothesis as the explanation of what happened to Redi's control group. Follow the two-step process and state
at least one of the assumptions that you use.

8:39 Revise your appraisal done as 8:18 or 8:19. To the extent that you are
able in a reasonable period of time, apply all the elements in FRISCO.

Diagnosis or Troubleshooting[2]

Diagnosis and troubleshooting also produce and test hypotheses about the cause of
a problem, but call for tests and analysis of symptoms. When either diagnosis or trou-

---

2. This discussion has been informed by the work of Scott D. Johnson and his associates. See their
*Application of Cognitive Theory to the Design, Development, and Implementation of a Computer-Based
Troubleshooting Tutor* (Berkeley, CA: National Center for Research in Vocational Education, 1992).

bleshooting require deliberate intervention to see what happens, then it is also experimenting. The reasoning patterns for diagnosis, troubleshooting, and experimentation are similar. Furthermore, the general principles of diagnosis and troubleshooting are identical. What to call it depends on the field (for example, medicine *versus* auto mechanics).

Diagnosis, or *troubleshooting*, is a type of activity that has the goal of finding out what is wrong with something that malfunctions. We all diagnose and troubleshoot. Some people do it for a living, but we all do it for personal reasons at least once in a while. Perhaps a flashlight does not work; perhaps a bicycle's gear shift is inoperative; perhaps one's own body has a problem: a fingernail breaks or one gets a headache. To diagnose or troubleshoot a problem with our bodies or a complex piece of machinery usually requires more knowledge than most of us have, so we are often very dependent on repair, maintenance, and medical people. In this section, you will see a few principles of diagnosis or troubleshooting. They can serve as guides to the things we can do for ourselves, but also as basic guidelines for professional troubleshooters and diagnosticians. You will also see some things that we can do for others to facilitate the diagnosing or troubleshooting that they do for us.

Do-It-Yourself Troubleshooting: The Inoperative Flashlight

Consider first this simple example of my troubleshooting a defective four-battery flashlight (which I shall call *F*). The flashlight did not operate when the switch was turned on. I happen to know that some of the things that can cause flashlights to be inoperative are these: bad batteries, extreme cold, a broken filament in the light bulb, corrosion on the switch and other contacts, and separation of the electrical contact between the body of the flashlight and the head. The basic strategy is to rule out possible causes, that is, to rule out hypotheses about what is causing the malfunction. When all but one are eliminated, then that one might well be the cause of the problem. But we have to check to make sure.

It was not cold, so I ruled out that possible cause. I decided to test things one at a time by putting the components in a similar flashlight that worked (which I shall call *Z*). *F* had brand new batteries. Even though *F*'s batteries were new, I tested them by putting all of them in *Z* and found that *Z* did not work. The batteries were in series; that is, any one's being bad was a sufficient condition for the flashlight not to operate. Note again the importance of background knowledge. I concluded that there was a defect in the set of batteries. Such a defect would have explained the failure of both flashlights, and there was almost certainly no other factor that would have explained the failure of *Z* because it had just worked with its own battery set. (This is another example, by the way, of best-explanation proof beyond a reasonable doubt.)

There might possibly have also been another problem, perhaps with the switch, perhaps with the bulb, perhaps something else. I had not yet ruled them out. I would have been careless to claim at that point that I had found the problem. I had found one sufficient condition for the malfunction, but there might have been another, for all I knew at that time.

Next, I was careful to keep the batteries identified as the *F* set and the *Z* set, each consisting of four batteries. Because I was interested in determining which one or ones of the *F* set were defective, I kept the *F* batteries lined up in order. Had the problem been more complex, I might have labeled them to make sure that they were not mixed up.

A simple procedure (and the thing that I did) was to put three of the original *Z* batteries in *Z* and try the original batteries one at a time as the fourth battery. That involved four more tests.

Efficiency

If testing had been very expensive or time-consuming (as it often is, though not in this case), the testing could have been done with fewer tests by putting two of *Z*'s original batteries in *Z* together with two of *F*'s batteries at once. Note that this is not varying one thing at a time. This shows that the method of varying one thing at a time, although the most thorough method, is sometimes too costly and inefficient to use.

If the flashlight worked, then with only one test I would have eliminated two possible causes, that is, two batteries as possible causes. I could then have tried each of the other two *F* batteries with three good batteries and thus located the defective battery or batteries. Even if the first of these two *F* batteries had been defective, I had to test the other battery because both might have been defective. I found that the fourth *F* battery was defective, and after replacing it in *Z* and checking to make sure that the replacement worked, put all four in *F*, which then tested satisfactorily. This last test was necessary because there might have been another problem in the flashlight.

If each test had taken an hour to set up, rather than the few seconds it takes to replace and test a flashlight battery, then it might have been worth seeking the fewer number of tests. I mention this because in complex items (such as a large computer, a computer program, or an airplane navigation system), we can achieve significant savings in time and money by organizing more efficient tests.

The principle to follow is this: To the extent that testing is expensive or time-consuming, organize your test plan to secure a maximum amount of information from each test. Ideally, each test should eliminate a maximum number of likely causes of the problem, if we make certain simplifying assumptions. Testing two batteries in one test does that. If the light works, we eliminate the two batteries being tested; if it does not work, we might have eliminated the other batteries as the cause. (But remember that there might be more than one problem.)

If testing is expensive, narrow down the possibilities as quickly as possible. Suppose that one test will check a whole series of components, and your understanding of the functioning of the whole system indicates that this series might well contain the cause. Then it might well be a good idea to use this test, and possibly rule out a large number of hypotheses at once. The assumption is that if a whole series of components works, then each individual one works and can be eliminated as a possible cause of the malfunction. This is usually a reasonable assumption to make.

A hypothesis is eliminated by its being found inconsistent with the test results, using denial-of-the-consequent reasoning. But there is always the possibility that it is the assumption that is faulty, rather than the hypothesis.

Alternative Diagnostic and Troubleshooting Strategies

There are three basic strategies. The efficiency strategy just described is especially appropriate when testing is expensive, but requires an experienced insightful person, especially if an understanding of the functioning of the whole system is to guide the selection of which subsystem to test first. Without such deep insight, understanding is still required in order to divide the whole system into (usually) equal parts. Differential cost of testing, however, is also a factor. Given two equally likely subsystems, the one to test first is usually the one that is least expensive to test.

A second approach to diagnosis and testing is the one I first mentioned with the flashlight batteries: systematic testing of every component in order, varying one thing at a time. If you do not understand the total system, or if testing this way is so easy that a complex test is not worth the trouble, this approach might be the best compromise.

A third approach to troubleshooting and diagnosis is the *memory approach*. This approach depends on the troubleshooter's remembering that specific symptoms have in the past been associated with specific causes. This approach does not require the deep expertise of the advanced efficiency approaches, but is sometimes the most feasible. One example of this approach is my habit of automatically replacing the light bulb in a house lamp when, immediately after turning on the light, there is a flash, and then the light is inoperative. I remember from experience that this combination of symptoms has always meant that the bulb is burned out.

Even though this memory strategy is effective, for a limited range of situations, I would rather leave difficult diagnosis and troubleshooting in the hands of someone with understanding. Such a person can deal with a wider range of symptoms, including those that deviate slightly from the pattern that is memorized and that might have radically different causes.

In actual practice, the best diagnosticians and troubleshooters use all three strategies and combinations thereof, combining them as appropriate in a given situation.

Perhaps we might add a fourth strategy for the person too ignorant to engage in the simplest troubleshooting, especially if the testing might be dangerous: Call in an expert. Even here, there is an important critical thinking process: applying the criteria of credibility not only in the initial selection, but as the services of an expert continue to be used.

Cooperating with Maintenance Specialists: Troubleshooting the Inoperative Radio

Like most of us, I am not competent to repair radios and many other items I use in daily life. But there are things that I can do to help specialists in their diagnoses. For example, when I was maintenance officer for an aviation club, there were many things I could do to help the radio specialists when a radio malfunctioned. Doing these things often saved the club both time and money, because otherwise the repairer would not have found the problem without expensive flight testing. It was important that I describe the complaint as fully as possible, stating the conditions under which the malfunction occurred, *and* those under which it did not occur.

One time a navigational radio needle became inoperative during a trip. To keep down costs, we needed to provide the radio repairer with more information than that. We determined and recorded the temperature, the altitude, and the location and frequency of the signal source, and tried both to reproduce the problem and to find out when it did not occur. In this case, when we experimented with it on the trip, the problem seemed to occur with every frequency ending in .9, and did not occur with any other frequency. This was very helpful information because the fact that it worked on all other frequencies enabled the repairer to eliminate a large number of hypotheses; and the fact that the radio did not work on the frequencies ending with .9 suggested to him a few hypotheses that he was then able to narrow down to one by further tests. This experimenting on our part was virtually at no cost because the airplane was flying anyway on its return home. (In modern aircraft, there are generally a number of alternate sources of the same navigation information; flying was safe in the prevailing weather conditions.)

Principles of Diagnosis and Troubleshooting

Although the particular strategy in diagnosis and troubleshooting depends on the facts of the situation and the expense involved, there are some general principles that fit into the hypothesis-testing approaches described earlier. Each possible cause corresponds to a hypothesis that explains the malfunction. Ruling out hypotheses narrows down the field of possibilities.

1. Be well-informed.
2. Do not assume that new parts always work.
3. If the symptoms are always associated with one cause, and you remember this, possibly you are in luck. Check this one if testing is inexpensive. But if this does not solve the problem, go on to the next step.
4. Identify as many possible causes of the problem as you can. Each possible cause has an associated hypothesis: namely, that it is the cause of the problem.
5. Try to eliminate as many of the associated hypotheses as you can, generally picking the most likely ones first (this choice requires expertise). When one and only one hypothesis remains, it probably represents the cause, if it was probable that you identified them all in the first place. Check it, though.
6. To the extent that testing is expensive, try to eliminate as many likely hypotheses as possible with each test. If you have the expertise, select the most likely subsystem first, given your understanding of the functioning of the system. However, if testing the most likely one is much more expensive than testing a less likely one, you must strike a balance.
7. If the problem does not have a definite set of known possible causes, then narrow down the problem to a particular sequence or area, study it, and try to come up with some further hypotheses. Vary things one at a time to test these hypotheses. When you are operating in unfamiliar territory, this conservative vary-one-thing-at-a-time testing strategy is also appropriate.
8. When turning over the problem to a maintenance person, provide details about the situation, and specify the conditions under which the problem appeared. If possible, also identify the type of conditions under which the problem regularly appears and the conditions under which it does not appear.
9. Check every conclusion you draw with some kind of test.

Do not memorize these principles. Understand them and practice applying them.

Implicit in the application of these principles to the situations I described (and others as well) are the elements of the FRISCO approach. The question, "What is the defect?," and the hypothesis, "The fourth battery is bad," provided the foci (F) at different stages in the investigation. The reasons (R) included the facts that Z did not work when a particular battery was in it, but did work when the battery was replaced. An alternative hypothesis was that the bulb was bad, but that was refuted (I) by its working when the batteries were replaced. Criteria of inference (I) that I used were the criteria of hypothesis testing (presented earlier in this chapter). An assumption made in testing complex and expensive-to-test systems is that if a whole sequence of components works well, then each is all right. This assumption also bears on inference (I). Important situational (S) factors included the expense and time involved in doing tests and the extent to which the possible causes of a particular kind of malfunction are known. There was no particular problem with clarity (C) in these cases, although it was important for me in reporting to the radio repairer to know the meaning of a number of key terms such as *frequency* and *omni*. Lastly, the overview (O) process consisted of checking over my thinking and the evidence.

Summary and Comment

Diagnosis, or *troubleshooting,* is an activity that has the goal of finding out what is wrong with something that malfunctions. The basic strategy is to eliminate hypotheses that identify possible causes of the problem, to be methodical about this, and to check the results. To the extent that the possible causes are known and to the extent that testing is costly in time or money, methods should be used that are likely to rule out a large number of hypotheses at each test. To the extent that we know few of the possible causes, a more conservative vary-one-thing-at-a-time strategy is appropriate. If we have good reason to believe that one and only one thing can cause the symptom of the kind reported, select that. But check it out.

Diagnosis and troubleshooting fit under the FRISCO approach to reasoning and investigation. All the elements are involved, as are all the critical thinking dispositions, especially the dispositions to take into account the total situation, to try to be well-informed, to look for alternatives, to endorse a position only to the extent that it is justified by the information available.

Check-Up 8E

True or False?
If false, change it to make it true. Try to do so in a way that shows that you understand.

8:40 The reasoning involved in diagnosis or troubleshooting is basically that of hypothesis testing.

8:41 In troubleshooting, it is sometimes a good idea to vary more than one thing at a time.

8:42 Because you might be wrong about it, it is generally best not to provide maintenance people with a description of conditions under which the malfunction regularly appears, and those under which it regularly does not appear. At most, you should tell what it is that is bothering you.

8:43 In efficient diagnosis and troubleshooting (testing a number of components at once), the following assumption is generally made: If a connected set of components functions correctly, then each individual component is probably all right.

Medium Answer

8:44 Suppose you have an eight-battery flashlight that is inoperative and that you have determined by putting the batteries in an otherwise functioning flashlight that the problem is with the batteries. Also suppose that it is very easy and quick to test individual batteries. The batteries in the flashlight are in series, that is, the operation of each is a necessary condition for the operation of the set. Describe an appropriate strategy to locate the problem.

8:45 Suppose that it suddenly has become very expensive to test batteries and that you have the same problem as in 8:44. Describe an efficient strategy, assuming that only one battery is bad.

8:46 Now suppose that a four-battery flashlight has been bouncing around in the trunk of a car for two years and is inoperative when you discover it. You want to get it working again because, as you remember it, it is basically a good flashlight. You are reluctant to take it to a repair shop because the repair shop would charge more than the cost of a new one. You have a battery tester and a circuit tester (a device to tell whether electricity will readily flow from one point to another). You also have an identical flashlight that works well. Describe in detail the steps you would take to troubleshoot and fix the inoperative flashlight. Take the process as far as you can. Explain why you do what you do.

Longer Answer

8:47 Describe a challenging diagnosis or troubleshooting situation in which you have been involved. Assuming that your audience is the membership of this class, describe and appraise in writing what you did, and what others did, if others were involved. Be prepared to tell the class about it orally. If there are any features of the situation or mechanism you are troubleshooting that are likely to be unfamiliar to the members of the class, be sure to include an account of how these things work.

Brain Teaser

8:48 A troubleshooting brain teaser for a rainy weekend: Suppose you have twelve pennies, eleven of which weigh the same, and one of which is off-weight, weighing either more or less than each of the others, but you do not know which. You also have a balance scale, on each side of which can be placed one or more pennies. The scale will show whether the weight on one side is equal to that on the other, or, if one side is heavier, will show which side is heavier. That is all the scale can do. It cannot be used to read weights. Suppose that it is very expensive to operate balance scales. Describe how to identify the off-penny efficiently, and to tell whether it is heavier or lighter than each of the others. Unfortunately, the difference in weight is too small for you to detect in any way but with this balance scale. If you can do this in three balancings, you are eligible for a Master General-Troubleshooter Efficiency Award.

Writing About Your Results

In writing about the results of your experimental, diagnostic, or troubleshooting work, the primary question to consider is "How will this report be most useful to the reader of this report (who might in fact be you, later on)?" The report should contain the information the reader needs to know in making future decisions.

Reports About Experiments

Experiments are usually conducted in order to develop knowledge about a topic, such as knowledge about the nature of meat spoilage and ways to prevent it, or knowledge about the factors that affect the learning of critical thinking. Although standard forms for such reports vary from field to field, certain sorts of things generally should appear in such reports. These include the identification of the question or hypothesis, including definitions of key terms; a discussion of the significance of the question or hypothesis; a review of prior work in the area, on which the experimental results should build; a description of the procedures used, including methods of measurement if these are not obvious; a report of results; a discussion of the results, including their bearing on the hypothesis and the question, and including your conclusion; suggestions for further research; and an abstract, which generally appears at the beginning. When you write a report of your experiment, these items might provide an outline and be useful as subheadings, but they should be adjusted to fit the field of your work and the likely interests of your reading audience.

It is important to prepare a written report of some kind. Otherwise, the work is likely to be lost. Even the results of the experimenting you do for your own interests are likely to be at least partially lost, even to you. Most people cannot keep such things fully in their memories.

Because actual report organization justifiably differs in format from field to field, I cannot provide much more general advice, but do urge you to read a number of reports in your field before you write yours. Perhaps you will want to make some changes in the standard form for the field. This is best approached from a knowledge of standard practices and their strengths and weaknesses.

Reporting the Results of Diagnosis and Troubleshooting

Reports of results of troubleshooting tend to be much shorter than reports of experiments, perhaps because the results are usually of interest to a much smaller audience, perhaps only the person whose body is being diagnosed or whose mechanism is the object of the troubleshooting. The results usually do not have general application, but there usually should still be a report when the results are significant, as in the repair of a car or the diagnosis and treatment of cancer. Such a report helps us to handle recurrences of the symptoms and to assess the adequacy of the treatment or repair.

Such reports always should describe the remedial action taken, if any, such as "Filter #3045 replaced" or "Methocarbomyl prescribed." It is also desirable that tests be administered and their results described. The dates of the tests and the remedial action are essential. Description of the original symptoms is also important so that others can assess the appropriateness of the tests and can check on the diagnosis. Can you think of any other essential items?

Check-Up 8F

Longer Answer

8:49 Write a report of the results of an experiment, preferably one you have done. Describe your intended audience. Use the subheadings suggested in the text, unless you have good reason to do it differently.

8:50 Write up the results of some troubleshooting or diagnosis you have done. Describe your audience and the situation. Cover the topics mentioned in the text, unless you have good reason to do it differently. If feasible, assume that you are doing it for pay and submit a bill that justifies your charge, probably combining your report and your justification of your charges.

Chapter Summary

In reasoning about experiments, we make assumptions of at least two kinds. One is that the experiment was done carefully and well. An assumption about comparability is of this kind. The other kind of assumption in reasoning about experiments involves the way things happen. Even though there is not a sharp line between the two kinds of assumptions, it is helpful to ask yourself about each. Because of the assumptions inevitably made in drawing a conclusion from an investigation, it is important that we be familiar with the subject matter of the investigation.

In simplified form, the reasoning to reject a hypothesis is deductive and has two steps: a denying-the-consequent step, which produces a denial of the conjunction of a hypothesis and a set of assumptions; and a step affirming one part of a denied conjunction, which produces a denial of the hypothesis but depends on the acceptance of the assumptions.

The reasoning to accept a hypothesis should adhere to the following four criteria; the first three are ideal necessary conditions, the fourth a desirable condition:

1. The hypothesis should explain some facts, given reasonable assumptions.
2. Other possible explanations should be inconsistent with facts, given reasonable assumptions.
3. The hypothesis should not be inconsistent with any facts, given reasonable assumptions.
4. The hypothesis should be plausible.

Overwhelming satisfaction of these criteria (assuming that we have made a strong effort to develop plausible alternative hypotheses) gives us proof beyond a reasonable doubt. If an alternative plausible hypothesis remains, then we should not endorse the original hypothesis.

Generalizing from the results of a few experiments to a large population is a topic reserved for the next chapter. However, representativeness is an important consideration.

In planning and executing an experimental investigation, we should control the variables to the extent that this is feasible. Generally this means the following: The variable or variables that are not being deliberately varied to see their effect should be held constant. One way to make sure that the groups start out the same is to assign members at random to the experimental and control groups. Other ways of ensuring comparability are often needed because random assignment is in many situations not achievable. If the experiment compares something with the same thing at another time, given the introduction of one (or perhaps more) experimental variables, then the other variables should be held constant from one observation to the next.

Controlling the variables has the function of ruling out alternative hypotheses (that is, satisfying criterion #2). If there is no other difference between two groups being compared, then alternative hypotheses that require such differences are ruled out.

Diagnosis, or troubleshooting, is an activity that has the goal of finding out what is wrong with some body or piece of equipment that malfunctions. Hypothesis testing reasoning applies to diagnosis and troubleshooting, but practical concerns such as expense and time are important. To the extent that the malfunction has a definite number of possible causes, we can be efficient in testing (and save money, if testing is expensive) by checking a combination of components all together. To the extent that we are not sure of the possible causes, a vary-one-thing-at-a-time strategy is generally appropriate. The basic strategy is to rule out more and more possible causes of the malfunction, that is, to rule out hypotheses.

When someone else is diagnosing or troubleshooting on our behalf, it is good to be able to provide that person with a description of the conditions under which the malfunction occurred, and even better to provide the conditions under which it regularly occurs and those under which it regularly does not occur. This enables the person more effectively to rule out alternate hypotheses. In any case, a methodical procedure and a check of the results are essential.

All the elements of the FRISCO approach apply to experimental reasoning, diagnosis, and troubleshooting. Assumption identification and application of hypothesis-testing criteria can fit into the *I*. The application of observation and credibility-of-sources criteria fits into the *R* of the FRISCO approach. The situation (*S*), clarity (*C*), focus (*F*), and overview (*O*) are also essential.

When you report the results of your experimentation, diagnosis, or troubleshooting, focus on what your audience needs to know. Follow the standard format for the field unless you have good reason to do otherwise, but in any case, be clear.

Suggested Answers for Chapter 8

Check-Up 8A

8:1 F **8:2** T **8:3** T **8:4** T

8:1 The control group is the group not exposed to the experimental factors, but supposedly otherwise the same as the experimental group.

8:5 **a.** The seeds in the empty dry open jar.

 b. Not very good, but not terrible either, assuming a student with a level of sophistication for which the experiment would be interesting. One difficulty was that the student did not avoid contamination of the earth with another possible factor, water. Some other difficulties are that only one source of earth was used, which might have been special, and that only one bottle and location were used, possibly also special. Furthermore, we have no assurance that the bottles were clean. But the control group did receive roughly the same treatment as the experimental group, except for what he assumed was the pure experimental treatment. The use of a control group is for many people a great step forward.

8:6 **a.** The heating of the soil ruined its seed germinating power.

 b. Fairly good at an elementary level. She did separate the soil and moisture variables, something that was not done in the previous experiment. But she did not secure samples of soil and water from different sources, so the result might have been attributable to the peculiarities of the water and soil used. She also did not guard against the hypothesis in *a*.

 c. Do a similar experiment, but use a variety of sources of soil and water and add another set of seeds to be planted in soils that are heated the same way and then wet again.

8:7 **a.** The first ten caught might be the weakest.

 b. That there was a cancer-producing substance accidentally available to the experimental rats during the Ultralight treatment, and it was eaten by them.

 c. If they had used just two rats, the experimental rat might have been going to get cancer anyway, just by chance.

 d. If all twenty rats had been exposed to Ultralight and had contracted cancer, but there had been no control group, then any number of other things that also happened to the experimental rats might have caused the cancer. For example, the food they ate might have been cancer-producing.

 e. Yes, it is fairly good. There was random assignment to experimental and control groups, equal treatment of experimental and control groups (except for the experimental condition), and a fairly good number of subjects.

8:8 **a.** That the students in the first class presured their parents to go to the game.

 b. No. There were too many alternative explanations of the results.

 c. Yes. Two suggestions: Do a survey of the two classes' parents' attendance before she began distributing the information about the team, in order to check the initial comparability of the experimental and control groups. Secure the information directly from the parents. (Perhaps the students were just trying to please her.)

8:9 Deliberately not included.

8:10 Check yourself: Be attentive to comparability of experimental and control groups, to seeing to it that the groups receive the intended treatments only, and to minimizing the possibility of plausible alternative explanations of the results.

Check-Up 8B

8:11 F   **8:12** F   **8:13** T   **8:14** F   **8:15** F

8:11 A dependent variable is one the investigator observes to see the effect, if any, of varying the independent variable.

8:12 Change *certain* to *likely*.

8:14 One advantage of control-group experimentation is that it usually is able to rule out time-related explanation factors.

8:15 "is very important, even if. . . ."

8:16 F: The conclusion is, "Triple-X Fuel Miser saves fuel."

R: The first four sentences are the reasons. We are assuming them to be true, but if the source is selling Triple-X Fuel Miser, there is at least some ground for suspicion of the evidence.

I: Some alternatives that occur to me are these:

He took a long trip after adding Triple-X Fuel Miser, whereas all previous mileage determinations were based on local driving.
The carburetor suddenly started to function better.
He failed to fill the tank last time.

So, I do not feel that the conclusion is established. The other possible explanations are not ruled out and are plausible possibilities.

S: The situation is insufficiently described. There is no way I can tell whether the narrator has a conflict of interest. I do not know why the narrator is giving us this information. And I do not know who might have been monitoring the experiment. However, I have some relevant information about the situation: If there were a fuel additive that could make a significant difference, then I would expect the automobile companies to make a fuss about its not being in the fuel in the first place. It is in the interest of the automobile companies for gasoline mileage to be good. But they have not made a fuss. So the proposed conclusion is inconsistent with this information about automobile companies' motivation.

C: The words seem clear.

O: After review I still feel that the first alternative hypothesis is such a plausible possibility that I should not accept the conclusion.

8:17 Deliberately not included.

8:18–8:20 Up to you.

8:21 Omit one at a time (five tests). Results: C and D are necessary; A and B, and E not necessary. Try only C and D together (the sixth test). Result: C and D are not by themselves sufficient. Try C and D together with each of A, B, and E (three more tests, making nine in all). Result: CDA works, CDB works, CDE does not work. Conclusion: C and D are each necessary and C and D and either A or B are jointly sufficient. E is not a factor.

Check-Up 8C
8:22 F   **8:23** T   **8:24** T   **8:25** T   **8:26** F   **8:27** F
8:28 T

8:22 Random assignment of subjects is an assignment in which each has an equal chance of being in either group.

8:26 Change *never* to *sometimes*.

8:27 Change *should always be* to *is often best*.

8:29 and 8:30 Deliberately not included. Be sure to be attentive to the meaning of the conclusions (the *C* in *FRISCO*), especially for 8:30. Your evaluation will depend heavily on your interpretation.

Check-Up 8D
8:31 T   **8:32** F   **8:33** F   **8:34** T   **8:35** T

8:32 Omit *more than two*.

8:33 If the results turn out otherwise than predicted, then the hypothesis or one of the assumptions is probably false.

8:36 **a.** One possibility: Differences in personalities of the teachers.
  b. One possibility: Teacher personality differences did not affect students' violence proneness.
  c. No, because the differences in the teachers' personalities might well have accounted for the results, as might the differences in the way they handled the subject matter.

8:37 Deliberately not included.

8:38 I shall assume that the experimental group meat was not contaminated with poison after it was assigned to the flasks to be covered. If this and certain other assumptions are correct, and if spontaneous generation occurred in the control group, then there would have been maggots in the covered meat. But there were none. So it is not true both that the spontaneous generation occurred in the control group and that the assumptions are true. There is good reason to believe that the assumptions are true. Therefore, spontaneous generation did not occur in the control group.

8:39 This one is yours.

Check-Up 8E
8:40 T   **8:41** T   **8:42** F   **8:43** T

8:42 Change *Because* to *Even though*. Omit the first *not*. Change *most* to *least*.

8:44 Identify all batteries by making two separate lines of batteries, or some other way. Put seven of the good batteries in the good flashlight, and check the ones from the bad group one at a time, being very careful to keep track of those that have been checked and found good, keeping them separate from those that have been checked and found bad. When finished, replace defective batteries with supposedly good ones, keeping track of the replacements, and check the whole group together.

8:45 Here is one possible specific procedure: Identify each group of batteries as before. Put four batteries known to be good in the functioning flashlight and add four batteries from the set containing one or more defective batteries. If the flashlight functions, put the tested batteries aside and label them *good* or put them in a special place for good batteries; label the other four as *X* batteries. If the flashlight does not function, label the four just-tested batteries as *X* batteries.

Now test the *X* set by taking two of its members and putting them in the functioning flashlight together with six batteries known to be good. If the flashlight functions, label these two *good* or put them in the special place for good batteries, labeling the other two as *Y* batteries. If the flashlight does not function, label these two just-tested batteries as *Y* batteries. We now know that the defective battery is in the *Y* set.

Now with seven good batteries in the functioning flashlight, test one of the *Y* batteries. If the flashlight functions, then the other *Y* battery is the defective one. If the flashlight does not function, then this *Y* battery is the defective one. We have now located the defective battery with three tests. We should then test the total set with the defective one replaced, just to be sure. That makes four tests.

8:46 There are a number of ways to troubleshoot a flashlight like this, but here is an overall scheme that would guide me. First, I would shake the inoperative flashlight (*F*) to see whether the whole system could function. If it works, this would be an efficient quick test of the bulb, all the batteries, and the integrity of much of the system, narrowing down the problem to a loose connection somewhere.

Batteries. If *F* does not work, I would try all the batteries from *F* in the flashlight that does work (*Z*). If *Z* works, then I have eliminated four possible causes (the four batteries) of the problem. If *Z* does not work, then I would probably check the batteries one at a time in *Z* with three batteries from *Z;* then I would replace the battery (or batteries) I discover to be defective and try out *F* with the resulting set of batteries. I would not use the two-battery-at-a-time test procedure because the one-at-a-time procedure is simpler and almost as easy to use. In any case, I will make sure that the batteries are installed in the direction shown in a diagram inside the flashlight. If no diagram is given, I will make sure that the electrical path through the batteries is all in the same direction (from bump end to flat end, for example).

Bulb. Assuming that the batteries are all right but that it still does not work, I would test the bulb next because that is also an easy procedure. To do this, I would put *F*'s bulb in *Z*. If it works, then I will put it back in *F*. If it does not work, I will try *Z*'s bulb in *F*. If it works, then I will buy a new bulb, put it in one of the flashlights, and check it.

Electrical connections. If *F* still does not work, I will inspect the interior of *F* to try to figure out the electrical path because electricity must go from one end of the battery set through the switch and bulb back to the other end of battery set. I will make sure that contact is made at all places. I will inspect for corrosion on the contacts, probably scrape the contacts anyway, and check *F*. Assume that it still does not work.

Switch. I have now eliminated batteries, the bulb, lack of contact in visible points, and corrosion on the visible contacts as possible causes of the malfunction, and have probably narrowed it down to the switch. I will check both sides of the switch with the circuit tester in various switch positions. If it shows no through passage of electricity (an "open") at all switch positions, then the problem is very probably in the switch.

The best I know for dealing with a flashlight switch is to spray tuner spray on the switch and work it back and forth. After doing this, I will try *F* again. I hope that it works because I do not know an economical way to replace a flashlight switch.

Sum. In doing this troubleshooting, I tried to rule out possible causes, as many as I could, as quickly as I could.

Note. In addition to troubleshooting and diagnosing strategy, I needed to know something about batteries, bulbs, switches, electricity, and tuner spray, showing the importance of knowledge about and understanding of the field in which you are working. If you have trouble following this example because of unfamiliarity with the materials, I apologize and hope that, even so, you understand the troubleshooting and diagnosing strategies I used sufficiently for you to use them in an area you do understand.

8:47 Remember to pay attention to the principles of troubleshooting and the criteria for hypothesis testing.

8:48 If I tell you the answer, it will not be a brain teaser. However, if you really feel that you need a hint, read on. Otherwise, stop reading now and go back to working on the teaser. The first balancing should be four against four, selected at random. Here is another hint: Try to develop some principles by working with a smaller group, perhaps four, seeing how efficiently you can locate the off-penny in a group of that size. Then apply these principles to the teaser, or invent and apply similar principles.

8:49 and 8:50 Up to you, but show it to a friend or associate to get reactions.

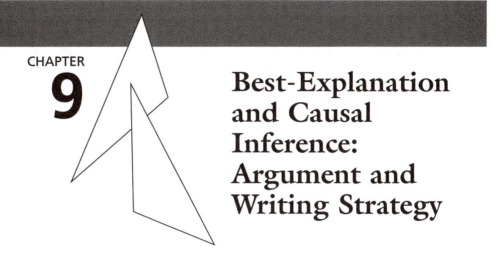

Best-Explanation and Causal Inference: Argument and Writing Strategy

Did Napoleon die from poison? Did Shakespeare intend Iago to be a melodramatic villain? Was Arlene's knife stroke only moderate in force? Was Pluto once a satellite of Neptune? Is there a sizable oil deposit beneath Seal Island? Does the Prime Minister intend to resign soon? Does Martine like Karl? Did Frank trip Pele on purpose, or just by accident? Does the president feel insecure? Why did the car crash into the pole? What caused the extinction of the dinosaurs? What did Thomas Jefferson mean by "equal"?

Best-Explanation Hypotheses

A proposed answer to each of these varied questions would be a fact-explaining hypothesis (or conclusion) that would be justified basically by its ability to explain the facts and the inability of its competitors to do so—or, to use a technical term, by its being the *best explanation*. Unfortunately, answers to these questions would be very difficult or impossible to obtain by experimentation. How then do we produce plausible answers to such questions, and how do we decide whether the evidence for such answers is strong enough? (This topic comes under the *I* for inference in *FRISCO* because we are talking about *inference* to best explanation.)

In this chapter, you will first see an approach to nonexperimental hypotheses that parallels the approach to experimental hypotheses that you found in the previous chapter. The basic criteria and reasoning are the same: Roughly speaking, hypotheses get their support from their ability to explain the facts and from the inability of their competitors to do so. But the types of evidence vary greatly from one type of situation to another, so a thorough familiarity with the area of inquiry is also necessary.

Because causation is at least closely related to the type of explanation under consideration here, a section of this chapter is devoted to causation. Furthermore, because many people need to put their hypotheses and their evaluations of them in writing, a section is also devoted to writing.

Different types of arguments have different criteria for their appraisal. Because you are now acquainted with two types of argument (deductive and best-explanation), and will encounter two more in the next two chapters, the question arises, "What criteria should you apply?" In this chapter, you will also find suggestions for dealing with this question.

First, let me clarify the distinction I have assumed between *hypothesis* and *conclusion*. A *hypothesis* is a proposition that gets its support from its ability to account for the facts and the inability of its competitors to account for them *and* that is a candidate for testing in the situation. Calling something a hypothesis implies that we have not yet decided that it is correct. When someone has judged it to be correct on the basis of the evidence, then it becomes, for that person, a conclusion. The tentative nature has then been abandoned. There are also cases in between, in which we might, for example, call something a tentative conclusion.

Not all conclusions, however, are former hypotheses. For example, some conclusions make value claims (such as "The habitat of every species should be preserved," "We should spray the area with Abate to kill the mosquito larvae," and "Arlene was wrong in what she did"), and do not account for anything. (But the hypothesis that someone *believes* one of those value propositions might account for some things that the person does. For example, the hypothesis that the judge *believed* that Arlene was wrong might account for the severity of the sentence he gave her.) These value claims are not hypotheses because they do not receive their support from their ability to account for the facts and are not alleged to account for facts. They receive their support in other ways, to be discussed in Chapter 11.

Henceforth, in order to avoid having to say both words, *hypothesis* and *conclusion*, I shall usually use only the word *hypothesis*. But consider what I say generally to apply also to conclusions that were or could have been hypotheses at some time. However, I shall use the word *conclusion* when talking about something that in the situation clearly is a conclusion.

Developing a Best-Explanation Hypothesis

When facing questions like those at the start of the chapter, it helps very much to be well-informed about the topic, so that we can avoid fruitless ideas and so that hypotheses from previous similar situations might stimulate a good one for this situation. It also usually helps to think hard about the question, but sometimes it is also a good idea to get away from it for a bit. It helps to talk to others, to imagine (at least temporarily) some of the constraints under which we are operating to be inoperative, and to be sensitive to hints that are present in the situation. Often it helps to modify and refine an unsuccessful hypothesis in a way that responds to its difficulties, and then to refine it some more, so that the production and testing of hypotheses interact with and contribute to each other. But there is no general set of rules that, if followed, produce good hypotheses. Much about it is intuitive, personal, and dependent on our already knowing quite a bit about the topic.

Given that we have a provisional hypothesis, produced by us or someone else, how do we judge it? To that topic we now turn.

Applying the Criteria to Be Satisfied in Accepting a Best-Explanation Hypothesis

The criteria for judging best-explanation hypotheses are the same as those for experimental hypotheses, which actually are one kind of best-explanation hypothesis. That is, whether or not we have experimented, a hypothesis is justified to the extent that, given reasonable assumptions, (1) it explains some facts, (2) alternative explanations of these facts are inconsistent with some fact or facts (if there is a plausible alternative hypothesis, then we must not endorse the hypothesis), (3) it is itself consistent with the facts, and (4) it is plausible. The difference is that, when we cannot do an experiment to create our evidence (the *R* in *FRISCO*), we have to search it out, as a detective does. An inference (*I*) that employs these criteria (whether experimental or not) is called a *best-explanation inference*. The term *best explanation* is used here because the acceptability of the hypothesis depends on its being the best explanation of the facts (as well as being a good explanation of the facts).

Let us apply the four best-explanation criteria to the pathologist's conclusion that the knife stroke was of moderate force:

1. The conclusion explains why the wound was only 2.5 inches deep.
2. An alternative explanation of the depth is that the stroke was strong in force but hit some bone. This alternative explanation was inconsistent, given reasonable assumptions, with the observation that there were no marks on the bones surrounding the wound. Another alternative explanation is that the stroke was strong in force, but the knife was slowed by a medallion worn by Al. Given the reasonable assumption that if there had been a medallion, someone would have reported it, this alternative explanation was inconsistent with the fact that no medallion was reported by anyone who examined Al. All other plausible alternative explanations also seem inconsistent with the facts.
3. The conclusion did not seem to be inconsistent with any facts, given reasonable assumptions. It would have been inconsistent with the observed depth, if we had assumed that Al was wearing a very thick studded leather jacket. (Under that assumption, a moderate knife stroke would not have penetrated even 2.5 inches.) But that assumption seemed unreasonable. No one mentioned such a jacket and the photo taken of Al on the dining room floor showed no such jacket—only a thin nylon jacket.
4. The conclusion was plausible—at least as plausible as any of the alternatives.

Therefore, the pathologist's conclusion that the stroke was of moderate force seemed justified on the basis of these criteria. As you can see, the criteria are not limited to experimental reasoning. They apply to many other types of hypotheses, including possible answers to the questions at the beginning of the chapter, which might be characterized as historical hypotheses, interpretations of author's meaning and intentions, and hypotheses about other people's states of mind (beliefs, likes, intentions, dislikes, fears, etc.)—or in general, hypotheses about events or states of affairs that are not observable or are difficult to observe.

The Reasoning Pattern in Rejecting a Best-Explanation Hypothesis

The reasoning pattern for rejecting a nonexperimental hypothesis is the same as for experimental reasoning. The first stage is showing that the falsity of an implication (i) of the hypothesis (h) plus assumptions (a) requires the denial of the combination of the hypothesis and the assumptions. For example, the hypothesis that the knife stroke was strong in force (call it *KS* for *knife* and *strong*), together with the assumption that there was *n*o *o*bstruction to the blow and the assumption that a strong *u*nobstructed knife stroke would have *p*enetrated more than 2.5 inches (*NOUP*), implied that the *w*ound would have been *m*ore than 2.5 inches deep (*WM*). Because it was not more than 2.5 inches deep, the conjunction of the hypothesis and the assumption must be false, as shown in the denial-of-the-consequent reasoning of Example 9:1, which depicts the first stage in the reasoning pattern.

Example 9:1

Two alternative symbolizations of the same reasoning:

1. If h and a, then i.	**1.** If KS and NOUP, then WM.
2. <u>Not i.</u>	**2.** <u>*Not WM.*</u>
3. Therefore, not both h and a.	**3.** Therefore, not both KS and NOUP.
Or: not (h and a)	Or: not (KS and NOUP)

Denial of the consequent; deductively valid

The schematic letters h, a, and i (for *hypothesis, assumption,* and *implication*) are used in the left-hand symbolization. The letter i is used for *implication* (rather than p for *prediction*) in the left-side symbolization because the word *prediction* is limited to what is expected in the future. Otherwise, this pattern is the same as the one in the previous chapter on experimentation. The pattern presented here is more general than, but includes, the pattern for experimental predictions.

The content-representative letters *KS, NOUP,* and *WM* are used in the symbolization on the right in Example 9:1. I could also have used p, q, and r. You should use whatever system of letters is most convenient for you.

The second stage is showing that the affirming of the assumptions then requires the denial of the hypothesis. We do this by claiming the assumptions to be true. In this case, the assumptions were that there were no obstructions and that an unobstructed strong knife stroke would have penetrated more than 2.5 inches. This pattern is shown in Example 9:2.

Example 9:2

4. Not both h and a	**4.** Not both KS and NOUP
5. a	**5.** *NOUP*
6. Therefore, not h	**6.** Therefore, not KS

Affirming one member of a negated conjunction; deductively valid

To review: Suppose the hypothesis is that the knife stroke was *strong* in force. One of the assumptions was that the knife stroke was unobstructed. Another was that an unobstructed strong knife stroke would have penetrated more than 2.5 inches. We simplify for the time being by considering only these assumptions (though there were more). If that hypothesis and the assumption are true, then Arlene's knife stroke would have penetrated more than 2.5 inches. (This conditional is line 1 in Example 9:1.) But the knife stroke did not penetrate more than 2.5 inches (line 2), so not both the hypothesis and the assumptions are true (line 3 of Example 9:1, which is repeated and numbered 4 in Example 9:2). I accept the assumptions (line 5 in Example 9:2). So I reject the hypothesis that it was a strong knife stroke (line 6 in Example 9:2).

Note that the rejection of the alternative hypothesis depends on the acceptance of the assumptions. For example, if the assumption that there were no obstructions to the blow is not acceptable, the hypothesis has not been refuted by this reasoning. Do not always blame the hypothesis for a false implication!

As with experimental reasoning, this reasoning pattern is somewhat idealized. Often, in practice, we need to loosen its strictness somewhat by adding words such as *probably, tends to,* and *generally.* For example, one of the assumptions I mentioned should probably include the word *probably:* "An unobstructed strong knife stroke would probably penetrate more than 2.5 inches." Accordingly, the rejection of the hypothesis would read, "The knife stroke was probably not strong in force." There are no mechanical rules for loosening deductive reasoning this way. One must use one's own good judgment, as was discussed in Chapter 7 under the heading *Loose Derivation.*

In sum, the criteria we use in rejecting a hypothesis are essentially the criteria of loose derivation (discussed in Chapter 7). This use of these criteria comes under the *I* in *FRISCO.*

Details and General Knowledge

I have given only a sketchy description of this example of the best-explanation way of looking at the reasoning. Without a much more complete grasp of the details in the situation, and without general knowledge about situations of this type, you are not in a position to decide whether the pathologist's conclusion was actually justified on the basis of the facts given. For example, the knife might have been very dull. If so, the alternate conclusion that the knife stroke was strong in force would have been consistent with the evidence, and could have given a good explanation of the depth of the wound. So a knowledge of the details is important. (Reminder: If there is a plausible alternative hypothesis, one should not endorse the hypothesis in question.)

Furthermore, for all I know, the chest bones and cartilage of an adult male might be so close together and so firm that a thin piece of steel could not slip through without great force. If so, the powerful-blow explanation would have been a good one. To rule out this alternative required general knowledge that applied to this situation. The pathologist was supposed to have such knowledge. We members of the jury did not have it. (Because of this sort of difference between experts and juries, experts are permitted to present their conclusions in courtroom testimony, as you will remember from Chapter 4.)

The general lesson here is this: If you do best-explanation reasoning or judge someone else's best-explanation reasoning, you must be well-acquainted with the details of the situation and have general knowledge about the things in the situation. Sometimes the general knowledge comes from one standard subject that has been organized for teaching in our schools (chemistry, for example), but often it does not, as in the moderate-blow case. Here the knowledge comes from a number of subjects —with the addition of a large dose of general knowledge from practical experience.

Other Types of Explanation

The word *explanation* applies to a variety of things. In hypothesis testing, it applies to a proposition or factor that *accounts for* something.[1] But there are other types of explanation, including process explanations (such as explaining how to swim), interpretation explanations (such as explaining the meaning of *deductive validity*), and justification explanations (such as explaining why you should, when driving, not change lanes without signaling). Best-explanation-reasoning explanations, in contrast, are supposed to *account for* something that is or was. Their explaining is not describing a process, stating a meaning, or justifying something. I mention these other types of explanation in order to help you avoid confusing their kinds of explaining with the explaining by a hypothesis or a conclusion that accounts for something. Do not look for these other kinds of explanation when looking for something that accounts for something (although these other kinds of explanation can be relevant to attempts to account for something).

Explanation and Partial Explanation

In the knife-stroke case, the "something" that was accounted for is the fact that the wound was only 2.5 inches deep. The proposition that was supposed to account for this fact is "The knife stroke was only of moderate force." That proposition was the pathologist's conclusion. It explained why the wound was only 2.5 inches deep.

---

1. + It also applies to *claims* that the proposition or factor explains why something happened, or accounts for, or caused, something. For example, the following could be hypotheses: "The moderateness of the knife stroke *explains why* the wound is only 2.5 inches deep," "The moderateness of the knife stroke *accounts for* the wound's being only 2.5 inches deep," and "The moderateness of the knife stroke *caused* the wound to be only 2.5 inches deep." In order to simplify the discussion, I shall forgo a detailed discussion of this form of hypothesis, which itself incorporates terms such as *caused, accounts for,* and *explains why*. I invite those who would find it interesting to perform the extension to this kind of hypothesis.

Factors, as well as propositions, can account for things. Viewing the knife-stroke case in terms of factors, instead of propositions, the factor was the (alleged) moderateness of the knife stroke. When a factor is offered in explanation, then the proposition that the factor obtained, or was in place, or was a characteristic of the situation (though often stilted) could be the hypothesis. Example: "Moderateness of the knife stroke was a characteristic of the situation." More idiomatically, we would say, "The knife stroke was moderate." Hypotheses are always propositions statable in the form of complete sentences. Factors are not stated in the form of complete sentences. The difference here between talking about a proposition and talking about a factor is generally a matter of convenience of expression.

Partial Explanation

A best-explanation conclusion does not need to be the total explanation of the fact to be explained. It can instead be part of the explanation, or a partial explanation. The difference is often in the way we look at things. For example, we might view the moderateness of the stroke as *the* explanation, given the conditions. Or we might view it as *part* of the explanation of the depth of the wound, the sharpness of the knife also being a part (a sharp knife encounters less resistance). Here is another way of saying the same thing: The sharpness of the knife might be deemed to be just a condition, or it might be deemed to be part of the explanation of the result. Given that a factor does play a role, we classify it as a condition, or as a partial explanation, or as *the* explanation, depending on what seems right to emphasize for purposes of assigning responsibility. Whether interpreted as the explanation or as a partial explanation, the moderate-force conclusion gets support from its ability to explain or help explain the facts (that is, to account for or help account for the facts).

If you are troubled in some cases by the idea of looking for *the* explanation of some facts, you might instead think of yourself as looking for something that, together with certain other circumstances, explains these facts. In our case, you might think of us as being concerned with the moderateness of the stroke as part of the explanation of the depth of the wound, another part being the sharpness of the knife. But because the sharpness of the knife is given, and the strength of the stroke is crucial, we are more interested in the latter.

As you might have guessed, the distinction among a condition that matters, a factor providing a partial explanation, and one providing the explanation, is a tricky one. Good judgment is required, paying attention to the details and goals in the given situation. It depends on how much responsibility you feel you are justified in allocating to the factor in the situation.

+ Explanation, Accounting for, and Causation

What sort of relationship is this accounting-for relationship? In particular, is it a causal relationship? This is a difficult and controversial question. Many people are reluctant to say so because causation seems to them to be a rigid, mechanical connection. If, on the other hand, causation is viewed as a broader concept, concerned with bringing something about, then the accounting-for relationship is more plausibly viewed as a causal relationship. It would then include the mechanistic type of causal relationships, but also many others, including those about motivation and those involving intentions and beliefs. For example, all of the following would be causal relationships under the broad interpretation of *cause:* "Arlene's motive for the stabbing was jealousy," "Her jealousy accounted for her stabbing Al," "Her jealousy brought about her stabbing Al," and "Her jealousy caused her to stab Al." Furthermore, all would be regarded as saying similar things. On this broad view of causation (which actually is my view), treating accounting-for as a causal relationship enables us to get guidance in making judgments about possible account-for relationships from some principles for guiding causal judgments that are discussed later in the chapter.

On the more narrow, mechanistic view of causation, judgments about account-for explanations are not all analyzed as causal. But these judgments can still be made and hypotheses can be judged because we often can tell whether one thing could account for another as easily as, on the broad view, we can tell whether that thing could have caused the other. For example, in the trial situation, it is obvious that Arlene's jealousy could have *accounted for* her killing Al, just as (on the broad view) it is obvious that her jealousy could have *caused* her to stab him.

Because this is a controversial topic, you must decide for yourself. But even if you construe causal relationships mechanistically, you can still usually make wise decisions about account-for relationships. Try it and see.

The FRISCO Approach Applied to the Moderate Force Conclusion

In using the moderate-force argument as an illustration of best-explanation reasoning, I have used the elements of the FRISCO approach, usually without saying so. Next, consider the explicit application of this approach to that example, now that you are familiar with the example and with best-explanation reasoning:

Focus: The pathologist's conclusion is that the knife stroke was only of moderate force.

Reasons: Some of her more important reasons are these:

1. The depth of the wound was only 2.5 inches.
2. There were no marks on the bones.
3. The knife blade was sharp.
4. There was no evidence of any exterior impediment to the knife stroke (such as a medal or a heavy jacket).

The reasons all seemed acceptable to the jurors. The first two we accepted on the word of the pathologist, who did well on the criteria for credibility. We did not need to take her word for the third because we were able to examine the knife ourselves. We were assured by the detective who sealed the knife as evidence that nothing had been done to it after he picked it up that night. The fourth reason seemed acceptable because the photos showed no evidence of external impediment and because no one mentioned any indication of external impediment. The prosecutor surely would have mentioned such evidence, if there had been any.

Inference: The conclusion satisfies the best-explanation criteria: It explains the depth of the wound. The primary alternative hypothesis (the strong-force hypothesis) is inconsistent with this depth, given the absence of an external impediment. The pathologist's conclusion is consistent with the facts as we knew them, and it seemed plausible.

In seeing that the hypothesis explained the depth, we assumed that the knife stroke was not obstructed by a heavy studded jacket or medallion. In rejecting the hypothesis that the stroke was strong in force, we made the same assumption, and also assumed that if the stroke had been strong and unobstructed, it would have penetrated more than 2.5 inches. The first assumption seems acceptable on the ground that if there had been an obstruction, the prosecutor would have mentioned it. For the last assumption, we had to depend on our own experience and on the credibility of the pathologist, who probably would not have drawn the conclusion if the assumption were false. Although there were other assumptions, these seem to be the most important ones.

Situation: The situation was taken into account in deciding on the alternative hypothesis of primary interest. If the stroke had been strong, then Arlene would have known that her blow would probably have caused great bodily harm. If she knew that, then she might have been guilty of murder. (Check-Up Item 7:8 in Chapter 7 provides the details of the murder charge, and will enable you to see why this is so, if you do not already know.) So the strong-force alternative was the important one. The situation was also taken into account in my noting that no one mentioned the presence of an external impediment to the blow. I had to know the situation to realize that. Also, the situation made the vagueness of the term *moderate* acceptable (a point to be elaborated under *Clarity*). The situation, according to my understanding of it, supported the pathologist's conclusion.

Clarity: In this situation, the meaning of the terms seemed clear enough and they did not seem to be used in more than one sense. In particular, the term *moderate,* which is vague, was precise enough for the purposes of the jury in that situation: Basically, we had to decide whether the prosecution had proved beyond a reasonable doubt that the defendant knew that her act caused a strong probability of great bodily harm, a key feature of the murder charge. On the basis of the pathologist's testimony and argument that the blow was moderate, we decided that this key feature of the murder criteria was not satisfied, and accordingly deemed Arlene not guilty of murder. The word *moderate* was clear enough in that situation for us to draw our conclusion. (Incidentally, please note the interdependence among the parts of FRISCO, especially among *I, C,* and *S,* a common occurrence.)

At this point in our deliberations, the meaning of the phrase, *proven beyond a reasonable doubt,* was not questioned, although it possibly would have been, had anyone thought that it had been proven beyond a reasonable doubt that Arlene knew that her blow created a strong probability of great bodily harm. For this situation, the phrase was clear enough. Later on, in considering whether Arlene was justified in using the force she used, that question was raised because one of the jurors who was resistant to Arlene's conviction for voluntary manslaughter was using a deductive notion of proof, it appeared. This situation is discussed at greater length in Chapter 12.

Overview: In reviewing, I note that the credibility criteria also apply directly to the conclusion because the pathologist stated the conclusion on the witness stand. The pathologist did well on these criteria: She had background experience and knowledge, she had no apparent conflict of interest, no one disagreed with her, she had a good reputation, I do not know about established procedures (a possible weakness), she knew of the risk to her reputation, she gave reasons, and I have no reason to think that she did not have careful habits.

After reviewing the evidence, the situation, and the way I applied the various criteria, I stick with my decision to believe the pathologist's hypothesis. Please realize that many details have been omitted from this appraisal—inevitably so. But the account does include the main concerns, and does illustrate the application of the

FRISCO approach to a real situation involving nonexperimental inference to the best explanation.

This strength-of-the-blow case, in combining the application of the credibility criteria with the criteria for best explanation, is typical of a wide range of cases. Often we are well-informed enough to apply the best-explanation criteria to some extent, but not well-informed enough to apply them with full confidence, in which case we need to make a judgment about the credibility of a source, for which we need credibility criteria.

Best-Explanation Reasoning in Figuring Out What Someone Believes or Thinks

When we conclude that someone believes or thinks something, our conclusion is a best-explanation conclusion. The inference to the conclusion depends on its ability to best explain the facts. For example, consider Pedro's conclusion that Jim believes that Martine was out with Karl at the Blue Cloud. This conclusion would explain why Jim said that he saw them out together. It would explain why Jim came running over to Pedro to give him the news (on the assumption that Jim believed that Pedro was in love with Martine, and would thus be very interested). It would explain why Jim avoided Karl the next morning, even though he needed Karl's help with his homework (Jim and Pedro being staunch friends). An alternate hypothesis, "Jim was trying to get Pedro upset in order to make Pedro easier to beat in a racquetball match," seemed inconsistent with what Pedro believed to be Jim's character. Can you see the best-explanation pattern here?

A more complex illustration of this pattern is to be found in Shakespearean critic A. C. Bradley's argument to support part of his understanding of Emilia, the wife of Iago, the villain in *Othello*. You saw the use of this part of Bradley's interpretation in an example of deduction in Chapter 7, where the conclusion was that Iago was not a melodramatic villain. One of the reasons for that conclusion by Bradley is his (intermediate) conclusion about Emilia's beliefs, namely that she did not suspect Iago of villainy. Bradley's argument in support of this intermediate conclusion appears here with the sentences numbered for convenience of reference. Sentence 1 is the conclusion of this passage, as I read it.

Example 9:3[2]

(1) She never dreamed he was a villain. . . . (2) Her failure, on seeing Othello's agitation about the handkerchief, to form any suspicion of an intrigue, shows how little she doubted her husband. (3) Even the tone of her speeches, and her mention of the rogue who (she believes) had stirred up Iago's jealousy of her, prove beyond doubt that the thought of Iago's being the scoundrel has not crossed her mind (IV.ii.115–147). (4) And if any hesitation on the subject could remain, surely it must be dispelled by the thrice-repeated cry of astonishment and horror, "My husband!", which follows Othello's words, "Thy husband

---

2. I am indebted to Bruce Warner for calling my attention to this example.

knew it all"; (5) and by the choking indignation and desperate hope which we hear in her appeal when Iago comes in:

> Disprove this villain, if thou be'st a man
> He says thou told'st him that his wife was false
> I know thou did'st not, thou'rt not such a villain
> Speak, for my heart is full.[3]

Remember, Othello has just killed his wife out of mistaken jealousy.

Bradley's extremely confident tone here might suggest that he has offered a deductive argument, but as it stands, the conclusion certainly does not follow necessarily. With the addition of appropriate assumptions, we can convert the argument into a set of deductively valid arguments, each of which yields the conclusion, but the assumptions we seem to need to add to make the arguments deductively valid also make the arguments weak because the assumptions (at least those that I can think of) are false.

For example, consider in Example 9:4 an argument, including a possible assumption that I have added (*b*), that makes use of her "thrice-repeated cry of astonishment and horror, 'My husband!'"

Example 9:4

    a. Emilia three times cried in a tone of astonishment and horror, "My husband!"[4]

    b. [Possible assumption: If a woman cries "My husband!" three times in a tone of astonishment and horror when she has just been informed that her husband has done a villainous deed, then she did not suspect him of villainy.]

    c. Emilia had just been informed that her husband had done a villainous deed.

    d. Therefore, Emilia did not suspect her husband of villainy.

The form of this argument, you will recall, is affirming the antecedent. This is a deductively valid form. The antecedent in this case is affirmed in reasons *a* and *c*. The whole conditional is the assumption, given in *b*.

The trouble with the argument in Example 9:4 is that the conditional proposition (*b*) appears to be false. A woman could fake the tone of astonishment and horror in such conditions. Also, she could still be astonished and horrified by the enormity of the deed even though she did suspect her husband of being a villain—just not that much of a villain. Or she could be astonished and horrified even though she thought he was a dreadful villain, but did not think that his villainy took him in this direction. Or she could be astonished and horrified by his acts of villainy, even though his being a villain of this sort was known to her. I am astonished and horrified by

---

3. A. C. Bradley, *Shakespearean Tragedy* (London: Macmillan and Co., Ltd., 1937), pp. 179–180.

4. You might have noted that I added *a tone of* in order to make clear what it was we could observe. If you want to leave it literally as Bradley presented it, then you must redo the example so that the best explanation inference goes from the observation made to the conclusion that she was astonished and horrified.

things done by terrorists, although I know in advance that there are terrorists and that they do dreadful things.

Bradley suggests that he has a proof beyond doubt. I feel that he is overstating his case. At least, as I have indicated, he does not have a deductively valid argument with true reasons. A sympathetic interpretation of his arguments applies the standards of best-explanation reasoning. The conclusion that she never dreamed that he was a villain could explain her crying "My husband!" three times in a tone of astonishment and horror. It could also explain her apparent choking indignation, her apparent failure to form suspicion of intrigue in the affair of the handkerchief, and the tone of the other speeches to which Bradley referred. All of this evidence also tends to make implausible the alternative hypotheses that she did suspect him of villainy. As a best-explanation argument, the evidence can pile up, but here no one piece is conclusive.

As usual, there is much more to be said. One interesting feature of this case is that Emilia is a fictional character. So the whole argument and interpretation takes place *as if* she were a real person.

Another interesting feature is Bradley's extreme confidence. If you read and discuss the play intensively, you might also decide that Bradley's extreme confidence is unwarranted, as I did. But I am only trying to show you a way to look at much of the reasoning we do, and you might well judge his confidence warranted. In the enactments of *Othello* that I have seen, Iago was not interpreted as a melodramatic villain. Bradley's view has apparently been generally accepted.

Summary

Deprived of the use of experiments, as we are for a variety of hypotheses, we still can use the best-explanation pattern of reasoning. The two-stage rejection of a hypothesis depends on other assumptions. The acceptance of a hypothesis depends on an elimination-of-other alternatives approach (using the same four criteria as with experiments) and is also dependent on assumptions. Both processes require a familiarity with details of the situation and knowledge of the sort of thing being studied. Often the reasoning must be loosened through the use of such words as *probably* and *generally*.

Evaluation of best-explanation conclusions is conveniently done by using the FRISCO approach. It is not a mechanical process. The elements, which are interdependent, are not necessarily applied in the order of presentation. They are applied, and often reapplied, in whatever order fits your developing grasp of the situation.

Here is the basic strategy for best-explanation reasoning: Know well the topic or field of study. Given reasonable assumptions, search for the hypothesis that seems the best explanation. Discuss it with others. Be open to a probably temporary relaxation of what you think are the constraints in a situation. Look for alternative hypotheses. Look for evidence that is inconsistent with the various hypotheses, including the favored hypothesis. If only one hypothesis remains after a thorough search for counterevidence, then—perhaps very tentatively—accept it. If you have made a strong effort to uncover alternative hypotheses, and if it is the only possible explanation, all the others being clearly unacceptable, accept it. But be open to new evidence that might make the hypothesis dubious. If you find some, consider refining the hypothesis, but sometimes it is best just to abandon it.

Much of our reasoning is best-explanation reasoning. Best-explanation reasoning applies to historical hypotheses, who-done-it hypotheses, hypotheses about the state of mind and belief and intentions of people, and various other hypotheses about things that we cannot possibly (or easily) experience directly. Best-explanation reasoning does not apply to value conclusions, though best-explanation conclusions are often relevant to them.

The type of explanation of concern here is that in which the explanation is intended to account for something. Other types of explanation are process explanation (explaining how), interpretive explanation (explaining the meaning of a term), and justification (explaining why something should be believed). Although these are often involved in account-for explanations, they are different and generally have different criteria for success.

+ The nature of the accounting-for relationship in best-explanation reasoning is complex and controversial. My view is that this accounting-for relationship is a causal relationship, construing causality quite broadly as a bringing-about kind of relationship that includes mechanical as well as other kinds of bringing about. But some people feel that the word *cause* indicates a mechanical relationship. If you feel this way, then stick simply with accounting-for as your interpretation of the type of explanation under discussion in this chapter. It will serve you well.

Check-Up 9A

True or False?
If false, change it to make it true. Try to do so in a way that shows that you understand.

9:1 In best-explanation reasoning, a conclusion receives support from its ability to explain facts that are offered in support of the conclusion.

9:2 In best-explanation reasoning, the ability of a conclusion to explain (that is, account for) some facts proves it true.

9:3 One way to cast doubt on a conclusion is to show that there are plausible alternative explanations of the facts explained by the conclusion.

9:4 If a conclusion satisfies the other criteria, then its being inconsistent with some evidence does not weaken its support.

9:5 The basic criteria for nonexperimental best-explanation hypothesis testing are the same as the criteria for experimental hypothesis testing.

Short Answer
In each of the following arguments, underline the final conclusion twice, label the fact(s) it is supposed to explain with *EF,* label alternative hypotheses with *AH,* and label any evidence that is inconsistent with an alternative hypothesis *IE,* but only if you have identified an alternative hypothesis. If your instructor has not made another suggestion, either use a photocopy of this page or copy the items by hand.

9:6 Arlene did not intend to hurt him severely. That explains why the blow was of moderate force.

9:7 Sandra did not flinch when I told her that Karl was out with Martine last night. That's why I think she knows already.

9:8 What is the problem? I'll tell you. The fuel filter is clogged with dirt. That explains why the car will not run.

9:9 George Orwell's intention in *1984* was to persuade the British that totalitarianism is bad. That explains why he depicted so many things that are offensive to the British people.

9:10 When I turn the key to my car, there is no sound. When I flip on the light switch, there is no light. When I turn on the radio, there is no sound or light. You might suspect that the battery connections are unhooked, but they are not. I looked. The car battery must be dead.

9:11 "I see that you have been to the cemetery," said the detective. "You have mud on your shoes that is the color of the mud at the cemetery. You are perspiring. You look upset. And you have a hint of a sunburn. If you had gone to the movies, the sunburn you have would not be there."

9:12 Said by the prosecuting attorney in an attempt to show that Arlene was not engaged in self-defense: "Arlene wanted Al to follow her. That's why she put his keys in her purse and zipped it closed. It's not true that she wanted the use of his car. She did not like his car, and was afraid to drive it."

Medium Answer

9:13–9:19 For each of the Items 9:6 through 9:12, supply a possible alternative hypothesis to try to explain some or all of the evidence presented. Try to make it as plausible as you can. If one is already presented (as in 9:10), then suggest a different one. You may write it in above. Here is an example of the first one:

9:13 (9:6) Arlene was weak at the time of the stabbing.

+ 9:20–9:26 For each of the alternative hypotheses you suggested in 9:13–9:19, imagine an evidence–assumption pair that would refute the alternative hypothesis (which you should repeat here). You might need to make up the evidence. Try to make it as plausible as you can. Note: the goal here is to give you practice in self-consciously identifying and formulating best-explanation evidence–assumption–refutation-of-hypothesis relationships to help you be more aware of the parts and their relationships to each other.

Please do this on a separate piece of paper. Here is an example pair for the first one, preceded by the alternative hypothesis:

9:20 (9:6, 9:13) Alternative hypothesis: Arlene was weak at the time of the stabbing.

Imagined counter-evidence: Arlene is muscular, weighs about 130 pounds, and was in good health at the time.

Assumption: If someone is muscular, weighs about 130 pounds, and is in good health, that person is probably not weak.

Longer Answer

In Items 9:27 through 9:31, for each piece of information, tell whether, if true, it would support the hypothesis, weaken it, or neither, *and tell why you think so*. Because the situations are so complex and the information can be construed in various ways if considered all by itself, there is generally no one right answer to these items. They are offered to give you practice in relating evidence to best-explanation hypotheses, and in justifying your decisions.

9:27 A popular hypothesis offered in explanation of the destruction of the dinosaurs, which is believed by many people to have happened 65 million years ago, is that a large meteor hit the earth 65 million years ago. Possibly, the resulting explosion created a large dark cloud that enveloped the earth for many years and shut off the sun, thus stopping photosynthesis and shutting down the dinosaurs' food supply, resulting in their starving to death.

a. An exceptionally large amount of iridium is found in the layers of the sea supposedly formed about 65 million years ago. Iridium is found in meteors in much higher concentrations than on the earth's surface. Does this support the hypothesis? Weaken it? Neither? Why?

b. It is determined that lava flow from volcanoes also contains a heavy concentration of iridium. Support? Weaken? Neither? Why?

c. The fossil record suggests that there were a number of small mammals developing at that time. These mammals did not die off at that time, and were presumably capable of stealing dinosaur eggs. Support? Weaken? Neither? Why?

d. It is believed that dinosaurs were cold blooded, meaning that they depended on the climate to keep warm. It is also believed that the shutting off of the sun by the cloud would have resulted in a severe winter lasting for many years. Support? Weaken? Neither? Why?

e. It is determined that all of our dating procedures are radically in error, suggesting that the dinosaurs died off only about 3,300 years ago and the layer of iridium was formed 3,300 years ago. Support? Weaken? Neither? Why?

9:28 Some historians have concluded that Napoleon died from arsenic poisoning administered by his own countrymen when he was in exile on St. Helena Island.

a. A sample of Napoleon's hair obtained while he was at St. Helena, but recently analyzed using a new technique employing nuclear bombardment, contains an abnormally large amount of arsenic. Arsenic poisoning leaves its traces in human hair. Support? Weaken? Neither? Why?

b. An alternative hypothesis is that he died of cancer, but some of his symptoms were nausea, chills, weakness, and increasing corpulence. These symptoms are judged by a cancer specialist not to be symptoms of cancer. Support? Weaken? Neither? Why?

c. These symptoms are deemed by an expert in arsenic poisoning to be typical symptoms of arsenic poisoning. Support? Weaken? Neither? Why?

d. A contemporary well-known French historian who teaches at the Sorbonne states that there is nothing to the arsenic poisoning story. Support? Weaken? Neither? Why?

e. It is established that arsenic in regular doses that are not noticeable to the recipient can kill the recipient. Support? Weaken? Neither? Why?

9:29 Dr. Frank Sulloway has recently advocated a hypothesis about the impact of being first-born among siblings, as compared to being later-born: First-borns tend to be conservative with respect to their immediate surroundings, whereas later-borns tend to revolt against the accepted views of their immediate surroundings. Consider each of the following pieces of evidence for its bearing on the hypothesis (which I have simplified a bit in order to make things more manageable).

a. The following people are later-borns: Charles Darwin, Rachel Carson, Karl Marx, Lenin, Fidel Castro, Ho Chi Minh, Marlon Brando, and George Eliot (female author of *Silas Marner* who abandoned religion and lived adulterously with a married man). Support? Weaken? Neither? Why?

b. The leaders of the extended reign of terror in the French Revolution were predominantly first-born, including Robespierre, whereas the ones killed by the guillotine were mostly later-born, including Danton, originally a revolutionary who began to feel that the revolution was going too far. Support? Weaken? Neither? Why?

c. Over the ages, first-borns were preferred by parents over the younger later-borns, and were given more privileges and greater inheritances because the first-borns would sooner be mature and able to help and were already past the greatest life-threatening dangers to children. Therefore, first-borns found it expedient to adopt the existing structure in the family or society. Support? Weaken? Neither? Why?

d. Sir Isaac Newton, who developed a new theory in physics that was dominant until Einstein's relativity, was a first-born. As a youth, Sir Isaac Newton hated his stepfather. Support? Weaken? Neither? Why?

e. Carlos, the Jackal, an international terrorist, was a first-born. His father was a deeply committed Marxist. Support? Weaken? Neither? Why?

f. There are those who are neither first-born nor later-born because they were the only child.

    g. You, the reader. Are you first-born, later-born, or neither? Support? Weaken? Neither? Why?

9:30 In a period of five weeks in 1987, fourteen humpback whales died in the Cape Cod, Massachusetts, area. Under ordinary conditions, it would take about fifty years for this many humpback whales to die in this area. What happened? A hypothesis advanced by Donald Anderson of the Woods Hole Oceanographic Institution is that they died from "red tide" (more specifically, paralytic saxitoxin produced by the dinoflagellate *Alexandrium tamarense*), which entered the whales' bodies in the mackerel and other fish that they ate while migrating.

    a. They did not die of hunger because they had abundant blubber and fish in their stomachs when they died. Support? Weaken? Neither? Why?

    b. They did not die of poison gas leaking from a nearby sunken submarine because there were no sunken submarines in the area. Support? Weaken? Neither? Why?

    c. The minimum lethal dose of saxitoxin for humans is seven to sixteen micrograms per kilogram of body weight. The whales' flesh contained an average of only 3.2 micrograms per kilogram of body weight. Support? Weaken? Neither? Why?

    d. Almost all of the saxitoxin in the mackerel was found in the mackerel's livers and kidneys rather than in their flesh. Support? Weaken? Neither? Why?

    e. Livers and kidneys in animals capture, metabolize, and excrete saxitoxin. Support? Weaken? Neither? Why?

    f. Each time whales dive, much larger amounts of blood and oxygen are sent to the heart and brain, bypassing the liver and kidney. Support? Weaken? Neither? Why?

9:31 In Shakespeare's *Hamlet,* the part of Polonius is, in my experience, usually played as a silly old fool. A hypothesis that has been advanced by a close associate of mine is that, instead of being a silly old fool, he is a sensible person, though set in his ways, who has adapted to the political pressures of serving a monarchy, just as many people these days try to seem agreeable to people in power and try not to rock the boat. Consider these pieces of evidence from the play and decide their bearing on my associate's hypothesis, defending your judgment.

    a. Hamlet, a sensitive person, several times refers to Polonius as a fool: "These tedious old fools" (II, ii). "Let the doors be shut upon him, that he may play the fool nowhere but in's own house" (III, i). "Thou wretched, rash, intruding fool" (III, iv). Support? Weaken? Neither? Why?

    b. In the play, Polonius formulates a possible alternative explanation for Hamlet's behavior (alternative to the new king's explanation that Hamlet is upset about the murder of Hamlet's father—the former king—and the quick remarriage of his mother to the new king). Polonius' alternative explanation is that Hamlet is upset about his rejection in love by Ophelia (Polonius' daughter), who has been told by Polonius to stay clear of Hamlet. Support? Weaken? Neither? Why?

c. Polonius gives sensible advice to his departing son, Laertes, including these bits of wisdom:

> Be thou familiar, but by no means vulgar.
> Those friends thou hast, and their adoptions tried,
> Grapple them unto thy soul with hoops of steel,
> But do not dull thy palm with entertainment
> Of each new-hatched, unfledged courage [spirited person].
>   Beware
> Of entrance to a quarrel; but being in,
> Bear't that th' opposed may beware of thee.
> Give every man thine ear, but few thy voice;
> Take each man's censure, but reserve thy judgment. . . .
> Neither a borrower nor a lender be,
> For loan oft loses both itself and friend,
> And borrowing dulleth edge of husbandry.
> This above all, to thine own self be true,
> And it must follow as the night the day
> Thou canst not then be false to any man. [I, iii]

Support? Weaken? Neither? Why?

d. Polonius also gives his son the following advice at the same time:

> Costly thy habit as thy purse can buy,
> But not in fancy; rich, not gaudy,
> For the apparel oft proclaims the man,
> And they in France of the best rank and station
> Are of a most select and generous chief [eminence] in that.
>   [I, iii]

Support? Weaken? Neither? Why?

e. Polonius forgets what he was saying when giving instructions to his agent: "What was I about to say? By the mass, I was about to say something! Where did I leave?" (II,i). Support? Weaken? Neither? Why?

f. When Hamlet mimics and makes fun of him, Polonius does not react angrily:

POLONIUS:	My lord, I have news to tell you.
HAMLET:	My lord, I have news to tell you. . . .

> POLONIUS: The actors are come hither, my lord.
> HAMLET: Buzz, buzz.
> POLONIUS: Upon my honor— [II,ii]

Support? Weaken? Neither? Why?

g. Polonius realizes that there is something reasonable behind Hamlet's wild talk:

> HAMLET: . . . The satirical rogue says here that old men have grey beards, that their faces are wrinkled, their eyes purging thick amber and plum-tree gum, and that they have a plentiful lack of wit, together with most weak hams. All of which, sir, though I most powerfully and potently believe, yet I hold it not honesty to have it thus set down, for you yourself, sir, should be old as I am if, like a crab, you could go backward.
> POLONIUS: [aside] Though this be madness, yet there is method in't.

Support? Weaken? Neither? Why?

9:32 There have been many reports (but only during the last five years) of premature wearing of the valve guides in certain piston engines (made by Manufacturer XYZ) of small aircraft. The valve guides are circular devices that hold the shafts of valves that either open to admit the air-gasoline mixture into the cylinder (the intake valve), or to let the burned gases out of the cylinder (the exhaust valve). The valve itself consists of a shaft that rides back and forth in the valve guide and an enlarged, roughly flat head that can close or open a hole into the cylinder, depending on the valve's position. One hypothesis is that rocker arms (that push the shafts of the valves) for exhaust valves were sometimes installed for intake valves, and vice versa, placing the oil-emitting orifice in the wrong place in each case, resulting in insufficient oil getting to the associated valve guide. Incidentally, the two rocker arms per cylinder are in a rocker arm box, one per cylinder.

See the drawing for the general relationship between a rocker arm, a valve shaft, and a valve guide.

a. The rocker arms for exhaust valves look identical to those of the intake valve, except for the placement of the small oil-emitting orifice, which supplies oil to the associated valve guide.

b. On inspection, five engines with premature wearing of one or more valve guides were found to have exhaust-valve rocker arms installed in the place of intake rocker arms in the position associated with the affected valve guides.

c. Some engines with premature wear on the intake valve guides

SCHEMATIC DRAWING

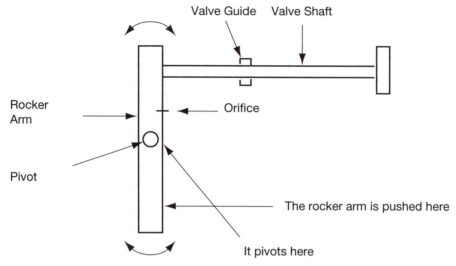

were found to have the correct rocker arms installed in all positions. (There are eight rocker arms on a four-cylinder engine, two per cylinder.)

d. Some engines had guides so heavily worn that they needed replacement after only 300 hours of operation (2,000 hours is expected minimum time). The rocker arms on these engines were in the correct places. That is, the intake and exhaust rocker arms were not exchanged.

e. It is learned that, about five years ago, manufacturer XYZ changed its valve guide manufacturing methods, and at least one production run of valve guides for the affected type of engine used a slightly different kind of steel.

f. On three engines, the valve guides on two cylinders show severe wear, whereas the other cylinders' guides show practically no wear. It is assumed that all the guides for these three engines (which were fairly new) were from the same production run.

g. Manufacturer XYZ changed the size of its valve shafts from $\frac{7}{16}$ inch to $\frac{1}{2}$ inch. Some mechanics suggest that this change could have caused the excessive wear.

h. The change in valve shaft size occurred about thirty years ago.

i. Excessive valve guide wear is found only in parallel valve XYZ engines, although the valve shaft size change was implemented in other types of engines as well.

j. On two engines (of the affected type with four cylinders and two rocker arms—in a rocker arm box—per cylinder) with correctly installed rocker arms, it is found that actual oil flow to the rocker arm boxes varies radically for different cylinders, with the pattern being haphazard. No oil was found after the first minute of idling operation. After two minutes of idling, two of the rocker arm boxes still had received no oil. After five minutes of medium-speed operation and two minutes of idling, the same two rocker arm boxes had received about 1/3 and 1/9 respectively of the amount of oil received by the other two rocker arm boxes.

9:33 In a book, newspaper, or magazine, or a speech or conversation that you can record in writing, find a presentation of a best-explanation conclusion together with evidence it supposedly explains.

   a. Attach it or a copy.

   b. Underline the best-explanation conclusion, label the facts it is supposed to explain with *EF,* label any alternative hypotheses with *AH,* and label any evidence that is inconsistent with any suggested alternative hypotheses *IE.*

   c. If no alternate possible explanations are offered that are inconsistent (given certain assumptions) with some evidence that is presented, then suggest one.

   d. State an assumption that would probably be made in showing each alternative hypothesis to be inconsistent with the evidence. If you have trouble finding a best-explanation argument, look at the range of questions in the first paragraph of this chapter. Arguments that support answers to these and similar questions are likely to be best-explanation arguments.

9:34 Apply the FRISCO approach to the argument in support of the conclusion about Polonius in 9:31 and report your results in writing element by element. In doing 9:31, you have already completed some of the elements. Be prepared to present the argument and your analysis to your class or group in an interesting way.

Necessarily Following: Deductive Versus Best-Explanation Inference and General Argument Strategy

In best-explanation reasoning, the conclusion does not necessarily follow from the evidence. If it did, then we could just go directly from the evidence to the conclusion (deducing the conclusion) and not worry about the explanatory power of the conclusion. The strategy in best-explanation reasoning is basically a process of showing that one possible conclusion could explain the evidence and eliminating other possible explanations as implausible, leaving only the one. But the conclusion does not necessarily follow from the evidence because one of the assumptions might be incorrect and because there might be still another plausible explanation that has not yet occurred to us.

   It does not necessarily follow from the depth of the wound and the lack of marks on the bones that the blow was moderate. Those reasons, which were the ones mentioned by the pathologist, do not rule out the possibility, for example, that the victim was wearing a medallion that deflected and reduced the strength of the blow. This alternative hypothesis did not occur to the jurors. If it had, it would probably have been rejected for the following reasons: If Al were wearing a medallion, then its presence would probably have been mentioned in the trial and its presence was not mentioned. In any case, we could not be absolutely certain that there were no other possibilities, so the conclusion did not follow necessarily from what she said.

A Possible Alternative: Transformation into a Deductively Valid Argument

Suppose instead that we transform the reasoning into deductively valid reasoning by adding a goal-filling reason as an assumption, shown in brackets:

Example 9:5

    a. The wound caused by the knife stroke was only 2.5 inches deep.
    b. There were no marks on the nearby chest bones.
    c. [If a wound caused by a knife stroke is only 2.5 inches deep, and there are no marks on nearby chest bones, then the stroke was only of moderate force.]
    d. Therefore, the stroke was only of moderate force.

By adding an appropriate reason (*c*), we have transformed the argument into one that is deductively valid. But that does not make the argument a good one because the added reason is not true. The medallion possibility shows this.

You can probably see from Example 9:5 (and from your experience with the items in Chapter 7) that you can transform any argument into a deductively valid one by adding a reason of the right sort. However, often a bad argument is produced because the argument often then contains a false reason. The deductive validity does not help the argument at all. Best-explanation is often then the best approach.

Choosing Between the Best-Explanation Approach and the Deductive and Other Approaches

Usually, when judging an argument, our purpose is to decide whether the conclusion is true or sufficiently well-established. Assume this to be our purpose. Because there are various ways of looking at an argument (deductive, loose deductive, best-explanation, generalization, and value judging—the last two of which have not yet been discussed in this book), we should choose the way of looking at the argument that gives the strongest support for the conclusion. If the argument, even when viewed in a way that makes it look its strongest, still does not provide strong enough support, then it does not succeed. However, if, when looked at in some way, it does provide sufficient support, then it succeeds.

If we can make an argument into a deductively valid argument by supplying it with additional reasons (in the form of assumptions) that are true, and if the original reasons are true, then we should take that route and accept the argument and the conclusion. We would then have shown that the conclusion follows necessarily from true reasons, and thus would have shown the conclusion to be true. What could be better than that?

But often any set of reasons that we can invent to produce deductive validity includes a false reason. Then the best-explanation approach can be the one to use. It can produce well-established conclusions, as it has done for most scientific conclusions. A familiar example of a well-established best-explanation conclusion is the prosecutor's conclusion that Arlene killed Al. See the beginning of Chapter 2 for a complex best-explanation argument in support of this conclusion advanced by the prosecutor. Best-explanation conclusions are sometimes very strongly supported, even though they do not follow necessarily from the evidence or true assumptions. The prosecutor's conclusion was very well-established. It was proven beyond a reasonable doubt, the best kind of proof you can get for a best-explanation conclusion, but the conclusion did not follow necessarily.

Another familiar example is the pathologist's argument for her conclusion that the knife stroke was of moderate force. This also is best-explanation reasoning, though it was not as strong as a proof beyond a reasonable doubt. Actually, in everyday life, best-explanation reasoning often does not yield proof beyond a reasonable doubt. But we are still often justified in basing decisions on it.

Often loose derivation (see Chapter 7) is the best kind of argument that we can find or construct to support a conclusion. Even though the conclusion does not necessarily follow, the argument can often be a good one, but good judgment is required here, in addition to the application of whatever criteria are appropriate.

Value-judging arguments cannot be expected to fit best-explanation standards because value conclusions do not account for facts. So different strategies (often loose derivation) are appropriate here. But the general idea still holds: Do the best you can for an argument (assuming that the goal is to decide whether the conclusion is acceptable) and then judge it carefully.

Complex Combinations

Often complex arguments consist of parts that satisfy different standards: possibly parts that satisfy deductive (or loose derivation) standards, parts that satisfy best-explanation standards, parts that satisfy generalization standards (to be discussed in Chapter 10), and parts that satisfy value-judging standards (to be discussed in Chapter 11). In Arlene's trial, the conclusion that she killed Al is a best-explanation conclusion. But the conclusion that she committed voluntary manslaughter follows necessarily from the satisfaction of the four conditions for voluntary manslaughter. The full set of conditions for voluntary manslaughter appeared as Example 7:1 in Chapter 7. If you have not seen these conditions, please go back and look at them now.

The first of these conditions, roughly speaking, is that she killed Al. This is a best-explanation conclusion (the prosecutor's argument for which was presented in Chapter 2). The conclusion that she was not justified in using the force she used (the fourth condition) is a value conclusion. The second and third conditions, which I have neglected here for simplicity's sake, call for best-explanation and value judging arguments. So the overall argument for her guilt under the voluntary manslaughter charge used at least three different kinds of inference: best-explanation inference, value-judging inference, and deductive inference. The deductive inference is from the satisfaction of the four conditions to the conclusion that she is guilty.

Not Necessarily

One frequently heard type of response to an argument is "Not necessarily" or "That doesn't necessarily follow." This is sometimes a misleading move in discussion, so beware.

Usually, the conclusion of an argument in real life does not necessarily follow, so the complaint, "Not necessarily" is usually correct, though sometimes misleading. But the danger is that these words will be applied to a good best-explanation argument, or some other kind of good nonnecessary argument, and we will think that somehow the argument has been shown to be a bad one.

For example, one of the jurors pointed out that the conclusion that Arlene killed Al did not necessarily follow from the evidence. Literally, this was correct, though misleading. That is, it was misleading if we then thought that the prosecutor's argument was a bad argument.

The requirement that a conclusion must follow necessarily is often the wrong criterion to apply, even in court cases where someone's life and freedom are at stake. There the criterion is *proof beyond a reasonable doubt,* an appropriate criterion, but not as strict as the criterion *necessarily following.* The prosecutor did prove beyond a reasonable doubt that Arlene killed Al, although this conclusion did not follow necessarily from the evidence.

Sometimes when people say "Not necessarily," they mean to be saying that the argument is not a strong one, and do not really mean only "Not necessarily." On the other hand, sometimes they mean the words literally. The thing to do, if possible, is to find out which is meant and to deal with the charge in terms of what is meant (the *C* of *FRISCO*).

If a person means the words literally and applies the charge to a best-explanation argument, one appropriate kind of response is, "That's right, but I didn't say that the conclusion followed necessarily." A more aggressive response would be, "That's right, but so what?"

Not necessarily is sometimes an unfair attack on an argument. Be ready for it.

Summary

Any argument can be transformed into a deductively valid argument by the addition of one or more appropriate reasons in the role of assumptions, but often the result is a bad argument because one or more of the added reasons are false. Best-explanation inference is often a good alternative when the conclusion is a factual rather than a value conclusion, that is, a conclusion that could account for facts.

A reasonable strategy for evaluating an argument is first to check to see whether it satisfies deductive standards and its reasons are true. If so, then accept it and the conclusion. If not, then apply inductive standards (best-explanation standards, which are discussed in this and the previous chapter, or generalization standards, which are discussed in Chapter 10), or value-judging standards (which are discussed in Chapter 11), or loose derivation standards (which are discussed in Chapter 7). Do not reject an argument until you have given it a fair chance. Many arguments are strong arguments, even though the conclusion does not necessarily follow from the reasons given.

Often an argument has different parts, calling for different standards for different parts. But the total argument is no stronger than its weakest necessary link.

Sometimes *not necessarily* is a deceptive way to condemn an argument's conclusion. Be clear what this phrase means in its context before judging whether it holds in that situation.

Check-Up 9B

True or False?
If false, change it to make it true. Try to do so in a way that shows that you understand.

9:35 The conclusion that Arlene killed Al does not necessarily follow from the evidence cited by the prosecutor.

9:36 Any argument can be transformed into a deductively valid one by the addition of one or more premises.

9:37 Some arguments are strongest when viewed as best-explanation arguments.

9:38 If the conclusion of an argument does not follow necessarily from the evidence, the argument is a bad argument.

9:39 Arguments that include both deductive and best-explanation elements are likely to be unsatisfactory because there is no way to judge them.

Medium Answer
The point of the following items is to illustrate the fact that construing an argument to be a deductive argument often results in your adding a reason that is quite implausible. The desirability of construing many arguments as best-explanation arguments is thus exemplified.

9:40–9:46 For each of Items 9:6–9:12:

    a. Invent one or more reasons that would transform the argument in support of the conclusion into a deductively valid argument. (This is like the simplified assumption identification you did in Chapter 7.)

    b. Tell whether you think that the deductively valid argument you have created is a good one and why.

Do this on a separate piece of paper. The first is done as an example:

9:40 (9:6)   **a.** If a person strikes a blow of moderate force, then that person does not intend to hurt the other severely.

    b. No, because the premise I added is very implausible. I might be very weak and strike a moderate blow, even though I intend to hurt someone severely. Also, I might strike a moderate blow in what I know to be a vulnerable place, intending to hurt someone severely.

+ Causation

Much, if not all, best-explanation reasoning involves causal relations. But because causation is a difficult and controversial topic, I have left it to the end of this two-chapter sequence on experimenting and best-explanation reasoning. Because causal reasoning fits the pattern of best-explanation reasoning, some of the ideas here have been presented earlier, but here the emphasis is on causal relations.

Because this section on causation is more theoretical than other parts of the book, the reader in a hurry might justifiably choose to omit it. But for dealing in depth with causal issues in many areas, this section can be useful.

A Distinction Between Singular Causal Statements and Causal Generalizations

When the pathologist asserted, "The stabbing caused Al's death," she was making a *singular causal statement*. To make a singular causal statement is to say that one particular thing (or set of things) caused another particular thing (or set of things). A singular causal statement is about one sequence. Although it might be a very complex sequence, it is only one sequence. The stabbing-death sequence was one sequence.

On the other hand, the statement, "Stabbing causes people to die" is a *causal generalization*. It is about an unlimited number of sequences of stabbing and dying, not just one.

Causal Generalizations

Here are some more examples of causal generalizations:

> Smoking causes cancer.
> Drinking causes accidents.
> Blowing a whistle causes people to quiet down.
> Lifting one's foot off the gas pedal causes the car to slow down.

Because these causal generalizations cover an unlimited number of possible sequences, they inevitably cover more than their evidence.

Vagueness

Furthermore, the proportion of positive instances in such generalizations is often vague. That is, they do not state even roughly a proportion of positive instances. For example, is smoking alleged to cause cancer occasionally, sometimes, often, usually, or always? The generalization does not say.

Because causal generalizations are vague in their ordinary bare form ("*X* causes *Y*" or "*X*s cause *Y*s"), a first step in deciding whether to believe them (and in formulating them in your own mind) is to clarify their meaning (the *C* in *FRISCO*). The clarification has two features: realizing that the phrase *under standard conditions* (or some such phrase) is always implicitly there, and determining what degree-of-universality qualification belongs in the generalization.

Here are examples of terms to indicate degree of universality: *always, almost always, usually, frequently, sometimes,* and *can cause.* When I say that drinking causes accidents, I do not mean that drinking always causes accidents, or merely that drinking can cause accidents. I think that drinking *sometimes* causes accidents (under standard conditions). When I say that blowing a whistle causes people to quiet down, I have in mind the idea that blowing a whistle *usually* causes people to quiet down (under standard conditions). When I say that lifting one's foot off the gas pedal causes the car to slow down, I mean that lifting one's foot off the gas pedal (under standard conditions) *always* causes the car to slow down. I realize that many degree-of-universality qualifications are vague, as is the phrase *standard conditions,* but causal generalizations are generally vague propositions.

Because of their inherent vagueness and generally unspecified degree of universality, causal generalizations require special care. We must keep in mind the standard-conditions qualifier and make sure that the degree of universality is clear enough for the situation. If the throttle spring breaks, then lifting one's foot off the gas pedal does not cause the car to slow down, but this does not show the generalization to be wrong. The conditions were not standard. What would show the generalization to be wrong would be repeated cases in which the car was functioning properly and conditions were otherwise standard, but lifting one's foot off the gas pedal did not cause a slowing of the car.

Suppose this happens going downhill in extremely hilly places in San Francisco. I would not treat these occurrences as counterexamples because for me and the people to whom I have imagined myself saying this (living in flat central Illinois), the steep hills of San Francisco are not standard. The concept *standard,* vague as it may be, is also situation-dependent.

If all the world were hilly like San Francisco, then the appropriate causal generalization might well be, "Lifting your foot off the gas pedal (under standard conditions) often causes the car to slow down." Or, if the situation called for explicit attention to the downhill factor, we might add another qualifier making hilly places an explicit exception to the original: "Lifting your foot off the gas pedal (under standard conditions) always causes the car to slow down, except when going down steep hills."

Thus, causal generalizations have a usually unstated and inevitably somewhat vague standard-conditions qualifier that depends on the situation, and also often have a vagueness (about their degree of universality) that can be clarified to some extent and that also depends on the situation. We must keep these ideas in mind when we develop causal generalizations, develop and evaluate arguments for and against causal generalizations, and try to apply these generalizations to new cases. We should also keep in mind the particulars of the situation (the *S* in *FRISCO*).

Causing, or Bringing About

Consider my general causal hypothesis about this book (discussed in Chapter 8): "Taking a course in critical thinking, using this book, tends to improve the critical thinking ability of students." Although I did not there use the word *cause,* the hypothesis is to my ear a causal hypothesis, restatable as follows: "A course in critical thinking, using this book, tends to cause improvement in the critical thinking ability of students." This should be understood to include the qualifier *under standard conditions* and obviously incorporates the somewhat vague term *tends to,* which to me means *more often than not* but certainly not *always* or *almost always.*"

If this proposed restatement of the hypothesis, using the word *cause,* seems to you to be an acceptable restatement, then you probably join me in thinking that causation is not necessarily mechanical. If the restatement bothers you on the ground that it makes the connection too mechanical, then you should probably substitute the phrase *bring about* for the word *cause* in this and many other places in this chapter. To my ear, *to cause* means the same as *to bring about,* so *bringing about* is—in neutral terms—the topic I intend to discuss here.

But what sort of evidence can support a general causal hypothesis? A number of types of evidence can be relevant, but often no single type is conclusive.

Instances of the Generalization

Strong support for a *can-cause* generalization about this book would be one case in which the following singular causal statement is well-established: "This critical thinking course, using this book, caused an improvement in the critical thinking ability of the students in this situation." (In Chapter 8, you read about strategy and problems in experimentally establishing such a singular causal statement.) More instances would establish a *can-cause* generalization even more firmly, perhaps justifying a *sometimes,* or even a *frequently* generalization.

Representativeness

The instances would have to be representative, or reasonably believed to be representative, of the group, area, or situation implicitly or explicitly referred to in order to make a more universal type of generalization, such as a *usually* or *tends to* generalization. A number of representative instances of an *X* having caused a *Y* supports a causal generalization that corresponds to the proportion of instances that are positive. That is, a group of eight out of ten positive representative instances supports the generalization of the form "*X*s tend to cause *Y*s." For example, suppose that in eight out of ten fairly representative situations, a shift to smaller classes from fifty students down to fifteen resulted in greater learning of critical thinking in the experimental than the control group. But in two, it did not. Then we could probably conclude that reducing class size from fifty to fifteen tends to improve learning of critical thinking. But to do this, it is crucial that the instances be representative of the sort of situation implicitly or explicitly referred to.

Support from Repeated Association

In some areas (such as that of the critical thinking book and course), it is difficult to establish with full confidence any individual singular causal claim (including the one I have been talking about). We cannot then build a generalization on a representative set of separately well-established singular causal claims because there are none. But a generalization can still get some support from a repeated association of the independent and dependent variables, such as the repeated association of the use of this text with improvement in critical thinking among students. But such evidence is by no means sufficient because there might be another explanation of the results. For example, in all these instances, the students might have come to the course with the strong intention to learn to think critically and have learned to do so despite the use of this book. Alternatively, the students might just have grown more mature or learned to think critically in their other courses or experiences. Repeated association is interesting, but dangerous to use by itself. The falling of a barometer and the later appearance of a storm is an example of a repeated association in which neither event causes the other.

An important feature of repeated association, if it is to be evidence, is that a cause must precede (or be concurrent with) its effect. A cause cannot occur after its effect.

Deliberate Intervention

The value of repeated association can be strengthened by the independent variable's having been introduced on purpose by someone. For example, my friend's deliberately turning the key a number of times when the motor is running, which is immediately followed by a loud noise, gives support for the generalization "Turning the key when the motor is running causes a loud noise" because there would seem to be no other plausible explanation of both the deliberate turning of the key and the loud noise that immediately followed every time. Similarly, support by the repeated association of the use of this book and improvement in critical thinking would be buttressed by an experimenter's having repeatedly introduced the book to half of a group of students who were not particularly interested in learning to think critically and having found that the ones who used the book thought more critically than the others. This support comes from the difficulty in coming up with alternative hypotheses to explain the results.

This deliberate intervention consideration is one of the chief reasons to support the use of experimentation over opportunistic data-gathering. Of course, there are disadvantages as well. Experimenters often disrupt the natural flow of things, so that the results do not fit the world as it really is.

The evidence need not come from the *addition* of a factor. If the first variable is deliberately *reduced* or *excluded* by the investigator, and if the relation between the two variables makes sense, then an ensuing reduction or elimination of the other gives good support for the causal generalization. This is the sort of reasoning used in connecting the eating of cholesterol with cholesterol coating in the arteries (which in turn is, at the time of writing, believed to cause heart attacks). Investigators reduced the level of eating cholesterol, found that it was followed by an average reduction in or elimination of the cholesterol coating of the arteries, and concluded that the first reduction caused the second reduction.

The Causal Chain

It is also important that the causal connecting path (or causal chain) between the independent variable and the dependent variable make sense (to satisfy the criterion that the hypothesis be plausible). Our knowing the causal chain from taking one's foot off the gas pedal through the closing of the flutter valve through the reduction of air and gasoline going into the engine to the slowing of the engine makes more plausible the causal generalization connecting the two ends of the chain. In the case of reducing the class size of a critical thinking course, on the basis of my teaching experience, I think that this causal-chain condition is satisfied. Reducing class size generally results in more discussion by each person, consequently more practice with examples. It also generally results in more individual attention by the instructor and more interaction between the instructor and student. These things in turn plausibly result in more learning of critical thinking.

Similarly, the causal generalization that drinking causes accidents is supported by the existence of a plausible causal chain from drinking through lengthened reaction time, less sharpness in judgment, and reduction of carefulness to the occurrence of accidents. Our understanding a plausible causal chain helps to justify our drawing conclusions relating causes to effects. If we cannot understand the causal chain, one must wonder whether the alleged causal relationship is possible.

But our knowing the causal chain is not absolutely necessary for us to be justified in inferring a causal generalization. The generalization that my friend drew, "Turning the key when the motor is running causes a loud noise," was justified by the repeated association and deliberate introduction of the independent variable. These things appeared to rule out any alternative explanation of the phenomena. My friend did not know anything about the causal chain. But still, the generalization is better established by being buttressed by knowledge of a reasonable causal chain connecting the turning of the key (while the motor is running) to a loud noise.

Support from Broader Causal Generalizations

A sixth kind of support comes from broader causal generalizations and laws. For example, the broader generalization "Reducing the air and fuel supply of a gasoline engine causes the engine to slow down" is support, given some reasonable assumptions, for the more narrow causal generalization "Lifting your foot off the gas pedal causes the car to slow down." Causal generalizations, then, can often be derived from broader and more basic causal generalizations.

Support from Being Asserted by a Credible Source

A seventh kind of support for a causal generalization can come from its being stated by a credible source (see Chapter 3). Our beliefs in many of our causal generalizations are justified in this way. For example, my believing that malaria is caused by an organism transmitted by the anopheles mosquito is justified primarily on the basis of its having come from credible sources. I have done no independent investigation of this generalization, and am not familiar with any evidence in its support, though there no doubt is much evidence.

Summary

So there are at least seven basic types of support for causal generalizations: the existence of a singular-causal instance of the generalization, the instance's being representative, there being a number of instances of association between the independent and dependent variables (the effect's not having occurred before the cause in each of these associations), the independent variable's having been deliberately introduced, an understanding of an intervening causal chain, the causal generalization being derivable from broader causal generalizations and laws (given reasonable assumptions), and their assertion by credible sources. These types of support rely on appeal to the four basic criteria for hypothesis testing that were introduced in Chapter 8 and extended to nonexperimental hypotheses in this chapter. This reliance holds even for support by showing a source to be credible (how else to explain the assertion by a credible source?). Credibility also counts independently of this reliance.

Singular Causal Statements

Singular causal statements are of the form "The X caused the Y" or something convertible into that form, such as "The X was the cause of the Y." Here are some examples:

> The stabbing caused Al's death.
>
> She performed the acts that caused his death.
>
> The disappearance of the baboons was caused by the approach of the lions.
>
> The faulty maintenance procedures were the cause of the crash.
>
> Her pointed reply caused a ripple of laughter.

Singular causal statements are in the past tense and are about one sequence. They do not explicitly go beyond the evidence; that is, they do not explicitly assert something about unstudied cases. For example, the first of my examples does not explicitly assert anything about the likelihood of death for the next person who is stabbed. It seems reasonable to think that there are some causal generalizations or law(s) underlying this singular causal statement, but the singular statement itself does not tell us what these are.

Singular causal statements are governed by the criteria for best-explanation reasoning. The conclusion that Arlene's stabbing of Al caused his death is the best explanation of the fact that he died. No plausible alternative explanations survived the scrutiny of the detectives and the pathologist. (A more complete argument for this conclusion was given in Chapter 2 as a selection from the prosecutor's summary remarks.)

Post Hoc Reasoning

Although a cause must occur before (or simultaneously with) its effect, a common error is to think that merely because one thing followed another (perhaps dramatically), the first caused the second. To reason this way, as pointed out in Chapter 8, is called *post hoc reasoning,* which is fallacious. For example, at a football game, Martin said that he hoped that the home team would lose. Immediately thereafter, the visiting team scored a touchdown. The scoring of the touchdown was caused by Martin's hoping for the loss, according to his friend. If the conclusion was based *only* on the fact that the touchdown immediately followed the expression of hope, then the reasoning was post hoc reasoning—and fallacious.

The relation might have been coincidental. Alternatively, it might be that both events were caused by something else, perhaps the coach's harsh words to the home team's quarterback, which Martin overheard. The harsh words might have caused Martin to hope that the team would lose, just to show the coach, and the harsh words might also have so upset the members of the home team that they allowed the touchdown. But in neither the coincidence situation nor the common cause situation is it correct to say that Martin's hoping the team would lose caused the touchdown.

Partial Causes and Conditions

There is always a large number of conditions that work together to produce an effect. Often we select one of these conditions and call it *the* cause or a *partial* cause. Making the distinction among the cause, a partial cause, and a condition depends on our interests and the practical situation. In the trial, the single most important factor in the death of the victim was the intentional stabbing, so it was selected, even though there were a number of other conditions that were important, such as Al's not wearing a thick leather studded jacket and the sharpness of the knife. Sometimes, because we think that more than one condition was significant, we call them partial causes, referring to each as *a* cause, rather than *the* cause. If, for example, Al had been warned to be wary of Arlene and to wear his leather studded jacket and his chain vest whenever he was with her, then we might have said that his failure to do so was a (partial) cause of his death and that the stabbing was only another (partial) cause.

How do you tell whether to call something a condition, a partial cause, or the cause? There is no easy straightforward answer to this question, but having been an abnormal occurrence (a stabbing is abnormal), a deviation from what should have been done (the stabbing was that), a deliberate human action (the stabbing was that, too), or a necessary condition given the other conditions (the stabbing was also that), argue for judging something to be a cause rather than a condition.[5]

The last-mentioned consideration (having been a necessary condition in the circumstances) is used in the *but-for* test in the law. Applied to the stabbing, it goes like this: "**But for** the stabbing, Al would not have died. So the stabbing was a cause." Unfortunately, this test does not yield certain identification of a cause. About the birth of Al, we could truly say, "But for his birth, he would not have died." Yet his birth is not considered to be a cause of his death. Furthermore, the *but-for* test does not always even give us a necessary condition for something's being a cause because

---

5. For discussions of these criteria, see Jonathan Bennett, "Event Causation: The Counterfactual Analysis," in James E. Tomberlin (ed.), *Philosophical Perspectives 1: Metaphysics* (Atascadero, CA: Ridgeview, 1987); John L. Earman, "J. L. Mackie, The Cement of the Universe," *The Philosophical Review, 85,* 1976, 390–394; Robert H. Ennis, "Mackie's Singular Causality and Linked Overdetermination," *PSA 1982,* Vol. 1 (East Lansing, MI: Philosophy of Science Association, 1982); H.L.A. Hart and A. M. Honore, *Causation in the Law* (Oxford: Clarendon Press, 1959); David Lewis, "Counterfactual Dependence and Time's Arrow," *Nous, 13,* 1979, 455–476; J. L. Mackie, *The Cement of the Universe* (Oxford: Clarendon Press, 1974); and Michael Scriven, "Causes, Connections, and Conditions in History," in William H. Dray (ed.), *Philosophical Analysis and History* (New York: Harper & Row, 1966), 238–264.

the effect might have been overdetermined in a way such that the nonoccurrence of the cause might have brought about something that led to the effect. To use an example suggested by Michael Scriven, the failure of a dike up the river caused the flood in the town. But had the dike been reinforced to the point where it did not fail, the surge of water would have gone past the dike at that point and broken a different dike at a point nearer the town, and the town would have flooded anyway. So the breaking of the dike was not even a necessary condition, even though it caused the flooding. Much more can be said about this and similar examples,[6] but for present purposes, that should be enough.

If one condition is sufficiently more important than the others, given the situation and our purposes, then it might well be picked out as the cause. Importance, given the situation and purpose, was in the background for the headline in my local newspaper, "Pylon care, not design, caused the DC-10 crash." It is misleadingly tempting, once we realize that there are always a number of conditions involved in producing an effect, always to refuse to pick one out. But the stabbing was the cause of Al's death. We were justified in picking that one out, given the situation, and calling it *the* cause.

In sum then, deviation from normality, deviation from what should have been done, something's being a deliberate human action, and something's having been a necessary condition, are criteria to consider in selecting one or more causes from the set of conditions, and for deciding whether one is *the* cause, or only a partial cause. You must use your understanding of the situation and your good sense in applying these criteria. None is absolutely a necessary condition for something's being a cause (although the *but-for* condition—the necessary condition—usually holds); rather, they are criteria that can be applied with judgment in a given situation to develop or appraise a singular causal statement.

To apply these criteria to the case of Arlene's knife stroke having been the cause of Al's death: Stabbing people is a deviation from the normal way people relate to each other. Stabbing him was something that should not have been done (in the eyes of the jury). The stabbing was deliberate. He would not have died at that time had he not been stabbed. Therefore, the claim that Arlene's knife stroke caused his death satisfies at least the first, third, and fourth criteria—and, for the members of the jury, the second as well.

Elimination of Alternatives as a Strategy for Identifying the Cause

There is a basic strategy for identifying causes in cases in which we think we know all the plausible, or, better still, all the possible causes. It is to investigate and rule out as many as we can. If only one remains, then it is probably the cause. You will recognize this strategy as a primary troubleshooting and diagnosis strategy discussed at the end of the last chapter. The strategy works best if we know all the possible causes, and even then we should be cautious, often needing to add a qualifying term such as *probably* to a causal conclusion. This strategy was pursued by a fire chief, who said about a hotel fire, "I feel it's doubtful that a motor started it. If we eliminate that, we have

---

6. See the items in the previous footnote for a flavor of the discussion.

eliminated all accidental causes. That would leave the cause to someone starting it. That would be arson." The chief's way of including a qualifier was to use the word *would* and not definitely state that the cause was arson. This basic elimination strategy provides a straightforward application of the elimination-of-alternative hypotheses criterion in cases in which we are knowledgeable about all the plausible or possible causes of an occurrence.

When any one of the lights in my home becomes inoperative, I use a variation of this strategy. Ever since I have lived here, when any one of the lights has become inoperative, this has always been because a bulb was burned out, the switch was broken, a circuit breaker had opened, or the power was out. If a light ceases to function, its switch behaves the way it usually does (in sound and movement), and the other lights in the same circuit work (ruling out the circuit breaker's being open and the power's being out), then the best explanation is probably a burned-out light bulb. The most practical thing to do is to replace the light bulb without checking every possible alternative hypothesis (such as a break in the wires) because the replacement is so much easier and cheaper than running an exhaustive check of alternative hypotheses. If replacing the light bulb does not do the job, then a more careful check of the alternative hypotheses would be in order because the most likely one (the defective-bulb hypothesis) has strong evidence against it. This simplified strategy is all right in situations in which there is usually one type of cause, and in which being mistaken in the remedy does not cost much.

The point is that sometimes there are practical reasons not to bother to check out every plausible possible hypothesis. In this kind of case, the defective-light-bulb hypothesis is so often the right one (given standard switch behavior and the other lights' being on) that the reasonable thing to do is to act provisionally as if it were true. If light bulbs were extremely expensive and were ruined by being removed from a fixture, or if replacing them were expensive or time-consuming (or life-threatening, if not the cause, as might result from a mistaken medical diagnoses), then it might be wise to check out the alternative hypotheses before replacing the light bulb. But this is not the way it is in my situation. My light bulbs are easy to replace.

Sometimes the situation is even less complicated. When there is only one kind of thing that can cause the sort of effect that occurred, then when that sort of effect occurs, we know what sort of thing caused it. For example, if only extreme heat can cause steel to turn a specified color in a swirling pattern, then we have conclusive evidence that this instance of a piece of steel's having turned that color in that pattern was caused by extreme heat.

The Causal Chain

In drawing singular causal conclusions (even more than with causal generalization), it is desirable, and sometimes necessary, to understand the causal chain by which the cause brought about the effect. The pathologist's concluding that the knife stroke brought about Al's death required that the pathologist understand the way the death came about (that is, understand the causal chain from the stabbing effort to the penetration to the loss of blood to the loss of oxygen to the death). The conclusion that faulty pylon maintenance caused the crash of a DC-10 required a tracing of a causal chain like this one: from maintenance procedures to the cracked pylon, to the loss of the engine, to the loss of flaps, to the stall, to the crash.

On the other hand, understanding the causal chain is not always necessary. As I noted earlier, a friend does not understand the mechanism by which a dreadful noise is caused by his turning the key when the motor of his car is already running. But he still was right to conclude that his turning the key caused that noise the last time he did it. He has three sorts of evidence for this conclusion: One is that there were a series of occasions on which turning the key when the motor was going was immediately accompanied by a similar noise. The two kinds of events kept occurring together. Second, the noise was produced not according to any schedule, but always exactly when he turned the key when the motor was running. He can think of nothing that both would have caused him to turn the key and caused the noise (so there probably was no common cause). There seemed to be no other explanation of this otherwise incredible series of coincidences than that turning the key when the motor is running always causes a noise (under standard conditions). His singular causal conclusion is an instance of this causal generalization.

The third type of evidence concerns the last time he did it, which is what the singular causal conclusion is about. That time the noise occurred exactly when he turned the key, and nothing else notable happened at that time, as far as he could tell. So, given that turning the key when the motor is running can and always does (under standard conditions) cause a noise like the one he heard, and given that he could see nothing else occurring at the time, then he justifiably concluded that turning the key that time caused the noise he heard. He has a right to conclude this, even though he does not understand the mechanism connecting turning the key and the noise.

Note that this is not a case of the post hoc fallacy. There is much more evidence than the mere one-time successive occurrence of the two events.

Note also that a stronger case is needed for the singular causal conclusion if we do not understand the causal chain. A case is easier to make if we do understand the causal chain. The car noise evidence had to be much stronger without an understanding of the causal chain than would have been needed, if the chain had been understood.

I remind you of the significance of the strategy of having human beings deliberately *introduce* the factor that is suspected of being the cause. If we introduce that factor at will (and its occurrence is immediately followed by the effect), then it is often difficult to think of an explanation of the pair of occurrences other than that the thing that we did caused the other.

Gaps in the Causal Chain

Understanding the causal chain is relevant to causal conclusions in another way. If we know the only causal chain (or chains) by which an occurrence could have brought about an effect, then if there was a gap in that chain (or those chains), the occurrence was not the cause. In the hotel fire, it was determined that the Christmas tree lighting was not plugged in, so the electricity that was needed to produce the heat in a short circuit in the Christmas tree lighting was not available. So a short circuit in the Christmas tree lighting was ruled out. There was a gap in the causal chain.

Another way of ruling out something as the cause is to show that it did not occur or was not present. Showing that lit candles were not present in the room where the fire started would rule out lit candles as the cause.

Credible Sources

A frequently used method of establishing a singular causal statement is to show that it is believed by a credible source. The pathologist's testimony that the knife stroke caused Al's death was accepted as establishing that fact.

Summary and Comment

Although causation is a difficult and thorny topic, there are loose criteria that we can employ in drawing and judging causal conclusions. The criteria summarized below do not by themselves produce correct answers. Good judgment, background knowledge of the facts that serve as reasons (R) and counterreasons, and sensitivity to the situation (S) are required in applying the criteria. The basic criteria are those of best-explanation reasoning (I), with special attention to the question "Is there another plausible explanation?"

The criteria do provide guidance for your exercise of your judgment. However, it is not true, as some people suggest these days, that there is no way to tell whether one thing caused or causes another. Often we are unable to do so, but often we are able to do it. We do it all the time, and if we follow the guidelines, are often right. But the challenge that we cannot be sure whether one thing caused another is often appropriate in the hard cases, such as determining whether Napoleon died of arsenic poisoning, and determining what the president knew and intended at a given time.

Causal generalizations *explicitly* apply to cases that are not part of the evidence for them. But they must be understood implicitly to include the vague limitation *under standard conditions* and they often do not specify the rough proportion of the cases that are positive. However, this specification can be made with such terms as *always, almost always, usually, frequently, sometimes,* and *can cause.* When stating causal generalizations, we might well include such a qualifying term, and in deciding whether to believe one, we first need to determine its degree of universality.

Support for a causal generalization is based on its ability to satisfy the four general criteria for hypotheses. More specific support can be of at least seven types, which can be justified by appeal to these criteria, but which it is useful to list here. Do not memorize these. Just make sure that you can think of an example of each.

1. The existence of a singular-causal instance of the generalization.
2. The representativeness of the instance.
3. The existence of a set of instances in which cases of the supposed cause are associated with cases of the supposed effect, even though in no one case was it established that X caused Y. In each case, the effect must not come before the cause.
4. The investigator's having deliberately introduced the independent variable (which is the supposed cause).
5. The plausibility of the causal chain.

6. The derivability of the causal generalization from a set of one or more broader causal generalizations or laws.
7. The assertion of the causal generalization by a credible source.

Singular causal statements can be, but do not need to be, made on the basis of an experiment. Crucial questions are whether they explain the facts, and whether there is another plausible explanation of the facts. In other words, the four basic criteria for hypotheses also apply here. More specific support for singular causal statements is of at least seven types, which may be justified by appeal to the four general criteria, but which it is useful to discuss and list separately. Again, do not memorize these. Just make sure that you can provide an example of each.

1. Eliminating all but one of the set of plausible causes or, even better, all but one of a set of possible causes.
2. Being clear about the causal chain by which the supposed cause could have brought about the effect.
3. Making sure that the supposed cause occurred and that it did not occur after the effect.
4. Showing that the supposed cause is an instance of the only kind of thing that can cause an effect like the one that occurred.
5. Showing that one or more of these four rough criteria are satisfied: that the supposed cause was an abnormal occurrence, was wrong or inappropriate, was a deliberate human action, or was necessary in the circumstances (the *but-for* condition).
6. Showing that the singular causal statement is an instance of an established causal generalization.
7. Showing that the singular causal statement was made by a credible source for that statement.

Post hoc reasoning is that in which we draw a singular causal conclusion *merely* on the ground that the effect occurred after the supposed cause. Although such reasoning is fallacious, the fact that something notable occurred just before the effect can be part of a set of evidence that supports the singular causal statement that the notable thing was the cause.

Singular causal statements do not imply universal causal generalizations. Furthermore, proving a universal one false does not show that a singular one that can be derived from it is false. For example, showing that the use of the critical thinking book caused improvement in one case does not show that it always does or will. And showing that the use of the book does not always do it does not prove that it will not do it in some particular situation.

This discussion of causation was basically a development of useful guides to causal reasoning, based on the principles of best-explanation reasoning. These principles are useful for those who are wondering how to start making a causal investigation. To those who are understandably wary of drawing causal conclusions, the principles and discussion should also be useful reminders that we can and do justifiably draw causal conclusions in everyday reasoning. It is easy to go wrong in causal reasoning, but we can get it right too.

There is more to be said and learned about the concept *cause*. This is a beginning on which you can build your refinements.

Check-Up 9C

Classification

Label each of the following as *S, G,* or *N*, according to whether it is a singular causal statement, a causal generalization, or neither.

9:47 Exercise causes heart attacks.

9:48 Hugh's smoking caused his cancer.

9:49 John's drinking caused the accident.

9:50 My assumption that she was generous caused me no little grief.

9:51 Practice makes perfect.

9:52 Reading good books tends to improve one's writing.

9:53 The rains came and we became wet.

9:54 The stirring speech brought down the house.

True or False?

If false, change it to make it true. Try to do so in a way that shows that you understand.

9:55 Causes never come after their effects.

9:56 One way of supporting a causal generalization containing an implicit *always* is by establishing a representative set of positive instances of it, each instance being a singular causal statement; and by trying unsuccessfully to find negative instances of it.

9:57 One way of supporting a general causal statement is by showing that it was made by a credible source.

9:58 If one type of thing generally occurs immediately after another sort of thing, this establishes that the first sort of thing tends to cause the second sort of thing.

9:59 One way of supporting a general causal statement is by showing that it follows from a broader general causal statement or statements, together with a reasonable set of assumptions.

9:60 One way of supporting a singular causal statement is by showing that it satisfies the best-explanation criteria for reasoning.

9:61 One way of showing that a particular thing caused a given effect is to show that of the various things that could have caused that effect, it was the only one that occurred.

9:62 One way of showing that a particular thing caused a given effect is to show that the effect occurred immediately after the particular thing occurred.

9:63 Causal reasoning fits under the general pattern of best-explanation reasoning.

9:64 Often a sufficient reason for picking out a causal condition as the cause in a particular case is its being an abnormal occurrence, or its being something that should not have occurred, or its happening before the effect happened.

9:65 Causal generalizations must be interpreted implicitly to contain the phrase *under standard conditions.*

Longer Answer

9:66 Consider all the evidence presented in *a* through *g* in Item 9:29 about the hypothesis that being the first-born tends to cause one to be conservative with respect to one's immediate surroundings, whereas being later-born tends to cause one to revolt against the accepted views in one's surroundings. Because this hypothesis is a causal generalization, pay heed to the seven causal generalization criteria as well as the four general hypothesis-testing criteria. Check your writing from the point of view of FRISCO, paying particular attention to the clarity of key terms in the hypothesis you are evaluating (including *conservative* and *revolt against the accepted views in one's surroundings*).

9:67 Take all the evidence presented in *a* through *e* in Item 9:30 about the hypothesis that the fourteen whales died from "red tide." Write two or three paragraphs in which you discuss the overall adequacy of the evidence from the point of view of the four criteria for judging hypotheses and the seven more specific criteria for singular causal statements. Assume that your audience is like this class. Check your writing from the point of view of FRISCO.

9:68 Do the same for all the evidence presented in *a* through *j* in Item 9:32 in support of the hypothesis that the interchange of rocker arms is the cause of the recent sudden increase of premature wear in valve guides in certain types of aircraft engines. Assume that there are no engine mechanics in your audience. You will probably become aware of the close relationship between singular causal statements and causal generalizations in the area of aircraft engines, so feel free also to apply the criteria for causal generalizations, where relevant. Check your writing from the point of view of FRISCO.

9:69 Do the same for all the evidence presented in the prosecutor's summary speech in Chapter 2. Consider again the first proposition that had to be proven beyond a reasonable doubt, for either voluntary manslaughter or murder: that the defendant performed the acts that caused the death of the victim. This proposition is a singular causal statement. Again, take the four general hypothesis-testing criteria into account as well as the more specific ones for singular causal statements. Check your writing from the point of view of FRISCO.

9:70 In about two pages, recount an investigation that you have performed that resulted in your drawing a general causal conclusion. Be sure to state the conclusion clearly (including a degree-of-universality term such as *usually*). Also, state whether and how your reasons for believing your causal generalization satisfy the general criteria for hypothesis testing, as well as the more specific criteria for general causal statements. Check your writing from the point of view of FRISCO.

9:71 Do the same for a singular causal conclusion you have drawn, paying attention to the general criteria for hypothesis testing as well as the more specific criteria for singular causal statements. Do not forget FRISCO.

9:72 Find a description of a causal investigation in a book, newspaper, magazine, etc., and supply a copy. Apply the FRISCO approach to it and report your results. Be sure to make it clear that you know whether the conclusion is a singular or general causal statement even if, in the case you pick, the distinction is not especially important. Also, pay heed to the general criteria for hypothesis testing and more specific criteria for causal statements.

Best-Explanation and Causal Reasoning in Position Papers and Other Argumentative Writings

In much argumentative writing, we use best-explanation and causal reasoning. Often our final conclusion is itself a best-explanation conclusion, as in the historian's written argument to support the conclusion that Napoleon died of arsenic poisoning. But often the final conclusion itself is not a best explanation or causal conclusion. Instead, some best-explanation or causal conclusions are intermediate conclusions offered in support of a final conclusion reached by some other type of reasoning.

One such example of writing that you have seen (in two different places in this book) is Bradley's argument that Iago is not a melodramatic villain, at least as I have construed his argument. Earlier in this chapter, you saw some best-explanation reasoning supporting the conclusion that Emilia did not suspect Iago of villainy. This conclusion was an intermediate conclusion in a larger argument, for it served as a reason in a deductive argument (presented in Chapter 7) leading to the final conclusion that Iago was not a melodramatic villain. This final conclusion is not a best-explanation conclusion, but was supported by a best-explanation conclusion. Furthermore, the final conclusion that Iago was not a melodramatic villain could itself become an intermediate conclusion used to support a value conclusion, "A person playing Iago should appear and act quite normally in front of almost everyone in the play." (Incidentally, this conclusion is not just a trivial addition in all situations. Some performers and directors might want to do things differently, playing Iago to look like a melodramatic villain to defy what is now tradition. Alternatively, some budding actors might not know what a melodramatic villain would be like and might not realize that melodramatic villains do not appear and act quite normally.)

It is common for arguments leading to value conclusions (such as "We should not use DDT to kill insects") to make use of intermediate best-explanation conclusions (such as "DDT weakens birds' egg shells"). The conclusion that DDT weakens birds' egg shells is a causal conclusion (*weakens* being a causal word, if one construes *causal* broadly, as I do), or at least a best-explanation conclusion, that serves as a reason for the value conclusion. Most value arguments have one or more of this type of reason in support of their conclusions. These reasons should be defensible. The defense can be testimony from a credible source (discussed in Chapter 3), a best-explanation argument (discussed in this and the previous chapters), or a combination.

General Writing Strategy

Sometimes the reasons in your argument are basic assumptions that you feel that you can expect your audience to accept. Alternatively, they might be observations you have made, testimony from others, or conclusions you have drawn in previous arguments. In any case, be aware of them and the sort of defense, if any, that you have for them. If you have no defense for one, be honest about it and note that your argument does depend on it.

In the course of your argument, keep in mind the situation and the point of view of the audience, that is, the person or people for whom you are writing. Your selection of reasons to elaborate and defend, and your selection of assumptions that you need not defend, depend in part on your audience. In presenting your argument, you are trying not only to make a good case, but to address their concerns. If your audience already accepts something as obvious, it is usually a waste of their and your time to prove it to them (although you might do so in order to point out to them that some of their beliefs do need to be defended). Continually ask yourself, "Will this make sense and be helpful to my audience?"

For the best-explanation parts of the argument, bring forward alternative explanations that have occurred to you, or that have been advanced by others. Deal with these honestly, noting their weaknesses and strengths. Indicate your reasons for rejecting them, if you do. Note any that still have plausibility. If there are challenges to your evidence, note them and deal with them. If any are plausible, make that clear.

When you write a position paper that combines a variety of types of argument or consists of several parts, you must figure out some reasonable and comprehensible order in which to put the parts. In the simplest and most direct form when writing arguments of a page or more, you start out by introducing the situation and your final conclusion, probably also summarizing the total argument. You end the position paper with a restatement of your final conclusion, alluding to the parts of your argument. I recommend this simple direct form when writing for readers in a hurry, and usually when the writing is being done by people who are not expert writers.

For filling in the arguments in between, or for short arguments, there are two major direct strategies, with many variations, which I shall discuss first. I call them *bottom-up* and *top-down* strategies. As you read about these strategies, think of some particular position paper or essay that you have written or are planning to write, and consider the extent to which it exemplifies these strategies.

Bottom-Up Strategy

A first strategy is to build your argument by starting with the basic reasons, the sort of things that appeared at the bottom of your diagrams in Chapter 2. (I suggest that you turn back now to the suggested diagrammed answers at the end of Chapter 2, if you are not visualizing the point.) On these basic reasons, you build one or more intermediate conclusions, one at a time. Then you put together the intermediate conclusions to develop the argument that rests on them, claiming no greater strength for your argument than it deserves. Items 2:51 (male sensitivity), 2:52 (female confidence) and 2:67 (SAT scores) in Chapter 2 exemplify a bottom-up strategy (reasons first, then conclusion).

Top-Down Strategy

The opposite of the bottom-up strategy is the top-down strategy, in which you start by giving your final conclusion, then your reasons, indicating somehow that you intend to defend its reasons (or if it is necessarily a short paper, that your reasons could be defended). Then you proceed to defend the reasons, each with an argument to support it. Bradley's argument to the conclusion that Emilia never suspected Iago of villainy (Example 9:3 in this chapter) exemplifies a simplified top-down strategy, as does Item 2:66 (research using animals) in Chapter 2 (conclusion first, then reasons).

Combination Strategies

As you might guess, there are various possible combinations of these two basic strategies. Examples 2:61 (schools' function) and 2:68 (conflict of interest) in Chapter 2 exemplify a combination of the two strategies (reasons, conclusion, more reasons). The prosecutor's speech in Chapter 2 exemplifies a different combination strategy that is appropriate for longer arguments (final conclusion, a series of arguments leading to intermediate conclusions, final conclusion repeated).

Indirect Strategies

Some situations call for one of a variety of indirect strategies. For example, sometimes you might not explicitly state the conclusion, as in Items 2:62 (homework) and 2:65 (street lights) in Chapter 2. Leaving your conclusion unstated sometimes makes the writing more interesting. Sometimes the writing becomes more effective, because the reader has to infer or construct the conclusion and then feels that the conclusion is his or her own conclusion. Sometimes such writing is more discreet because in the situation, the reader would feel affronted by your forwardness in a direct aggressive statement of the conclusion. This latter situation is common in cultures where people are expected not to thrust themselves forward.

A major danger in not stating your conclusion is that your audience will not figure out your conclusion—or, more seriously, will misread you and hold you responsible for a view you do not hold. An occasional danger is that an audience in a hurry will just not want to take the time to figure it out. Perhaps the audience should be willing to take the time, but many do not. Furthermore, often they are not expert enough to draw the appropriate conclusion, and need help.

Not stating the conclusion can be a deceptive technique. It is a way of avoiding responsibility for a conclusion that you want to draw, but really cannot defend very well. Then you can always say, "I never said that!" On the other hand, if the conclusion is justified, but you would get in trouble from narrow-minded readers for asserting it, it can be useful to avoid stating it—just to keep out of trouble, which under some regimes can be serious: possibly prison, execution, or torture.

Another indirect strategy is to talk around the issue, sometimes introducing irrelevant material (that is, material of interest and on the topic, but that is not supportive of the conclusion or its denial, and that does not help to show the significance of the conclusion). Such material can increase interest and, like avoiding stating the conclusion, can help avoid the charge that the writer is thrusting himself or herself forward by presuming to suggest what is relevant and what is irrelevant.

Talking around the issue can serve these purposes well. But the dangers are that some readers will miss the argument and will lose patience with the extra time required. For other readers, these are not problems.

Summary

You must choose your strategy after analyzing the situation, including your audience. Be ready to alter your strategy, depending on its reception by the audience. In any case, be aware of your own and your audience's probable assumptions. Make sure that your own are made clear and that theirs are addressed. Note and deal with alternative hypotheses and possible challenges to your evidence, as above. Be sure to claim no greater (or less) strength for your argument than it deserves.

The most straightforward position paper writing strategy is to present your conclusion, discuss its significance and your argument plan, offer your reasons, consider counterarguments, and summarize. Other strategies have advantages and disadvantages, the most common of which is failure to communicate your point.

Check-Up 9D

9:73–9:79 Reread and revise each of Items 9:66–9:72 in light of the advice given in this last section about writing involving hypothesis formulation and judgment. Make sure that you have a thesis, which might be the hypothesis, might be that the hypothesis is probably false, might be that there is insufficient evidence to establish or refute the hypothesis, etc. Make sure that you are aware of your organization plan and that you are aware of the role of each sentence in your paper. Be ready to read the result to the class as a prelude to discussion of the issue.

Suggested Answers for Chapter 9

Check-Up 9A

9:1 T   9:2 F   9:3 T   9:4 F   9:5 T

9:2 Change *proves it true* to *helps to support it*.

9:4 Change *does not weaken* to *severely weakens*.

9:6 <u>Arlene did not intend to hurt him severely.</u> That explains why <EF> the blow was of moderate force.

9:7   <EF> Sandra did not flinch when I told her that Karl was out with Martine last night. That's why I think she knows already.

9:8   What is the problem? I'll tell you. The fuel filter is clogged with dirt. That explains why <EF> the car will not run.

9:9   George Orwell's intention in 1984 was to persuade the British that totalitarianism is bad. That explains why <EF> he depicted so many things that are offensive to the British people.

9:10   <EF> When I turn the key to my car, there is no sound. <EF> When I flip on the light switch, there is no light. <EF> When I turn on the radio, there is no sound or light. You might suspect that <AH> the battery connections are unhooked, but they are not. <IE> I looked. The car battery must be dead.

9:11   "I see that you have been to the cemetery," said the detective. <EF> "You have mud on your shoes that is the color of the mud at the cemetery. <EF> You are perspiring. <EF> You look upset. And <EF & IE> you have a hint of a sunburn. If <AH> you had gone to the movies [end of AH], the sunburn you have would not be there.

9:12   Deliberately omitted.

9:13 (9:6)   A possible alternative hypothesis is suggested with the item.

9:14 (9:7)   Sandra no longer cares for Karl.

9:15 (9:8)   The fuel line is bent so severely that it is closed.

9:16 (9:9)   George Orwell was just trying to make a good story with well-motivated characters.

9:17 (9:10) The wires behind the dashboard to the ignition, lights, and radio are loose or detached.

9:18 (9:11) It is a hot day and you have been searching unsuccessfully in the field for your dog. The mud in the field is the same color as the mud at the cemetery.

9:19 (9:12) Deliberately omitted from answers.

+ 9:20–9:26 You might well have come up with different responses:

9:20 (9:6, 9:13)   Possible answers are suggested with the item.

9:21 (9:7, 9:14)   Sandra told me this morning that she is in love with Karl. Assumption: Sandra was telling the truth.

9:22 (9:8, 9:15)   I inspected the fuel line and found it to have no sharp turns. Assumption: If a fuel line has no sharp turns, then it is not bent so severely that it is closed.

9:23 (9:9, 9:16)   Orwell said that he was not just trying to make a good story by depicting those consequences. Assumption: Orwell was telling the truth.

9:24 (9:10, 9:17) I inspected the wires behind the dashboard and found nothing loose or detached. Assumption: My inspection was thorough.

9:25 (9:11, 9:18) I could find no mud in the field that is the same color as the mud in the cemetery. Assumption: I looked everywhere in the field.

9:26 (9:12, 9:19) Deliberately omitted from the answers.

9:27–9:32 Varying judgments about these items are possible, depending on what else you assume about the situation and the facts. The important thing here is that you give a reasonable justification of the answer you choose. I shall give mine, but yours might reasonably differ.

9:27 **a.** Support, because the hypothesis' meteor would explain the exceptionally large amount of iridium in that layer.

b. Weaken, because this is an alternative explanation of the iridium.

c. Weaken, because this suggests an alternative explanation of the disappearance of the dinosaurs, and because the mammals' food supply would probably also have been shut off, thus providing evidence that is inconsistent with the hypothesis.

d. Strengthen, because this item provides a way that the dinosaurs could have been killed without the warm-blooded mammals also being killed. So the inconsistency just mentioned in *c* is resolved.

e. Weaken the specific 65-million-year hypothesis because the meteor is now placed at about 3,300 years ago. (But the occurrence of the meteor could still explain the destruction of the dinosaurs.)

9:28 **a.** Support, because the arsenic in his hair could be explained by the hypothesis.

b. Neither, because this is not inconsistent with the cancer hypothesis. He might also have had cancer.

c. Support, because the hypothesis could explain the symptoms.

d. Weaken, because (assuming the French historian to be a credible source who is not influenced by a conflict of interest) the historian's statement is in conflict with the hypothesis.

e. Support, because it helps to make the hypothesis plausible.

9:29 Deliberately omitted.

9:30 **a.** Support, because this evidence rules out an alternative hypothesis.

b. Support, because this evidence rules out an alternative hypothesis.

c. Weaken, because (assuming that whales have at least as much resistance as humans, and that the dosage is retained) this dosage is inconsistent with the hypothesis. If the hypothesis were true, we would expect a much stronger concentration.

d. Neither, because I cannot think of any fact explained by, or inconsistency suggested or resolved by, or plausibility affected by, this information.

e. Support, because this information suggests a way to resolve the inconsistency noted in *c*.

f. Support, because this information also suggests a way that the inconsistency in *c* could be resolved.

9:31 Deliberately omitted.

9:32 **a.** Support, because this information helps to provide a way that the hypothesis could explain the data, suggesting that the oil could have been sent to the wrong place.

b. Support, because this is more evidence that is explained by the hypothesis.

c. Weaken, because here is evidence that is not explainable by the hypothesis (and the hypothesis was the only explanation offered).

d. Weaken, because here is more evidence that is not explainable by the hypothesis.

e. Weaken, because this is an alternative hypothesis that could explain the evidence.

f. Strengthen, because this evidence is in conflict with the hypothesis suggested in *e*. (If the type of steel explains the defects, why were there good guides in those engines?)

g. Weaken, because this is a plausible alternative hypothesis.

h. Strengthen, because this evidence is in conflict with the alternative hypothesis mentioned in *g*. If this hypothesis were true, then the problems would have started to develop thirty years ago.

i. Strengthen, because this evidence is inconsistent with the alternative hypothesis mentioned in *g*. One might well expect the valve shaft size change to affect all engines (although it might not).

j. Weaken, because selective oil starvation might explain the worn guides.

9:33 and 9:34 These are up to you.

Check-Up 9B
9:35 T   **9:36** T   **9:37** T   **9:38** F   **9:39** F
9:38 Replace *is* with *might be*.
9:39 . . . can be satisfactory, although there are different ways to judge the elements.

9:40 (9:6) Answer suggested with item.

9:41 (9:7) **a.** If a person does not flinch when told that her boyfriend is out with another woman, then she knows already. Karl is Sandra's boyfriend.

b. No, Sandra might be accustomed to having Karl do that and has hardened herself. Alternately, she might not really care.

9:42 (9:8) **a.** Whenever the car will not run, the fuel filter is clogged with dirt.

b. No. There are many other possible causes of the car's not running.

9:43 (9:9) **a.** If an author depicts many things that are offensive to the people of a nation, that author is trying to persuade them that totalitarianism is bad.

b. No. Authors have many possible motives for depicting offensive things. They might simply want to be objecting to the offensive things, or might simply be trying to shock people in order to sell books.

9:44 (9:10)   **a.** If there is no sound when the key is turned, no light when the lights are turned on, no sound or light when the radio is turned on, and the battery connections are hooked, then the battery is dead.

  b. No. There might be a loose wire somewhere else.

9:45 (9:11)   **a.** If anyone has mud on her shoes the color of the mud at the cemetery, is perspiring, looks upset, and has a hint of a sunburn, then he or she has been to the cemetery.

  b. No, there are other ways to get the mud, to perspire, to be upset, and get a sunburn.

9:46 (9:12) Deliberately omitted.

Check-Up 9C

9:47 G	**9:48** S	**9:49** S	**9:50** S	**9:51** G	**9:52** G
9:53 N	**9:54** S	**9:55** T	**9:56** T	**9:57** T	**9:58** F
9:59 T	**9:60** T	**9:61** T	**9:62** F	**9:63** T	**9:64** F
9:65 T					

9:58 Change *establishes* to *by itself does not establish*.

9:62 Omit *One way of*; add *not sufficient* before *to show*.

9:64 Replace *happening before the effect happened* with *being a deliberate human action*.

9:66–9:72 Up to you. Make sure that you have stated your position clearly, and that you have considered all relevant criteria. Have you had FRISCO in mind when doing each of these?

Check-Up 9D

9:73–9:79 Again up to you. Make sure that you have stated your thesis clearly, even though the hypothesis you are considering might itself not be clear enough, that you have applied the relevant criteria, that you have had FRISCO in mind, and that your organization plan makes sense.

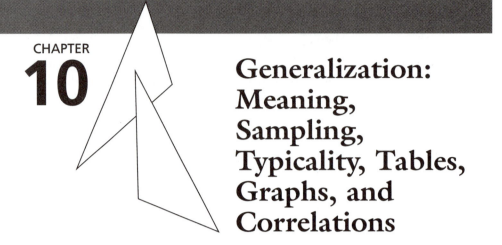

Generalization: Meaning, Sampling, Typicality, Tables, Graphs, and Correlations

Do you believe the following generalizations?

1. A person in trouble is more likely to get help from a group of witnesses to the person's problems than from a single individual.
2. Mental patients are usually not dangerous to other people.
3. The most successful women in what is still pretty much a man's world are most often those with older brothers.
4. Public opinion polls are often accurate within one or two percentage points.
5. Friendships are more likely to be formed between opposites than people who are similar to each other.
6. You are apt to forget more in the first few minutes after learning something than in the next several hours.

According to Gregory R. Kimble, author of *How to Use (and Misuse) Statistics,*[1] who was at the time the chair of the psychology department of Duke University, the odd-numbered generalizations are false and the even-numbered ones are true. On the basis of an application of the criteria for credibility, I am inclined to believe him, although there are a few problems with interpreting and applying this set of generalizations.

The ideas in this chapter should be of use not only in reading and evaluating others' ideas, but in your own writing. You will encounter ways of expressing various types of generalizations, ways of presenting them visually, and ways of justifying them.

Types of Generalizations

First, let us be clear about what generalizations are. A *generalization* is a statement about a number of cases. Generalizations can be categorized according to whether they go beyond the data on which they are based and according to their degree of

1. (Englewood Cliffs, NJ: Prentice Hall, 1978).

universality. Some best-explanation hypotheses are generalizations, but not all. Furthermore, not all generalizations are best-explanation hypotheses.[2] For example, the statement "A rising barometer is usually accompanied by improvements in the weather" is an example of a generalization that is not a best-explanation hypothesis. It does not account for the weather improvement last week (although it justified a prediction of probable improvement). Satisfying the criteria for best-explanation hypotheses (when they are relevant) can provide good support for generalizations, but in this chapter, I shall focus on other kinds of support.

Limited-to-the-Data and Inferred Generalizations

Limited-to-the-Data Generalizations

These cover only the cases that have been examined. Suppose that we examine the eye color of everyone in the room, counting the number of blue-eyed people and the total number of people, and find eight blue-eyed people out of twenty-two. The resulting generalization "Eight out of the twenty-two people here have blue eyes" is a limited-to-the-data generalization. It does not go beyond the data provided by our counting.

These generalizations appear to be the easiest to establish because they do not go beyond the data, generally requiring only counting. However, some difficulty often springs from the meaning of the terms involved, from bias by the investigator, or from the difficulty of securing access to countable things. For example, the generalization "All countries have social class structures (as opposed to being classless societies)" could be a limited-to-the-data generalization, but it might well suffer from all three of those problems. Deciding how to tell whether a country has a social class structure could be quite difficult. The investigator might well be biased, and access to information in many countries is difficult.

For an illustration of these difficulties in a different field, suppose we examine fifty mental patients and judge that only four are dangerous to other people. We might then state the generalization "Four of these fifty mental patients are dangerous to other people." This generalization does not go beyond our counting data, but there are still two standard problems. One problem is in determining what actually counts as evidence—in this case, of dangerousness in a patient. A second standard problem is in avoiding bias of the investigator—in this case, bias in determining whether a particular patient is dangerous. The problem of access might also be quite difficult, but in this case, I assumed that problem had been handled.

These three kinds of problems hold for inferred generalizations also, and must always be kept in mind. They come under at least the *C* and *S* in *FRISCO*, and inevitably the *I* as well.

Inferred Generalizations

For the rest of the chapter, I shall focus on *inferred generalizations*. They go beyond the data on which they are based by claiming that the characteristic holds for a larger group. As I interpret Kimble's generalizations, they are all inferred generalizations.

---

2. See Robert H. Ennis, "Enumerative Induction and Best Explanation," *The Journal of Philosophy, 65* (18), 1968, pp. 523–530.

For example, his generalization about mental patients applies to mental patients in general, not just to those studied.

Some inferred generalizations are about a population, each member of which could be identified and studied if we had time and resources, such as a generalization about all practicing physicians in Urbana, Illinois, based on a sample of those physicians. Other inferred generalizations are about limitless populations, not all of whose members could be identified and studied, such as all mental patients, some of whom are dead, some of whom are not yet patients of any kind, and some not yet even born. We cannot secure the much-desired random sample of them. (There is more about random samples in the next section.) Generalizations that apply to limitless populations are theoretically the most difficult to evaluate because the nature of the population in the studied cases might be significantly different from the population in the cases we cannot study, rendering the generalization inapplicable. All of Kimble's generalizations apply to limitless populations.

Degree of Universality

Universal generalizations hold that every member of the class being considered has the stated characteristic. They have the form "All *A*'s are *B*'s." Here are three examples:

1. All of the people in this room are adults.
2. Every action has an equal and opposite reaction.
3. Societies always develop class systems, even when organized with the goal of being classless.

The first of these universal generalizations is also a limited-to-the-data generalization because I looked at everyone in the universe that was mentioned (people in the room) and found only adults. The other two are universal inferred generalizations (and come under the *I* in *FRISCO*). Not all of the cases to which these last two generalizations apply have been examined.

Less-than-universal inferred generalizations claim that the characteristic holds for some (loosely or precisely specified) subclass of the members of the class. All six examples from Kimble's list are less-than-universal inferred generalizations, as is the following probability generalization: "The probability of getting a four on one roll of a die is 1 in 6." According to this probability generalization, one-sixth of the rolls, in the long run, should be fours. This is less than universal because it says neither that every roll will be a four nor that none will be a four.

Gambler's Fallacy

One danger in applying a probability statement is to fall into the trap of the gambler's fallacy. Suppose that the last ten rolls of the die have not been fours. Does that increase the chances of getting a four this next roll? To think so, assuming that the die is an honest one, is to commit the *gambler's fallacy*. If the six faces of a die have equal chances of coming up on top, then the past history does not affect the next roll at all. The chances of getting a four on the next roll are still 1 in 6, even though the last ten rolls have not been fours. But remember that I said, "assuming that the die is an honest one." If a long-run record shows something significantly different from one out of six, then there is reason to suspect the die.

Streak Theory

Suppose that the last two rolls have been fours. Does that increase the chances of getting a four on the next roll? Suppose you have been having a run of especially good hands at cards. Does that mean that the next hand is more likely to be better than average? According to the *streak theory,* the answers are both *yes.* The streak theory holds that if you have been having a streak of one kind of thing, then the next shot is more likely to be that kind of thing. But if the die and the cards are honest, the streak theory is wrong also. The probabilities do not change with history.

Getting three fours in a row does not prove wrong the statement that the probability of getting a four is 1 in 6. (It is just that such a result is unlikely, if the probability statement is correct.) Similarly, finding one mental patient who is dangerous to others—or finding several—does not prove wrong the generalization about mental patients.

A Trade-off: Ease of Support Versus Utility in Application

In general, a few counterexamples do not prove a less-than-universal generalization wrong because the generalization does not claim to tell us what to expect or believe for every case. It tells us roughly what to expect in the long run for some amount of the cases. But there is a trade-off. The more a generalization is insulated from counterexamples, the less guidance it provides about what to believe or do. Even those that loosely specify a proportion or probability give us more guidance than those that use words such as *sometimes* and *often.*

Examples of less-than-universal generalizations that specify a proportion very loosely are Kimble's examples numbered 1 (*more likely*), 2 (*usually*), 3 (*most often*), 5 (*more likely*), and 6 (*more . . . than*). In these cases, the loose proportion is over one half. In contrast, a precise proportion (1 in 6) is specified in the probability generalization about the die.

But some less-than-universal generalizations indicate only a rough absolute number of cases (rather than a proportion or a probability). For example, generalizations containing the word *often* often (!) do not give us even a rough proportion. Consider this one: "Loud music often emanates from automobiles at this corner." This generalization tells us that loud music occurs at this corner with a frequency that is significant, but it could be only 10 percent of the time. All that is required to satisfy the requirements imposed by the word *often* is that it happen a good number of times, but not a high percentage of times. The word *often* is less helpful in giving us guidance than one that uses the word *usually,* which would require at least over 50 percent in the long run.

The meaning of *often* is heavily dependent on the situation and people's desires and expectations. In the case of an annoyance such as (for me) loud music emanating from cars, one in ten would be considered often. But one would not say "The salespeople at this store are often helpful" if they are helpful only 20 percent of the time. On the other hand, you might say "I often find $20 bills on my porch" even if it happens only once every two or three months.

This does not imply that nonproportional less-than-universal inferred generalizations are useless. Sometimes they are very useful. The fire chief who was mentioned in the previous chapter knew that arson can be a cause of fires. He knew—that is, a nonproportional less-than-universal generalization. If he had eliminated all the other possibilities, as he thought, then he had good reason to believe that it was arson that caused the fire. This shows that such *can-cause* knowledge can be quite useful. *Can-cause* generalizations are less than universal.

Here is another useful one: "Standing up in a canoe often causes it to tip over." This nonproportional, less-than-universal generalization is important for people who are learning to operate canoes. It specifies a danger that under most conditions should be avoided, even though we do not have a proportional statement to offer.

Consider the problem of the meaning of the terms in this generalization: "Three out of five doctors recommend Zenith Aspirin." What does that mean? Is it about a certain set of five doctors (method of selection unspecified), three of whom recommended Zenith Aspirin? If that is all that it means, then such a limited-to-the-data generalization is very easy to prove (and is uninformative, again illustrating the trade-off principle). To prove it, all we need to do is find three doctors who recommend Zenith Aspirin and two who do not. Then in the sense specified, three out of five doctors recommend Zenith Aspirin. But this could be quite misleading. One danger is that there could be a shift in the meaning of the words used in the generalization, so that the buying public would think that the generalization is about a proportion of a much larger population of doctors. Then it would appear to give information that is significant, although it could well be absolutely false.

All these facts about the meaning of the words in a generalization serve as a warning to be very attentive to clarity in considering and applying generalizations (the *C* in *FRISCO*). Generalizations often appear to say more than they do. The less they say, the easier it is to justify them, but often, consequently, the less useful they are (a generalization!).

Inference to Generalizations

If the words "Three out of five doctors recommend Zenith Aspirin" are used to express an inferred generalization, then presumably the data consist of a set of doctors, three fifths of whom recommend Zenith Aspirin. The generalization makes a statement about more doctors than those in the data. But who are these other doctors?

First, we need to distinguish among three groups: the group actually studied, a larger group (from which the sample, the group actually studied, has been drawn), and an even larger group, which includes the previous two groups and in which we are most likely to have the greatest interest. But ordinarily, the third group is too large to allow us to draw a random sample from it. So we want to extend our conclusions about the second group to the third group. The extension assumes that the smaller group is typical of the larger group. We cannot automatically go from a conclusion about the smaller group to a conclusion about the larger group, even if we could legitimately infer to the smaller group from the studied group.

Accordingly, there are two inferences, one from the studied group to the group from which the studied sample was drawn, and one from this group to the even larger group. People often forget about the fact that they are making this second inference, thinking that it is automatic, but it is not. The sampled group might not be representative of the larger group, even if the sample (the studied group) is representative of the sampled group.

For example, suppose that the doctors in a random sample of the doctors in Urbana, Illinois, are asked whether they recommend Zenith Aspirin, and that three fifths of this random sample reply affirmatively. Leaving aside for the moment some concerns about the meaning of the question, we might then justifiably conclude that three out of five doctors in Urbana recommend Zenith Aspirin. The doctors covered by this conclusion are all the doctors in Urbana, although only a random sample of these doctors were questioned. This first inference is legitimate if good jobs of random sampling and follow-up were done. But then someone might also conclude, "Three out of five doctors recommend Zenith Aspirin." This seems to be about a different and much larger population of doctors, possibly English-speaking North American doctors, perhaps even a larger group (all North American doctors? all doctors in the world?). The justification for extending the generalization would depend on the Urbana doctors' being typical of English-speaking North American doctors, or the even-larger group. I doubt this typicality, so would discourage this inference.

But if I had not been so specific about the identities of the sampled group and the larger group, the inference might pass unnoticed. Suppose that I said that three out of five doctors recommend Zenith Aspirin, and added in a footnote that this conclusion is based on a scientifically determined sample of doctors. That way of putting it neglects the distinction between the group sampled and the group that the ultimate generalization appeared to be about and, consequently, neglects the inference step from one to the other. I have often seen this distinction and the associated inference swept under the rug, not only in advertising, where we might expect it to happen, but in many other areas as well.

For example, in child psychology, we often find people talking about all children, basing their statements on a very restricted sample. They use terms such as *the child* or *children* that suggest that their statements apply to all (or almost all) children, when the evidence is about a sample of a limited population that is in many ways not typical of all children. An example is this statement by Jean Piaget, an influential Swiss psychologist: "We . . . describe the development of propositional logic, which *the child* at the concrete level (Stage II: from 7–8 to 11–12 years) cannot yet handle"[3] (emphasis added). The problem of the meaning of some of the terms in this statement (*propositional logic, 11–12,* and *handle*) is severe as well.[4] But the point here is to note the contrast between the universality of the statement and the size and nature of the group actually sampled: middle-class Swiss children. Please be warned that there is much more to this issue than is possible to indicate here, including the problem of inferring from the children actually studied even to middle-class Swiss children.

This problem of breadth of coverage is a general problem in the meaning of generalizations that we develop ourselves, as well as those asserted by others. We must try to be aware of the extent to which the generalization makes a statement about things or people that were not investigated or studied. That is, we must be alert to the meaning of the general terms in a generalization. To what do they refer? An

---

3. Barbel Inhelder and Jean Piaget, *The Growth of Logical Reasoning from Childhood to Adolescence* (New York: Basic Books, 1958), p. 1.

4. See my "Children's Ability to Handle Piaget's Propositional Logic: A Conceptual Critique," in Sohan and Celia Modgil (Eds.), *Jean Piaget: Consensus and Controversy* (London: Holt, Rinehart and Winston, 1982), pp 101–130.

all-too-frequent occurrence is a statement maker's acting as if the investigation justified reference to a larger group, when in fact the typicality of the smaller group is dubious. We shall return to the problems of sampling and typicality.

Another question of meaning in this case, postponed earlier, is the meaning of the phrase *recommend Zenith Aspirin*. What sort of evidence does it take to establish that a doctor recommends Zenith? Does it mean that the doctor recommends only Zenith Aspirin, or that the doctor recommends Zenith as well as other kinds of aspirin and some other pain relievers as well? Because it is in the interest of advertisers (and others) to get us to buy the products advertised (and to do other things), we must be duly cautious about the meaning of the words used by them.

Summary

Generalizations are either limited-to-the-data or inferred, and either universal or less-than-universal. Less-than-universal generalizations are either proportional or loosely numerical (using terms such as *often, sometimes,* and *at least some*). Proportional generalizations are vague (using terms such as *usually* and *generally*) or precise (stating probabilities or percentages). In general, the more informative a generalization, the more difficult it is to defend; and the less informative, the less susceptible to defeat by counterexamples (the *trade-off principle*).

Inferred generalizations are sometimes the result of an inference from a sample to a population from which the sample was drawn, and are defended on the basis of the method of sampling (a topic to be discussed soon). Sometimes the generalization goes beyond the population from which the sample was drawn and is about an even larger population. The justification of the larger-population generalization depends on the extent to which the sampled populations is typical of the larger population. The leap from the sampled population to the broader population often slips by unnoticed, a danger.

The degree of satisfaction of the four best-explanation criteria is relevant to those generalizations that are best-explanation hypotheses. But in this chapter, we are focusing on support by representativeness.

Probabilities for honest items (such as dies and cards) do not change with history. To think that a run of one sort reduces the chances of getting another of that sort is to accept the gambler's fallacy. To think that the chances are thereby increased is to accept the streak theory. Both are errors.

Check-Up 10A

True or False?
If false, change it to make it true. Try to do so in a way that shows that you understand.

10:1 Universal generalizations hold that every member of the class or group being considered has the characteristic in question.

10:2 A characteristic of proportional generalizations is that they go beyond the data on which they are based.

10:3 Although generalizations are usually relatively simple in structure, their meaning must frequently be carefully considered.

10:4 The generalization in 10:3 ("Generalizations are usually relatively simple in structure") is a less-than-universal generalization and is informative as it stands.

10:5 The following is a probability generalization: "The chances of getting heads in the toss of a coin are one half."

10:6 According to the generalization in 10:5, one half of the tosses of the coin, in the long run, will turn out heads.

10:7 If the generalization in 10:5 is true and the last three tosses turned up tails, then the chances are better than even that the next one will turn up heads.

10:8 If the generalization in 10:5 is true and if the last three tosses turned up tails, then the chances are better than even that the next will turn up tails.

10:9 It is legitimate to extend a generalization to a population larger than the population from which a random sample was drawn, as long as we are assured that the sample was indeed random.

Longer Answer

10:10 Consider the generalization "Societies always develop class systems, even when organized with the goal of being classless." Assume that a class system is a system within a given society consisting of a prestige and power hierarchy (resulting in some identifiable classes' being of higher status and power) and in which somehow there is considerable passage of the class status of parents to their offspring.

   a. Cite examples and, if you can, counterexamples to this generalization.

   b. Revise the generalization if you feel that it needs revision in order to be true.

   c. Write a short defense of the generalization, as revised (if you revised it). Heed FRISCO.

10:11 Find a generalization in a newspaper, magazine, research report, etc. Copy it and give the source.

   a. Tell what type of generalization it is (limited-to-the-data or inferential, universal or less-than-universal).

   b. Comment on its meaning. Is it misleading? State its meaning in other words than those in which it is written.

   c. Tell whether you think that the evidence supports the generalization. Explain why you think as you do. (Do not expect to do a perfect job here. Just do the best you can. But do not neglect such considerations as credibility of sources, and actual reports of the data on which the generalization is based.)

Sampling and Typicality

In 1936, the magazine *Literary Digest* surveyed public opinion in an attempt to predict who would win the United States presidential election: the republican, Alfred Landon, or the democrat, Franklin Roosevelt. Ten million ballots were sent out to find out how that sample of the voting population felt about the candidates. Over two million of these ballots were returned. On the basis of these returns, the *Literary Digest* concluded that more voters would vote for Landon than for Roosevelt (an inferred less-than-universal generalization). As it turned out, however, Franklin Roosevelt won 60 percent of the votes and was reelected. This error in prediction is a classic one in the history of sampling.

At least part of the problem was that the people chosen to receive the mailing were selected from telephone books, lists of subscribers to the magazine, and lists of owners of automobiles, resulting in a systematic bias in favor of the well-to-do, who were more likely to vote republican. The sample selected for study was not representative of the voters of the United States.

Furthermore, the fact that the prediction was based on a return of only slightly more than a fifth of the people solicited leaves room for more bias. Were voters for Landon or voters for Roosevelt more likely to return the ballots? What do you think? Opinion surveys that depend on the people surveyed to return their answers generally obtain a return of much less than half, always raising a question of bias. People who return survey forms are different from those who do not. The difference might make a difference in the outcome. This is not to say that one should automatically disregard results of surveys that depend on the people surveyed to return an answer. Rather, this is an important factor to consider. We should always try to ascertain the percent return in a survey and consider what difference there might be between those who returned an answer and those who did not.

Ways that survey makers can reduce the problem include providing a stamped self-addressed envelope, making it very easy to respond to the survey by asking few questions (or only one), following up on a survey request with a barrage of further requests to comply, perhaps appealing to the conscience of those being surveyed, and actually interviewing each person personally. There are problems with each of these approaches, as you can imagine, and no solution is perfect.

Random Sampling

How can a sample be selected that is representative of the population from which it is selected? Securing a random sample of sufficient size is the standard ideal answer. To say that a sample is *random* is to say that each member of the population had an equal chance of being selected. Securing a random sample requires that we have access to the entire population, so that each member has an equal chance of being included.

Suppose that we want to determine whether student opinion supports the thesis of a president of a university stated in a speech published in the student newspaper. The thesis is, "Tuition and fees at this university are reasonable." Assume that there are 10,000 students. Suppose that it is too much trouble or too expensive to query all 10,000 students in a way that will produce sincere answers, so we decide to select a random sample of about 1,000 students, ordinarily a sufficient number for a random sample. In order to give each an equal chance of being selected, we need to have a list of the entire student body. We could put all the names in a large drum, mix them well, and draw out 1,000 names, making sure that there were no mechanical problems, such as two names sticking together, or a name being caught in a crevice. To avoid such problems, we could write the names on 10,000 ping pong balls and mix them in a large sphere. It is not easy mechanically to give every name an equal chance of being selected, even if we have a complete list, but having the list is a necessary condition.

A simpler way than using names written on ping pong balls or slips of paper would be to use a table of random numbers from a book of statisticians' tables. Such tables consist of long lists of randomly selected digits, from 0 to 9. Here is a part of a table I have on my bookshelf: "2315754859018372599376249708695." It goes on, and on, and on. We could go through the list of students and assign each student in order a digit from the table. For example, starting from the beginning of the series just presented, the first student gets a 2, the second a 3, the third a 1, the fourth a 5, etc. Then we could arbitrarily choose one digit by closing our eyes and touching down in the middle of a table with a pointer. Suppose the pointer points to a 5. Then we could include in our sample every student who had been assigned that particular digit. That is, we pick all students who had been assigned 5. That procedure would give us about 1,000 students selected at random from the 10,000.

Another way to use the table would be to number the students from one to 10,000 and, starting at some arbitrary point in a table of random numbers, select a series of 1,000 four-digit numbers, neglecting any duplicates. The students who have those numbers would be in the sample. Starting at the third digit of the sequence in the last paragraph, students with the following numbers would be included in the sample: 1,575, 4,859, 183 (neglecting a beginning zero), 7,259, 9,376, 2,497, 886, etc. (Even if there were only 8,000 students in the population, we could proceed this way, just ignoring all numbers over 8,000.) Can you suggest a number to assign to the 10,000th student, given the four-digit procedure?

Random sampling does not guarantee representativeness, especially with a small selection. I took a random sample of eight people from a population of forty-eight people in a group composed of thirty-six males and twelve females. Of the eight people in the sample, three were females and five were males. In the sample, then, three-eighths were females, although in the population only one-fourth, or two-eighths, were females. A sample of eight people is a very small random sample if representativeness is important to us. On the other hand, a random sample of several thousand members is very likely to be representative. Of course, several thousand was impossible in my sample from forty-eight people, but with such a small population, sampling is often unnecessary anyway. Sampling is most useful when the population is so large that examination of every member is too difficult or expensive.

Even after selecting a random sample from 10,000 students, there would still be problems in determining the opinions of these selected students: Some might be out of town or ill, some might be reluctant to answer, and the questions we ask might be misleading to some. But the point here is that a random sample can be drawn from a population to which we have access. Giving each member of the population an equal chance of being selected is feasible.

The absolute size of the sample, rather than the percentage of the population selected, is of primary importance in sampling. If the *Literary Digest* had actually secured a random sample of only 1,000 of the voters in the entire United States and had determined how each one of these people was going to vote (not missing one), then it would very likely have come within a few percentage points of the actual vote. These facts (the importance of the absolute size rather than the relative size and the adequacy of a random sampling of 1,000 for most purposes) are facts about random sampling that surprise many people.

Because it is often extremely difficult to secure a random sample of even 1,000 and to examine *every* member, there would still have been good reason for concern. Securing a random sample was practically impossible for the *Literary Digest* because of the problems of developing accurate lists and of securing valid information from every person selected for examination. The expense and difficulty of identifying and securing valid information from pure random samples bring people to seek substitute methods.

Systematic Sampling

An alternative that makes the process of selecting the sample slightly easier is systematic sampling. Instead of using a random selection process, a systematic process is used, such as selecting every tenth student on our list of 10,000 students, starting with an arbitrarily picked one of the first ten. The mechanics of this procedure are easier, leaving the selection process less susceptible to error (an advantage), but there is the possibility of systematic variation in the way that students are listed, a variation that might make the sample unrepresentative. I do not see much chance of this sort of thing in the ways that I imagine students would be listed, so I would settle for a systematic sample in this case. But a systematic sampling procedure would not have helped the people from the *Literary Digest*. They still would have needed complete lists and would have needed to secure returns from those sampled in a way that did not bias the results. Furthermore, systematic sampling would not have increased the efficiency of sampling. They would have had to do just about as much work one way or the other.

Stratified Random Sampling

Because of the difficulties involved in securing valid results from each member of a selected sample, stratified random sampling is sometimes used. *Stratified random sampling* consists of breaking up the population into groups, and then randomly sampling each group. It enables us to reduce—to some extent—the size of the group selected without losing accuracy, if we stratify on variables that are correlated with the characteristic we are estimating. Consider again the survey of student opinion about the president's thesis about tuition and fees.

We might expect the freshmen to view the thesis somewhat differently from the seniors, and perhaps the juniors and sophomores will differ from each other as well as from the others. We want to be sure that each group is fairly represented in the final sample. Males and females might differ from each other also, as might people from different departments and ethnic backgrounds. In order to explain this idea, I shall neglect departments and ethnic backgrounds, but they should certainly be considered in a sampling of this sort. The goal is to use the groupings that make the most difference. For present purposes, I shall assume that gender and class level make the most difference.

Suppose that there are 2,500 in each class and that half of each class is female and half male. Then there would be eight groups of 1,250 members each. See Table 10.1. We would then take a random sample from each group, ensuring equal numbers of females and males, and equal numbers from each class in the total sample.

If there is a high relationship between class or gender and opinion about the president's thesis, we can manage with fewer people sampled without losing validity of results. In this case, we might be able to reduce our sample size by 30 percent, maintaining the same degree of accuracy. Stratified sampling down to about 88 people per group (about 700 in all) to study carefully would actually be an improvement over studying 125 per group (1,000 in all) less carefully. Their remarks could then be given more consideration, missing returns could be pursued more effectively, and interviews would be more feasible. Viewed differently, the cost of the interviewing without increasing the care of the work would be less with stratified sampling, not a full 30 percent less, but significantly less, if the interviewing is expensive. In any case, however, we would need a complete list of all the members of the population to make sure that everyone in each subgroup of 1,250 had an equal chance of being chosen.

Cluster Sampling

In its simplest form, *cluster sampling* calls for selecting a sample of groups (or clusters) from the total population being studied, and then sampling within the groups that are selected, but only from those groups. In effect, the *Literary Digest* people did cluster sampling, but they apparently did not sufficiently consider whether the groups they selected were representative of the total population. In fact, it is clear that these groups were not representative because they included only people with a telephone, or an automobile, or a subscription to *Literary Digest*.

One advantage of cluster sampling is that we are not required to list the entire population being sampled. In its simplest form, we are required to list the populations of the clusters that have been selected, so that we can do a pure random sample (or stratified random sample) within those groups.

TABLE 10.1   Eight Cells from which to Draw a Stratified Random Sample

	Gender	
Class	*Women*	*Men*
Freshman	x	x
Sophomore	x	x
Junior	x	x
Senior	x	x

Note: An "x" indicates a cell from which to take a random sample in order to secure a stratified random sample, stratified according to gender and class. Each "x" represents 1,250 people.

The trick is to secure a set of clusters that represent the total population. The election pollster's dream is a small town that is representative of the entire state, province, or country of which it is a part. Then a single cluster (the town) would be enough, and all we would have to do is to study it intensively. This intensive study might itself consist of selecting a set of representative subclusters, perhaps city blocks, and doing intensive study within the selected blocks. Ultimately, a random sample, or complete enumeration, would be made, but only then would it be necessary to do the onerous task of completely listing and locating people, even the reluctant ones. Unfortunately, the pollster's dream town cannot be identified with complete assurance until after the fact, but pollsters do have techniques that they feel give them reasonable assurance that they can identify representative clusters throughout a voting area, clusters that can then be studied intensively.

A cluster sampling of the 10,000 students might mark out a set of dwelling areas or units, list these units, and randomly select one third of the units (or clusters), which would each then be studied by random sampling within the clusters. In order to attain the same accuracy of sampling, one would ultimately need to draw a sample of more than 1,000 students, but the larger number would be more geographically concentrated and thus easier to locate. Furthermore, one would not need to obtain lists of the members of the units not sampled. For roughly the same precision of estimation, then, one might actually have less trouble, depending on how much more trouble it is to track down people as geographically separate as those in a pure random sample. Incidentally, if the sampled units are not roughly equal in size, then the results for the units must somehow be weighted in accord with the size of the unit.

A simpler but less accurate alternative: If there is some class hour when almost all students are in class, then a randomly selected sample of classes (clusters) can be drawn from classes meeting at that hour, and each selected class examined, either by random selection within the selected classes or by securing the opinions of all the students in the selected classes. It might actually be easier to secure the opinions of all the students within a class, given that the class and the teacher have to be interrupted anyway, if only a simple question is asked. If all the students within selected classes are to be queried, one might pick at random about one-sixth of the classes (or clusters) for study for roughly comparable accuracy, though more than 1,000 students would be examined. With a planned random sampling of one-third of the students in the selected classes, we might select one-third of the classes at random for comparable accuracy.

The numbers required here are vague—with only rough approximations—because of a variety of technical factors in determining the accuracy of estimation. Consult a text on sampling for more details. But from this account, you should now have a fairly good idea of the broad outlines of the process and the type of problems involved.

A Danger in Sampling, and the Case-Study Alternative

Although random sampling and its variations seem to some people to be the only scientific way to estimate a characteristic without examining the whole population, there are those who disagree. The basis for the disagreement lies in the fact that examination of a large number of people often results in a superficial examination of each. Even though random sampling can reduce the number needed to somewhere between 100 and 2,000, depending on the accuracy desired, that still requires a large number of people, if the characteristic being estimated is not easily identified or measured. Eye color is easily enough determined for large numbers of people. Prospective voting intentions are less easily determined because people might be reluctant to tell the truth to someone they do not know. They might fear ridicule or rejection. Furthermore, they might not have thought about the matter enough at the time of the query, and make a snap judgment that would later be reversed.

Characteristics such as fluency, numeracy, critical thinking ability, and self-confidence are much more difficult to determine. Even one person's opinion about the president's thesis in her speech is not easy to determine because such opinions are likely to be very complicated and to consist of varying shades of agreement and disagreement. The simplicity of the questions required for surveys of characteristics can result in distortion of the characteristics.

An alternative that is often suggested is the case-study approach, or some variation thereof. A case study calls for intensive, extended, and thoughtful observation and interpretation of one, or a few, cases. In-depth interviewing of a few of the 10,000 students, selected to make sure that they are different from each other, would be an example. Each student interviewed would be asked for reasons, descriptions of the background situation, opinions of other students, descriptions of discussions with other students, etc. The primary rule for the investigators is to keep their eyes and ears open in sensitive, careful, and creative ways. This approach enables the investigators to secure a much better picture of the entire situation and to better analyze what students really think about a president's thesis, so its proponents argue.

Difficulties with case studies, according to their critics, are that generalization from case studies is not easy (or not possible), and that the reporter often puts his or her own subjective interpretation on the situation. The relative value of case studies is a controversial issue.

Inferring to a Broader Population

It is tempting to draw a conclusion about a broader population based on a sampling from a population that is contained within that broader population. For example, we might be tempted to draw a conclusion about all university students in the country, based on a random sample of the opinions of the students in one particular university. You saw earlier the danger in inferring to all doctors from a random sample of a population of Urbana doctors, even though the random sample is a representative sample of Urbana doctors. And you saw the result of inferring to the United States population of voters in 1936 from a sample drawn from people with a telephone, automobile, or subscription to the *Literary Digest*. But such inferences are not always wrong. It depends on whether the sampled population is typical of the broader population.

In agricultural research, where the techniques of sampling are used extensively, inferences to broader populations are regularly made. For example, a study based on a sample of a type of wheat this year is generalized to apply to the same type of wheat next year. We could not have sampled next year's wheat because it did not exist when the sampling was done. But on the assumption that this year's wheat of the given type is typical of wheat of that type (an assumption that is defended by examination of its characteristics), we are ready to extend the generalization beyond the population from which a random sample was drawn.

Unfortunately, the rules for judging typicality do not have the clarity and precision of the rules for random sampling. You must keep your eyes and ears open and be well-informed. Because of what we know about wealth and voting habits, we know that the *Literary Digest* people had no right to generalize from the populations from which they sampled to the population of the United States. On the other hand, because of the regularity of characteristics of species of plants, we feel comfortable inferring to a generalization that is about more than the wheat from which we drew a random sample.

But there is more to keeping your eyes and ears open and being well-informed. The best-explanation reasoning pattern can be applied here. If we make a number of studies of wheat, voting preference, or opinions about the college president's thesis, even though these are not of randomly selected clusters of the population and they respectively turn out about the same, then we might justifiably infer that the trait pervades the population if there is no other plausible explanation of the agreement among the results and if we responsibly have searched for one. Thus, a judgment of typicality can be buttressed by the best-explanation approach to reasoning.

Summary

One standard way to justify an inference from a group to a broader population containing the group is to have the group be a random sample of the population. A *random sample* is a sample drawn in such a manner that each member of the population has an equal chance of being selected for the group. For the estimate to be accurate, the sample must be of fairly good size, somewhere between 100 and 2,000 depending on the confidence one seeks to have in the accuracy of the estimate. In securing this confidence, the size of the sample is much more important than the size of the population. A random sample of 1,000 from a population of 10,000 justifies not much more confidence in accuracy than a random sample of 1,000 from a population of 200 million, even though the proportions selected are very different (1 in 10 versus 1 in 200,000).

Problems with studies using random sampling can include having a low percentage return from the sample that is selected (leaving it open that the returns do not represent the population), inability to make the complete list required for randomly selecting the sample, difficulty in locating and securing returns from the ones selected, misinterpretation of questions and refusal to answer them truthfully, and the oversimplification that is sometimes required in order to secure countable answers.

Alternatives to pure random sampling include systematic sampling, stratified random sampling, cluster sampling with random sampling within the clusters, and variations and combinations of these. All require a sample of good size. The stratified random sample can be somewhat smaller than a pure random sample for the same degree of confidence in accuracy if the variables of stratification are well-correlated with the characteristic being investigated. The cluster sample approach generally requires a larger-sized sample than the pure random approach, but does not require listing of all members of the broader population, and often facilitates access to the sample because the members are usually grouped together geographically.

There is much more to say about sampling than has been said here, much of it being fairly technical. For more details, I recommend a standard text on sampling.

Because of the problems with random sampling and its allies, some people recommend as an alternative the use of intensive case-study techniques, which they feel give more of the full flavor of a situation. On the other hand, random sampling and allied methods, their proponents often maintain, are the only scientific way to study a population without studying every member.

In any case, inferences that go beyond a population sampled or studied depend on the typicality of that population. Being well-informed, keeping one's eyes and ears open, being sensitive, and using best-explanation reasoning techniques are the keys to determining typicality.

Check-Up 10B

True or False?
If false, change it to make it true. Try to do so in a way that shows that you understand.

10:12 A sample in which the person selecting the sample did not deliberately bias the selection is a random sample.

10:13 A pure random sample is necessarily representative.

10:14 A pure random sample with a size of 2,000 drawn from a population of 100 million would for most purposes provide an estimate in which we could have sufficient confidence.

10:15 A sample produced by drawing a random sample of groups and then drawing a random sample of individuals within the selected groups is called a systematic sample.

10:16 A case-study approach is thought by its supporters to be superior to a random-sampling approach in part because it does not force an over-simplification on complex and deep social phenomena.

10:17 One difficulty with a pure random sample of a size greater than 1,000 is that it is likely to be unrepresentative of the population.

10:18 There is no basis for inferring to a larger population than the population from which a random sample has been drawn, even though the larger population includes the population that has been sampled.

10:19 A stratified random sample can justify a smaller sample, if the variables of stratification are related to the variable being studied.

Medium Answer
10:20 A tennis ball machine produces 2,000 tennis balls per hour. In order to check on the quality of the production, the inspectors systematically select 500 tennis balls (every fourth one) from the first hour of an eight-hour production run and the same number from the last hour of

the production run, securing 1,000 tennis balls altogether. Each of the 1,000 balls is given the bounce and squeeze tests, and is visually inspected for apparent defects. The thinking is that if the production is all right at the beginning and end of a run, it is no doubt all right in the middle.

a. What do you think of these inspection procedures, and why?
b. What would you do, and why?

10:21 The school board of a large city containing 100 elementary schools wants to secure an estimate of the number of third-grade students who understand and are able to use contraposition and avoid conversion in everyday situations. An interview-type test has been devised that takes about thirty minutes of a student's time, but the number of students is too large for the test to be given to every student. Assume that there are four classes of about 25 third-graders in each of the 100 schools, making 10,000 third-graders altogether. Tell how you would draw a sample of about 1,000 third-graders for testing, and explain why you make the choices you do. Because you do not know all the details about this school system, you will need to make some assumptions about the situation.

10:22 Find a report of a sample-based survey that tells the size of the population sampled, the size of the sample, the method of sampling, and the conclusion that was drawn. Apply the FRISCO approach to this report and include a copy of the report with your comments.

10:23 Design a sampling study that is intended to answer a significant question. (1) State the question, (2) describe the population of interest (including approximate size), and (3) describe the population from which the sample will be drawn if it is different from the population of interest. If it is different, also (4) explain how you will justify inferring to the population of interest, (5) describe your sampling plan (including numbers), and (6) describe the technique for securing information about the selected individual (for example, if you will ask one or more questions, state them and give your plan for interpreting them). Prepare to describe your planned study to your class or group.

Interpretation of Data: Tables, Graphs, and Correlations

Tables, graphs, and correlations are useful ways of presenting data and of developing and testing hypotheses about relationships. Because most of you have learned about tables and graphs elsewhere, I shall here only do a quick review of some important features. Although this section is primarily for those who feel somewhat uncomfortable with tables, graphs, negative and positive relationships, and correlation relationships, others will find some interesting questions here. First, let us examine a table of numbers related to highway fatalities (Table 10.2).

TABLE 10.2 **Traffic Fatalities, Population, and Registered Vehicles for Sixteen Southern States and Washington, D.C., 1976**

1. State	2. Highway Fatalities (thousands)	3. Population (millions	4. Registered Vehicles (millions)	5. Highway Fatalities per 100,000 Population (Column 2 x 100 /Column 3
Texas	3.24	12.60	8.97	26
Florida	2.02	8.35	5.85	24
North Carolina	1.58	5.46	3.89	29
Georgia	1.30	4.98	3.33	26
Tennessee	1.28	4.23	2.81	30
Alabama	1.14	3.65	2.58	31
Virginia	1.06	5.05	3.30	21
Louisiana	1.00	3.88	2.34	26
Kentucky	.90	3.44	2.35	26
Oklahoma	.86	2.77	2.21	31
South Carolina	.83	2.84	1.77	29
Mississippi	.72	2.37	1.45	30
Maryland	.68	4.13	2.51	16
Arkansas	.53	2.12	1.35	25
West Virginia	.52	1.83	1.04	28
Delaware	.14	.58	.36	24
Washington, D.C.	.08	.70	.37	11
Average	1.05	4.06	2.73	25.5

What is the meaning of the number 3.24 at the top of Column 2? A glance at the column heading tells us that 3.24 is in the column containing numbers of highway fatalities in thousands. It is in a row labeled *Texas*. Therefore, the number 3.24 is the number of highway fatalities (in thousands) in Texas, or roughly 3,240. The title of the table tells us roughly what we can expect to find in the table. Actually, three very important places to look in a table of numbers are the title of the table, the column headings, and the row labels. Sometimes, in order to avoid clutter in a table, footnotes are added to explain some special fact. These must be examined also.

The number 3.24 was stated in terms of thousands and rounded off for convenience. The exact figures would have made it more difficult to see the relationships in the table as a whole, and probably are not absolutely accurate anyway.

Comparing the number 3.24 with the numbers by the names of the other states gives us some idea of how serious 3.24 is. But we must be careful. Of course, a rate of 3,240 highway fatalities is serious no matter what the number is in other places. But relative to the other places, did Texas have the most dangerous highways that year? A quick and careless look at Columns 1 and 2 might suggest that, of the places listed, Texas has the most dangerous highways because 3.24 is the highest number in Column 2. But note that Texas had more people and more vehicles than any of the other places, so it does not seem fair to judge it the most dangerous without taking into account the size of the population exposed to traffic fatalities. West Virginia has .52 in Column 2. Does that mean that West Virginia had safer highways? No, because it had a much smaller population than Texas (1.83 million, as can be seen across from West Virginia in Column 3). There were many fewer people available to be hurt on the highways.

Looked at another way, the number of fatalities in Texas was about three times the average for all of these states (given at the bottom of Column 2), but that does not show that Texas was three times as dangerous as the average. It has about three times the average population of all these states (see the bottom and top of Column 3).

One way to make a comparison is to make a ratio of the number of fatalities to the number of people, and compare these ratios. Roughly speaking, such a ratio shows the chances, if you were a member of that population, that you had of being a fatality, neglecting other factors than just living there. I have calculated the ratios (Column 5) and find that the highway fatalities per hundred thousand people were 26 for Texas and 28 for West Virginia. (Because I worked with rounded numbers, these figures are not precise. They are close enough for us to say that the rates were about the same.)

The important point here is that comparisons can be misleading. When reading or making tables of figures, we should seek fair comparisons. Often, some note of warning should be included, unless one's audience is sophisticated enough that the warning is not needed. Of course, the date of the information should be noted. Things might well be different now, and the year studied might have been an exceptional year. Is there reason to think that conditions in 1976 were significantly different from now?

It is easy to be misled by tables. One must stop and think about the numbers. Numbers do frighten some people, but simple numbers like these need not be frightening. Just stop and think about their meaning (the *C* of *FRISCO*). A higher number of fatalities does not by itself mean that a place is more dangerous.

Graphs

Graphs that show relationships can be intimidating. But all it takes is reading the titles and thinking about the meaning of the points and lines. Look at Graph 10:1, which shows a point for each place plotted on two axes: one for fatalities and one for population. The line at the bottom on the horizontal direction is called the horizontal axis, and here it shows population. The line in the vertical direction is called the vertical axis; here it shows traffic fatalities. In looking at a graph, one first thing to do is to become familiar with what each axis represents, and of course, to read the title.

Each place has been represented by a point (shown by an *x*), determined by going straight up from its population number and going straight across from its fatality number. Anywhere on a horizontal line across the graph indicates the number of fatalities shown by the number it crosses at the left. Anywhere along a vertical line drawn up from the bottom indicates a population of a size given by the number it crosses at the bottom. To get a point for Texas, we go across from 3.24 for fatalities, and go up from 12.60 for population. That point represents fatalities of 3,240 and population of 12.60 million, as one can tell by going back to the axes: going straight down from the point we cross the horizontal axis at 12.60, and going across from the point we cross the vertical axis at 3.24.

The display of points in a graph like that of Graph 10.1 is called a *scatterplot*. (I

Graph 10:1 Traffic Fatalities vs. Population in Sixteen Southern States and Washington, D.C.

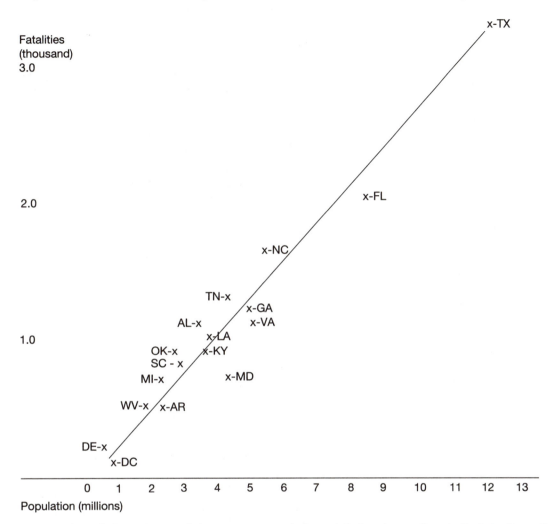

plotted the points and they are scattered about.) I also drew a line (called the line of best fit) that represents a hypothesis about the relationship in that set of places between population and fatalities in the year studied. Because the line does not go directly through all the points, there must be other things than size of population that influenced the number of fatalities.

Until I drew the line, I was engaged in limited-to-the-data generalizing. But the line suggests that there is a relationship that holds for population sizes not represented in the data. For example, it could be the basis of a prediction that if Texas had a population of only 11.0 million, there would have been somewhere around 2.8 thousand (or 2,800) fatalities. (Draw a straight line up from 11.0 million until it touches the line of best fit that I drew. Then, from the point of touching draw a line straight over to the vertical axis at the left and see where it hits—about 2.8.) The line of best fit represents an inferred generalization that goes beyond the data.

The limited-to-the-data generalization is this: For these seventeen places, larger populations tended to have more highway fatalities in the year studied. An inferred generalization is this: Places with larger populations are likely to have larger numbers of highway fatalities. This inferred generalization seems plausible, but I do not intend to defend it further.

Here is another limited-to-the-data generalization: In the areas studied, there tended to be fewer fatalities per person in and around the capital of the United States than in places away from the capital. Here is another inferred generalization: The people who live in and around Washington, D.C., tend to be more cautious on the highways. What do you think of these generalizations? They illustrate the distinction between observation and inference that I drew back in Chapter 4, if you are willing to think of the limited-to-the-data generalization as a set of observations. If not, then at least the distinctions are parallel and the warning the same: We generally must be more wary of inferences that go beyond the data than of the data on which they are based.

Positive and Negative Relationships

In the highway fatality case, the line of best fit shows a positive relationship between population and fatalities. That is, it suggests that as the population gets larger, the number of fatalities increases as well. A line that slopes up as it goes to the right shows a positive relationship. As one variable gets larger, so does the other. In contrast, a negative relationship is one in which, as one variable gets larger, the other gets smaller. See Table 10.3 for an example.

To secure the information in Table 10.3, a copilot recorded information from a set of aircraft instruments as the pilot took off and climbed to 5,000 feet en route to the destination. The primary purpose was to see the relationships between altitude and temperature, but a number of other items were recorded as well. In order to secure accuracy of estimates, the same operation should be repeated a number of

TABLE 10.3   Altitude, Temperature, Airspeed, Vertical Speed, and Distance from Airport on a Routine Takeoff and Climb

Altitude (feet)	Temperature (Fahrenheit)	Airspeed (miles per hour)	Vertical Speed (feet per minute)	Distance from Airport Center (nautical miles)
756[a]	72	no reading	0	0.5[c]
1,000	70	115[b]	1,100	1.1
2,000	67	115	1,050	2.8
3,000	63	115	980	4.4
4,000	60	115	920	5.9
5,000	56	115	850	7.5

Notes:
a. The top row gives the data just before takeoff. The airport is 756 feet above sea level.
b. The pilot was attempting to maintain a constant indicated airspeed
c. This information can be directly read from an instrument called a DME (Distance Measuring Equipment).

Graph 10:2. Altitude vs. Temperature on a Selected Flight

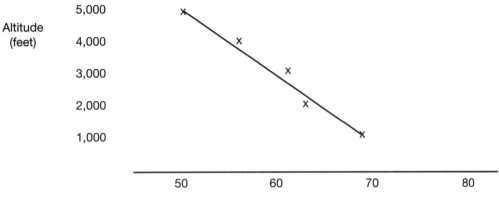

times (three is often a good number of times) and the results averaged to get a good estimate, because precise reading of these instruments is not possible, and because mistakes can creep in. But my purpose here is to illustrate relationships, using tables and graphs, so for the sake of simplicity, let us neglect the securing of multiple readings. These few pieces of data do not by themselves establish relationships, but they are striking enough to give one good reason to believe that there are some significant relationships here. (Other data and theoretical considerations do, however, support trends evident here.)

What do the data tell us about the relationship between altitude and temperature? We can see that the temperature went down as the altitude increased. (A general rule at these low altitudes, by the way, is that the temperature usually decreases about 3°F for each thousand feet of altitude—a well-established generalization.) This relationship is plotted in Graph 10:2.

Note that the line goes up to the left, not to the right. This means that the relationship is a *negative* relationship. As the altitude increased, the temperature decreased.

Note also that the variable on the horizontal axis does not start at 0. Can you see that if it had ranged from 0 to 80, the line would have been much steeper in slope? See Graph 10:3, based on the same data, and compare it to Graph 10:2. The lesson here is that relationships and differences can be made to appear in different ways by excluding or including selected portions. There are other ways of being fooled by the way the scale is set up. One in particular is the use of logarithmic scales. If you remember logarithms, you might imagine how this can occur.

Next, look at a scatterplot with a line of best fit for altitude and indicated airspeed for this flight in Graph 10:4. The line of best fit (a perfect fit this time) goes straight up and down. No matter what the altitude (in this sequence of observations) the indicated airspeed was the same. So there was no apparent relation in this sequence, something that we can see from the line's being straight up and down. However, we do not learn anything from this about the possibility of a real relationship between attitude and indicated airspeed because the pilot deliberately kept the indicated airspeed at 115 mph as the airplane climbed. At constant power and verti-

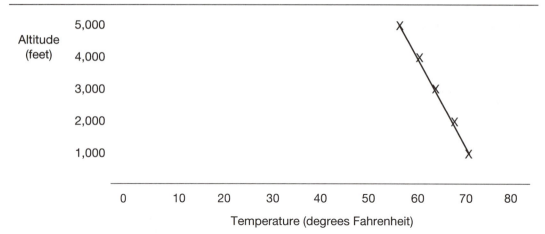

cal speed, the indicated airspeed would in fact have declined as this aircraft climbed.

What would you infer from a line of best fit that goes straight across, not slanted at all? Similarly, it would indicate no apparent relationship in the data because it would tell us that there was no change in the variable on the vertical axis when there were changes in the variable in the horizontal axis. If you do not see that, then study the graph a bit until it becomes clear.

Draw or imagine a scatterplot using altitude and distance from the airport. You should get a line that slopes upward to the right, showing a positive relationship for this particular segment of this particular flight. Does that show that climbing causes an airplane to be farther from the airport? Not in ground distance. The airplane could just as easily have circled and arrived at 5,000 feet when it was just over the place where it started. The ground distance from reference point on the airport could then have been the same as at departure. Climbing does not cause airplanes to be farther away across the ground from a position. Although there was a relationship in this flight, it was what some people call a *spurious* relationship. I think that the word *spurious* is a bit strong because it implies that the relationship is counterfeit or false. I suggest instead calling it a noncausal association because, in that situation, there really was a relationship. What do you think?

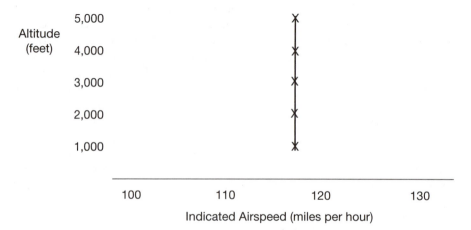

Correlations

Correlation coefficients are a numerical way of expressing the degree of relationship between two variables. They range from +1 to –1, with 0 indicating no relationship at all. +1 indicates a perfect positive relationship; –1 indicates a perfect negative relationship. If a relationship is *perfect,* then there is a formula for precisely calculating either one, given the other. A high negative relationship is stronger than a low positive relationship. For example, a relationship of –.9 is stronger than a +.3.

For some examples of correlation coefficients, consider some data and graphs presented earlier in this chapter. The correlation coefficient for the relationship between traffic fatalities and population in Graph 10:1 is .98; the correlation coefficient for the relationship between altitude and temperature presented in Graph 10:2 is stronger than –.99; and 0 is the correlation coefficient for the relationship between altitude and indicated airspeed (no relationship in this particular study) in Graph 10:4. The first two are very high correlations compared with those commonly obtained in the social sciences. For example, the correlations between college entrance tests and grades in college tend to run less than +.50 and are regarded as significant.

Making scatterplots like those in the graphs is helpful in visualizing the situation, but the correlation coefficient is an efficient means of reporting the relationship, and has other uses as well. See a statistics book for some of these uses.[5]

As with other generalizations based on data, one must be careful in inferring beyond the data on which the correlation is based. For example, it would be a mistake to infer from the data given here that the correlation between altitude and indicated airspeed is generally zero. In fact, it is not. The greater the altitude, the less the indicated airspeed, other things remaining equal. What made the 0 relationship in this case was the pilot's deliberately maintaining an indicated airspeed of 115 mph by adjusting the controls. This warning is often ignored in the social sciences, which make heavy use of correlations. Instead, investigators and interpreters often blithely assume that their sample is representative of the general population or of the population to which they desire to apply the correlation. For example, people often assume that a high correlation between a multiple-choice test of English usage and good writing will hold of groups for whom the multiple-choice test has become a high-stakes test. (An example of a high-stakes test would be an admissions test or advanced placement test for which getting a good score is very important to some people.) People often train to take such tests, thus reducing the actual relationship between the test and good writing.

Although correlation coefficients can be very useful, be careful. Figures do not lie, but liars certainly do figure (and suggest misleading interpretations of the figures).

Summary

Key features of tables and graphs are their titles and the labeling of their horizontal and vertical axes. Then one must also determine whether the numbers or lines mean what they might at first seem to mean. One way to do this is to see what bearing a

---

5. The type of correlation coefficient employed here is the most common kind, the Pearson Product–Moment Coefficient of Correlation. It is used for linear relationships, those that can be represented by a straight line.

conclusion drawn from data might have on you. For example, does the highway fatality table tell you that you would be at greater risk in Texas than in other places considered?

A good way to see whether there is a relationship between two variables is to make a scatterplot. Each point marked with an *x* shows an individual person or thing. Its location is determined by its value on each of the axes. After all the points are marked, a line of best fit is drawn. It represents a beyond-the-data hypothesis about the relationship between the variables for the data that were used. Such lines of best fit do not tell us which of either variable is a cause of the other, nor that there is a causal relationship between the variables. They might be arbitrarily related, as is the relationship between altitude and distance from the airport. Neither was a cause of the other. And they might be really related, as are altitude and indicated airspeed for that type of aircraft; but the relationship might be masked, perhaps by the investigator's procedures, as in the case when the pilot deliberately maintained an indicated airspeed by adjusting the trim control.

A positive relationship is one in which, as one variable grows larger, the other does also. Positive relationships appear as sloped lines going up to the right (and down to the left) in standard ways of using axes. Negative relationships are those in which as one variable grows larger, the other grows smaller. Negative relationships appear as lines that slope up to the left (and down to the right). Lack of relationship is shown by lines that are either horizontal or vertical, or by no drawable line of best fit.

Correlation coefficients (which range from +1 to −1) are often used to show the strength and nature of relationships. A strong positive relationship is shown by a high positive decimal number that is close to, but not larger than, +1. A strong negative relationship is shown by a high negative decimal number that is close to, but not lower than, −1. A number hovering around zero indicates no relationship.

Check-Up 10C

True or False?
If false, change it to make it true. Try to do so in a way that shows that you understand.

10:24 A negative relationship, using standard ways of labeling axes, slopes up to the left.

10:25 If the points on a scatterplot all appear on the same line and the line slopes one way or the other, there is an apparent relationship between the variables for the data used.

10:26 The entire possible range of a variable should appear on its axis.

10:27 A correlation of +1 indicates a strong negative relationship.

10:28 A correlation of +.8 indicates a stronger relationship than a correlation of +.4.

10:29 A correlation of +.4 indicates a stronger relationship than a correlation of −.8.

Medium Answer

10:30 Make a scatterplot for altitude and distance from the airport for the data in Table 10.3. Draw a line of best fit.

10:31 Make a scatterplot and line of best fit for altitude and vertical speed when the airplane is flying.

    a. Why did you select the range you did for the variable altitude?

    b. Is the indicated relationship positive, negative, or neither?

    c. Do you think that the relationship is causal? Explain. If you cannot answer this or explain why (because you are not familiar with the facts), then just read the suggested answer.

10:32 Make a scatterplot and line of best fit for highway fatalities and registered vehicles from the data in Table 10.2.

    a. Is there an apparent relationship between these two variables? If so, is it positive or negative?

    b. Do you think that there is a real causal relationship between these two variables? Defend your answer.

10:33 Make a scatterplot and line of best fit for temperature and distance from the airport, based on the data in Table 10.3.

    a. Is there an apparent relationship between these two variables? If so, is it positive or negative?

    b. Do you think that there is a real causal relationship between these two variables? Defend your answer.

    c. Can the data be generalized to a general relationship between distance from the airport and temperature (for example, "The farther one gets from this airport, the colder it is")? Why?

Longer Answer

10:34 Do a study in which you gather data that can be put in a table and a graph. Make the table and a scatterplot and line-of-best fit graph. Give the titles to the table and graph, and label the rows, columns, and axes.

    a. On your scatterplot, did you start both variables at zero? If so, why? If not, why not?

    b. Is there a positive or negative relationship, or neither?

    c. Is there a causal relationship between the variables? If so, in which way? Explain.

Suggested Answers for Chapter 10

Check-Up 10A

10:1 T	10:2 F	10:3 T	10:4 T	10:5 T	10:6 T
10:7 F	10:8 F	10:9 F			

10:2 Add *sometimes*.

10:7 Change *better than even that the next will turn up heads* to *still one half that the next will turn up heads.*

10:8 Change *better than even that the next will turn up tails* to *still one half that the next will turn up tails.*

10:9 It is legitimate to extend a generalization to a population larger than the population from which a random sample was drawn as long as the population from which the sample was drawn was typical of the larger one.

10:10 and 10:11 These are up to you.

Check-Up 10B
10:12 F   **10:13** F   **10:14** T   **10:15** F   **10:16** T
10:17 F   **10:18** F   **10:19** T

10:12 A random sample is one in which every element in the population sampled had an equal chance of being selected.

10:13 A pure random sample of sufficient size is probably representative.

10:15 Change *systematic sample* to *cluster sample*. (Instead of this, you could give a definition of systematic sampling.)

10:17 A pure random sample of a size greater than 1,000 is likely to be representative of the population.

10:18 There is a basis for inferring to a larger population than the population from which the random sample was drawn, when the smaller population is typical of the larger one.

10:20   a.   By neglecting the middle six hours, they risk missing problems that develop in those six hours but that are not causing trouble at the beginning and end.

b.   It would probably be better to select every sixteenth ball (a systematic sample for the whole day). But perhaps the machine is systematically making every sixteenth ball badly and everyone is missed. It would probably be better to select at random six five-minute periods in each hour and to select at random one-eighth of the balls produced in each selected five-minute period. Again, 1,000 balls would be selected. I do not know enough about tennis ball production to be more specific.

10:21 Deliberately omitted.

10:22–10:23 These are up to you.

Check-Up 10C
10:24 T   **10:25** T   **10:26** F   **10:27** F   **10:28** T
10:29 F

10:26 The entire possible range of variables is often not included on a graph so that a certain range can be examined more thoroughly.

10:27 Change *negative* to *positive*.

10:29 Change *stronger* to *weaker*.

10:30

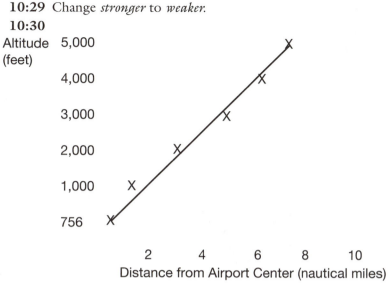

10:31

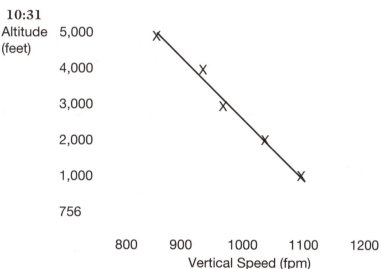

    a. This was the range in the table.

    b. Negative. (We cannot give a value for the altitude of 756 because we do not know what the vertical speed is at takeoff. The 0 vertical speed reading was obtained before the airplane was flying, as can be seen by the concurrent airspeed reading.)

    c. Yes, because the airplane's power and the density of the air on which the propeller can get a "bite" reduce with the altitude. (Giving a good answer to this question requires knowledge of the field. If you figured it out, good for you!)

10:32

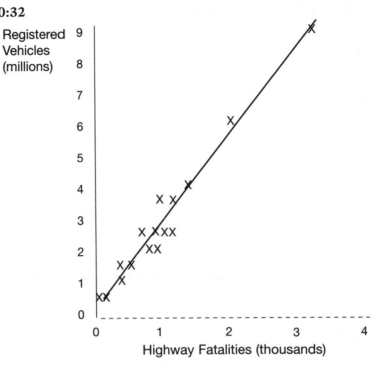

a. Yes.

b. Yes, because a greater number of vehicles results in more chances for accidents, providing that usage is about the same.

10:33 Deliberately omitted.

10:34 This is up to you.

11   Making Value Judgments

When we, the members of the jury, decided that Arlene was not justified in using the force she used, we made a value judgment. In effect, we were saying that, given the circumstances, she was wrong in using that much force.

The making of value judgments is a controversial topic. Almost everything one can say in this area can arouse disagreement by someone, but I shall do my best to make some sense, and walk the fence between severe controversy and emptiness.

Even the distinction between value statements and factual statements is in dispute, but for our purposes, a distinction is needed and can be made. However, because the distinction is so basic, it is difficult to find other words that clarify it.

The Distinction Between Value Statements and Factual Statements

Roughly speaking, a *factual statement* attempts to describe, whereas a *value statement* places a value (positive or negative) on the way things are (or were, or could be). Here are some examples of statements that in the context were value statements:

1. Arlene was wrong in using that much force.
2. Shakespeare makes better reading than Agatha Christie.
3. Physicists should have refused to cooperate in the making of nuclear weapons.
4. It is generally right to promote democracy in nondemocratic lands.

Here are some statements about the same topics that in those contexts were factual statements:

5. Arlene stabbed Al.
6. These days more people read Agatha Christie than read Shakespeare.
7. Many physicists cooperated in the making of nuclear weapons.
8. Democratic countries never try to promote democracy in nondemocratic lands.

There can be false factual statements (such as #8) and false value statements, such as "Every scientist is a higher-quality person than any politician."

I am including statements using the words *should, ought,* etc., in the value statement category if they imply value statements using words such as *right, wrong, good,* and *bad.* For example, statement #3 is a value statement because it roughly implies the following value proposition: "It would have been a good thing for physicists to have refused to cooperate in the making of nuclear weapons." On the other hand, the following statement containing the word *should* is not a value statement: "If you want the quickest way to Sacramento at midday, then you should use the Bay Bridge." It is not a value statement because it simply informs us of the fact that the Bay Bridge route is the quickest at midday. This is a matter that can be determined by observation and generalization from observation. To decide that the quickest way is the most desirable way, on the other hand, would be to make a value decision.

The distinction between factual and value statements is not absolutely clear. There are statements that combine factual and value elements. For example, the statement "The meeting was dominated by that arrogant group" clearly has both elements. It seems to be a largely factual question whether that group did dominate the meeting, but it is a value question whether the group's behavior is objectionable enough to be judged arrogant.

For theoretical reasons, some people hold that all factual statements are based on values; others hold that all value statements are really factual statements, but for our purposes, we need not go into these topics. The distinction between value and factual statements is useful at the level of practical critical thinking, though not totally clear in all contexts and for all purposes.

It is useful because it tends to separate statements that assert two radically different kinds of things and that can be supported in sometimes radically different ways. By just inspecting the eight examples I have given, you should be able to see the radically different kind of assertion made by value and factual statements.

Although value and factual statements share some ways of being supported, there are ways that they do not share. Value and factual statements share, as ways of being supported, deduction or loose derivation from acceptable principles, and assertion by acceptable authorities. Pure value statements, on the other hand, cannot serve as hypotheses that (causally) account for ordinary descriptive facts, and so cannot be the direct product of best-explanation inference. Value statements are not the simple direct result of observation. These differences in kinds of support make it useful to draw the distinction. It helps us decide what kind of support to seek for a statement.

When the Congress of the United States asked in the mid-1960s for a study of the extent of equality of educational opportunity in the United States, it was asking for more than a scientific study. James Coleman, the sociologist who took charge of this classic study, needed to make value judgments about what was to count as equality of educational opportunity. The danger is to think that all he had to do was a factual, scientific study, using only direct observation, generalization, and inference to best explanation. That would be to neglect the value judgment he had to make. The value–factual distinction conceptually enables us to see that he had more to do than a factual scientific study, so the distinction can be helpful.

In drawing this contrast between value and factual statements, I do not mean to imply that we can never be confident about value statements. We can be quite confident about some value statements, such as "It was absolutely wrong for the Nazis to kill six million Jews."

It is partly because we can justifiably be quite confident about some value judgments that I promote a factual statement–value statement distinction, and avoid using the oft-promoted fact–opinion distinction. The fact–opinion distinction suggests that whatever is not factual is mere opinion.[1] But my statement about the Nazis, though not factual, is not merely an opinion. If you think otherwise, then we are both in trouble, and I hope that you will read the discussion of relativism later in the chapter.

This chapter deals with how to decide about value statements, with some attention to how to write a defense of a value statement. Do not expect neat automatic formulas that generate answers, because there are none here. Instead, expect only some rough guidelines and warnings. Your own judgment is crucial here.

Arriving at and judging value statements comes directly under the *I* in *FRISCO,* although the situation (*S*) is always important, as is clarity (*C*). Let us start by looking at one kind of inference to value statements, loose derivation.

Loose Derivation from Principles and Factual Statements

In deciding that Arlene was not justified in using the force she used, we relied on some value principles and the factual situation. The key element in the factual situation was that Arlene had the readily available alternative of fleeing into her parents' room, if Al had, as she claimed, threatened to kill her. (We believed that she would have been safe in her parents' room.) One value principle that we assumed was that it is wrong to stab another person if the person is not threatening you. Another value principle we assumed was that it is wrong to stab a person who is threatening you if there is a peaceful alternative readily available.

More explicitly, the reasoning went as follows:

Example 11:1

Either (1) he threatened her or (2) he did not threaten her. Consider each alternative:

---

1. Incidentally, an alternative to the factual–value distinction is a three-way distinction among fact, opinion, and reasoned judgment. A third alternative is the distinction between observation and conclusion. The popular fact–opinion distinction seems to incorporate and confuse all three of these distinctions, all of which seem worthwhile when separated from each other. When combined, they invite us to denigrate all value judgments (as mere opinions), to label as facts propositions such as "The earth is flat" (because it is factual), and to label as opinions propositions such as Boyle's law or the law of gravity (because they are not observation statements). For an interesting discussion of the fact–opinion distinction, see Perry Weddle's "Fact from Opinion," *Informal Logic, 7* (1985), 19–26.

1. Under the assumption that he threatened her:
   a. Al was threatening Arlene.
   b. It is wrong to stab a person who is threatening you if there is a peaceful alternative readily available.
   c. Arlene had the readily available peaceful alternative of fleeing into her parents' room.
   d. Therefore, it was wrong for Arlene to stab Al.

2. Under the assumption that he did not threaten her:
   a. Al was not threatening Arlene.
   b. It is wrong to stab another person if the person is not threatening you.
   c. Therefore, it was wrong for Arlene to stab Al.

Under each alternative, we reached the conclusion that it was wrong for Arlene to stab Al. Although the state had not proven beyond a reasonable doubt that Al had not threatened to kill Arlene, we concluded that under either alternative (that is, whether he threatened her or not), it was wrong for Arlene to kill Al, and thus that she was not justified in using the force she used.

Under either alternative, the conclusion was derived. Because the two alternatives exhaust the possibilities, the conclusion was apparently established (although there is an assumption problem, to be discussed shortly).

The reasoning process here is enough like deduction for us to call it *loose derivation*. Note two ways in which this reasoning process is loose:

Most importantly, the general value principles are not to be interpreted as universal requirements. Consider one of our principles, "It is wrong to stab another person if the person is not threatening you." There certainly are exceptions to this principle. It might be all right to stab another person to protect a baby, or to protect a whole set of people from torture or death, even though you are not threatened. Consider the second principle, "It is wrong to stab a person who is threatening you if there is a peaceful alternative readily available." There are exceptions to this one as well. It might be that the peaceful alternative would result in great physical damage or risk of physical damage to the one being threatened, such as walking on the ledge of a tall building. Or it might be that the person who is threatening you is ultimately trying to get past you to assassinate the prime minister, or the president, and the only way to stop the person is by stabbing.

Value principles generally have so many exceptions that one cannot specify them all in advance. If we could specify them, we would add a description of the exceptions to the value principles. Instead, the thing to do is to keep in mind that there might be exceptions to the principles and that particular applications of a principle might not actually be justified, even though the principle, as a broad general principle, is justified. One way to keep this sort of thing in mind is, after you assert a principle, to say under your breath, "unless there is a (really) good reason to believe or do otherwise in the specific situation."

Just to make the point more firm, let us consider the value principle "One should not lie" or, if there is doubt about the meaning of the word *lie*, "One should try to tell the truth." This is a good principle, but there are exceptions. Suppose that an anxious mother wants to know whether her son, who died on a battlefield, died painlessly. Suppose further that he actually had an extended period of agony before death. Should you tell the mother the truth? At least many people would say that you should lie in this case; they may also say, if asked in another context about lying in general, that lying is wrong. The best way to resolve this apparent inconsistency is to understand that people have an unspoken qualification to the principle, "unless there is a (really) good reason to believe or do otherwise in the specific situation." (Sometimes the shorter phrase *prima facie*—meaning *on the face of it*—is used, as in "Lying is *prima facie* wrong.")

A second source of looseness in the reasoning results from a degree of vagueness in the terms used. The terms *peaceful alternative, threaten,* and *readily available* are vague. Would making a verbal threat against an assailant be a peaceful alternative? Is it threatening for someone to say, "I'm going to frighten you?" Is jumping out the window of a one-story house a readily available alternative? A two-story house? The words in our talk about values are often vague, making application to cases difficult. The neatness of ideal deduction eludes us in the area of values, even though the strategies of deduction are often useful.

Summary

A statement of the worth (positive or negative) of some thing or action is a *value statement*. Value statements differ from factual statements. *Factual statements* (which can be specific, general, and even theoretical) attempt to describe, but not evaluate, the worth of a thing or action. The distinction is not a precise one, although it is useful.

Both kinds of statement can be the conclusions of a process similar to deduction, although there tends to be more looseness when dealing with values. In particular, value principles generally have an implied qualification, "unless there is a (really) good reason to believe or do otherwise in the specific situation," and terms in value statements are often vague enough to require a judgment about whether and how they apply.

Value statements cannot serve as hypotheses to be evaluated by best-explanation procedures and are not merely reports of direct observation. Value questions cannot be settled by scientific research only, although scientific research can contribute. These facts, and the apparent difference in the kinds of things asserted by the two kinds of statements, are good reasons to make the distinction between factual and value statements.

Check-Up 11A

True or False?
If false, change it to make it true. Try to do so in a way that shows that you understand.

11:1 One way of defending value statements is by showing that they can be loosely deduced from an acceptable principle and one or more facts.

11:2 One way of defending a value statement is by showing that it can account for the facts and that alternative possible explanations of these facts are inconsistent with some facts.

11:3 Typically, a good value principle has no exceptions.

11:4 Factual statements are all true.

11:5 Factual statements attempt to describe, sometimes simply, sometimes theoretically.

Short Answer

Decide whether each of the following statements is a factual or a value statement. Assume that the context is a normal one.

11:6 The United States should have stayed out of World War I.

11:7 The United States entered World War I.

11:8 The United States stayed out of World War I.

11:9 It is wrong to give information to an authority if it might hurt a friend.

11:10 You should do unto others as you would have them do unto you.

11:11 Students are reluctant to tell a teacher if a friend cheats.

11:12 The basic human dignity of every person should be respected.

11:13 All is fair in love and war.

More Short Answer

For each of the following arguments, (a) identify and state the conclusion. Then (b) tell whether the conclusion follows from the reasons (assuming for each case that it is not an exception to the value principle). In each case, defend your decision by using Euler circle diagrams, propositional logic principles, or both.

11:14 The United States should have stayed out of wars that did not strongly affect its basic interests. World War I did not affect the basic interests of the United States. Therefore, the United States should have stayed out of World War I.

11:15 If you tell Martine that Karl is not interested in a reconciliation, then you would be lying to her, even though you believe that she is better off without Karl. If you lie to her, then you will not be respecting her basic human dignity. Therefore, you should not tell her that Karl is not interested in a reconciliation. The basic human dignity of every person should be respected.

11:16 My friend cheated on a test. It would be wrong to tell the teacher about it because it would be wrong to give this information to the teacher, if it might hurt my friend. Telling the teacher about my friend's cheating on the test might hurt my friend.

11:17 Michael's intercepting and destroying Bill's love letter to Juanita was unethical. I realize that Michael is in love with Juanita, but to interfere with someone's attempt to communicate with a loved one is to fail to show respect for her basic human dignity. It is wrong not to show respect for the basic human dignity of every person.

11:18 Michael's intercepting and destroying Bill's love letter to Juanita was not unethical. All's fair in love and war, and Michael is in love with Juanita.

Facts About the Past; Future Consequences

It is surprising how often value reasoning goes wrong because the facts are ignored or because the alleged facts are not really facts. In our reasoning to the conclusion that Arlene was not justified in using the force she used, many facts were important, and two predominantly factual matters were crucial: Did Al threaten to kill Arlene (more specifically, did he say, "Arlene, I'm going to kill you," as she claimed), and was there a peaceful alternative for her to pursue?

Factual Claims

If he had so threatened, then on grounds of self-defense, she might have been justified in using the force she did (neglecting the peaceful alternative question for the time being). If he did not threaten her, then, assuming that she had no other justifying circumstances, she was not justified in using the force she used. Because the defense attorney had offered no other justifying circumstances, because it was his job to do whatever he could on her behalf, and because he seemed very competent, we had a right to assume that there were no other justifying circumstances. Therefore, the question of whether he threatened her was an important one.

Unfortunately, this factual question could not be settled to our satisfaction because the only eyewitness source of information (Arlene) had a strong conflict of interest. Because of this conflict of interest, her testimony on the matter could not settle it for us. But he might have threatened her, and of course he might not have done so. This important factual matter could not be resolved satisfactorily.

Unstated Facts

For a long time, although the fact that she had a peaceful alternative was staring us in the face, we jurors ignored it. Facts do not advertise themselves as relevant, and they often remain not only ignored, but unstated. Nobody had stated for us the fact that she had a peaceful alternative. The prosecuting attorney might have done so, but he did not. For a long time, none of the jurors realized that this was a fact and that it was relevant. When one of the jurors realized and stated this fact, the rest of us immediately recognized it as a fact, a fact that was quite important. We then used this fact to reason to the conclusion that she was not justified in using the force she used.

Because of the importance of facts in making value judgments, it is crucial to make sure that we have the facts. Misinformation can do much harm. It is important to be familiar enough with the situation to be sensitive to facts that have not even been formulated. Unformulated facts, like the fact that she had a peaceful alternative, are often ignored.

Consequences

It is often helpful to force ourselves to think about the probable or possible future consequences of accepting a value judgment. Claims about what the future consequences will be are factual claims, so here we have another way in which facts can be important. But it is generally more difficult to be sure about factual claims about the future than factual claims about the past, so one must be especially careful here. Think of the times that you have confidently predicted what would result if a particular course of action were followed—and been wrong. Have you ever decided it would be good to offer a loan to a friend, predicting that the friendship would then be even firmer, and had it turn out otherwise? Have you ever decided that you should not tell a friend the whole truth about your feelings, thinking that your relationship would otherwise be damaged, and discovered otherwise? It can happen.

However, it is still important to try to look at the probable or possible consequences of accepting a judgment about what is a good thing to do or a good way to be. The consequences are usually relevant. Suppose the question is whether it is a good idea to allow dogs to run unleashed in the park. One of the bad consequences of not allowing such freedom is that the dogs in the area will be less likely to get exercise and self-expression. Some good consequences of not allowing the freedom are fewer dog fights, and reduced frightening of people who are afraid of dogs. These consequences (and others) should be considered in deciding whether it is a good idea to allow dogs to run unleashed in the park. Because there are good and bad consequences, just looking at the consequences and judging them separately are not enough. The good and bad ones must somehow be weighed against each other. We shall return to this topic shortly.

Sometimes, consequences and situations can arise of which the value is uncertain: They do not seem to come under any value principle we already have, or they contain elements that do not come under any value principle we have. Consider dog fights.

There was a time in my life when I knew of no justified value principle that covered dog fights. Then I witnessed several and decided simply on the basis of the full presentation of the details of these dog fights that they are not a good thing. This is the way that some of our justified value judgments are formed. We consider in detail one or more examples of a type of situation, are sensitive to them, probably reflect on them, and form a judgment about their worth. This is the way I came to object to dog fights.

I have never seen a cockfight, and suspect that my judgment about them would be the same, but I cannot be confident about that without a presentation of details. My imagination and knowledge of the kinds of things that would happen are just not good enough. The vivid depiction of details is important to this way of forming values.

What assurance do we have of the correctness of a judgment about a consequence, given that it was made perceptively and sensitively with a clear idea of the details of the consequence? No guarantee is possible. Reasonable disagreements sometimes develop. But this is the best we can do when there are no acceptable value principles to guide us, or when acceptable value principles are in conflict and there is no higher-level acceptable value principle or authority to resolve the issue.

Furthermore, even when acceptable value principles or higher-level principles are there to guide us, it is a good idea to look at the consequences of following them. The case under consideration might be an exception to the principle. Even though it is not possible to guarantee a correct judgment as a result, in the long run, your judgments will probably be improved by your attending to both principles and consequences.

Consequences of the Jurors' Judgments

This jury was not expected to apply the method of looking at the consequences (for the defendant) of the particular judgment I have been discussing. That is, one consequence of the judgment that Arlene was not justified in using the force she used was, if the other conditions were satisfied, that she would serve a term in prison. Our society has assigned to the legislature and the judicial system the job of deciding whether this consequence is appropriate. For us to take this consequence into account in deciding whether she was justified would have been to take over the work that is assigned to the legislature and the judges. We were told not to take it into account in making our decision.

However, we could have considered the consequences of the value principle we assumed about peaceful alternatives if we had identified and wondered about this assumption. That is, we could have imagined the consequences for society of holding the principle that it is wrong to hurt people severely who threaten your life, when there is a peaceful alternative. We might have imagined the probable consequence (assuming other factors remain the same) that there would continue to be men bullying and threatening physically weaker women. We might also have imagined a set of people (mothers, sisters, brothers, fathers, and children of a person who threatens, and might otherwise be severely hurt) who would be happier without the injury or death. In that situation in the jury room, we did not imagine these consequences. As soon as the point was made that she had a peaceful alternative, we immediately felt that we knew that she was not justified in using the force she used.

Some associates[2] have, as I noted earlier, challenged us for not having made the assumption explicit and for accepting it without question. What do you think?

Weighing Reasons

When we have evaluated each of the consequences and have applied principles directly, we will probably find that we have some reasons in support of a conclusion (pro reasons) and some against (con reasons)—and some in between. How do we decide?

Decision Theory

Elaborate methods have been worked out to try to give guidance in answering such questions, often going under the name *decision theory*. These methods ask us to assign numbers, often amounts of money, to each consequence, viewed as a value or disvalue (a negative value). Thus, for example, we would have to assign a numerical value in terms of money (or some other unit) to the good health of dogs and to human fear. This sort of thing I feel we cannot do, but if you feel that we can, then you might well consult a text about decision theory, which should include calculating and comparing expected values of alternative courses of action. There is a vast literature on the topic, but I do not go into it here because I have never felt able to assign num-

---

2. Including Professor Anita Silvers of San Francisco State University, who was the first to point out this assumption to me.

bers to things that some people value very highly (such as clean air, friendship, love, and self-respect) and to value principles themselves, such as "Lying is wrong."

When it is possible to assign numerical values to all the important factors and to estimate the probability that each will occur, then decision theory can be useful. But beware: It is tempting to neglect factors to which we cannot assign a numerical value, in order to fit a decision-theory system.

The Ben Franklin System

For most cases that you actually do face, I recommend instead a simple method suggested by Ben Franklin. It does not generate a decision, but can be an aid to your considering and weighing the pro and con reasons.

List on one side of a piece of paper all the positive aspects of some value choice and on the other side all the negative aspects. If you find an aspect on one side that is of about equal importance to an aspect on the other side, then cross them both off. If an aspect on one side seems roughly as important as two on the other side, then cross off the one and the two. When one side has something left and the other side has nothing left, then you should consider choosing the side with something left; how strongly depends on how much is left. I have done this sort of thing in Table 11.1, numbering each reason. In preparing the table, I did not cross out reasons for fear of confusing you. Instead I shall tell you in successive steps what I did.

The various stages in my thinking follow.

Assuming that the focus is clear (which it is in this case), make sure you consider the alternative ways of handling the problem. The opposite of the conclusion being considered is to allow dogs the free run of the park. Because this is in effect the con side of the argument, this alternative is being considered already. Two other alternatives have occurred to me (listed under 6): to prohibit dogs completely or to license only certain dogs to be in the park without being leashed. These special dogs would have to pass a test and maintain good behavior in the park, just as automobile drivers do in order to maintain their driving rights. The first of these two alternatives seems overly severe and the other seems administratively burdensome and unworkable, so I reject them. This rejection gives support to both alternatives because the elimination of competitors generally gives at least some support to the remaining possibilities. So I put these two rejected alternatives in the middle to show that their rejection does not affect the balance. Next, I concentrate on the remaining pro and con sides of the proposed conclusion.

Pro-1 and Con-1 seem to have about equal strength. Cross out the pair.

Pro-2 and Con-2 seem to have about equal strength. Cross out the pair.

Although Pro-3 seems stronger than Con-3, cross them out as a pair, remembering that the Pro side has an edge here.

Pro-4 seems stronger than the combination of Con-4 and Con-5, so cross out all three, remembering that the Pro side has an edge here as well. Actually, Con-5 seems to be a very weak reason because I assume that dogs are not as important as humans. But what do you think?

In any case, that leaves Pro-5 without compensating counterreasons. This uncompensated counterreason, together with the edge for the Pro side and the unworkabil-

TABLE 11.1   Conclusion Under Consideration: Unleashed Dogs Should Not Be Allowed in Pulaski Park

Pro	*Con*
1. This prohibition would result in fewer dog fights.	1. It is inconvenient for owners to keep dogs leashed.
2. Dog-fearing people would be less likely to be frightened by dogs.	2. This prohibition is likely to cut down on dogs' exercise; lack of exercise makes dogs irritable and harms their health.
3. Intrusions on people's activities such as Little League baseball games, tennis, basketball, informal ball games, frisbee, chess, reading, etc., would be less likely.	3. Well-trained non-offending dogs would have their freedom restrained unnecessarily, as would their considerate owners.
4. Dogs would be unlikely to jump on people, lick them, and knock them (especially children) down.	4. Dogs also have a right to jump and to express themselves.
5. Dog bites would be less frequent.	5. This prohibition is in conflict with the principle that dogs are important too.

	6. Other alternatives that have occurred to me seem unworkable:
	  a. Excluding dogs from the park completely seems unnecessarily severe.
	  b. Allowing only dogs that pass obedience tests and actually maintain good behavior seems unworkable.

ity of two other alternatives (mentioned in 6) appear to justify the conclusion under consideration for Pulaski Park.

On reviewing the reasons, I see no additional ones that are relevant and strong. One occurs to me, but I reject it. It holds that if leashes are required, there would be less spreading to young children of some diseases contained in dog droppings. I reject this on factual grounds: I see no reason to expect less spreading from leashed dogs than from unleashed dogs. My weighing of the reasons still seems satisfactory, so I maintain my conclusion. What do you think?

This approach enables us to retain the vagueness that is inevitably there, and it avoids assigning monetary or other numerical values to things, but it does assume some comparison of the strength of reasons. It gives a way to make a decision when the situation (including consequences and appropriate principles) is fairly clear, and when a look at the reasons leads one to feel that one side does outweigh the other. One danger is that the approach can lead to our thinking of only two alternatives: pro and con. In using the approach, we must deliberately try to think of other alternatives and other ways of looking at some of the problems addressed.

The Franklin approach is not a decision procedure. That is, it does not automatically generate a decision, and reasonable people might well differ on comparing the strength of individual reasons. It is only a convenient way to organize your thoughts. Furthermore, some problems seem too difficult to resolve this way, but it is often helpful. I know of no better way for cases like that of the dogs in the park. Perhaps you can develop a better way. I invite you to try.

FRISCO

Consider the extent to which I made use of the FRISCO approach in appraising the value judgment about dogs in the park. Remember that these phases of FRISCO, though presented in the FRISCO order here, should be applied with various orderings, emphases, and repetitions, depending on the situation:

F: It was important to know the conclusion that was under consideration. It appears at the top of Table 11:1.

R: It was important to know the reasons. They are the body of Table 11:1. A large number of factual beliefs were relevant here. Most of the items listed under *Pro* and *Con* are factual beliefs about consequences, such as the belief that the prohibition would result in fewer dog fights.

Some value beliefs on which my conclusion rests are the beliefs that dog bites are bad, that dogs knocking down children is bad, that dog fights are bad, that intrusions on our free activities are better avoided, that dogs' physical and mental health is important, that dogs have a right to express themselves and to be free, that trouble to people and dogs should be avoided where feasible, that people are more important than dogs, and that dogs are important too. Defending each of these involves us in another argument, but perhaps you will agree with most or all of them. Do you?

In any particular value argument, we cannot defend everything, but these seem to me to be acceptable starting points. If I encounter someone who disagrees with one, then we must discuss that one and argue its pros and cons.

I: One alternative to prohibiting unleashed dogs is explicit—the con side—permitting unleashed dogs. Others are permitting no dogs at all in the park, and permitting dogs without leashes if the dogs have special licenses. I rejected each of these other alternatives without explicitly going through the Franklin system for them. But if there had been any serious doubt about either rejection, then it would have been appropriate to use the Franklin system on them as well.

I made a tentative decision, based on a weighing of the reasons and a consideration of the situation and the clarity of the words involved. The decision is subject to revision, as it should be, if other important considerations develop.

S: Familiarity with the situation involving dogs and parks in general was required in predicting the consequences of accepting the conclusion. Also required was familiarity with the situation in Pulaski Park. It covers the space of about one city block and is surrounded by families with small children.

C: I deliberately used terms whose meaning was somewhat vague, but seemed precise enough for the circumstances. For example, the word *unleashed* in the conclusion under consideration does not specify a maximum length for a leash. Does a 100-foot rope count as a leash? I deliberately left that vague, thinking that the meaning was clear enough in the situation, and that specifying a meaning for *unleashed* would unnecessarily complicate matters at this stage. Furthermore, I repeatedly used terms that do not specify an exact amount, such as *fewer dog fights* and *less likely*. This degree of vagueness is appropriate for the situation at this time, although if the problem becomes more difficult, more specificity would be needed.

As far as I can tell, there are no crucial ambiguities or misleading ways of putting things.

O: I have reviewed the decision arrived at under FRISCO's *I.* It still seems right to me. You might have come to a different conclusion.

Writing a Value Argument

Much of the argumentative writing we do is aimed at supporting value conclusions —conclusions that hold that either something is good (or bad) or something should be done (or not be done). By *argumentative,* I remind you that I am not talking about hostile or aggressive writing, although it might be that; rather, I am talking about writing that has a conclusion and offers reasons in support of the conclusion.

Strategies

Naturally, it is important that you have an audience in mind, and that you write to that audience. It is also important that your audience realize what your conclusion and reasons are. The most obvious way for the audience to know your conclusion is for you to say what it is at the beginning. When you or your audience is in a hurry, or under stress, that is generally the best way. But there are other ways, such as drawing your conclusion at the end, leaving it up to the audience to figure out your conclusion, even to appear to be drawing a conclusion that is just the opposite of your real conclusion.

The trouble with these indirect strategies is that they often do not work. Often, the audience does not realize what your conclusion is. It takes greater writing skill, an audience with more reading skill, a point and a topic that are fairly simple, and usually more time devoted by both you and the audience, in order to use the indirect strategies effectively. But they are possible.

If you have used the Ben Franklin approach to organize your thoughts, then the content of your position paper or memo has already been developed for you, but it must be organized in a way that flows from one point to the next. One simple, straightforward way is to break up the paper or memo into three major sections, possibly labeled *reasons, counterarguments,* and *on balance.* Another way is to take the supporting reasons one at a time and work the challenges into a discussion of each of the supporting reasons. It often helps to start out with a concrete example. A third way, which is more difficult, is to weave a complex pattern that ends up considering all of the pros and cons, but does it in a complex mosaic.

Strength

In any case, it is important to give strong arguments and to claim for your conclusion no more strength than you have justified in your reasons. Your reasons can include general value principles, statements of fact that show that the case fits under the principle, and statements of factual consequences of accepting the conclusion and of failing to accept it. Often these consequences are most persuasive, and provide the greatest strength for your argument, if they are stated in detail. Concrete examples help here.

Temperance

Although this depends on your audience and the rest of the situation, it is often best not to be hard and uncompromising in stating your arguments and conclusions. Temperate language is usually best, not only because it allays suspicion of prejudice, but because it helps you be in a frame of mind that is open to alternatives. It certainly is a good idea, if there is space, to consider and evaluate alternatives to your conclusion and your reasons. That does not mean that you have to accept the alternatives. You might mount strong arguments against them, but be fair.

Factual Bases

Some of your argument might support the factual bases for your value statements. In the dog-leash case, for example, you might offer arguments to support or challenge the factual claim that there would be fewer dog fights if unleashed dogs were prohibited in Pulaski Park. These arguments in support of your factual claims might try to show that your source is credible, that your factual claim is a best explanation, that it is a justified generalization, that it follows (tightly or loosely) from some principle otherwise established, that the observation and reporting conditions were good, or all of the above.

Checklist and Revisions

In Chapter 1, you were provided with a position-paper checklist (starting with "1. Is there a thesis?"). It is a good idea to look this over before you start writing, to keep it in mind, and to check your drafts against this list. I said *drafts* because ordinarily you should revise what you write several times before giving it to your audience. "Revise, revise, and revise some more" is one of the cardinal principles of good writing. Very few people write a good first draft.

Analogical Argument

One type of argument that has not yet been discussed in this book is the *analogical argument*. In this type of argument (which can be used to support factual as well as value conclusions), the arguer offers another case on which it is assumed there is agreement about the conclusion. The arguer also urges that the other case and the present one are similar enough for the other conclusion to be transferred to this case. Here are some examples:

Example 11:2

    a. Cockfights are like dog fights. You know that dog fights are ugly and should be stopped and avoided. Similarly, cockfights should be banned.

    b. Allowing the Revolutionary Army free speech on the radio is like giving oxygen to a burning building.

    c. The earth is like an apparently healthy human being with a developing heart artery defect. Unless we take steps to reverse the deterioration, the earth and its inhabitants will die.

The other person might well point out that there is a difference. In the argument of Example 11:2a, one might point out that dogs and roosters are different, so it does not follow that cockfights are ugly and should be stopped and avoided. Other differences are that cockfights are generally organized for the amusement of human beings, and that the roosters are trained to fight under controlled conditions. Always at issue in analogical arguments is whether the two cases are sufficiently similar in relevant respects.

The principal guideline available for dealing with the question of relevant similarity is to see whether both cases come under the same acceptable principle, making analogical arguments judgable by the principles of loose deduction or derivation, discussed in Chapter 7 and the early part of this chapter. In this case, the generalization might be that fights between animals are generally ugly and should be stopped and avoided if possible, from which it follows loosely that cockfights are ugly and should be stopped and avoided if possible. This principle, you will realize, is open to exception, and depends on judgment, so appeal to a broader principle is not a guarantee of a reasonable decision. But such an appeal is a step beyond just asking whether the difference is relevant. At least the search for a principle provides some guidance about relevance.

One advantage of analogical arguments is that they help open our eyes to possibilities that we had not seen before, sensitizing us to the details of a situation. Seeing cockfights as similar to dog fights reminds me of the pain, blood, and unhappiness that accompanied dog fights, and sensitizes me to these possibilities in cockfights. Similarly, seeing free speech on the radio to be like oxygen shows the importance of the free speech to the health of the Revolutionary Army, in the eyes of the speaker. Seeing the environmental deterioration as similar to that of a cardiac artery shows how crucial the speaker sees the environmental changes to be. Analogies help us to see things from the other's point of view and bring out the vitality of the situation.

As you might guess, the use of analogical arguments is somewhat controversial. Some people feel that they are generally worthless. Others feel that they are fine, as long as the cases are relevantly similar. I have urged a middle ground that depends on treating analogical arguments as loose derivations and depicting consequences in detail. Think about it, but do realize that there is much more to be said about merits and problems of cockfights and about the merits and problems of analogical arguments.

If you use analogical arguments in your value-judgment writing, be aware of similarities and differences, and try to fit both cases under a broader acceptable value generalization. Also try to make use of the appeal of details, but be wary of the differences between the cases. There always are differences that might be used to challenge your point.

Summary

Neglect of the facts, failure to notice the facts, and failure to collect facts are often the source of disagreement and problems in making value judgments. So a first step is to make sure that the supposed facts actually are facts. In particular, it is usually important to consider the prospective factual consequences of accepting a value judgment. These consequences are judged by acceptable value principles, most of which have accrued over time and are part of the cultural tradition. But sometimes consequences occur that are not covered by acceptable value principles, or that are possible exceptions to acceptable value principles. Then it is important to examine them in detail, formulating original value principles on the basis of a perceptive, sensitive, and reflective examination of these consequences.

It is often helpful to list the pro and con sides of a value issue in two columns on a piece of paper. Then eliminate sets of reasons that are of equal importance for each side, and see what is left. If there are still strong reasons on one side, then that one is probably the one to take. Although this Ben Franklin strategy is imprecise, tempts us to neglect alternative ways of defining problems, and does not generate a solution that automatically resolves differences among reasonable people, it is often useful.

Critical thinking about values is subject to the FRISCO approach. The elements are the same: Focus, Reasons, Inference, Situation, Clarity, and Overview. They should be applied interactively. That is, every element or phase should interact with each of the others, and may be repeated in various ways. They are not sequential steps, although for purposes of summarizing, they may be presented in order.

Reasoning in the value area is imprecise and open to challenge. But it is not totally worthless and useless, as some relativists would have us believe.

Much of our argumentative writing leads to value conclusions. Various strategies are possible, assuming that the arguer is well-versed in the relevant facts, has explored the pros and cons for a particular position (possibly using the Ben Franklin approach as a decision-making process), and can state the conclusion. It is usually a good idea to be temperate in language, to use examples, often one right at the beginning, and to claim no greater strength for the conclusion than has been established.

Analogical arguments are commonly used to support value conclusions, and always depend on whether the relevant similarities are strong enough to outweigh the dissimilarities. Assimilating analogical argument to loose derivation and to depiction in detail of the consequences is helpful here.

Check-Up 11B

True or False?
If false, change it to make it true. Try to do so in a way that shows that you understand.

11:19 The FRISCO approach is inapplicable to reasoning about value judgments.

11:20 Both facts and acceptable value principles are very important in making decisions about value judgments.

11:21 The Benjamin Franklin approach that calls for us to list and cross off reasons is more precise than most decision-theory approaches.

11:22 The consequences of accepting a value judgment should usually be considered before accepting the judgment.

Medium Answer

11:23 Pick a local value issue with which you are familiar, or a personal decision issue that you face. Use the Ben Franklin strategy for making a decision and keep the FRISCO advice in the back of your mind. Your report of your effort should include a list of the pro and con reasons, should show how you balance them against each other, and should state your conclusion with some indication of how strongly you stand by it.

11:24 Now use your results from 11:23 as the content for a two- or three-page position paper on the issue. Make sure that you have an audience in mind. Pay heed to the Chapter 1 position-paper criteria.

11:25 In a page or two, appraise my handling of the proposed leash rule for Pulaski Park. Assume that Pulaski Park is near to where you live or, if you live in the country, is in the city nearest to you. Apply the FRISCO approach in your thinking. Assume that you are writing this to go in a letter to me. Again, pay heed to the Chapter 1 position-paper criteria.

11:26 Apply the Ben Franklin procedure to the question "Should our society adopt the principle that it is generally wrong to react with violence to a threat on your life, if there is a peaceful alternative readily available?"

11:27 Now use your results from 11:26 as the content for a two- or three-page position paper on the issue. Have an audience in mind, perhaps the readership of your newspaper. Pay heed to the Chapter 1 position-paper criteria.

11:28 Put yourself in President Harry Truman's position in the summer of 1945 and use the Ben Franklin approach to help decide whether to order the dropping of the atomic bomb on Hiroshima.

11:29 Now use your results from 11:28 as the content for a two- or three-page position paper on the issue. Have an audience in mind, perhaps the readership of a nationally distributed newspaper (give its name). Pay heed to the Chapter 1 position-paper criteria.

11:30 Consider the analogical argument about cockfights in Example 11:2. Assume that it is offered in your home town in defense of an ordinance forbidding cockfights. Appraise the argument, taking into account the phases of FRISCO.

11:31 Reproduce and appraise an analogical argument that you find in a newspaper, a magazine, or a conversation with some friends. Describe the situation and take into account the phases of FRISCO. Prepare a letter to the editor (or a friend) in which you evaluate this argument and defend your evaluation.

+ Relativism

Although a variety of differing doctrines are called *relativism,* two relativistic value judgment doctrines appear repeatedly and are significant enough to deserve discussion. These two doctrines are called *cultural relativism* and *personal relativism.* Roughly speaking, these doctrines respectively hold that what is right (or good) depends exclusively on what a culture approves (cultural relativism) or a person approves (personal relativism). In this sense of *culture,* the culture of a large group of people consists of all of their joint beliefs, attitudes, and ways of living.

Cultural Relativism

Three general types of cultural relativism can be identified, which I shall call *basic cultural relativism, factual cultural relativism,* and *sophisticated cultural relativism.*

Basic Cultural Relativism

John Zadrony's *Dictionary of Social Science* contains the following definition:

Definition   Cultural Relativism—the point of view in which each cultural group is evaluated in terms of its own value system.

One common form of this view holds that a practice or act of a person or group is supposed to be judged by the standards of the culture of that person or group. I shall call this view *basic cultural relativism.* For example, the fact that Western culture approves eating the meat of cattle makes it all right, according to this view, for people of the West to eat the meat of cattle; the fact that the culture of many Hindus in India holds that eating the meat of cattle is wrong makes it wrong for them to eat the meat of cattle. Furthermore, it follows from this that it would be wrong for the people of the West to try to induce Indians to eat the meat of cattle, just as it would be wrong for the Indians to try to prevent Westerners from eating the meat of cattle. These things would be wrong because they would be interference with the ways of a particular culture; basic cultural relativism assumes the ways of a particular culture to be right for the people in that culture.

There are problems with basic cultural relativism.[3] For one thing, according to it, all moral reformers are wrong because they are proposing things that, at the time the reform is proposed, are disapproved by the culture, which the reformers are trying to change. According to this view, a person who tried to get rid of slavery at a time when slavery was accepted by a culture was at that time wrong. It is a suspicious view that condemns reforms without looking at their individual merits and weaknesses and that is committed to support of the status quo, no matter how bad it may be.

Secondly, the view is self-contradictory in some situations: Relativism both endorses and condemns interference with an interfering culture. For example, a culture that, as one of its basic ways, tries to spread its religion, or its respect for human dignity, to another culture that does not accept this religion or respect would be trying to interfere with the other culture. Because doing this is one of the ways of the

---

3. This discussion of basic cultural (and personal) relativism draws heavily on W. D. Ross' *Foundations of Ethics* (Oxford: Oxford University Press, 1939), 22–26, 59–63.

interfering culture, relativism must endorse the interference. But because the ways of culture being interfered with are held to be right for that culture, relativism must condemn the interference. Thus, basic cultural relativists are committed to inconsistent recommendations in this common type of situation.

This difficulty could perhaps be avoided by holding (as an exception to the general rule) that whatever is endorsed by a culture is what the people in that culture should do unless it is, or results in, interference with another culture. Such an exception would avoid the self-contradiction, but would then require all cultures *not to* interfere with a culture that practiced slavery of, or discrimination against, people of one particular skin color or one gender, to pick some significant examples.

Each of these points could be explored more fully, and the arguments can get very complex. Instead of pursuing them here, I invite you to engage in these explorations of basic cultural relativism with your associates, so that I can turn to two other types of cultural relativism, which are more plausible.

Factual Cultural Relativism

The fundamental principle of factual cultural relativism, the second type of cultural relativism, is that the value statements supported by different groups are often different and conflicting in a very fundamental way. This difference is a factual matter, exemplified by the difference in evaluation of eating the meat of cattle.

Different cultures often do disagree about many value statements, so factual relativism seems to be a correct view. But the fact that two cultures do disagree does not show that both are right, or that neither is right, or that neither can be established as right, although we might be led to think so, if we are careless about distinctions among different kinds of relativism. That is, we might be led to think so if, from the establishment of factual relativism, we infer that some other type of relativism is true. Because they say different things, establishment of one does not establish another.

Sophisticated Relativism

Sophisticated relativism is the view that there is not any way of establishing one value principle as correct. Sophisticated relativism takes a sophisticated value position, and is difficult to prove wrong or right without already assuming that it is wrong or right. Sophisticated relativism gets its appeal in part from the difficulty of showing that some value principle or position is correct without assuming some other, more basic value position, which can then be challenged by the sophisticated relativist. Ultimately, there is no further position to appeal to when the most basic position is questioned. If you keep asking "Why?" you eventually run out of even-more-basic principles to use in giving an answer. Try it on any value position you hold.

In discussing sophisticated relativism, I shall not try to appeal to an authority because (among other things) any authority I select would be suspected by a large segment of my readers. So I would like to pursue the more precarious course. The basic strategy is to show that people who express this position do not actually believe it, as evidenced by their own strongly held views about various contemporary issues that affect them. There are such issues for all those I have heard express the position. Self-respect, employment, war, military service, education, taxation, honesty, medical treatment, delinquency, imperialism, equality, capital punishment, genocide, birth control, and euthanasia are likely issues on which people expressing sophisticated relativism do have a stand that they are willing to defend by giving reasons. That a person is willing to take a stand and give reasons implies that the person thinks there is at least some justification for the position and that the position is better than the alternatives.

In any practical situation, then, the location of a particular issue on which sophisticated relativists are willing to take a stand and give reasons should convince them that they do not really accept sophisticated relativism. If we should uncover a person who sincerely is unwilling to take a stand on any issue, then I do not think there is anything to do but wait until that person becomes a human being.

Alternatively, a sophisticated relativist could take a position on one of those difficult issues, but admit that he or she cannot offer any reasons in support of it, and leave it at that. I have never found such a person. All the sophisticated relativists I have ever met would be embarrassed to say that they cannot give any reasons or evidence for their positions, and in fact do give reasons. They not only take stands on some of those issues, but are also willing to give reasons that suggest that they think that their positions are justified. Thus, they are not really relativists. They just talk that way when they are not deeply and intimately involved in an issue.

The previous discussion of sophisticated relativism was abstract. Let me try to offer a sample dialogue so that you can check out your understanding and can apply some of these ideas to your own deeply held value positions. In the following dialogue, let *SR* mean *sophisticated relativist* and let *F* mean the relativist's *friend:*

Example 11:3

SR: Although it would be nice to be able to defend our value statements, ultimately there is no way to show that one is any better than another.

F: Does that include all of *your* value statements?

SR: Of course.

(Later)

SR: The prevalence of politicians who take bribes is disgusting. However, it's the fault of the system, which needs radical change.

F: Why do you say that?

SR: The ordinary person is neglected and exploited, and stymied in his or her efforts to do anything.

F: Is that bad?

SR: Of course it is. Special privileges are unfair.

F: Why?

SR: Well just look at what happens right here on this street. Look at Ms. Mills, who works hard, is totally honest, helps her neighbors, makes an important contribution, but is unable to provide care for her sick mother. In contrast, Mr. Jark, who is careless and inconsiderate, gets a lucrative city contract for doing nothing, just because he makes a large contribution every year to the right people. His sick father receives fine care. That is obviously not fair.

F: I'm persuaded.

Note what has happened here. SR, although denying that there is any way to show that one value judgment is any better than another, seems to belie his assertion. He defends his value judgment. Furthermore, when he runs out of higher-order reasons, he appeals to a consideration of the details of a situation. So he really does not believe what he says as a sophisticated relativist.

I offer this story as typical and invite you to check any self-proclaimed sophisticated relativists you know and see whether they do the same thing when dealing with things that really matter to them. Let me know if you find anyone who really sticks by his or her sophisticated relativism.

Personal Relativism

Similar in some ways to basic cultural relativism, *personal relativism* locates its ultimate justification in the approval of the person making the value statement. Instead of "Whatever is approved by the culture is right," the doctrine is "Whatever is approved by me is right." There is an initial plausibility to this view as well, for it would be very odd for a person to say (without qualification), "I approve of something that is wrong." Try saying to yourself about some particular action: "I approve of that action even though it is really wrong (not just judged wrong in our culture)."

A problem arises when we consider a situation in which one person claims that a particular act or thing is good and another claims that it is bad. The nature of this problem depends on the way in which we interpret personal relativism, as a definition of *right* or as a doctrine setting forth a nondefinitional sufficient condition for something's being right.[4]

In the definition case, all ethical disagreement disappears because the apparent contenders are simply talking about different things: the reaction of one and the reaction of the other. When Jane says that it was right for John to cheat on the history test, she would simply be saying that she approves of it; when Frank says that it was wrong, he would simply be saying that he disapproves. Given this definitional interpretation of personal relativism, each party would have to admit the truth of the other's contention (assuming that Jane does approve and that Frank does disapprove). That is, Jane would admit that Frank disapproves of the cheating, and Frank would admit that Jane approves of it. Thus, each would admit all that the other had supposedly claimed. The disagreement that we all know exists has been whisked away by definitional personal relativism. When Frank says that the cheating was bad and Jane says that it was good, it should be clear that they really are disagreeing and that neither does in fact think that what the other is saying is true. Definitional personal relativism magically, but falsely, eliminates real disagreements.

Given the nondefinitional, sufficient-condition interpretation of personal relativism, then, either contradictory judgments are both judged correct or the person advancing the position is insufferably arrogant. If Jane's approval is a sufficient condition for the cheating's being good and Frank's disapproval is a sufficient condition for the cheating's being bad, then this kind of personal relativism generates and endorses conflicting views: The cheating was both good and bad. If, on the other

---

4. Again, I lean on W. D. Ross, *ibid.*

hand, it is only the approval and disapproval of the person advancing personal relativism that matters, then the view does not generate such a conflict, but it is unacceptably arrogant. Thus, personal relativism has difficulties.

Absolutism Versus Relativism

One common form of argument offered in favor of relativism is exemplified by the following passage:

Example 11:4

We cannot assume that there are absolutes in morals. In fact, it is obvious that there are no absolutes. Look at the differences among cultures that are reported to us by anthropologists. For example, Margaret Mead tells of sexual freedom on Samoa. Point to an absolute and I will show you that you do not really regard it as an absolute. You say that a son should honor his father? I ask you then to think of the father who introduces his son into a life of crime. Should that son honor his father? Obviously not. Absolutism is false. Relativism is the only other way.

Before you read my commentary on this argument, think of what you would say about it.

In what follows, note the extended attention I have given to clarity of meaning (*C*). Later on, I shall refer to this argument and my treatment of it in discussing strategy and tactics for dealing with problems rooted in meaning.

In the situation (*S*) in which this argument was presented, it seemed that the conclusion was that relativism is a correct doctrine. The primary reason offered is that absolutism is an incorrect doctrine. The defense for this reason is based in part on a fact about Samoa that is a counterexample to factual absolutism (the view that all cultures are agreed on value judgments). It is also defended by a denial that value principles are universal. This denial is supported by an exception to the principle that a son should honor his father.

We should note that the argument assumes that there are only two alternatives: absolutism and relativism. This assumption should be examined. But there are several ways in which the term *absolutism* can be taken in this argument, so there are several possible interpretations of the assumption. We must look at the argument as a whole several times, each time using one of these senses of *absolutism* all the way through the argument.

Here I shall interpret *relativism* only to mean sophisticated (cultural) relativism, in order to keep things relatively simple. Basic cultural relativism seems wrong, I have argued, and factual relativism is probably true, but not relevant here. We could add to the complexity of the treatment by adding factual relativism as an interpretation of relativism, but then the conclusion in favor of relativism would be a factual one about what people do and what they believe they should do. It is not about what people should do, nor about what values they should accept, though such "should" conclusions are what the arguer, in my experience, wanted. That is, the arguer wanted me to accept that I should not draw value conclusions that apply to what other people should do.

This will be difficult reading. Among other things I am illustrating an argument strategy for dealing with possibly shifting meanings. I will refer to this example in Chapter 13, when the topic of shifting meanings will be emphasized. Read slowly, and read again.

1. Assume that absolutism is the belief that all cultures agree on a basic set of values. Then, although absolutism might be false, the assumed strong either–or proposition, "Either absolutism **or** relativism is right," is false as well, because a person who denies this sort of absolutism might consistently believe that there still is one proper way to do things. Hence, the argument's assumption is false, when *absolutism* is interpreted as the denial of factual relativism, and the conclusion is not established, given this sense of *absolutism*.

2. Assume that absolutism is the belief that there is a set of value principles that we know and that can be applied clearly and without exception. Then again, absolutism is probably false. Value principles generally do have exceptions and borderline cases. But is this kind of absolutism the only alternative to relativism? No. A person could believe that there is a set of rough principles—not exceptionless—that are basically correct. Thus again the assumed strong alternation is false, given this interpretation of *absolutism*. Again, the conclusion is not established, given this second sense of *absolutism*.

3. Lastly, make the supposition that absolutism is the belief that the principles by which we operate are at least for the most part true, and that although there are many borderline cases, there are at least some things that are clearly wrong and some that are clearly right. (I realize that this interpretation is confusing and does violence to what most of us mean by *absolutism*, but some people, in my experience, do sometimes interpret it this way.) In this case, the assumed strong alternation might in fact be true, but absolutism in this sense has not been shown false. Again, the conclusion is not established, given this third possible sense of *absolutism*.

My appraisal of the pro-relativist argument consists of a denial of the assumed strong alternation (either absolutism **or** relativism) unless *absolutism* is interpreted in the third way, in which case, absolutism has not been shown false. Thus, the conclusion is not established, whichever way we interpret the argument.

Although this presentation is simplified and the points and counterpoints can get much more complex, the basic strategy should be clear. Whether or not you agree with the overall appraisal, I hope that you understand the one-interpretation-at-a-time strategy. Table 11:2 summarizes this use of the strategy.

TABLE 11.2   **The One-Interpretation-at-a-Time Strategy Applied to an Argument that Offers Relativism and Absolutism as Exclusive Alternants**

Interpretation of Absolutism	Appraisal of the Argument
1. Factual Absolutism: All cultures actually agree on values	1. The reason "Absolutism is false" is true, but the alleged exclusive alternation is false, so the argument is defective.
2. Value Absolutism: There is one and only one set of justified value principles, and these can be applied clearly and without exception.	2. The reason "Absolutism is false" is probably true, but the alleged exclusive alternation is false, so the argument is defective.
3. Loose Absolutism (which is probably mislabeled when called absolutism): Many of our principles, though there are borderline cases and exceptions, are at least for the most part true.	3. The reason "Absolutism is false" is dubious and certainly has not been shown to be true, although the exclusive alternation, under this interpretation of *absolutism,* might well be true or close to it, so the argument is defective.

In sum, the argument is defective, no matter which of these three senses of *absolutism,* is chosen. Is there another?

Summary

There are two broad types of value-judgment relativism, cultural and personal. Cultural relativism in turn has three primary types: basic cultural relativism, factual relativism, and sophisticated relativism. I could also have broken personal relativism down into three comparable types, but to save time and space, only considered the kind of personal relativism that is comparable to basic cultural relativism.

Basic cultural relativism is the view that whatever is approved by a culture is right for the people of that culture. It suffers from at least two difficulties: It automatically condemns all moral reformers and leads to inconsistency or to excessive restraint.

Factual cultural relativism is the view that there are actual disagreements among different cultures about value judgments. This view is probably correct, but it does not thereby establish the two other types of cultural relativism.

Sophisticated cultural relativism is the view that there is not any way of establishing one value principle or judgment over another. In my experience, the adherents of this view do not actually accept it when dealing with things that really matter to them.

Personal relativism has the problem that either it eliminates value disagreements that we know do exist, or it forces one to say conflicting or insufferably arrogant things.

The argument for relativism that leans on an alternation between absolutism and relativism, and on showing that the first alternant must be wrong, does not work. Depending on the interpretation of *absolutism,* there is either another alternative to the two suggested, or the defectiveness of absolutism is not shown. There is much more to be said about this argument and about the topic of relativism, but these things should get you started and should dispel some elementary mistakes that some are inclined to make.

In this section on relativism, as well as in the entire value judgment chapter, there has been much emphasis on clarity of meaning, the *C* in *FRISCO*. Meaning often assumes great importance when the topic is abstract and difficult.

You have probably noticed that this section on relativism consisted mostly of argument. In Chapter 13 in a section on argument strategy and tactics, I shall use some of these arguments as examples.

Check-Up 11C

True or False?

If false, change it to make it true. Try to do so in a way that shows that you understand.

11:32 Basic cultural relativism holds that whatever is approved by a culture is right for the people who belong to the culture.

11:33 Factual relativism is the view that basic cultural relativism is correct.

11:34 Sophisticated cultural relativism is the view that there is no way of deciding among conflicting values.

11:35 Personal relativism, as here challenged, holds that whatever is approved by the speaker is right.

11:36 One accusation that cannot fairly be made against basic cultural relativism is that it leads to inconsistent judgments.

11:37 If what the speaker approves is by definition what is right, then (if they are sincere) both sides in an argument about a value judgment are right in this sense of the word *right*, but that is a contradiction.

Medium Answer

For each of the following, write a one-page essay starting with your conclusion, and then giving reasons for your conclusion. Pay attention to the criteria for a position paper given in Chapter 1. Use examples in giving your reasons.

11:38 Argue in support of the conclusion that value judgments endorsed by different cultures do in fact differ sometimes.

11:39 Argue against the view that democratic countries should not attempt to change the totalitarian ways of other countries. Assume that the view you are arguing against is grounded on the basic cultural relativist assumption that whatever is in a culture is right for the people of that culture. Be sure to include a challenge to this basic cultural relativist assumption and give your reasons for this challenge.

11:40 Refute this argument: It is right for Jones to cheat on a law school aptitude test because whatever a person approves of is right for that person to do, and Jones approves of the cheating. Be sure to show one or more problems with this personal relativist view.

11:41 Plan a survey in which you will try to find out the percentages of people in a certain group (or population) who accept each of the three kinds of cultural relativism. In your plan, make it clear how you will tell whether someone accepts each of the three types. (For example, state the question that you will ask and tell how to interpret the possible answers.) Make this easy enough for you actually to do the survey, paying attention to the principles of sampling and generalizing in Chapter 10. Do not expect perfection, but be aware of, and specify, the limitations of your procedures.

11:42 Do the survey you planned in 11:41 and write a report for an audience you specify, or orally present a report to this class.

Suggested Answers for Chapter 11

Check-Up 11A

11:1 T   **11:2** F   **11:3** F   **11:4** F   **11:5** T

11:2 Change *a value statement* to *some factual statements*.

11:3 Typically, even the best value principles have exceptions.

11:4 There can be both true and false factual statements.

11:6 Value   **11:7** Factual   **11:8** Factual   **11:9** Value

11:10 Value   **11:11** Factual   **11:12** Value   **11:13** Value

Note: In discussing Examples 11:14, 11:15, and 11:17, I have used concepts from Chapters 5 and 6. If these concepts bewilder you, then you might find it helpful to reexamine the relevant parts of those chapters.

11:14 **a.** The United States should have stayed out of World War I.

b. It follows, as shown in the following diagram:

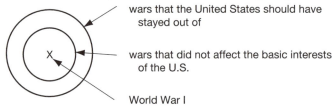

wars that the United States should have stayed out of

wars that did not affect the basic interests of the U.S.

World War I

11:15 Deliberately omitted.

11:16 **a.** It would be wrong to tell the teacher about it.

b. It follows: the antecedent has been affirmed.

11:17 Deliberately omitted.

11:18 **a.** Michael's intercepting and destroying Bill's love letter to Juanita was not unethical.

b. It follows, assuming that whatever is fair is not unethical, as shown by the following diagram:

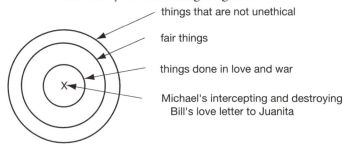

things that are not unethical

fair things

things done in love and war

Michael's intercepting and destroying Bill's love letter to Juanita

Check-Up 11B

11:19 F   11:20 T   11:21 F   11:22 T

11:19 Change *inapplicable* to *applicable*.

11:21 Change *is more precise* to *is often more practical* or *is less precise*.

11:23–11:31 These are up to you. Have you reviewed and revised?

Check-Up 11C

11:32 T   11:33 F   11:34 T   11:35 T   11:36 F

11:37 F

11:33 Factual relativism is the view that the value judgments supported by different groups are often different and conflicting.

11:36 Change *cannot* to *can*.

11:37 Omit the last clause, *but that is a contradiction*.

11:38 An argument of this sort appeared in the discussion of this topic. I hope yours used a different example than the eating of the meat of cattle, and I hope that you stated your conclusion clearly, making apparent that it is your conclusion.

11:39 In your argument you might well have shown how the assumed view leads to contradictory recommendations. You also might well have pointed out some of the incredibly vicious practices of some totalitarian governments, practices that a democratic government is committed to avoiding. Again, I hope that you stated your conclusion clearly and indicated that it is your conclusion.

11:40 You are on your own on this one.

11:41 Again you are on your own, but make sure that you have satisfied this question: Do your questions (or other ways of deciding what people think) actually work fairly well?

11:42 I hope that you found it interesting, and that your audience did also.

12

Reported Definition and Definition Forms

In the jury room, the phrase *proven beyond a reasonable doubt* caused great difficulty. In trying to decide whether Arlene was justified in using the force she used, we were concerned with whether Al had hit her and threatened to kill her, as she had claimed. She had been examined the night of the killing and no bruises were found on her. Other evidence was presented to show that she had not been beaten. Furthermore Arlene's little brother reported that he only heard Al say, "Arlene, I want to talk to you." The prosecutor held that she was not justified in using the force she used. But had the state *proven this beyond a reasonable doubt*? Might Al actually have hit her and threatened to kill her?

After much discussion about the issue, some jurors felt that we needed a definition of *proven beyond a reasonable doubt*. We decided to send to the judge a request for a definition of this set of words. About a half hour later his reply came back: "There is no definition of *proven beyond a reasonable doubt*. Do the best you can." This unexpected response threatened to end the deliberation. So I decided to hazard a definition off the top of my head without having had the time to formulate a definition carefully. Something was needed, even though, in a way, we all knew what the phrase means. I thought that the meaning could be stated, albeit vaguely (because the concept itself is somewhat vague), and made the following hasty suggestion: "To say that something is *proven beyond a reasonable doubt* is to say that it would not make good sense to deny that thing." What I was trying to do was to report a meaning in accord with standard usage of that set of terms, which is what dictionaries try to do.

Thinking about it later, I realized at least one improvement that I could have made in order to make definition a more accurate report of standard usage of the words *proven beyond a reasonable doubt*. Can you think of any improvements in my hastily formulated definition?

When I was giving that definition in that situation, I was not telling people anything they did not already know. But the situation called for a restatement in other words of the idea of proof beyond a reasonable doubt. The other jurors had a degree of special respect for me because they knew me to be a professor and teacher of logic and critical thinking. Thus, they had an understandable report of the standard usage of the crucial phrase from someone who appeared to satisfy the criteria for credibility. So they took my word.

We did finally decide that it had been proven beyond a reasonable doubt that she was not justified in using the force she used. The definition I gave, despite its defects, enabled us to discuss the matter. In this situation, I believe that the defects in the definition did not affect the argument.

This chapter and the next are concerned with definition. The *C* of *FRISCO* will thus be emphasized. But other elements will be emphasized also because definitional acts take place in situations in which other things are happening.

We shall begin with a look at one very common kind of thing people try to do under the label *definition:* Report meanings that are in accord with usage. It is what I was trying to do with *proven beyond a reasonable doubt.*

Reported Definition

A *reported definition* is an attempt to give the meaning of a word as the word was or is used. Usually (as in dictionaries), the attempt is to give standard usage of a term or phrase. That is, the attempt is to give the meaning of the word as the word is conventionally used. I tried to do this with the phrase *proven beyond a reasonable doubt.* A reported definition is then a factual statement. It can be correct, incorrect, or "roughly speaking" correct, etc. My reported definition of *proven beyond a reasonable doubt* was, roughly speaking, correct; it was sufficiently correct to get the discussion moving again without confusing anybody in that context.

Actually, my use of a reported definition was not typical in that I was telling them something they already knew. Usually, we give a reported definition to tell our audience something that it does not already know. In Chapter 4, I gave the following reported definition of *hearsay:* "Roughly speaking, *hearsay* is testimony that reports what someone else said with the intention of persuading the listener of the truth of what was said."

My intention was to inform you in case you did not already know. In the jury room I gave a simpler but similar reported definition of *hearsay* when a juror wondered what hearsay is. Again, my intention was to inform someone by reporting what I believed to be standard usage.

Sometimes a reported definition is not of standard usage, but only a report of how a particular person used a term on a particular occasion. When one juror asked to be reminded what the pathologist meant by *moderate stroke,* the response of another juror was a reported definition. It was a report of the pathologist's usage of that term on that occasion. The other juror did this by repeating the pathologist's demonstration of the speed of the arm movement that the pathologist called *moderate.* This was an informal sort of definition, but in that case, as with the pathologist's original definition, acting it out was the best way to convey meaning in those circumstances. More about the way to present definitions later. The point here is that reported definitions do not always report standard usage. Sometimes they report a special usage of a term.

Roughly speaking, a reported definition is satisfactory to the extent that it reflects the usage it is intended to reflect, given the situation, assuming that it is put in a way that the audience can understand it. My definitions of *proven beyond a reasonable doubt* and *hearsay* were satisfactory to the extent that they reflected standard legal usage for those phrases and were put in a way that the jurors understood. The juror's definition of *moderate stroke* was adequate if it adequately reflected the pathologist's usage of the term *moderate stroke* and was understandable.

Testing a Reported Definition

To test a reported definition that is intended to reflect standard usage, it is often a good idea to try to think of various examples that come under the term being defined. Then see whether they come under the other part of the definition, and vice versa. For example, consider this reported definition of *pencil:*

Example 12:1

A *pencil* is a writing implement containing graphite.

Pencil is the term being defined. The rest of the definition (that is, the defining part) is *writing implement containing graphite.* (A definition has two parts: the term being defined, and the part doing the defining.)

To apply the test, think of examples of pencils and then see whether the defining part also fits these examples. That is, see whether these examples are writing implements containing graphite. Then do it the other way around. Find examples of writing implements containing graphite. Then see whether they are pencils. By and large, if one part fits, but not the other, then you have found a counterexample to the definition. The ideal is to have no counterexamples. This ideal would be rarely attained if the goal of reported definition were to present universal truths. But producing universal exceptionless truths should usually not be the goal of a reported definition. Rather, the goal should be to produce a definition that is adequate for the situations in which it might be used. For example, we might have a piece of chalk with a piece of graphite jammed into it for some reason. This would not be a pencil, but it would not prove the definition inadequate. The definition is adequate for the situations in which I envision its use. Reported definitions are to be judged according to whether they are good enough for the situation (the *S* in *FRISCO*).

Consider these two definitions of the word *triangle:*

Example 12:2

A *triangle* is a closed figure consisting of three straight line segments.

Example 12:3

A *triangle* is a figure with three sides.

Although Example 12:3 is easier to understand (and thus might be better to use for initial teaching of the idea of a triangle), there are obvious counterexamples to Example 12:3. Imagine a three-sided figure with its sides made up of lines each shaped like an *S,* as in Diagram 12:1:

Diagram 12:1

The figure in Diagram 12:1 is not a triangle, although according to Example 12:3, it would be a triangle. Therefore, this figure is a counterexample to Example 12:3. Example 12:2, although more difficult to understand, is less vulnerable to counterexamples. It is a more accurate report of the standard usage of the word *triangle.*

Using Circles to Exhibit Defects and Success in a Definition

Sometimes it helps to draw circles to exhibit the relationship between the two parts of a reported definition. In Example 12:3, the word *triangle* is the term being defined; the phrase *three-sided figure* is the defining part. Note that I have omitted the word *is,* which works like an equals sign (=) in an ideal definition.

A diagram of the relationship between these two parts of the definition in Example 12:3 shows the circle for the defining part outside the circle for the term being defined.

Diagram 12:2

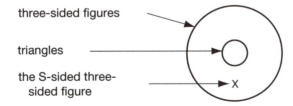

This diagram states that the definition has the defect of having the defining part represent a class that is larger than the other class or, in this case, that there are three-sided figures that are not triangles. (The S-sided three-sided figure is an example.) Circle diagrams are a way of explaining this sort of defectiveness to other people.

Note that in contrast to the use of circles to test the deductive validity of

arguments, these circles all represent actualities, not possibilities. The circle for triangles represents all triangles. The circle for three-sided figures represents all three-sided figures, not just an unruled-out possibility that there are three-sided figures that are not triangles.

Example 12:4 is another defective definition, if treated as a reported definition of the term *car* in its standard meaning.

Example 12:4

A *car* is a four-wheel land motor vehicle mainly for use on public roads.

Can you think of any clear and obvious counterexamples to this definition?

One counterexample to this definition of *car* is my neighbor's pick-up truck. It is not what I would call a car, yet it fits the defining part. Another counterexample is the car that won last year's Indy 500. It is a car, yet it does not fit the defining part. It was not designed for use mainly on public roads. Here is a circle diagram of this situation:

Diagram 12:3

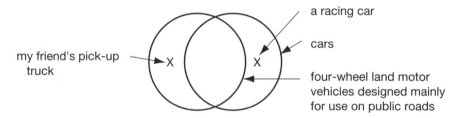

This diagram of two overlapping circles shows that there are cars that do not fit the defining part (racing cars) and that there are things that fit the defining part that are not cars (pick-up trucks). The car definition is both too restrictive and too liberal. (Do not be bothered by the fact that the size of the circles and the overlap are not truly proportional.)

You have seen a definition that was defective because the defining part included too much. You have seen one that was defective because the defining part included too much and also was too restrictive. A third way that a reported definition can be defective is by only being too restrictive:

Example 12:5

Proof beyond a reasonable doubt is proof that is deductively valid and that has true premises.

This definition is too restrictive because there are proofs beyond a reasonable doubt that are not deductively valid. One example is the prosecutor's proof (in

Chapter 2) of his conclusion that Arlene performed the act that caused Al's death. This proof, because it is not deductively valid, is a counterexample to the definition, and shows that the defining part is too restrictive. A circle diagram can show this situation:

Diagram 12:4

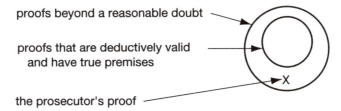

proofs beyond a reasonable doubt

proofs that are deductively valid
and have true premises

the prosecutor's proof

In this case, the deviation from standard usage mattered because one of the jurors was using the deductive definition, resulting in his refusing—for a while—to accept any other kind of proof.

The ideal for a reported definition is to have the two parts cover exactly the same area, that is, to have coextensive circles (circles that lie on top of each other and appear as only one circle), as in Diagram 12:5, which diagrams Example 12:2:

Diagram 12:5

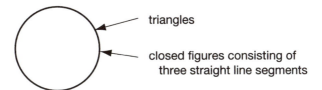

triangles

closed figures consisting of
three straight line segments

Actually, it is difficult to satisfy this ideal completely for terms in everyday use. For example, would you call Diagram 12:6 a triangle? I am reluctant to do so, yet it satisfies the defining part of Example 12:2, according to one way that we might interpret the words *closed figure* in that definition.

Diagram 12:6

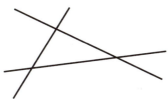

I invite you to try to make a true precise reported definition of some term in its standard meaning that has no counterexamples. Then see whether a friend can produce a counterexample. It is instructive to do this, both to make the definition and to try to produce a counterexample. Because you have not yet read about different ways of formulating definitions, it might be difficult even to start making such a definition, but give it a try. You already know something about formulating definitions because you have often done it. Furthermore, trying to make some definitions will help you get warmed up for the next part of this chapter.

When you are offering a reported definition in a discussion, take steps to avoid being sidetracked by challenges that do not bear on your basic points. First of all, try to state the definition correctly, avoiding obvious counterexamples. Second, you might well include loosening qualifiers such as *roughly speaking* and *by and large*. Third, it is often wise to admit in advance that there are borderline cases that do not affect your main point, which provides the situation (*S*) for the definition, but make sure that these borderline cases really do not affect your main point.

After thinking more about my definition of *proven beyond a reasonable doubt*, I developed the following definition: "To say that a conclusion is *proven beyond a reasonable doubt* is to say that the evidence supports it so strongly that it would not make good sense to deny it." If I am roughly right about this reported definition, then the diagram looks roughly like this:[1]

Diagram 12:7

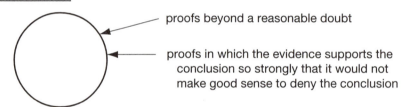

proofs beyond a reasonable doubt

proofs in which the evidence supports the conclusion so strongly that it would not make good sense to deny the conclusion

Diagram 12:7 represents the ideal in reported definitions of terms in their standard meaning: coextensive circles. Seek this ideal, but do not expect perfection.

Reported Definitions as Best-Explanation Hypotheses

As I indicated earlier, one of the jurors appeared to use *proof beyond a reasonable doubt* in its deductive sense. My belief to this effect was a best-explanation hypothesis, as are most reported definitions. The definition best explains the things that people (or in this case, the person) say and do. In this case, some of the things explained were the juror's answers to several questions I asked him about whether certain things are proven beyond a reasonable doubt. For example, I asked him whether the prosecutor had proven beyond a reasonable doubt that Arlene had killed Al, and whether it

1. A definition in *Black's Law Dictionary,* 6th Edition (Minneapolis: West Publications, 1991), goes roughly as follows: To *prove something beyond a reasonable doubt* means to establish it by virtue of the probative force of the facts. It has never been fully clear to me why the judge did not offer us this or some similar definition, but possibly he felt that the words *probative force* would mystify us. In content, I feel that my definition, as amended, amounts to about the same as that in this dictionary. What do you think?

had been proven beyond a reasonable doubt that the moon causes tides. He responded negatively to both questions. He justified his response by noting that it was logically possible for the reasons to be true, but the conclusion false. My hypothesis that he was using the term in the deductive sense explained why he answered in the way that he did. There was more evidence, but that should be enough for you to see the reasoning pattern here. Formulating reported definitions is a creative/critical activity that employs the criteria for best-explanation hypotheses.

It was important in this situation for us to realize that this juror was using a different definition of proof from the one that we and the court (even though the judge refused to state the definition) were presuming. Then we were able to point this out to him and say that in using his definition, he was not responding to the murder criteria as they were intended.

Defining Terms Any Way We Please

There is a common view that you may define a term any way that you please, as long as you let your audience know the meaning. An extreme form of this view is expressed by Humpty Dumpty in Lewis Carroll's *Through the Looking Glass*:

> "When I use a word," Humpty Dumpty said, in rather a scornful tone, "it means just what I choose it to mean—neither more nor less."

There is a germ of truth in this slogan: Every word could actually have meant something different from its actual meaning in our language. But in giving a reported definition, we are obligated to try to provide a true account of usage, and are not free to define a word any way we please.

This freedom-of-definition view is much more appropriate for a type of definitional act that we shall be considering in the next chapter: arbitrarily stipulating a meaning for a term.

Summary

A reported definition is the most common type of definition. Most of the time, when we are puzzled about a word, we merely need to know how it is used. Reported definitions are supposed to provide us with this sort of information. For reports of standard usage, this is something that is often imprecise. We usually cannot expect perfection. But for purposes of communication, knowing roughly how a word is used in our society at this time is very important. Otherwise there is no basis for expecting to understand each other. Furthermore, for purposes of communication and understanding, knowing how a particular person is using a word and how a word is used in some other societies or groups are both very helpful. We use reported definitions to convey this information.

Because reported definitions are information, it is false that you can define a term any way you please if reported definition is the type of definition you are doing.

Circles can be helpful in exhibiting defects (or success) in reported definitions that attempt to reflect standard usage.

Check-Up 12A

True or False?
If the statement is false, change it to make it true. Try to do so in a way that shows that you understand.

12:1 A reported definition is a factual statement.

12:2 The intention in a reported definition is to reflect usage; this is usually standard usage, but if not, then the usage of some particular person or group.

12:3 If a reported definition that is intended to reflect standard usage is successful, then its Euler diagram will consist of two overlapping circles, each with a part outside of the other.

12:4 The definitions in dictionaries are reported definitions.

12:5 To be satisfactory, a reported definition must have absolutely no counterexamples.

12:6 A counterexample to a reported definition is a case that fits one part of the definition, but not the other.

Medium Answer
For each of the following reported definitions intended to reflect standard usage, decide whether it is correct. If not, identify a counterexample (be specific), and draw a circle diagram that exhibits the defect in the definition. The term being defined is italicized.

Do this on the basis of what you believe the term to mean, consulting a dictionary if you choose. The point here is not to see whether you know the standard meaning of these terms, but rather to give you practice in handling definitions, based on what you believe the standard meaning to be. Use a separate sheet of paper.

12:7 A *circle* is a plane curved figure.

12:8 A *glacier* is a large body of ice.

12:9 A *sovereign state* is one with complete control over all its affairs.

12:10 A *poem* is a literary work with meaning beyond the actual literal meaning of its words.

12:11 The *scientific method* is a method consisting of all of the following activities. (If any one is missing, the method is not scientific. If all are present, the method is scientific):

  a. Stating the problem
  b. Formulating hypotheses that are possible answers to the problem
  c. Observing
  d. Measuring
  e. Calculating
  f. Using instruments
  g. Experimenting
  h. Drawing a tentative conclusion
  i. Testing the conclusion with further experiments

12:12 An *artery* is a muscular tube that carries blood away from the heart.

Another Medium Answer

> **12:13** Formulate a reported definition that is intended to reflect the standard usage of a term you use in your everyday life. Try to do it in such a way that there are no counterexamples. Be prepared to offer it to others for their scrutiny.

The Classification Definition Form

So far, you have been considering one type of activity that goes under the label *definition:* reported definition. Next, you will examine one form in which definitions, including reported definitions, can be formulated: the classification definition form. Reported definition and classification definition are not mutually exclusive categories. Rather, they exemplify two different dimensions of definition: type of activity and form.

The most commonly recommended form of definition is the classification form. It is often a very useful form for a definition, though not always so. Basically a *classification definition* consists of a general class and distinguishing features. In the previous section, the definitions of *pencil, triangle, car, hearsay,* and one of the definitions of *proven beyond a reasonable doubt* are classification definitions. As a reminder, here they are again (the term being defined is italicized, as is the general class term):

Example 12:1

A *pencil* is a writing *implement* containing graphite.

Example 12:2

A *triangle* is a closed *figure* consisting of three straight line segments.

Example 12:3

A *triangle* is a *figure* with three sides.

Example 12:4

A *car* is a four-wheel land motor *vehicle* mainly for use on public roads.

Example 12:5

Proof beyond a reasonable doubt is *proof* that is deductively valid and that has true premises.

Example 12:6

Roughly speaking, *hearsay* is *testimony* that reports what someone else said with the intention of persuading the listener of the truth of what was said.

In these examples, the words *implement, figure, vehicle, proof,* and *testimony* are the general class terms, although it is sometimes an arbitrary matter what is deemed to be the class term. For instance, in Example 12:2 I could have called *closed figure* the general class term, rather than *figure*. In any case, when making a classification definition, be sure to include a general class term. Roughly speaking, the general class term refers to a class that includes what is being defined.

The rest of the defining part of a classification definition is supposed to distinguish what is being defined from the other members of the class. In Example 12:1, the words *writing* and *containing graphite* distinguish pencils from other implements. The word *writing* excludes various other kinds of implements, such as farm implements and tools; the words *containing graphite* distinguish pencils from other writing implements, such as pens. The word *is* roughly means the same as *equals* (=) and asserts that the term being defined is equal to the defining part (which in turn consists of the general class term and the terms for the distinguishing features).

Rules for Classification Definition

Thus, two basic rules for classification definition are these:

1. A classification definition must contain a general class term.
2. A classification definition must contain features that are supposed to distinguish what is defined from the rest of the general class.

If the general class term and distinguishing features are well-chosen, then the third rule is satisfied:

3. The defining part and the term being defined should be equal in coverage. The defining part should be at least as broad as, but not broader than, the defined term.

Rule 3 is the one we were testing with circles earlier in this chapter. If Rule 3 is satisfied, then a circle diagram consists of coextensive circles (the same circle for both the term being defined and the defining part).

Negatives

Although sometimes unavoidable, it is usually a mistake to include a negative in a definition. The reason is that negatives usually do not exclude enough. For example, suppose I define pencil as follows:

Example 12:7

A *pencil* is a writing implement that is not a pen.

The negative phrase *not a pen* fails to rule out some writing implements that are not pencils. For example, it does not rule out a piece of chalk, or a stick used to write in the sand. So we have Rule 4:

4. Definitions usually should not include negatives.

The reason for the *usually* is that some terms express negative ideas and need a negative of some sort in the definition. An example is the term *bachelor*. A crucial feature of being a bachelor is not being married. The definition of *bachelor* needs a negative (such as *not*) in it. Can you think of any other negative concept?

Circularity

A *circular definition* is one that makes no progress, generally because it uses the term being defined (or something like it) to do the defining. A fifth rule is the noncircularity rule:

5. Generally, a term should not be used to define itself.

The rule is probably violated in Example 12:8:

Example 12:8

Marxism is the ideology of Marxists.

If *Marxist* is then defined as a person whose ideology is Marxism, Example 12:8 seems circular and in violation of Rule 5. If, instead, we know what Marxists believe, but are not sure whether their doctrine is called Marxism, then the definition is not circular. Furthermore, the word *ideology* adds something to the definition in some situations. To many people, an ideology is a doctrine that is held unthinkingly to some extent. If the point of the definition is make this claim about Marxists, then the definition is not circular. (It would then not be a reported definition, but rather a positional definition, a type to be discussed in the next chapter.) Many Marxists object to having their views labeled *ideology,* although they often claim that the views of their opponents are ideology. So, to include Marxism in the general class *ideology* is in some situations to say something about the crucial issue. The situation and assumptions are therefore important in making a decision about whether a definition is circular. Circularity is relative to the situation and assumptions (coming under the *S* and *I* of *FRISCO*).

Summary

The classification form of definition is the most popular form of definition. It is brief, precise, and usually convenient. A classification definition is a definition consisting of a general class and distinguishing features (Rules 1 and 2). The term being defined and the defining part are supposed to be equivalent, neither one broader nor narrower than the other (Rule 3). Generally, negatives should be avoided in classification definitions (Rule 4). The use of the term being defined (or terms like it) should be avoided, unless the repetition does not interfere with the purpose of the definition in the situation (*S*) in which it occurs (Rule 5).

Check-Up 12B

True or False?

If the statement is false, change it to make it true. Try to do so in a way that shows that you understand.

12:14 A classification definition mentions a general class and distinguishing features.

12:15 In a classification definition, the defining part is supposed to be equal in meaning to the term being defined.

12:16 An ideal reported classification definition has no counterexamples, but for everyday terms there are few that satisfy this ideal.

12:17 In a classification definition it is sometimes all right to use a term in the defining part that is similar to the term being defined.

Short Answer

For Items 12:18 through 12:22, give the distinguishing features of Examples 12:2 (triangle), 12:3 (triangle), 12:4 (car), 12:5 (proof beyond a reasonable doubt), and 12:6 (hearsay). The first is done as an example:

12:18 (12:2) *closed, consisting of three straight line segments.*

More Short Answer

For each of the following classification definitions, tell which, if any, of the five rules for classification definition it violates. If you think that a definition violates more than one rule, choose the lower-numbered rule. Assume some ordinary situation in making your decisions.

Again, the point here is not to see whether you know the standard meaning of these terms, but rather to give you practice in handling definitions, based on whatever you believe to be the standard meaning.

12:23 A *tariff* is when you pay extra for something you buy.

12:24 *Nationalism* is where people support their country.

12:25 An *ex post facto law* is a law that is ex post facto.

12:26 A *circle* is a plane closed figure.

12:27 A *glacier* is a large body of ice.

12:28 *Snow* is precipitation that is not rain.

Still More Short Answer

Make reported classification definitions of each of the terms suggested in Items 12:29–12:35. Try to reflect standard usage, but do not seek perfection. Instead, seek definitions that are adequate for the situation (the *S* in *FRISCO*).

12:29 Define *argument* for a college class in critical thinking.

12:30 Define *experiment* for a high school science class.

12:31 Define *folk dancing* for a close friend.

12:32 Define *conclusion* (as the term is used in this book) for an average college freshman.

12:33 Locate and define a term that is best defined using a negative of some sort. Describe the situation for which you think your classification definition is appropriate, and identify the term clearly.

12:34 Choose your own term and situation. Describe the situation for which you think your classification definition is appropriate, and identify the term clearly.

12:35 Define *validity* for a close friend. Describe the features of your friend's background that make your definition at an appropriate level of sophistication for your friend.

Some Alternatives to Classification Definition

You might have had some difficulty defining *validity* in Check-Up 12:35 because it is not easy to find a general class term that includes validity. Problems also arise for other sorts of terms. Classification definition cannot directly be used for adjectives and other parts of speech that are not nouns. Furthermore, classification definition gives an appearance of precision that is sometimes unwarranted. That is, some terms are more vague than a classification definition would make them appear.

Consider how you might define the following terms: *proof, parallel, if,* and *scientific method*. None is readily amenable to classification definition.

Equivalent-Expression Definition

The difficulty I experience in trying to define the words *proof* and *validity* is in finding a general class. When you have difficulty finding a general class, one useful strategy is to develop an equivalent-expression definition. My original and amended definitions of *proven beyond a reasonable doubt* are of this type. The amended one goes as follows:

Example 12:9

To say that a conclusion is *proven beyond a reasonable doubt* is to say that the evidence supports it so strongly that it would not make good sense to deny it.

In this definition, I put the expression to be defined inside a larger expression and equated the larger expression with another expression. The larger expression (containing the expression to be defined) is as follows:

to say that a conclusion is proven beyond a reasonable doubt

The other expression is as follows:

to say that the evidence supports it so strongly that it would not make good sense to deny it

In the definition in Example 12:9, these two expressions are equated. Hence the name *equivalent-expression definition*. The word *is* again divides two parts of the definition and serves as an equals sign (=). A classification definition of *proof* might look like this:

Example 12:10

A *proof* is a combination of propositions or evidence that establish a conclusion.

Here is an equivalent-expression definition of *proof*:

Example 12:11

To say that a proposition is *proved* is to say that it is established by the evidence and other propositions offered in its support.

The two definitions (Examples 12:10 and 12:11) seem about equally understandable, but (as is often the case) the equivalent-expression definition was easier to formulate because it did not require finding a general class term. Finding general class terms is often difficult for abstract concepts, and not always necessary, as is shown by Examples 12:10 and 12:11.

An equivalent-expression definition of *deductive validity* might look like this:

Example 12:12

To say that an argument is *deductively valid* is to say that the conclusion follows necessarily from the premises.

This is smoother than a classification definition, which might go like this:

Example 12:13

Deductive validity is the quality of having the conclusion follow necessarily from the premises.

The general class term *quality* was not easy to think of, and furthermore is not very helpful for understanding the concept.

My definition of *reported definition* at the beginning of this chapter is an equivalent-expression definition: "To *report a meaning* is to report how a term is (or was) used." But note that I changed the words slightly before I put the term to be defined in the larger expression. I used the words *report a meaning* instead of the words *reported definition*. In my equivalent-expression definition of *deductive validity*, I used the words *deductively valid* instead of *deductive validity*. Similarly, in my discussion of *proven beyond a reasonable doubt* and *proof* I shifted back and forth between the words *proven* and *proof* for the sake of convenience. This changing and shifting is allright as long as the definition conveys what needs to be conveyed to the audience. Did my definitions make sense to you?

One standard way to make an equivalent-expression definition is to start with the words *to say that;* then to add an expression containing the word to be defined; then to say *is to say that;* and then add an expression that is equal in meaning to the previous expression. The form looks like this:

Example 12:14

To say that . . . is to say that. . . .

In the first space goes the expression containing the word to be defined. In the second space goes the expression that does the defining work.

Another approach to definition, when the term to be defined is an adjective, is to add a noun of which the meaning is clear and unproblematic, and then to define the combination in classification form. Example 12:15 is such a definition of the word *parallel,* which is an adjective. When the word *lines* is added, the combination becomes definable in classification form, even though the original word *parallel* was not so definable.

Example 12:15

Parallel lines are lines in a plane that do not meet, however far extended.

Here the word *lines* is a useful helper. Repeating it in the defining part does not make the definition circular because its meaning is clear and unproblematic.

Still another way of dealing with words that are not nouns is to convert them into nouns, and then give a standard classification definition of the noun. For example, to explain the meaning of *free* we could define *freedom* in classification form:

Example 12:16

Freedom is lack of restraint.

For most purposes, this definition conveys the meaning of the word *free,* as many people use the term. More about this term later.

But this conversion-to-noun approach does not always work. It does not work well for *parallel.* The corresponding noun would be *parallelism,* leading to a stilted definition:

Example 12:17

Parallelism is the quality of being in the same plane but not meeting, however far extended.

The approach does not work at all for particles, such as *or* and *if.* There is no noun conversion available for them. Instead, the standard equivalent-expression form works best:

Example 12:18

Roughly speaking, to say "*If p,* then *q*" is to say that *p* implies *q.*

The approach to choose depends on the individual term to be defined and the situation.

Strictly speaking, the standard equivalent-expression form has the limitation of defining a term only as it appears in the given expression. But this form is still very useful for many situations. I often use it when I need a definition quickly, and also use it to avoid awkwardness and other problems.

Range Definition

For some terms, the precision of a classification definition is inappropriate. Check-Up 12:11 presents a precise classification definition of *scientific method,* but the precision is misplaced because the concept has vague boundaries. As a reminder, here is the definition that was presented:

> **12:11** The *scientific method* is a method consisting of all of the following activities. (If any one is missing, the method is not scientific. If all are present, the method is scientific):
>
>   **a.** Stating the problem
>
>   **b.** Formulating hypotheses that are possible answers to the problem
>
>   **c.** Observing
>
>   **d.** Measuring
>
>   **e.** Calculating
>
>   **f.** Using instruments
>
>   **g.** Experimenting
>
>   **h.** Drawing a tentative conclusion
>
>   **i.** Testing the conclusion with further experiments

Any such list of distinguishing features of scientific method is likely to have exceptions. For example, most astronomers do not run experiments, nor do they test their conclusions with further experiments, although their methods are scientific. On the other hand, the nine activities listed are very commonly present in cases of scientific practice, and are often essential. They are part of the fabric of science, although not always is each absolutely necessary for a method to be scientific. The conditions listed, although very important, are not necessary conditions because the concept itself does not have precise boundaries.

The range form of definition accommodates this sort of vagueness in boundary. It was named by Max Black[2] after ranges of mountains because of the vagueness of boundaries of mountain ranges. A glance at a map confirms that mountain ranges do not have exact boundaries, yet there is something there to be named. This comparable imprecision in our language is recognized by the range form of definition. A *range definition* is one consisting of a set of crucial criteria, such that most of these criteria can be expected to hold for any given application of a term (although most or all of them are not necessary conditions). Example 12:19 is a reported range definition of *scientific method:*

Example 12:19

Scientific method is a method of investigation characteristically involving stating a problem, formulating hypotheses that are possible answers to the problem,

---

2. Max Black, *Problems of Analysis* (Ithaca, NY: Cornell University Press, 1954), pp. 3–23.

observing, measuring, calculating, using instruments, experimenting, drawing tentative conclusions, and testing the conclusions with further experiments.

The key term in that definition that shows the boundaries to be imprecise is *characteristically*.

Note that there is still a general class term used: *method of investigation*. Thus, this range definition is a modified classification definition, modified to accommodate the loose boundaries of the term. It is a combination of the classification form with the loose spirit of the range definition. Alternately, the equivalent-expression definition form could have been modified to make a range definition:

Example 12:20

To say that the *method* a person is using is *scientific* is to say that by and large it consists of the activities of stating a problem, formulating hypotheses that are possible answers to a problem, observing, measuring, calculating, using instruments, experimenting, drawing a tentative conclusion, and testing a conclusion with further experiments.

The key phrase in that definition that shows the boundaries to be imprecise is *by and large*.

Example 12:19, the classification range definition, gives us *method of investigation* as the general class. Example 12:20, the equivalent-expression range definition, gives us no general class. If the imprecise term to be defined conveniently fits under a general class, the classification range form is better. If not, the equivalent-expression range form is better.

Actually, the precision to give to the boundaries depends to some extent on the level of sophistication of the discussion (the situation again!). For example, at a low level of sophistication, the word *democracy* might well be defined in standard classification form:

Example 12:21

Democracy is a form of government in which the people rule.

At a more sophisticated level, a range definition is appropriate because at that level the boundaries are not precise:

Example 12:22

Democracy is a form of government characterized by selection of lawmakers by the governed; freedom of speech, press, religion, and other forms of expression; and equality of all of the governed.

In this definition, the key words indicating imprecise boundaries are *characterized by*.

Example 12:22 does more justice to my concept of democracy than Example 12:21, partly because Example 12:22 is in the range form. My concept of democracy is somewhat vague in boundaries. For example, I do not insist in all cases that all law-makers be selected by the governed, but by and large expect this. In this case, the level of sophistication of the discussion is a crucial part of the situation. Thus, the situation (*S*) again plays a role in deciding what sort of definition to use.

Other Forms of Definition

The equivalent-expression definitions, range forms of definition, and combinations thereof are the most useful ways to convey at least most of the meaning of a term for most situations. Some other ways of conveying meaning are giving a synonym, using a term in a situation, giving examples and negative examples, and operationally defining a term. Because operational definition is seldom useful for most people, I shall neglect it here. If you are interested, I refer you to an article I wrote on operational definition.[3]

Synonyms

Giving a synonym is very common, as in Example 12:23.

Example 12:23

Lugubrious means gloomy.

Although usually not absolutely identical in meaning, synonyms can be very helpful because they are so quick and convenient.

Examples and Negative Examples

In many circumstances, giving an example and a negative example is a very useful way to convey the meaning of a term. (A *negative example* is a case that is not an example.) Often it helps to give examples and negative examples in conjunction with classification, equivalent-expression, or range definition, but sometimes an example or a negative example by itself will do the job.

In teaching a child the meaning of the word *square,* it helps to give examples of squares, but it also helps to show rectangles (negative examples), and to state that they are not squares. Consider this somewhat abstract definition of *irony:*

Example 12:24

Irony is a mode of expression in which the implied attitudes are opposed to those literally expressed.

This definition might be helped by an example. The use of the word *noble* in "The noble Brutus has told you that Caesar was ambitious" is an example of irony.

---

3. Robert H. Ennis, "Operationism Can and Should Be Divorced from Covering Law Assumptions," in Leonard I. Krimerman (Ed.), *The Nature and Scope of Social Science* (New York: Appleton-Century-Croft, 1969), pp. 431–444.

But the example must be familiar to the audience, if it is to help convey meaning. If the audience is not familiar with Shakespeare's *Julius Caesar,* then the example is not much help.

Hamlet's use of the phrase *slings and arrows* in his comment about the *slings and arrows of outrageous fortune* is a negative example of irony, and can be helpful, if the audience is familiar with *Hamlet.*

When someone uses a word or a definition you do not understand, sometimes all you need is an example. Asking for examples is a good habit to have. Asking for negative examples is also a good habit, though one that is much less common. A negative example helps tell you where the person is drawing the line.

Using a Word in a Situation

Although using a word in a situation is sometimes useful for teaching someone, it is often not useful because you usually want to tell someone what you mean by a word you are using or have used in the situation. Using it was not enough. In the beginning of this book, it would not have been enough for me to have let you figure out what I meant by *argument.* It was much better for me to tell you. Using it in the situation was not enough.

Summary

Although the classification form of definition is understandably the most common form of definition, other forms are better for certain circumstances. The equivalent-expression definition is one of my favorites because it is so easy to formulate and understand. It does not require a search for a sometimes awkward-appearing general class term, it gives the meaning in a context, and it is readily usable with words that are not nouns.

The range form of definition is useful in displaying the vagueness many concepts have. The classification form gives an appearance of precision that is sometimes misleading, though perhaps acceptable at a low level of sophistication. The range form can be an adaptation of the classification form or the equivalent-expression form.

Examples and nonexamples help bring abstract concepts down to earth and to mark the boundaries. It is a good idea to learn to ask for them in situations in which the meaning of a word or a definition is murky.

Any attempt to formulate a definition requires close attention to the situation.

Using Definitions in Your Writing

It generally helps others to grasp your meaning in a position paper if you define your terms. Often, the classification form is the one to use, but do not neglect the other forms, especially for abstract terms and terms that are not nouns. The range form is helpful when the term's boundaries in the context are not precise and you want to avoid needless quibbling about a term. However, challenges to a definition are often not just quibbling, especially when the definitions embody a point of view (making them positional definitions, not simple reported definitions). Positional definitions are discussed in the next chapter.

In any case, you now have a set of forms from which to draw in explaining to others the meaning of the terms you use. The choice among these forms should depend on your appraisal of which form is likely to communicate the meaning most effectively in the situation. Sometimes a simple example or synonym will do it. But often the more elaborate forms are needed. It depends on the situation, which includes the nature of your audience, the topic under consideration, and the actual content of the definition.

In the next chapter, you will see some of the roles definitions can play in controversial aspects of your writing and discussion. In the current chapter, the emphasis is on effective communication.

Check-Up 12C

True or False?
If the statement is false, change it to make it true. Try to do so in a way that shows that you understand.

12:36 An advantage of the classification form of definition is that it can be used for defining words that are not nouns without making any changes in the words.

12:37 An advantage of equivalent-expression definition is that such definitions are easy to formulate.

12:38 An advantage of range definition is its precision.

12:39 The word *characteristically* is more likely to be found in a range definition than a pure classification definition.

12:40 A negative example can help mark the boundaries of a concept.

Medium Answer
For each of the following situations, formulate a classification and an equivalent-expression definition. In each case, tell which definition you prefer for the situation given and tell why.

12:41 Explaining to fifteen-year-olds the meaning of *self-evident* as it appears in the *Declaration of Independence*.

12:42 Explaining the meaning of *compatible* to a close friend.

12:43 Explaining to a college class in critical thinking the meaning of *necessarily follows*.

12:44 Explaining to an introductory art class the meaning of *symmetric*.

12:45 Explaining the meaning of *eclipse of the moon* (or *lunar eclipse*) to a ten-year-old child. (If you are not familiar with this term, look it up first.)

12:46 Explaining the meaning of *resistance* to a group of people. You decide the situation, but describe it.

12:47 Explaining to a chance adult acquaintance in the supermarket the meaning of *implies*.

More Medium Answer
For Items 12:48–12:55, give a reported (standard meaning) range definition of each

of the terms, as you understand them. If you think there is more than one standard meaning, choose only one. Consider your audience to be a close friend. Make adjustments for terms that are not nouns.

12:48 Home economics

12:49 Poetry

12:50 Sophisticated

12:51 Psychology

12:52 Music

12:53 Friendship

12:54 Language

12:55 Sovereign

12:56 From your conversations within the past few days, choose a term that needed defining. Describe the situation and underline and define the term as you understand it, explaining why you chose the form you used. Also tell why you used or did not use an example and a nonexample.

12:57 Take out a recent position paper you have written. Select a key term, the definition of which might help your paper. Using each of the forms of definition that have been considered, formulate a definition of this term, if that is possible, and discuss the activity. More specifically:

    A. If possible, formulate a definition of the term in accord with each of the following forms:

        1. Synonym
        2. Classification
        3. Equivalent-expression
        4. Range
        5. Example and negative example
        6. Using a term in the situation

    B. Were you unable to make a definition using any of the forms? If so, try to explain why you were unable.

    C. Which of the resulting definitions best suits your circumstances? Why?

Suggested Answers for Chapter 12

Check-Up 12A

    12:1 T   **12:2** T   **12:3** F   **12:4** T   **12:5** F   **12:6** T

    12:3 Replace *two overlapping circles, each with a part outside of the other* with *two coextensive circles.*

    12:5 Replace *have absolutely no counterexamples* with *be good enough for the situation.*

12:7 Incorrect. An ellipse is a plane curved figure, but is not a circle.

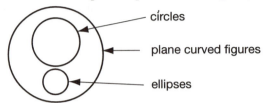

circles

plane curved figures

ellipses

12:8 Incorrect. A frozen lake is a large body of ice. Diagrammed like 12:7.

12:9 Deliberately omitted.

12:10 Incorrect. The short story "The Lottery" is a "literary work . . .," but it is not a poem.

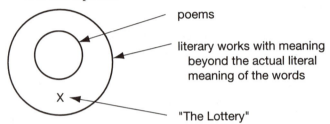

poems

literary works with meaning
beyond the actual literal
meaning of the words

X

"The Lottery"

12:11 Deliberately omitted.

12:12 This is all right at my (low) level of sophistication.

12:13 This is difficult, but not always impossible. Try it on your friends.

Check-Up 12B

12:14 T   **12:15** T   **12:16** T   **12:17** T

12:18 Done as an example.

12:19 *with three sides*

12:20 *four-wheel land motor, mainly for use on public roads*

12:21 Deliberately omitted.

12:22 *that reports what someone else said . . . what was said*

12:23 #1

12:24 #1

12:25 Deliberately omitted.

12:26 #3

12:27 Deliberately omitted.

12:28 #3 (also #4)

12:29 An *argument* is a set of propositions consisting of a conclusion and one or more reasons offered in support of the conclusion.

12:30 An *experiment* is an attempt to learn by deliberately changing something and noting what happens.

12:31 Deliberately omitted.

12:32 A *conclusion* is a proposition that someone is trying to establish in an argument.

12:33 A *bachelor* is a man who is not married. Appropriate for young children who are increasing their vocabularies.

12:34 This is up to you.

12:35 *Validity* is the quality of having the conclusion follow from the evidence. This is a stilted definition, I admit, but my friend is quite literate and good with language.

Check-Up 12C
12:36 F   **12:37** T   **12:38** F   **12:39** T   **12:40** T

12:36 Substitute *equivalent-expression* for *classification*.

12:38 Substitute *imprecision* for *precision*.

12:41 Classification: *Self-evidence* is the quality of being obvious. Equivalent-expression: To say that something is *self-evident* is to say that it is obvious. I prefer the equivalent-expression form here because it is less stilted and easier to formulate.

12:42 Classification: *Compatibility* is the quality of being capable of coexisting in harmony. Equivalent-expression: To say that two people are *compatible* is to say that they can coexist in harmony. I again prefer the equivalent-expression form here because it is less stilted and easier to formulate.

12:43 Deliberately omitted.

12:44 *Symmetry* is the quality of being balanced by being the same on both sides. To say that a design is *symmetric* is to say that it is balanced as a result of being the same on both sides. I again prefer the equivalent-expression form for the same reasons. But even the equivalent-expression definition seems overly abstract and needs supplementation with examples and negative examples.

12:45 Deliberately omitted.

12:46 *Resistance* is the quality of tending to hold something back. To say that I have increased the *resistance* in an electric circuit is to say that I have increased its tendency to hold back the current. The circumstance is a discussion of an electric iron with a close friend. Again I prefer the equivalent-expression form for the same reasons.

12:47 Deliberately omitted.

12:48 *Home economics* is a field of study characteristically concerned with cooking, sewing, home budgeting, child rearing, decorating and designing home interiors and exteriors, informal education, family life, and the research and disciplinary study underlying these activities.

12:49 Deliberately omitted.

12:50 A *sophisticated* person is one who is by and large worldly wise, complicated, refined, experienced, and subtle. Note that range form is combined with something that verges on equivalent-expression form here because *sophisticated* was embedded in a larger expression, which was then equated (using the word *is*) with another expression.

12:51–12:55 Deliberately omitted.

12:56–12:57 These are up to you.

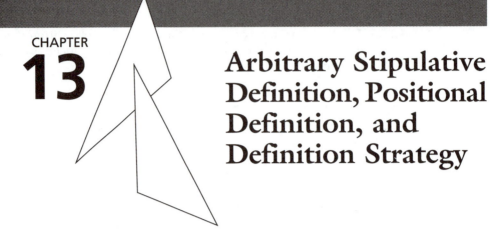

CHAPTER 13

Arbitrary Stipulative Definition, Positional Definition, and Definition Strategy

Not all definitions are reported definitions. Sometimes, when giving a definition, we are accomplishing (or trying to accomplish) something else. In the following examples, only 13:6a is a pure reported definition:

Example 13:1

Let *p = I will miss band practice*.

Example 13:2

The *C* in *FRISCO* shall stand for *clarity* (of meaning of words).

Example 13:3

By *argument* I mean a set of propositions including a conclusion, generally explicitly stated, and one or more reasons, again generally explicitly stated, offered in support of the conclusion.

Example 13:4

(In my automobile insurance policy) *Car:* a four-wheel land motor vehicle designed mainly for use on public roads.

Example 13:5

We define a *segregated* school as any school in which the percentage enrollment of any minority group varies more than fifteen percentage points from the percentage of that group in the school system as a whole.

Example 13:6

    a. Some people identify *freedom* with the absence of social direction and physical constraint.

    b. But rightly conceived, to say that someone is *free* is to say that the person possesses the power to think reflectively in an intelligent manner (a paraphrase of statements made by John Dewey in *How We Think*).

Arbitrary Stipulative Definition and Positional Definition

In contrast to reported definitions, arbitrary stipulative definitions and positional definitions are not attempts to *make factual statements* about standard or other usage. Instead, they attempt to *give* a meaning to a term, phrase, or symbol, or to *express a position* on an issue. This way of looking at definitions emphasizes what a definer is *accomplishing or trying to accomplish,* rather than just the content of the definition and the form of the words used. The same words can be used to accomplish different things, just as a tool can be used to do different things. For example, a screwdriver can be used to turn screws, but can also be used to pry things loose, or to serve as a paperweight.

Because most people do not consciously distinguish among these three types of definitional activity (reporting, arbitrarily stipulating, and expressing a position), they do not consciously choose to do one over the other. But these are three identifiable, important, and different definitional activities. You will find it helpful to be able to distinguish among them, so that you can assess the defense available for the definition in the context in which it is offered. Different definitional activities require different types of defense.

Arbitrary Stipulative Definition

A person giving an *arbitrary stipulative definition* suggests or requests that we, the audience, agree to a meaning for a term for the sake of communication. (Note my use of the equivalent-expression form here.) In effect, an arbitrary stipulative definition provides a communication agreement to which we are invited or requested to assent. Henceforth, for the sake of brevity, I shall just call these definitions *stipulative,* leaving out the word *arbitrary,* though keeping it in mind. (This itself is a stipulated definition of *stipulation*.)

Examples 13:1 and 13:2 were clear cases of stipulative definition when I offered them earlier in this book. In each case, I was the definer and was inviting you to understand my symbols in the way specified so that you could understand other things that I was saying. If you did not understand what I meant by *p* or *C,* then you would not understand what else I was saying. I was asking you to use those symbols in the given way. I needed some symbol or term for the concepts of interest, and selected those.

The primary motivation in a stipulative definition is convenience of communication. Only when convenience of communication is an appropriate primary motive is Humpty Dumpty's freedom-of-definition view fairly close to being valid, and often not even then. (Reminder: He said, "When I use a word, it means just what I choose it to mean—neither more nor less.") However, a background presupposition in cases of stipulation is that the idea involved is important enough for our attention, so even pure cases of stipulation involve a judgment.

The basis for an apparently stipulative definition can be a reported definition. For example, I did not just invent a wild definition of *argument*. Based on and to some extent justified by a reported definition of *argument* in the field of critical thinking, I was both stipulating and (implicitly) reporting it. Similarly, in a class in English literature or a class in physics, the instructor might at one and the same time stipulate and report a meaning for *irony* or *work*. Part of an instructor's job is to teach students the standard meanings of special terms in the field of study. But the definitions are usually presented as requests, suggestions, or commands, as well as reports of usage. Thus, such definitions are usually partly stipulative (backed up by authority) as well as partly reported.

Positional Definition

To give a *positional definition* is to express a position or point of view on some issue. This is a third kind of definitional activity. The definition of *murder* that was given to my jury (see Chapter 7, Check-Up Item 7:8) was a positional definition. Roughly speaking, the position expressed by that definition of murder is that an act that fits those criteria is among the most serious of crimes, deserving of serious punishment. Generally, the primary thing to defend in a positional definition is the position expressed by the definition.

Examples 13:5 (*segregated*) and 13:6b (*free*) were clearly positional definitions in the context in which they appeared. The goal was not simply convenience in communication. The people giving those two definitions were trying to attach criteria to a term in a way that will have some impact above and beyond the communicative function of a definition. These definitions incorporate a position on an issue. In our culture and social fabric, these two terms already have some kind of positive or negative connotation.

Segregation has a negative connotation. That is, the prevailing feeling in our culture at the time of writing is rejection of segregation, and there are legal objections to segregation. Members of our society generally feel pressure to eliminate whatever is labeled *segregation*. This has happened in the State of Illinois, where the given definition has been used. The definition incorporated a position by some officials of the State of Illinois against what was defined as *segregation* in Example 13:5, and people felt pressure to eliminate it.

It is similar with Dewey's definition of *free*, except that *free* has a positive connotation in our culture. Generally, whatever is labeled as free is lauded by being so labeled, and whatever is labeled as a denial of freedom is condemned by being so labeled. Definition 13:6b is an attempt to get certain things labeled by the word *free*. For example, some people might judge compulsory education to be an infringement on the freedom of parents and children. According to the definition of *freedom* that

Dewey rejected (13:6a, "absence of social direction and physical constraint"), compulsory education reduces the freedom of the students and their parents. This is so because the students are required to attend school, and the parents are required to see to it that their children attend school. Social direction and physical constraint are not absent under compulsory education, so freedom (in the sense that Dewey reported and rejected) is to that extent diminished. Thus, to say that compulsory education interferes with freedom (as it truly does, in this sense of *freedom*) is to assert that compulsory education has at least some weakness. This sense of the word *freedom* (that Dewey rejected) is sometimes called *negative freedom*. The word *negative* in *negative freedom* is not to be confused with the word *negative* in *negative connotations*. The same goes for the word *positive*.

The positional definition of the word *free* offered by Dewey in Example 13:6b provides one version of what is sometimes called *positive freedom:* the power to do. . . . According to the definition in Example 13:6b, compulsory education does not infringe on freedom, but rather promotes it, assuming that compulsory education actually does facilitate the possession by students of *the power to* think reflectively in an intelligent manner. Compulsory education usually contributes to learning to read and write. The ability to read and write presumably contributes to the power to think reflectively in an intelligent manner (depending on the further positional definition of reflective thinking and intelligence).

One danger in the positive definition of freedom as "the power to do . . ." is that the definition is vague about what comes after the word *do*. Totalitarians who have no respect for negative freedom can accept a positive definition of *freedom,* such as "the power to do what one is supposed to do," with the totalitarian definer specifying what one is supposed to do.

This problem even arises to some extent with Dewey's definition, which is considerably more explicit than "the power to do. . . ." The terms *reflective thinking* and *intelligent* are themselves in need of some interpretation. The interpretation provided could radically affect the worth of Dewey's positive freedom. Suppose that it is assumed that *acting in an intelligent manner* is intended to mean *acting in accord with the will of the leader.* Then the definition could be used in service of totalitarianism. I am not saying that Dewey interprets *intelligence* this way. I am only trying to show that the positive definition of *freedom* can be used to oppose freedom in the standard sense of the term (assuming that the negative definition gives the standard sense of the term). We must beware when people start shifting the meanings of terms in our language. (I am not saying that such shifting is always wrong—just warning you to beware.)

These positional definitions clearly incorporate a position about some issue or question. They are not merely innocent attempts to find a convenient neutral meaning for a term. When positional definitions embody controversial value judgments and are offered without defense, they are often called *persuasive definitions.*

Example 13:4, the definition of *car,* is from my insurance policy. It is partly stipulative and partly positional. A company that sells automobile insurance needs to be quite precise about what sort of thing it is insuring because some vehicles are more risky to insure than others. The definition is not intended to be a reported definition of the word *car* in its most standard sense because it includes pick-up trucks and vans under the category *car,* and does not include racing cars. But the company's purpose in writing the insurance policy was not to report the standard meaning of the word *car*, but rather to specify one kind of thing that it offers to insure to a certain extent for a stated price. Given the insurance deal the company offers for cars, its definition of *car* is a positional definition. On the other hand, the company could easily have chosen another word in the place of *car* (perhaps *automobile*) and defined and used the word *car* differently. So, in a way, the definition is stipulative.

The line between stipulative and positional definition is not sharp, but, roughly speaking, more defense of the implicit value judgment is needed for a positional definition. Usually no defense at all is needed for a pure stipulative definition. Often, if a person wants to define a term in a particular way for the purpose of communication, then the person has a right to do that. However, one important thing about which we should then be concerned is the convenience of the stipulation. Another concern is the importance of the associated idea.

A third concern can arise from confusion caused by the difference between the stipulated meaning and the standard meaning, depending on the particular term and the situation. For example, in our contemporary society, offering the above definition of *segregation* (Example 13:5) as a mere stipulative definition would usually be misleading. This is because the word *segregation* (when applied to schools) already is built into the public mind as referring to something bad. Most of us are not flexible enough to treat Example 13:5 as *only* a request to understand that the specified kind of situation is what the speaker is referring to when he or she says *segregation*. Rather, we will feel some pressure to treat whatever is accordingly labeled *segregation* as wrong.

If, on the other hand, we are in a group of flexible people who actually will treat the definition of *segregation* in Example 13:5 merely as a rule to facilitate communication, then the definition can appropriately be stipulated. But we must be sure that no positive or negative impact accompanies the word in that situation. In most situations, that definition should not be presented as a mere stipulation because people are not ordinarily that flexible.

I am not saying that segregation (so defined) is acceptable or unacceptable. Rather, I am saying that offering that meaning for the term as a mere stipulation might illegitimately have the impact of persuading people—without an accompanying justification—that segregation (so defined) is wrong. It is a mistake to treat that definition as a stipulative definition (needing little or no defense) because it will probably have an impact that needs defense.

Unfortunately, there is a possible confusion built into the use of the term *stipulate*, as I have stipulated its meaning here. Positional definitions are stipulated in the everyday sense of *stipulate*. For example, John Dewey was, in a way, stipulating his definition of *free*. That is why I started out by talking about arbitrary stipulation. For these purposes, please accept my stipulation that the word *stipulation* (in the pure case) shall refer only to arbitrary attempts to establish convenience of communication —without implying an answer to basic underlying issues, except the issues regarding whether the idea concerned is important and whether the stipulation is convenient. To say that a decision is *arbitrary*, in the sense in which I am using it here, is to say that it does not matter which way the decision goes. (Note that I have just given an equivalent-expression stipulative/reported definition of *arbitrary*.)

TABLE 13.1 Three Dimensions of Definition: Form, Activity and Content

	Activity		
Form	*Report a Meaning*	*Arbitrarily Stipulate a Meaning*	*Express a Position*
Classification	13:6a (freedom)		13:4 (car)* 13:5 (segregated)* 13:6b (free)
Equivalent-Expression			
Range	13:3 (argument)*		
Example/Negative Example			
Use in Context			
Synonym		13:1 (p), 13:2 (C)	

↘ Content

Note: 1. For purposes of illustration, some cells are filled in with example numbers.
2. Because the existence of the content dimension is obvious (that is, it is obvious that definitions can differ in content) and because this paper is only two-dimensional, the content dimension is shown by an arrow that should be visualized as coming out of the page.
*3. Example 13:3, the definition of *argument,* is borderline between arbitrary stipulative and reported. Example 13:4, the definition of *car,* is borderline between arbitrary stipulative and positional. Example 13:5, the definition of *segregated,* is borderline between classification and equivalent expression, although it is closer to being of classification form.

At this point, it might be helpful to examine Table 13:1, which depicts the form, activity, and content of a definition as three different dimensions of definition. Every definition given by someone is a composite of these three dimensions. Examples 13:1–13:6 are placed in the table.

Summary

Arbitrary stipulative definitions are attempts to specify a meaning for a term for the sake of convenience in communication. Little or no defense is required, but one should be careful to avoid stipulating a meaning for a term with positive or negative connotations in a situation in which the participants will not be flexible enough to leave these connotations out of their thinking. For the sake of brevity, I generally leave out the term *arbitrary* in labeling these definitions.

Positional definitions are those that express or incorporate a position on an issue. Often the position is controversial. When this is so, and defense is not provided, they could also be called *persuasive definitions.* Although defense for positional definitions need not always immediately accompany them, defense should be available, and we should be ready to request a defense for positional definitions when they are offered to us.

Check-Up 13A

True or False?

If false, change it to make it true. Try to do so in a way that shows that you understand.

13:1 A positional definition expresses a position on a question or an issue.

13:2 A stipulative definition has as its primary purpose convenience in communication.

13:3 Humpty Dumpty's statement that a word means just what he chooses it to mean is acceptable in situations calling for stipulative definition.

13:4 Humpty Dumpty's statement is acceptable in situations calling for positional definition.

13:5 The following is a positional definition of *educated:* "An *educated* person is one who is a critical thinker and is well-informed about this and other cultures" (offered by a professor in a discussion of the general goals of the University of Illinois).

Medium Answer (less than one page for each)

13:6 Choose one of the following often-contested terms. Imagine and describe a situation in which you would offer a positional definition of the term, and state your positional definition of the term for that situation.

equality of opportunity	genocide	education
science	a responsible person	teaching
art	a friend	proof
justice	democracy	home economics
fascist	healthy	literacy
sexual harassment	critical thinking	person

13:7 Defend the positional definition you gave in Item 13:6.

13:8 Judge the following (partial) positional definition of *love* and defend your judgment:

Love is not having to say that you're sorry.

13:9 In a newspaper, magazine, textbook, or lecture, find a definition that is a stipulation offered primarily for the sake of convenience. Quote and cite it. Judge whether the definition provides convenience, given the situation, and defend your judgment.

13:10 Judge the positional definition of freedom (*positive freedom*) that I attributed to John Dewey (Example 13:6b). Defend your judgment.

+ Definitional Strategy

Reporting a meaning, stipulating a meaning, and expressing a position through a definition are very different things. In discussing issues with others, developing oral and written material for presentation to other people, and understanding what others have done, you must make sure that these activities are not confused.

The Need for Defense of Positional Definitions

One principal danger in dealing with positional definitions is acting as if they are stipulations for convenience and need no defense. The rule that you can define a term any way you please does not apply to positional definitions. These must be justified. For the *segregation* definition, the wrongness of situations that would thereby be judged segregated needs to be shown. For the positive-freedom definition, it must be shown that it is generally more important to help students to think reflectively in an intelligent manner than it is to eliminate school-related constraints on them.

Both of these issues are more complex than I have indicated, but I hope you get the flavor. Problems of definition and meaning like this tend to be the most complex and difficult critical thinking problems.

Because offering a positional definition often amounts to assuming crucial support for a conclusion, we have a right to ask for reasons. The simplest way to handle this problem is to ask "Why?" That is, "Why should that definition be accepted?" The answer "I have a right to define my terms however I like" is not acceptable for positional definitions. If someone gives you such an answer, then, in reply, you can point out some consequences that would arise from accepting the definition and point out different consequences that would arise from accepting a competing definition. Then you can point out that these differences must be defended.

Introducing Confusion with a Stipulative Definition

Another possible danger lies in the use of definitions that are claimed to be stipulative, but in fact are not, and risk throwing a discussion off the track:

Example 13:7

J: Please don't argue with me about this. I want you to meet the Ramirez-Craigs.

M: (in a nasty voice) I don't want to. (angrily) You're bothering me. Go away!

J: I asked you not to argue.

M: I'm not arguing.

J: What do you think you're doing, then?

M: Just telling you how I feel about it. I haven't given you any reasons; I've just told you how I feel. It's my intuition. I have no argument. Now leave me alone. You're making me angry.

J: You are arguing. You always argue, it seems for the sake of annoying me.

M: Look, this is silly. We are using the word *argument* in different ways. In order to avoid confusion, let's define *argument* as an attempt to prove something by offering reasons in support of it. In that sense of *argument*, I am not arguing with you.

J: All right, in that sense of *argument* you are not arguing with me. Then I wonder why you always disagree with me in that nasty way of yours. And I wonder why you do not want to meet the Ramirez-Craigs.

The putative stipulative definition of the word *argument* offered by M did not solve their basic problem and risked throwing the discussion off the track, even though it in fact is the definition I stipulated earlier in this book. (Note the importance of the situation.) But, given J's flexibility about the meaning of the word *argument* (in the last entry), M's definition did not prevent them from discussing their problem. The dispute about whether M was arguing was a fruitless dispute, introduced by M. It turned out that J was flexible enough, and immediately stated the two issues without using the word *argument*. If J had not been that flexible, then M's stipulation might have succeeded in confusing things. You might also look at M's stipulation as a deliberate device to throw J off the track, but J did not fall into the trap. J stated the two issues without using the word *argument*.

One way to handle such attempts to throw a discussion off the track is to be flexible, like J. Express your concerns in ways that adhere to someone's stipulative definition, as J did.

Another way is to refuse the stipulation. J might have said that M knows very well what J meant, and in that sense of the word *argument,* M and J were arguing. This strategy is appropriate if you have trouble being that flexible, or if there are other people listening, or somehow involved, who would have trouble being that flexible.

Using a Positional Definition to Avoid the Issue

Another way of misusing definitions is to argue for (or assume) a positional definition of a term, draw a conclusion using the term in that sense, and then apply the conclusion in a way that actually ignores the real original issue, although the application may appear to bear on the original issue. This, in effect, is defining the problem out of existence. Consider this discussion:

Example 13:8

J: You were selfish in cutting into that lunch line when those people weren't looking.

M: So what? I just did what anyone would do.

J: That's not true, but it doesn't matter whether other people would do that. It was selfish.

M: Let's define our terms. To be *selfish* is to act in accord with your very own desires. Right?

J: Hmm. I'm not sure.

M: That's an enlightened definition of the word *selfish*. It makes deciding about whether someone is selfish purely a factual matter. People have desires. If they act in accord with them, then they are selfish. It's as simple as that. This definition leaves out the subjective meaning that some people have for the word *selfish,* so it is a better definition.

J: I follow you so far. Go on.

M: Good. Now you should be able to see that everything everybody does is really selfish. That's because people really act in accord with their desires all the time. If they did not desire to do what they do, they would not do it.

J: So?

M: Because everything everybody does is selfish, you cannot condemn me for doing something selfish. That wouldn't be fair.

What do you think J's response could be? M has managed to make it appear that cutting in line is no worse than anything else anybody does. Under M's definition of *selfish,* (together with M's assumption that people always act in accord with their desires), being selfish is unavoidable behavior. The position expressed by M's definition is that there is nothing wrong with what M did.

One response could be just to say, "Nonsense." This might well be appropriate on some occasions, but if M is serious about it, this response does not help.

Another response could be for J to be flexible and accept M's definition and argument (which only defends the *selfishness* of cutting in line). J should then claim that M's cutting into line was still *unfair* to the people who were displaced.

Alternately, still accepting M's definition, J could distinguish among types of selfishness, perhaps praiseworthy selfishness, neutral selfishness, and condemnable selfishness. Then J could make the point that M's cutting into line was condemnable selfishness. Except for the change in wording, this is the same point J tried to make in the first place. Two difficulties with this strategy are that it requires flexibility on J's part (and that of M and the audience, if any), and that it takes time. It also requires quick thinking. Producing useful distinctions on the spot is often difficult.

A third kind of reply is to refuse to accept the positional definition of *selfish*. This could involve defending the so-called subjective element in the word *selfish*. The word *selfish* in my desk dictionary is defined as "concerned chiefly or only with oneself, without regard for the well-being of others." J could say that it was easy to see that M's cutting into line was done without regard for the well-being of others. So it was not difficult to show that the "subjective" element (acting without regard for the well-being of others) applies in this case. So the concept indicated by the reported definition in my dictionary is not defective in the way alleged by M. That concept does not need to be replaced, J could conclude. J could also note that not all people are selfish, in this dictionary sense, because many people act out of regard for the well-being of others, thus undercutting M's claim that everything everybody does is selfish.

Equivocation: Shifting Meaning in Mid-Argument

Watch for definitional wizards who develop a stipulative or positional definition, draw a conclusion on the basis of the definition, and then apply the conclusion using the term in its standard sense. Consider this example:

Example 13:9

S: The question is whether the State proved beyond a reasonable doubt that Arlene was not justified in using the force she used.

Q: That depends on what you mean by *proof beyond a reasonable doubt*. The best definition of this phrase is *absolutely airtight proof, so that the conclusion could not possibly be mistaken*. If the conclusion could possibly be mistaken, then there is room for reasonable doubt. We need high standards like this because we certainly don't want to convict an innocent person.

S: So?

Q: So the proof that Arlene was not justified is not so airtight that it could not possibly be mistaken. We can possibly be mistaken about anything, so we can possibly be mistaken about this. Therefore, the State has not proven beyond a reasonable doubt that Arlene was not justified in using the amount of force she did.

In applying his final conclusion to the situation (in the last sentence), Q was in effect using the phrase in its standard meaning, because in the question that the court asked the jurors, the court used the phrase in its standard meaning. But the conclusion's following depends on the term's being interpreted in accord with the positional definition Q offered and defended.

Let me elaborate. Q first argued for his positional meaning. According to his positional meaning, the State has *not* proven its case beyond a reasonable doubt. But the court asked the question in the standard meaning of the phrase, so to answer "No" is—in this situation—to make the statement ("It has not been proven beyond a reasonable doubt") in its standard meaning. If the positional meaning and the standard meaning differ, then Q has committed the fallacy of equivocation. To commit the fallacy of *equivocation* is to exploit a shift in meaning in arguing for a conclusion. (Note the convenience in the immediately preceding sentence of the equivalent-expression form of definition for the word *equivocation*.)

Something very much like this occurred in my jury room. What is an appropriate response to what Q has done? Stop reading and think about what you might have said if you were in the jury room.

In this case, it was not possible to be flexible and let Q have his way with the phrase *proven beyond a reasonable doubt*. The phrase is so deeply embedded in our legal system that proof beyond a reasonable doubt is a necessary condition for conviction. When a term is so deeply embedded in our culture that its use is a crucial part of our legal system, flexibility is the wrong stance. We might agree with the definition or we might disagree, but agreement simply to accommodate someone does not make sense. To do that is to settle the issue without thinking about it. One had to argue against Q's positional definition in that context, if one believed it to be different from the standard meaning.

One thing to have done was to show that elsewhere Q had not done justice to his own concept because by his definition the prosecutor had not even succeeded in proving beyond a reasonable doubt that Arlene performed the act that caused Al's death. Q himself had agreed earlier that the prosecutor had succeeded in doing this. The basic strategy here would be to secure a counterexample from the things the speaker has done or said (turning a person's position back on the person).

Another possible move was to show that according to Q's definition, there should never be any convictions because proof beyond a reasonable doubt would be unobtainable. That would be a totally unacceptable situation, so the phrase could not possibly mean in that courtroom situation what Q claimed it to mean. This sort of move is sometimes called *reduction to absurdity* (that is, showing an absurd consequence of a position).

Can you think of any other possibly appropriate responses to Q?

Impact Equivocation

It is often difficult to establish that the arguer consciously exploited a meaning shift. Therefore, I have invented a name for a fallacy that is like equivocation, because it has the impact of equivocation, even though we are not sure what the arguer is actually doing. This name is *impact equivocation*. To commit the fallacy of *impact equivocation* is to use a different meaning for a term than the meaning the audience is likely to understand it to have, with the impact on the audience being the same as if equivocation had been committed.

Whether or not the juror was consciously equivocating, at least this impact-equivocation fallacy was being committed by the juror in the example dealing with *proof beyond a reasonable doubt*. Regardless of whether he was consciously exploiting a meaning shift, his conclusion (that the case had not been proven beyond a reasonable doubt) was bound to be interpreted by the other jurors, the judge, and all others concerned in accord with the standard meaning of the phrase. Thus, his argument would have had the impact of an equivocal argument.

This problem holds for the other two examples in this section on definition strategy. In Example 13:7, M (in offering the critical-thinking definition of *argument* in that situation) was risking (perhaps even inviting) having J interpret M's conclusion in the sense of *argue* that J was using. Thus, M's verbal wizardry risked having the impact of equivocation.

In Example 13:8, M's verbal maneuvers invited having the conclusion interpreted as a denial of the charge that M had been selfish (in the standard sense of that term). Thus, again there was the danger of having the impact of equivocation.

The term *reliability* is an example from the field of psychometrics (testing). As the term is defined by psychometricians, the *reliability* of a test is, roughly speaking, its consistency in producing the same score for the same individual, regardless of whether the score is a valid indicator of the individual's accomplishments or prowess in the thing named by the test. For example, a multiple-choice test that measures one's degree of low-level rote memorization of facts and details in a field, say physics, might be very reliable in the psychometrician's sense of *reliable*. But if such a test is called a physics achievement test, then there is danger of impact equivocation, for its reliability might well be interpreted by the non-psychometrician public as indicating that the test can be depended on to give us a good estimate of a person's understanding of physics. It would probably not be a reliable test of physics achievement in the everyday person's sense of the term *reliable*, but could well be a reliable test in the psychometrician's sense of the term. This sort of problem often arises with technical terms in specialized fields, but can be serious in cases like this, in which the unsuspecting public is often invited to accept a conclusion that is not supported by the data.

The extent to which a person has committed the impact equivocation fallacy depends on the audience. That is, it depends on the extent to which the audience is likely to be fooled into accepting the conclusion in one sense of the key term rather than the sense in which the arguer claims to be using. In order to avoid this fallacy, we have a responsibility to try to know the audience and to take steps to warn the audience, if there is danger of their being misled. If a warning will not provide adequate protection (perhaps because the audience is too inflexible to handle the ambiguity), then the arguer has a responsibility to avoid the ambiguous use of terms.

Considering Several Possible Meanings

One basic (though often complex) strategy for dealing with possible equivocation, impact equivocation, and other problems arising from the meaning of terms is that of evaluating the argument several times, each time interpreting the key terms in accord with each of their possible meanings. Then the argument is judged separately for each of its possible interpretations. Roughly the strategy goes as follows: If the meaning is Y, then the judgment is such and such. If the meaning is Z, then the judgment is such and such (and so on, for as many plausible interpretations as exist). Then, if every judgment is that the argument is defective, and if there are no other plausible meanings for the key term (or terms), then the argument is given a final judgment of defective. Simply put, the final judgment would then consist of the following summary statement: "Whatever the interpretation, the argument is defective. Therefore, the argument is defective." This overall judgment follows from the individual judgments and the assumption that all reasonable interpretations have been included.

This strategy could be applied to the example dealing with selfishness. Consider the case of M, who was accused of selfishness: On the special interpretation that M gave to the word *selfish*, it follows that everybody is selfish all the time, but it does not follow that M's cutting into line was all right because that action was in addition unfair. Therefore, the argument is defective, using M's special sense of *selfish* throughout the argument. Furthermore, on the standard interpretation of *selfish*, it is not true that everybody is selfish all the time, so it does not follow that M's behavior was all right. In fact, it seems that M's behavior should be condemned because it was without regard for the well-being of others. Thus, the argument is defective in the other sense of *selfish*. No matter which sense of the term we use, given that we consistently carry the argument all the way through in each rendition of the argument, the argument is defective.

At the end of Chapter 11, you saw an argument about absolutism and relativism. It did not seem possible to report one consistent meaning of the term *absolutism* because it was not clear what meaning was in use in that argument. So the strategy I adopted was to identify the most likely and examine the argument from beginning to end for each meaning, making sure that only that one meaning was considered throughout that particular examination of the argument. This strategy requires flexibility on the part of the reasoner and the audience.

A Simpler Strategy

A simpler (but less thorough) strategy would have been to pick only one meaning for *absolutism*, defend the choice of that meaning, and then (assuming that meaning) examine the argument. For example, I could have offered the following more simple response:

Example 13:10

The speaker assumes that we have only two choices, absolutism or relativism. By *absolutism*, I think the arguer probably means the view that value principles are universal, exceptionless truths. This is what I have found most people to mean who offer arguments like this. If this is what the arguer means, then the arguer's complaint against absolutism is justified. I can think of exceptions to at least most broad value principles. But then we must object to the arguer's assumption that there are only these two alternatives, absolutism and relativism. There is the additional alternative that value principles can be generally correct. If so, then the conclusion that we should accept relativism does not follow. It has not been proved because it has not been shown to be the only alternative to absolutism.

In this simpler strategy, one picks the most likely interpretation and argues against the position, assuming that the position is employing that interpretation. The strategy accomplishes much. If someone wants to push the issue further, it is still possible to become flexible with the meaning of the word *absolutism* and go back to the more thorough strategy: Consider the argument once for each meaning (or combination of meanings) of the key term (or terms).

The strategy of considering several possible meanings could have been even more complicated. Suppose that there are two terms in an argument, one of which could be interpreted in two ways, the other in three ways. Then an exhaustive treatment would require six (two times three) evaluations of the argument, one for each of the six possible combinations of the meanings of the key terms. For practical reasons, this complexity must sometimes be replaced by the simpler strategy of working initially with the one set of meanings that we think the speaker has probably intended.

Summary

Although there is no sharp line between arbitrary stipulative and positional definitions, they are very different at their extremes. A pure *arbitrary stipulative definition* is a suggestion, a request, or a demand that the audience agree to a meaning in order conveniently to conduct the business at hand. We have much freedom in giving arbitrary stipulative definitions, although we are limited by the flexibility of the audience. A standard *positional definition,* on the other hand, expresses a position or point of view on some issue. In giving positional definitions, we are bound by the limits that the situation sets for the word or phrase in question. Often the word has positive or negative connotations, and the positional definition is an attempt to capture these connotations for things that would then be labeled by the word or phrase.

Both are quite different from reported definitions, which are factual statements that claim to reflect usage, usually standard usage. The criteria for judging one kind of definitional act are different from those for judging another. You should not perform one definitional activity and behave as if you have performed a different one. Sometimes a definition is partly one kind and partly another. Then, criteria for each kind apply.

For the sake of brevity, I often refer to arbitrary stipulative definitions as *stipulative definitions.* But to avoid confusion in some situations, the full term, *arbitrary stipulative definitions,* should be used.

Because all three acts (reporting, stipulating, and expressing a position) are definitional activities, it is tempting to confuse them. It is also tempting to change meanings and introduce new ones. Often this is all right, but one common error is to act as if positional definitions need little or no defense because stipulative definitions often need little or no defense.

+ It is sometimes dangerous to introduce into a discussion a definition that differs from a correct reported definition. This is often done by engaging in a different definitional act than the one that is appropriate (Q, for example offered a positional definition of *proven beyond a reasonable doubt* rather than a reported definition; M offered a putative stipulative definition of *argument* and a positional definition of *self-ish,* rather than reported definitions).

+ Another potential error is to shift meanings of a term in midargument, often by proving a conclusion that incorporates one meaning of a term and then applying the conclusion, using a different meaning. Exploiting a shift in meaning in midargument is called *equivocation*.

+ *Impact equivocation* is the interpretation of a term in an argument in a special way when there is danger that the audience will take the term in a different way and be misled. The misleading impact is like that of equivocation, but can be unintentional.

+ Ways of handling such definitional wizardry include the following:

Making sure that there is a defense of the position expressed in a positional definition. This usually requires at least a defense of the value judgments implicit in the position (using elements of FRISCO). One way to ask for a defense of the position is to say "Why do you define it that way?"

Being flexible (if the situation allows) and reformulating one's concern in other words.

Rejecting a new definition, perhaps because a true reported definition is called for and there are clear counterexamples to the definition, or because the audience is too inflexible to incorporate the different meaning, or because (if it is a positional definition) there are good reasons not to attach the suggested criteria to the term.

Examining an argument several times, once for each possible meaning (or combination of meanings) of the key term (or terms).

Applying a definition to a concern of the definer to check to see whether the definer really wants to live with that definition.

Showing that accepting the definition actually has serious unacceptable consequences (reducing to absurdity).

Showing that a key term is used in one sense in one part of the argument and in another sense in another part of the argument, and that the argument depends on a shift in meaning from one to the other.

There are many variations on these basic ideas.

The *S* and *C* in *FRISCO* are especially important when dealing with problems of definition and +equivocation. We must try to be clear, and we must keep the situation in mind, continually asking ourselves to consider the consequences when performing or accepting the verbal maneuver under consideration.

+ Check-Up 13B

True or False?
If false, change it to make it true. Try to do so in a way that shows that you understand.

13:11 Positional definitions may not be offered and accepted just as a matter of convenience.

13:12 Positional definitions, like any position, need defense.

13:13 If a term has a standard usage in a given situation, and if that usage is the one by which people will interpret your use of the term, then it is all right for you to give a positional definition of the term that differs from its standard usage.

13:14 In the situation described in 13:13, it is all right for you to give a stipulative definition of the term that differs from its standard usage.

13:15 It is not possible to report a stipulative definition of a term.

13:16 It is not possible to report a positional definition of a term.

13:17 Although flexibility in accepting others' definitions is useful, there are times when one should not be flexible in accepting and operating with others' definitions.

13:18 We have a right to stipulate any meaning for any term in any situation, and use the term in accord with that meaning, as long as we tell people what we are doing.

Medium Answer (one page or less)
Comment on each of the following dialogues. Tell whether each participant is doing appropriate things, and defend your judgments.

13:19 Assume that the background issue is whether the statue being discussed should remain in its prominent place on campus:

    T: Is the new statue *Hawks in Repose* a fine piece of art? I'll tell you something. It's not art at all. It's just a pile of junk, welded and bolted together. *Art* may be defined as an attempt to express a thought in an appealing way that is understandable to the everyday common person. Obviously, because we do not understand that statue, it is not art.

    P: Just for the sake of discussion, I'll accept your definition of *art*. Then I'll restate my question. Is the new statue good enough to leave out there in the middle of the campus? And why?

13:20   **H:** I hear that the Jitzy Mitz are coming to town and are going to play their dreadful music at the Roxy.

    K: They are an offense to the ear. We should do something to stop them from performing.

    H: Much as I dislike their sounds, and much as I know that there will probably be some trouble at their concert, I don't think that we should do that. It's a free country. The people who go know that there might be trouble, and they like that stuff.

K: Freedom doesn't mean that people can do anything they want, regardless of the quality of what they do. We have a responsibility to protect society from such trash. True *freedom* is having the power and opportunity to do what is in accord with the interests of the group. It's clear that in this city, most people do not like this music, and it is likely to encourage defiance and deviation from our way of life. Permitting it is against the interests of the majority.

13:21   **D:** *Theft* may be defined as the act of taking something from someone without that person's consent. We all know that the Internal Revenue Service takes money from us without our consent. But we are forced to pay, under threat of severe penalty. So, in reality, the Internal Revenue Service consists of a set of bandits stealing what we have toiled so hard to earn.

G: No, that's not what *theft* means. There is another important element: To be a theft the taker must wrongfully take something. The Internal Revenue Service does not take our money wrongfully—with some exceptions of course. It is to everyone's advantage that the government tax us. How else could we "insure domestic tranquility, provide for the common defense, and promote the general welfare?"

Longer Answer

For each of the following, reproduce the dialogue, specifying the context, and evaluate each participant's actions, justifying your evaluations.

13:22   A dialogue you have heard or seen in which the positional definition of a term played a key role in producing equivocation or impact equivocation.

13:23   A dialogue or exchange in a newspaper (such as a pair of letters to the editor) or magazine in which a positional definition was misused somehow.

Writing That Consciously Takes Account of Definitional Activities

In writing a position paper, you often need to make clear just how you are using specific terms. For example, when I write position papers in the area of critical thinking, I need to say what I mean by *critical thinking*. Otherwise, people wonder. So I start by offering a reported definition of *critical thinking*: "reasonable and reflective thinking that is focused on deciding what to believe or do." This is a reported definition because it captures as well as I can the central meaning of this term as used in the English-speaking world. I might be wrong about it, but it is the best I can do, and it does provide a basis for whatever else I want to do in the paper.

But sometimes a stipulated or positional definition, or some combination, is appropriate. The important things are that you define all terms of which the meaning might not be clear to your audience, and that you know what you are doing. That is, you should know what sort of act you are performing (reporting, stipulating, or expressing a position, or some combination) so that you know and have available the sort of defense that is needed for that act. For example, I do not expect to defend my definition of *critical thinking* as convenient, nor do I expect to defend its position on some controversial issue. Rather, I expect to defend it as the best explanation of the varied usage that I have found for the term in the English-speaking world.

Unfortunately, people often offer positional definitions that express controversial positions, and defend them by saying that they, like Humpty Dumpty, have the right to use terms in any way they please. For example, I have seen someone define *fetus* as *a human being from three months after conception to birth*. Someone else defined *fetus* as *the organic mass that becomes a human being at normal birth*. Each definition expressed a controversial position on the issue "Is a fetus a human being?," but neither speaker offered a defense or felt one was needed. Each definer felt as if it were his or her right to define a term however he or she chose to define it, as is appropriate with stipulated definitions. But these definitions expressed controversial positions, so the freedom from obligation for a defense does not extend to them.

When you offer a positional definition, be sure that you do not behave as if it is your right to define terms any way you please, without obligation to provide a defense. You should be able to provide at least some defense, although you are not necessarily obligated to provide it in the paper. That depends on the situation, including the audience. There is no point in proving something to the converted when time and space are at a premium, as they usually are.

You need not always provide definitions. If the meaning is clear to the audience, you are wasting their time with definitions. But often the mistake goes in the other direction, when definitions are needed but not provided. You must decide, based on your appraisal of the situation.

Check-Up 13C

True or False?
If false, change it to make it true. Try to do so in a way that shows that you understand.

13:24 A position paper should always contain definitions of its key terms, if the paper is to be clear.
13:25 No defense need be available for a reported definition.
13:26 A defense should be available for a positional definition.

Longer Answer
13:27 Select and provide a copy of a position paper that you have written in the past year, and see whether you have handled the definitional problems appropriately.

    a. If not, revise it, and in a separate paragraph or two, defend your revision.
    b. If so, defend your handling of the definitional problems.

+ **13:28** Select (and provide, if needed) a classic position paper. Evaluate the handling, or avoidance, of definition(s). Justify your evaluation. Here are two possible examples, both of which are available in Richard D. Heffner's *A Documentary History of the United States,* as well as many other sources:

  a. James Madison's *The Federalist #10* (in which Madison defines *faction* in his defense of the ratification of the United States Constitution).

  b. Alexander Hamilton's letter to George Washington, in which he defends the constitutionality of a national bank and offers the following definition of *necessary:* "*Necessary* often means no more than needful, requisite, incidental, useful, or conducive to."

+ **13:29** Do the same for an editorial in a newspaper. Be sure to provide a copy for your instructor to see.

Suggested Answers for Chapter 13

Check-Up 13A
13:1 T   **13:2** T   **13:3** T   **13:4** F   **13:5** T

13:4 Insert *definitely not* between *is* and *acceptable.*

13:6 Make sure that your description of the situation makes it clear whether the term has positive or negative connotations in that situation, and makes clear the nature of the attachment.

13:7 In effect, you have probably defended a value position here. You might have mentioned prospective consequences of accepting and of not accepting your definition, as well as other important facts. If you drew on general value judgments (and you probably did), you should have made them clear as well. Show your response to a friend before you turn it in.

13:8 Same advice as in 13:7.

13:9 This is up to you. Deciding about convenience is easier than deciding about a position.

13:10 There are many interesting things written on this topic, including John Stuart Mill *On Liberty* (1859) and R. H. Tawney's *Equality* (1929).

Check-Up 13B
13:11 T   **13:12** T   **13:13** F   **13:14** F   **13:15** F
13:16 F   **13:17** T   **13:18** F

13:13 Insert *not* before *all right, unless you have a defense.*

13:14 Insert *not* before *all right.*

13:15 Delete *not.*

13:16 Delete *not.*

13:18 Add: *if the stipulation is convenient and not confusing to the audience.*

13:19 T is offering an undefended positional definition, possibly thinking he has the right to stipulate any meaning he wants for the term *art*. In this definition, he takes a position that he does not defend. This position is that something must be understandable by the "everyday common person" in order to be art. T thus avoids arguing whether the status is good, but achieves his apparent goal of condemning the statue (without defending this condemnation). He has not defended the value judgment implicit in this condemnation.

P's flexibility is appropriate if the only issue in the situation is whether to leave the statue in the middle of campus. If that is the only issue, then two important questions are: "Is the statue understandable by the common everyday person?" and "Is it important that a statue in the middle of campus be understandable by the common everyday person?" However, because *art* generally has positive connotations in situations like that, it would often be a mistake for P just to let T have his positional definition of the word unless P agreed with T's positional definition. Rather, P might well have asked T for a defense of the definition. P might have then said, "Why do you define *art* that way?"

13:20 I shall leave the details of this one up to you, and invite you to discuss it with a friend and in a group of people or your class. But be alert to what K is doing with the word *interests* (as well as the word *freedom*). It first seems that a group's interests are whatever is good for the group. But then it seems that a group's interests are what a majority of the group likes or desires. Does this latter interpretation of *interests* make K's position more acceptable in any situations? Also be alert for the value judgments implicit in the situation.

13:21 Deliberately omitted.

13:22 and 13:23 These are up to you. Be sensitive to the elements of FRISCO.

Check-Up 13C

13:24 F   **13:25** F   **13:26** T

13:24 Change *should* to *need not*.

13:25 At least some sort of defense should be available for a reported definition.

13:27–13:29 These are up to you.

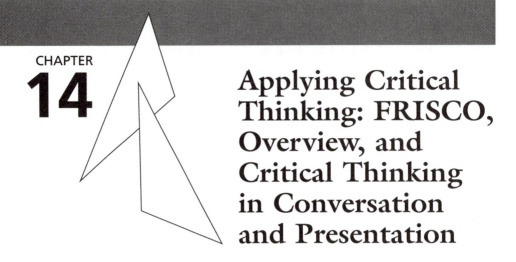

Applying Critical Thinking: FRISCO, Overview, and Critical Thinking in Conversation and Presentation

The chapter organization in this book emphasizes one aspect of critical thinking at a time. But real situations always involve many aspects of critical thinking at the same time—plus other things as well—and you must put them all together. In this, the last chapter, I invite you to join me in putting the pieces together in approaching a decision, considering it, judging it and the support you have for and against it, gathering more evidence, stepping back and reflecting, and applying your insights in oral presentations and discussions. You have, I hope, been continuously trying to apply all aspects of critical thinking in your writing, and in particular to formulating a position, writing a position paper, and evaluating your own and others' ideas and arguments.

Broad Critical Thinking Elements: FRISCO

Those of you who have read through this book have now considered in some detail each of the first five elements of FRISCO. In the following brief summary of FRISCO (which was introduced in Chapter 1), it covers both the evaluation and development of positions and arguments.

Those of you who have not read the other chapters of this book will find some unfamiliar language here. For the most part it is defined, but some terms describing types of inference, such as *deduction, loose derivation, induction, generalization, best-explanation inference,* and *value judging* might not be clear to you. There is no simple set of definitions and accompanying strategies. They are developed throughout the book, but be patient. Read the rest of the book. For the time being, the major strategy is to use whichever set of inference standards makes the reasoning look best, if you are only trying to tell whether the conclusion is justified. With a different goal, a different approach could be appropriate.

FRISCO in Making a Decision
About What to Believe or Do

F: In making a decision about what to believe or what to do, you first must be clear about the question or issue at hand. What are you trying to decide about? What is your question? You should state this question to yourself as clearly and sensitively as possible, because if you do not know what your question is, it is difficult to proceed. Until you have stated your question as clearly as possible, you do not even know how to tell whether you are making progress. Questions can be of all sorts, and can be simply the question of whether a particular hypothesis is justified.

Getting clear about the question, conclusion, or hypothesis comes under Focus (the *F* in *FRISCO*). The focus can simply be a decision that you or someone else has made or recommended. The question then is, "Is this decision reasonable?" Remember that the decision can be about an action, as well as about what to believe.

R: You must also familiarize yourself with the situation and the relevant facts, often investigating and gathering more information. A decision should not be made in ignorance, if at all possible. The relevant information provides the **R**easons for and against the decision. You must identify and evaluate these reasons.

I: The reasoning step that goes from your information to the decision is the **I**nference. A good decision requires good information, but the inference step to the decision must be justified as well. You can have fine information, but make a bad decision. Important parts of this inference step are identifying assumptions and searching out and considering alternatives—not only alternative decisions, but also alternative interpretations of the situation and the evidence, and alternative points of view.

S: Understanding the **S**ituation helps you be clear about your question (the *F*), and also helps you to know the meaning of key terms with which you are dealing and to know the often-relevant interests and concerns of various participants. Always keep the situation in mind, even after you have determined your question.

C: **C**larity about your own and others' meanings of the terms you are using is essential. Otherwise, confusion reigns, and you do not know what you are about, nor how to apply your decision.

O: At the **O**verview stage, which you should be doing repeatedly in the decision-making process, you step back and check it all over, reflecting on various alternatives and how well you handled each of the elements of FRISCO. In other words, you go through it all again, making sure that you see the whole picture. The completion of the final overview, however, does not mark the end of critical thinking about a question. Even after you have made the decision, it is important to be open to more information and to other points of view and ideas, and to be willing to change your mind, if warranted.

The above FRISCO elements might all seem like common sense, and in a way they are. In part, they amount to a person's being open to new ideas, caring about getting it right and being careful and well informed, trying to be honest and clear about things, and caring about the worth and dignity of others. These are basic critical thinking dispositions (elaborated later in this chapter).

Most of these elements of FRISCO receive special emphasis in various parts of the book: Focus receives special emphasis in Chapter 2. Reasons receive special emphasis in Chapters 2–4. Inference is emphasized in Chapters 5–11. Situation is emphasized throughout, as is clarity, although Chapters 12 and 13 emphasize definition and meaning. Overview is emphasized in this chapter.

Inventing, Checking for Quality, Reformulating

As you go through this FRISCO-guided decision-making process, you are constantly inventing, checking the quality of what you are doing, and reformulating, a continuous evaluative and creative set of interdependent processes. The reason that most of this book is about the quality-checking parts of this activity is that there is much more to be explained about checking for quality. Furthermore, the quality-checking parts continually inform the inventing and reformulating parts and provide the ultimate control of our thought.

Overview

So far, you have seen a brief summary of the FRISCO elements. I shall now elaborate the *O* element, the overview, with emphasis on inference-evaluation procedures and on the interdependence of the elements, as well as openness to revision, even after the decision is made. This strategy is sequential, just to make sure that all aspects are covered, although the original decision-making process skips around a good deal.

The overview element should actually be applied at every point in the decision-making process, from formulating your question—through gathering information—to making your decision, although it can be more detailed at the advanced stages of decision-making. Furthermore, an overview is a necessary final step before provisional acceptance of the decision to believe something or to do something. You should do these overviews when you evaluate the arguments of others, as well as when you develop your own. Basically the whole idea is to keep track of what you are doing. Be reflective about it.

Focus and Reasons

First of all, try to be clear about the focus (*F*), the question or conclusion at issue (Chapter 2). In doing so, you will need to take the situation into account. Actually, the selection of the question is sometimes a decision, so it might call for an initial overview by itself. Next, determine what information and reasons (*R*) are given or available, and get clear about how the reasons join together to provide support for a conclusion. If there is not enough information, get more. Check the information. Is there good reason to believe it? Is it from a credible source (Chapter 3)? Were adequate observation procedures used (Chapter 4)? Answering each question itself calls for some sort of overview (because each question calls for a decision), so repeated overviews are necessary.

Inference

Look at the inference (*I*). If the goal is only to tell whether the conclusion or decision is justified, use the following strategy of successful application of different standards. If the goal is otherwise (such as trying to figure out what a particular person is thinking and arguing, and to judge that), then a different strategy might be appropriate.

If the question or conclusion requires a value judgment, then make sure that you consider the consequences of acting on it, and check the factual information, if any, offered in its support. Also check the value principle(s) on which it is based. There usually are one or more value principles in the background. Decide whether, in the given situation, the conclusion at least loosely follows from these principle(s). In doing so, consider whether the argument takes account of all relevant consequences and principles. (Value judging is discussed in Chapter 11.)

If the conclusion is an inferred factual conclusion, first check to see whether it is supported by a deductively valid argument with acceptable reasons. (Deductive logic is discussed in Chapters 5 and 6, with applications shown in Chapters 7–9 and 11.) Do the reasons come from credible sources, are they acceptable observation statements, or are they acceptable conclusions that you have previously drawn? Judging the argument might well require you to contribute one or more assumptions that fill, or help fill, the deductive gaps (Chapter 7). When attributing assumptions, do the best you can to help the argument if your ultimate concern is whether to accept the conclusion. It might well be that the best that you can construct is a loosely deductive argument—a loose derivation (Chapters 1 and 11) from acceptable reasons. Then you must make a judgment about whether the argument is good enough, given the situation.

If you cannot construct a satisfactory deductive argument or loose derivation for an inferred factual conclusion, then consider whether a good inductive argument has been, or can be, constructed by adding acceptable assumptions (again assuming that your primary interest is whether to accept the conclusion). Roughly speaking, there are two kinds of inductive arguments, generalization and best-explanation arguments, although some conclusions can be supported by both types—that is, best-explanations that are also generalizations.

If the reasoning generalizes from a series of instances (inductive generalization), are the instances likely to be representative of the population that is the subject of the generalization (Chapter 10)? Consider whether the generalization is consistent with your own experience and whether it is in agreement with the claims of credible sources. Again, pay attention to whether the evidence or reasons are acceptable.

Suppose instead that the conclusion is a hypothesis that gets its primary support from its ability to explain the facts (best-explanation inference). Are there any facts that appear to be inconsistent with it? Are there any plausible alternative explanations (Chapters 8 and 9)? Have appropriate experiments been done (Chapter 8)? Has a reasonable effort been made to uncover alternative explanations? Does the hypothesis fit in with the larger body of knowledge that you accept? Is the hypothesis in agreement with the views of credible sources? (This agreement is not a necessary condition, but it helps to make the hypothesis plausible.)

If the total argument is a combination of smaller arguments, then you must evaluate them one at a time, using the successive evaluation strategy of the previous paragraphs. A total argument is no stronger than its weakest necessary link. However, an argument might be a strong one even if one of the parts is weak, if that part is not a necessary part of the chain or if the other parts do not depend on it for support or help. The other parts might be strong enough by themselves. You must balance and judge.

Situation

Have you kept in mind the situation (S) as you did these other things? Did you keep in mind the basic concern when you decided about the strength of the inference and the meanings of the terms? Have you successfully looked at things from the point of view of others, and have you attempted to discount any unfairness resulting from your own deeply held assumptions? (These questions represent crucial critical thinking dispositions. Some others are listed below.) Are you well-informed? Check with other people and books (Chapter 3). Do they give you reason to wonder? Investigate (Chapters 4, 8, and 10).

Clarity

Make sure that you know the intended meanings of key terms and, if not, try to find out (C). Are the terms clearly defined, if definition is necessary (Chapter 12)? If you cannot ascertain a single intended meaning for each key term, you might need to appraise the argument anew for each meaning, or meanings, of key terms (Chapter 13). If there is even one interpretation that gives you a good argument from the beginning all the way to the application, accept it. The argument is a good one.

Finally, you must check your tentative decision. Make sure that it is no stronger than is warranted by the evidence or reasons (evidencing a crucial critical thinking disposition on your part). You should be open to making revisions, especially if new relevant information of ideas develop. Your conclusion should also be clear enough to provide guidance in the situation. Qualify your decision, as appropriate, and always be open to considering new information and points of view (another crucial critical thinking disposition).

Critical Thinking Dispositions

Here is a more complete list of critical thinking dispositions, all of which should be functioning throughout the overview (and of course, all the elements of FRISCO). There is overlap here, even with FRISCO itself, but I hope you will not mind. Read this set slowly, thinking about a particular decision you made, and asking yourself whether you were like this when you made the decision.

Ideal critical thinkers are disposed to do the following:

1. Care that their beliefs are true and that their decisions are justified; that is, care to "get it right" to the extent possible, or at least care to do the best they can. This includes the interrelated dispositions to do the following:

    A. Seek alternatives (hypotheses, explanations, conclusions, plans, sources), and be open to them.
    B. Endorse a position to the extent that, but only to the extent that, it is justified by the information available.
    C. Be well-informed.
    D. Seriously consider points of view other than their own.

2. Represent a position honestly and clearly (theirs as well as others'). This includes the dispositions to do the following:

   A. Be clear about the intended meaning of what is said, written, or otherwise communicated, seeking as much precision as the situation requires.
   B. Determine, and maintain focus on, the conclusion or question.
   C. Seek and offer reasons.
   D. Take into account the total situation.
   E. Be reflectively aware of their own basic beliefs.

3. Care about the dignity and worth of every person. This includes the dispositions to do the following:

   A. Discover and listen to others' views and reasons.
   B. Take into account others' feelings and level of understanding, avoiding intimidating or confusing others with their critical thinking prowess.
   C. Be concerned about others' welfare.[1]

The elements of FRISCO and these dispositions might seem like a great deal to manage all at once. But with practice, a short review list such as FRISCO in the back of your mind can help you do it without an explicit question about each one.

Check-Ups

Those of you reading this chapter before reading the others should know that there will be periodic Check-Ups that you should use for review and application. They usually start with true–false questions that are intended primarily as a review of the main points, and in a way constitute a summary, which is usually also provided. But true–false questions cannot reach deeply enough, so there are more open-ended activities. It is important to do the Check-Ups, at least to the point that you feel confident about the ideas in the relevant section.

Check-Up 14A

True or False?
If false, change it to make it true. Try to do so in a way that shows that you understand.

   14:1 If an argument is not deductively valid, then it cannot be a good argument.

---

1. A few interpretive comments: Several of the dispositions (1 D, 2 E, and 3 A) contribute to being well-informed (1 C) but are separate dispositions in their own right.

   The expressed concern with true belief accepts the view that our concepts and vocabulary are constructed by us, but also that (to oversimplify somewhat) the relationships among the referents of our concepts and terms are not constructed by us. We can have true or false beliefs about these.

   The disposition (#3) to care about the dignity and worth of every person is not required of critical thinking by definition, but in order that it be humane. I call it a correlative disposition, by which I mean one that, although this disposition is not part of the definition of *critical thinking,* it is desirable for all critical thinkers to have it, and the lack of it makes the critical thinking less valuable, or perhaps of no value at all.

14:2 If an argument includes a reason that is clearly false, then the argument cannot provide adequate grounds for believing the conclusion.

14:3 If an argument is deductively valid, then if you accept the reasons, you must accept the conclusion.

14:4 Once the conclusion or question is identified, the situation is no longer of interest in decision-making.

14:5 If a key term is ambiguous, then showing that the argument is a good argument—in at least one of the senses of the key term—is enough to show that the argument is a good one.

14:6 If the conclusion is factual, then if an argument is not deductively valid, there is still the possibility that it is inductively valid.

14:7 There are two kinds of inductive arguments or relationships: generalization from particulars and inference to the best explanation.

14:8 Both consequences and principles are relevant to making value judgments.

14:9 The overview process is appropriate only at the end of the decision-making process.

14:10 The elements of FRISCO are independent of each other when applied to a decision.

14:11 Quality checks on the decision-making process should be made throughout.

FRISCO Argument Appraisal

14:12 Apply FRISCO to the following argument. Do a more thorough job than you did in Item 1:23. You are now much better informed about the reasons and assumptions of this argument than you were at the beginning of the book. Suppose you have overheard the argument offered to someone about to take the same course. Imagine and specify further details of the situation.

Argument: You should not bother to do your homework in this course in critical thinking because critical thinking is difficult to learn.

14:13 Apply FRISCO to one of the following arguments (a or b), simpler versions of which appeared earlier as Items 2:51 and 2:52. Imagine that you are thinking of advancing as your own the argument you have selected, and that the first proposition (italicized) is in part based on your own experience, and in part on any other evidence that you might have on the subject. (The italics here do not mean that the italicized proposition is the conclusion.) Imagine and specify further details of the situation as you envision it, including the audience and the probable medium of presentation. Decide whether the argument justifies the conclusion.

    a. *Men generally have difficulty being sensitive to others.* If it is desirable for our society to consist of fully developed human beings, then those who are sensitive should make a special effort to help those who are not. Generally, this means that women should make a special effort to help men to be more sensitive, just as the rich should share their wealth with the less fortunate—through a system of income taxes. I say this even though some might feel that it places an unfair burden on women.

b. *Women generally do not have confidence in themselves, or they find it difficult to maintain confidence.* Therefore, if we are to achieve true equality, hiring preference should be given to women in cases where men outnumber women, just as a painting should be balanced. To some people this might at first appear to be unfair to men, but I think that on reflection they will change their minds.

+ **14:14** Apply FRISCO to the following argument. Imagine and specify further details of the situation as you envision it, including the audience, facts about the presenter (here called "Chris Individ"), and the medium of presentation.

Chris Individ argues as follows: "There is absolutely nothing wrong with even the most extreme forms of selfish individualism. All people can be expected to be selfish, that is, to do what is best for themselves, including wasting food and driving expensive sports cars when others are starving and without sanitation. This is because people always do what they really want to do. Otherwise, they would not do it. Because being selfish is doing what you want to do, everybody is selfish all the time. So there is nothing wrong with being selfish, just as there is nothing wrong with being human. How could it be wrong to do what all people are doing every minute of their waking lives, and to do what all people unavoidably do?

Thinking Critically When Discussing Things with Others

Up to now, we have been considering the practice of critical thinking in situations in which you have as much time to think as you want. You have applied numerous critical thinking strategies, principles, and insights to a variety of examples that I provided and to some that you have located yourself. But in all cases, you had time to reflect and revise before "going public" with your proposals and judgments.

However, in discussion with other people, you generally do not have the luxury of time to reflect and revise before you respond in public. You often think and work things out as you talk. When other people say things, there ordinarily is no chance to have these things recorded and played before you need to respond. So discussion provides a special critical thinking challenge. I shall begin with some general advice, and then give some specific advice, including the suggestion of a wide array of specific strategies, questions, challenges, and responses.

General Advice

The first piece of general advice is that it takes practice—and more practice—to think critically in discussion. Find nonthreatening situations and try out my suggestions, as well as your own ideas. Think about what happened, and try again in other situations. Then practice some more.

A second piece of general advice is that you need to keep track of many things at once. You cannot just focus on one thing and ignore what else is going on. You will need to do the following:

Keep the situation and the focus in the back of your mind.

Make sure that the focus is agreed on, in case it is not explicitly stated.

Make sure that the focus is not changed in mid-discussion, unless there is good reason for changing it.

Make sure that the reasons and evidence are out in the open.

Judge the reasons and evidence.

Listen to what the speaker (including yourself) is saying.

Note the reactions of other people.

Make sure that what is being said is clear enough for the situation.

See how the given reason(s) bears on the general focus in the situation (that is, check the reasoning that is going on).

Look for assumptions.

Be thinking about possible alternative conclusions or explanations that are consistent with the acceptable reasons and evidence.

See how it all applies to concrete examples, if the discussion is abstract.

These are some specific things to do, but the general point here is that you must concurrently do them all, to the extent that you are able. Quite a juggling act! But you need to do it—in committee meetings, open hearings, meetings of your organization, jury deliberations, small group discussions around a table, talks you give to large groups and to small groups, as well as private discussions with someone to whom you are close. Do not expect to be very good at it at first. But with self-conscious practice, your competence will develop.

A third general piece of advice calls for open-mindedness. That is, try to look at things from others' points of view, try to be aware of your own deep assumptions, and be open to changing your views. Adopt the other critical thinking dispositions as well.

I hope that you agree with these three general pieces of advice, but I also suspect that you would like something more specific. You shall have it, but remember that any specific suggestion is valuable only to the extent that it fits into the second and third pieces of general advice.

The rest of the chapter is organized around four discussion activities: seeking clarification, challenging, responding, and presenting. They are distinguished for purposes of presentation of my suggestions, but in a real discussion, they usually flow from one to another and back again. You will find that generally there are threatening and nonthreatening ways to pursue your inquiry, but whether a particular question or challenge is threatening depends not only on its words, but on the tone of voice, on the situation, and on the nature of the person addressed. In almost all cases, I recommend the least threatening way that will get the job done.

Seeking Clarification

It is useful to distinguish between seeking clarification of a position and challenging it. But the distinction is sometimes elusive because some clarification efforts are in fact a challenge to a position, some are perceived as a challenge even if not so intended, some challenges result in clarification, and some apparent challenges are actually intended to achieve clarification. However, let us start with questions explicitly seeking clarification. The reason for starting here and for emphasizing clarification is simple: If we are not clear about what is being said, we cannot respond to it reasonably.

Six basic types of questions that we use to clarify a position (which I shall exemplify shortly) are general clarification questions, those asking for the main point, those asking for the reasons, those asking for the connection between the reasons and the conclusion, those asking for the meaning of certain words, and those asking for the import or significance. The clarification questions deal with more than the *C* for *clarity* in FRISCO (which was concerned only with word meaning) because they attend to identifying the focus and reasons, determining the basis for the inference, and determining the situational significance.

I shall list some illustrative questions, generally arranged in order of decreasing gentleness within each category. One of my purposes in listing these questions is to encourage you to feel comfortable in using them. Another purpose is to give a range that you can use in the coming practice exercises and elsewhere. You should practice using, receiving, and responding to all of them. Try to develop a facility for thinking of them quickly in appropriate circumstances. A third purpose is to encourage you to use the less-threatening ones rather than the more-threatening ones. The less-threatening ones are just as effective logically, and make it easier for your associates to feel comfortable in opening up and revising their views.

As you read these questions of clarification, read slowly enough to enable you to imagine yourself asking these questions in some discussion you were in during the previous week. Then think about how each question might have worked in that situation. Then practice using them!

All of these questions can be asked more informally. I leave it to you to add the slang and short cuts. I present them this way because with just bare print and no body language or facial expressions, they are more clear in this form than in their more informal versions. But many colorful modifications can be made!

General Clarification Questions

1. Would you say a little more about that?
2. Why did you say that?
3. What do you mean?

Main Point Questions

1. Let me see if I have it right. Is this your main point? [State what you think is the main point.]
2. I take it that your main point is this: [state what you think is the main point.]
3. I'm afraid I don't quite see what you're driving at. Could you say a little more about it?
4. What is your main point?
5. Just what exactly is your thesis?
6. What's this all about?

Reason-Seeking Questions

1. Could you say a little more about your reasons for saying that?
2. Perhaps you could elaborate on why you believe that.
3. Why did you say that?
4. Why do you believe that?
5. Do you have reasons for that conclusion?

Questions Seeking the Connection Between the Reasons and the Conclusion (Relevance).

1. I want to understand you. Could you elaborate on the connection between the reason and the conclusion?
2. Are you assuming that. . .? [Specify a likely assumption.]
3. You are assuming that . . ., are you not? [Specify a likely assumption.]
4. I'm not sure I see the bearing of this point on your conclusion.
5. Would more evidence help? How would you get it?
6. How does that support the conclusion?
7. How is that relevant?
8. What does that statement [a statement made by the speaker] have to do with your conclusion?

Questions Seeking Clarification of Word Meaning

1. I'm not sure how you are using this word.
2. Could you give an example of. . .?
3. Could you give a negative example of. . .? [This question is unfortunately rarely used, though it can be very useful and is sometimes devastating to a position that really does not say anything. A *negative example* is a case that is instructively not an example.]
4. Would this be an example. . .? [give an instructive possible case.]
5. Perhaps we are talking past each other. Are we using this word the same way? [This question is often asked much later in a discussion than it should be. Consider it when you see people looking at the same facts, yet still disagreeing with each other. Often the disagreement in such cases is merely verbal, though not always.]

6. What do you mean by. . .?
7. By . . ., do you mean. . .?
8. Do you know what . . . means?

Questions Seeking the Import or Significance of the Conclusion

1. Could you tell me roughly how your conclusion (or thesis, or view) might apply in this situation: [describe a situation of interest to which there is possible application]?
2. Could you comment on the significance of your view for this situation?
3. Suppose you are right in what you say; what should I [or someone else] do differently?
4. What difference does it make?
5. Does it make any difference?

Summary and Comment So Far

In discussion, you usually have ready access to the other person, and can use this access to clarify what the person is saying. This goes beyond word meanings, the concern under the *C* in *FRISCO*.

Questions of clarification are not limited to the beginning of a discussion. Often, things that need clarification are not apparent until well into a discussion. So be ready to use these and similar questions at any time. But some of them are almost always appropriate at the beginning of a discussion.

Specific questions of clarification can try to get the focus or main point out in the open, can get the reasons out in the open, can try to ascertain the relevance of the reasons, can seek clarification of ambiguous or unfamiliar terms, and can seek the practical significance of the position, among other things.

I have suggested a range of questions for each of these activities. The questions range from less threatening to more threatening. I urge you to use the less-threatening ones whenever you can. Any question can be somewhat threatening, especially if the person addressed does not immediately see a good answer.

The three general clarification questions are ones that you should always be ready to ask. Of the three, the second and third questions, "Why did you say that?" and "What do you mean?," are sometimes more threatening, and are more specific than the first, but usually are good general questions. The first question, "Would you say more about that?," although vague, is very useful. It often provokes the speaker to see what needs elaboration. Then the speaker can provide the elaboration, if he or she knows it and wants to provide it. Usually people do want to make clear what they are saying. The question "Would you say more about that?" is also useful for the questioner who feels confused and is not sure exactly what is lacking. The question helps to get the dialogue going.

Before you go further, you need to practice using all of these questions. It would be best if you could practice with someone else. Find a partner and do one or more of Check-Up Items 14:15–14:18 together. Schedule a significant block of time in order to make this activity worthwhile.

Check-Up 14B

14:15–14:18 Find a partner and address one of the arguments in Items 14:12 through 14:14 in Check-Up 14A. For each argument, imagine further details in the situation as necessary. Then one of you play the role of the arguer while the other asks the arguer each of the suggested questions in the first three groups (general clarification, seeking focus, and reasons). The one playing the arguer role should then try to answer the questions. Then switch roles and the former arguer should ask the new arguer each of the questions in each of the last three groups (relevance of reasons, seeking word meaning, and significance). The new arguer should respond to each of the questions. Do this orally. After each question and response, discuss with your partner the quality of the question and response, and how each of you felt. Go slowly and plan to spend several hours doing this. Then write out an answer to each of the following questions:

    a. What additional details in the situation did you imagine?
    b. Which questions were most useful in this situation? Why?
    c. Which questions were least useful in the situation? Why?

14:19 Find a partner. Do the same thing as in 14:15–14:18 for an argument that you find in your daily life such as from a newspaper editorial page, a magazine article, a talk show, a debate, a discussion with a friend, or a meeting you attended. The most instructive argument here would be one about an issue on which you and your partner disagree. In your written report, present the total argument and describe the situation in full. Also answer questions *b* and *c* that appeared under 14:15–14:18.

Challenging a Position

Challenging a position can result in its rejection, but rarely is a position destroyed simply by a challenge. Challenge often results in a clarification or a modification, especially if the challenge is presented gently, in a nonthreatening way. As you read these forms of challenge, imagine yourself trying to apply each to an extended discussion you have had in the past week that included an argument (not necessarily involving a hostile disagreement). Try to see whether the likely reply might have clarified the position, resulted in its modification, or been grounds for rejection. Again, the important thing is to practice asking these questions to yourself and to think about the import of possible responses. Stop now and think over the discussion and argument you select before you proceed.

    Possibly not all of the following suggested challenges are applicable. But at least try to see whether each applies in your discussion.

Producing an Apparent Counterexample

A *counterexample* is a case that seems inconsistent with the generalization offered or assumed. (Examples of counterexamples to definitions appear early in Chapter 12. A counterexample to the spontaneous generation hypothesis appears at the beginning of Chapter 8.) Even though you might think that a counterexample you offer will refute a position, often the result is clarification or modification.

1. How would your view deal with a case like this: [describe a case that appears inconsistent with the view being presented]?
2. Here is a situation (or case). It seems inconsistent with what you said. Is it?
3. What you said is not consistent with my experience: [describe the experience].
4. If what you said is true, then we would expect this also to be true: . . ., but it is not true.
5. That could not be right because there is this case: . . . [describe it].

Suggesting a Possible Inconsistency

The trouble with inconsistency is that no more than one of two inconsistent things can be right. The person who makes two statements that are inconsistent with each other must withdraw at least one, on pain of having said nothing.

Ralph Waldo Emerson is often quoted as urging that foolish consistency is the hobgoblin of small minds, but he was not talking about straightforward inconsistency between two statements. Rather, he was chiding someone for unwillingness to change his mind in the face of good reason to do so.

Here are some questions that can be used to challenge a possible inconsistency:

1. Here you said this, and there you said that. Do they conflict with each other?
2. These two things you said appear incompatible. Are they?
3. You have contradicted yourself. You said this, and you said that. They can not both be true.

Dubious Reasons or Evidence

If the explicitly stated reasons or evidence (the *R* in *FRISCO*) are dubious or false and if the argument depends on them, then the argument is suspect. But remember, that does not show the conclusion to be false.

Because you now probably have the idea about the range from less-threatening to more-threatening questions, I shall henceforth only give one or two fairly non-threatening questions to illustrate the challenge. You can supply others.

Sample Challenge: "You stated that . . . [give the stated reason]. I wonder about that because the college newspaper reported otherwise."

Weak Source

Often the credibility of a source is suspect. A challenge to the credibility of this source is then appropriate, and should probably refer to one or more of the criteria for credibility listed in Chapter 3.

Sample Challenge: "That source has a conflict of interest, because. . . ."
Another: "Why should we take that person's word?"

False or Dubious Assumption

A position is no stronger than its assumptions. A standard challenge technique is to claim that the position assumes a proposition and that the proposition is false or dubious.

Here is a sample challenge:

"Aren't you assuming that . . . [give a dubious proposition that you think the argument needs in order to be the best argument that it can be] ?"

This technique is more speculative than the dubious-explicit-reason technique because it is difficult to be sure that one has actually identified an assumption on which the argument or the position depends. (See Chapter 7.) Unfortunately, people often claim to identify an assumption when the assumption is not needed by the argument for the argument to be a good one.

An example of the identification of an unneeded assumption was a juror's claiming that the defense attorney made the following assumption: "A person who kills in defense against a threatened attack should be judged innocent of murder as well as voluntary manslaughter." (The defense had argued, you probably remember, "My client is innocent because she was defending herself against attack.") The juror then proceeded to reveal that he interpreted the word *attack* very broadly (including verbal attacks) and argued that the assumption was false because we did not think that defending yourself against the threat of insults generally justifies killing someone. But this was not relevant because the defense attorney did not need such a broad assumption and is unfairly burdened with such a sweeping assumption. Real physical attack was enough for his assumption to be about. So it is important to make sure that the assumption is needed by the position or argument, if refuting it is to count heavily against the position or argument. But despite the danger of misattribution of assumptions, attempted identification of a false assumption is useful at least in probing a position, and often in challenging it.

Circular Argument

Sometimes an argument does not make any progress because it starts by explicitly assuming what it tries ultimately to prove. Usually, because of verbosity, this is less obvious than in the following example: "Our industry remains volatile. Therefore it is subject to change."

Sample Challenge: "Your argument seems circular."
Another: You seem to begin your argument by assuming your conclusion, though in different words.

Changing the Subject

Often, in discussion, one person argues for something that is unrelated to the question at hand. Sometimes the shift is subtle, as occurred in the argument regarding selfishness (Item 14:14). Sometimes the shift is not subtle, as when the other person attacks you personally for your ignorance (or bad memory) about something that is not part of the issue. In the language of logical fallacies, such a personal attack is sometimes called *argumentum ad hominem*. I mention this label because having heard of the label might help you avoid being intimidated by someone's using it. I do not recommend that you use it. I prefer the equivalent label *personal attack argument*. I used that label in Chapter 3, when I noted that some personal attack arguments (*ad hominem* arguments) are relevant. In any case, it is often easy to be distracted by changes in the subject, whether they are subtle or not.

> Sample Challenge: "Have you changed the subject? I thought that we were talking about. . . ."
> Another: "What does that personal attack have to do with the issue we are discussing?"

These challenges are much easier to see when you are not involved in a heated discussion and when you are not the butt of the personal attack, so you need to keep them in the back of your mind at all times.

Insufficient Reason or Evidence

There are a variety of ways that the reasons and evidence offered can be insufficient. I shall mention a few:

Other plausible explanations. Sometimes a hypothesis does explain the evidence, but the evidence is not sufficient to rule out alternative hypotheses. See Chapters 8 and 9. To assert the hypothesis that one thing caused another, simply on the ground that the first preceded the second, has a special fallacy label: *post hoc reasoning*. Again I do not recommend that you use this label, but that you be familiar enough with it to avoid being intimidated when someone else uses it.

> Sample Challenge: "Here's another plausible explanation of that evidence: . . ." [Challenger offers the other plausible explanation.]

An undefended positional definition. Sometimes an undefended proposed definition embodies a position, and has value consequences, if it is accepted. (For example, "I define freedom as the power to do the right thing.") Such a definition needs defense. See Chapter 13.

> Sample Challenge: "Why should we accept that definition?"

Overgeneralization. Often, people draw general conclusions that apply to things or populations of which the evidence is not representative. See Chapter 10.

> Sample Challenge: "Have you overgeneralized?"

Oversimplification. It is often tempting to oversimplify complicated situations by stating one or two simple principles and deriving a conclusion from them. Then one might neglect the fact that most acceptable value principles, and many others as well, have exceptions. See Chapter 11. Another standard kind of oversimplification is the assumption that there are only two alternatives, when in fact there are others (sometimes called the *either–or* fallacy).

Sample Challenge: "But there are exceptions to that rule (or generalization). Here's one: . . ." [Challenger describes an exception.]
Another: "There are other alternatives. It's not just either this or that. It might be both, or it might be this other possibility: . . ." [Challenger offers another alternative.]

Emotional language without sufficient substance. People often appeal to slogans or use words (including *glittering generalities* and *name-calling*—some popular fallacy labels that are self-explanatory) that set off emotional reactions in many of us but do not offer substantial reasons.

Sample Challenge: "These are high-sounding phrases (or bad names), but now tell us your reasons."
Another: "That's good rhetoric. Now let's get down to substance."

Faulty analogy. An *analogical argument* (discussed in Chapter 11) proceeds by showing that two things are alike in some respects, and concludes that they are therefore alike in some other respect. Some analogical arguments are strong; some are faulty. Their potential weakness lies in the respects in which the two things are different, and there are always differences. For example, one might argue that all the nations of the world could successfully join together because they are like the thirteen states that joined together to form the United States. A challenger could note that the cases are different because the United States had external enemies against which the states needed to protect themselves, whereas the world has no such external enemies. As you can see, the argument could go on and on, possibly acquiring validity as it approximates one of our standard forms: deduction, loose derivation, induction (generalization or best-explanation), or value judging.

Sample challenge: "There's a significant relevant difference between these two cases: . . ." [Challenger describes the difference.]

Neglect of a point of view. Often, a conclusion depends on the point of view of the arguer. It sometimes helps to show that from another point of view, the evidence is insufficient.
Our point of view, as jurors in judging Arlene guilty of voluntary manslaughter, was nonconfrontational. That is, we assumed that if a person is threatened and there is an easy way to escape, that person should take that way of escape. From the point of view that women should fight back and confront threatened violence with violence, our evidence was insufficient to show that she was not justified in using the force she used.

Sample Challenge: "But look at it from this point of view: . . ." [Challenger describes it.]

General failure to follow. Sometimes, we feel bewildered by the claim that a conclusion follows from the reason(s) or evidence because we cannot see how anyone could have thought it did, or we just do not understand the alleged connection. In that case, a general challenge is appropriate.

Sample Challenge: "I do not see the connection between the reason(s) and your conclusion."
Another: "Could you explain how this is relevant to your conclusion?"

(There is a special term used for a general-type failure of a conclusion to follow from its support: *non sequitur.* I mention this term so that you will not be intimidated by its use, though again I do not recommend that you use it. To say that something is a *non sequitur* is to say only that the conclusion does not follow. I was disappointed when I learned that this impressive phrase meant only that. I had expected the term to have a more specific meaning. How about you? Anyway, now you know.)

That completes this suggested set of ways that the sufficiency of the evidence or reason(s) could be challenged. You might think of others, but these are enough for now. You might even want to put the next item, equivocation, in this group. But elegant categorization of ways of going wrong is not our concern here.

Equivocation

Sometimes an argument can look good, but not be so because it depends on the shifting of meaning of a key term during the course of the argument (see Chapter 13).

> Sample Challenge: "Have you changed the meaning of [state term] in drawing your conclusion?"
> Another: "No matter which interpretation of [state term] we use, your argument is defective. Look. On this meaning, there is a problem here. On that meaning, there is a problem there. There do not seem to be any other plausible interpretations."

Fallacy Labels

As you may have noted, I have tried to work a definition and brief discussion of some of the major fallacy labels into this discussion of challenge questions. To apply a fallacy label to someone's thinking is in effect to raise a challenge question.

The danger with fallacy labels is that for many of them, activities that they fit are often not fallacious; that is, they are often not mistaken. For example, *appeal to authority* is a fallacy label (presented in Chapter 3), but many instances of appeal to authority are perfectly all right. We do it when we provide citations to support a reason we are using, and often this is perfectly legitimate.

On the other hand, some fallacy labels, such as circularity and *non sequitur,* if applied correctly, label only mistakes. In any case, it is helpful to be familiar with the most common fallacy labels, in part because they sensitize us to common sources of error, and in part because they provide an efficient way to communicate complaints (to those who understand their meaning). You will find definitions of a number of popular fallacy labels in the Glossary.

Summary and Comment

Although I could have categorized these kinds of problems and challenges differently, no one listing being perfect, I hope I have conveyed a number of different kinds of challenges that might be used in a discussion. These include claiming that:

> There are possible counterexamples.
>
> There is an inconsistency.
>
> The evidence or reasons are false or at least dubious.

The source is not credible.

An assumption is false or dubious.

The argument is circular.

The subject has been changed.

The evidence or reasons are insufficient because

> There is another possible explanation.
>
> A positional definition is undefended.
>
> There is overgeneralization.
>
> There is oversimplification, including using exceptionless principles and the either–or fallacy.
>
> There is emotional language without sufficient substance.
>
> The analogy is faulty.
>
> A legitimate point of view has been neglected.
>
> There is some general failure to follow.

Equivocation occurred.

For each of these defects, I have suggested one or more possible challenge questions. You might not always be justified in your use of these challenges, but—with people of goodwill and understanding—challenges like these can at least help clarify.

Many fallacy labels were used in this section, and some others have been introduced in various other parts of the book. These labels can be useful because they warn of standard places where people go wrong and because they provide an efficient way to communicate a complaint—if the person being addressed knows the meaning. They are dangerous because they often intimidate people who do not know the meaning of these labels and because they seem to invite being applied simplistically. Beware.

Before proceeding to look at ways of responding to challenges directed at you in the next section, please practice using the above challenges and similar ones that you develop for yourself, as in Check-Up Items 14:25 and 14:26.

Check-Up 14C

True or False?
If false, change it to make it true. Try to do so in a way that shows that you understand.

> **14:20** Challenging a position is dangerous because it will not result in clarification.
>
> **14:21** A counterexample is an example that appears to count against a position or a definition.
>
> **14:22** A *circular argument* is one that starts by explicitly assuming what it ends up trying to prove.

14:23 *Post hoc* reasoning is reasoning that concludes that one thing caused another simply because it preceded the other.

14:24 Anything accurately labeled by one of the fallacy labels is a mistake.

Application of Challenge Questions

14:25 Find a partner. Each of you choose and adopt one of the arguments in Items 14:12–14:14 on which you have not yet practiced, or find another argument in this book. Imagine a context for the argument(s) chosen. Then one of you should try to formulate a challenge of each of the types listed above (in the immediately preceding section *Summary and Comment*). The challenge should apply to the argument that your partner has chosen. The partner should try to respond. Next, reverse roles and select another argument. The previous challenger should become an arguer, and the previous arguer should become the challenger, again trying to frame each of the types of challenge listed above. Then write out answers to the following questions:

   a. Which arguments did you choose? Describe the situations you have imagined.
   b. Which of the challenges seemed most useful? How so?
   c. Which of the challenges seemed least useful? How so?

14:26 Find a partner. Select an argument that you find in your daily life, such as from a newspaper editorial page, a magazine article, a talk show, a debate, a discussion with a friend, or a meeting you attended. It can be the same one you selected for Check-Up Item 14:19, but you might find it more interesting to find another. Join together to try to formulate a challenge of each of the types listed above (in the immediately preceding section *Summary and Comment*). If you have ready access to the arguer, deliver the challenge and record the response. If you do not have ready access to the arguer, imagine what the response might be (if you can) and record that. Then:

   a. Provide a copy of the argument.
   b. Specify important features of the situation.
   c. Provide a copy of the (possible) responses.
   d. State which of the challenges seemed most useful, and why.
   e. State which of the challenges seemed least useful, and why.

Responding

By now, you should have a fairly good idea of the straightforward questions of clarification and challenges that I have presented. You have, I hope, practiced asking them and have offered some responses to them. Next I shall present some overall strategies for responding to these straightforward questions and challenges, and then some strategies for responding when things seem to be going wrong.

Responding to Straightforward Questions of Clarification and to Challenges

Knowing what to expect is half the battle. However, that is not all there is to it. You still need to be alert and well-informed, and of course you should try to give an honest, helpful answer. But beyond this, the following strategies for dealing with straightforward questions of clarification and challenge can be helpful:

Restate the question. It often helps to rephrase the question and reflect it back to the questioner. ("Is this what you are asking. . . ?" or "This is what I think you are asking. . . ." [restate the question, using other words].) Doing this not only ensures that you are communicating with the person, but gives you time to think and ensures that everyone else has heard and understands the question. This strategy is especially valuable when the question is vague.

If there are several questions from one person, deal with them one at a time. Sometimes in large groups, a questioner will try to ask a number of questions in a row. Often it is a good idea to interrupt after the first question and try to answer it, saying that if the questioner goes on, you will forget the question and your prospective response.

Actually, a trick that veteran presenters sometimes use to fend off challenges is to allow the challenger to offer several challenges, and then to respond only to one, the weakest of the lot. This is sometimes effective persuasive strategy on the part of the presenter. In order to avoid its being used on you when you are raising challenges in a large group setting (and you are not a designated respondent), it is usually best to offer the strongest one first, and then seek full discussion of it. Then, if there is more opportunity after it is discussed fully, you might try to offer another.

Summarize your answer when you are finished. Unless the question is a simple "Yes" or "No" question, it usually helps to summarize your answer. Then you and the other(s) know what the central features of your answer are.

Admit the weaknesses of your memory, but compensate. Often, when asked how you know something, you cannot remember your exact source. Say so, but offer to try to find it and supply it later, if the person so desires. Then do try to find it and supply it to the person at some later time. Another response is to ask others in the discussion whether they also believe the reason, and whether they know a source. Sometimes, if your claim is commonly accepted knowledge, just say so. But be careful. Perhaps your reason really is dubious.

Do not feel embarrassed by not being able to remember all your sources of evidence. Just show good faith in responding and take your time.

Admit possible problems with your position when they are pointed out. If someone has offered what looks like a good challenge and you cannot think of an answer, admit it. There are often possible answers that you are not able to think of on the spot. Tell the person that you will think more about it and, if this is feasible, let the person know the result. On the other hand, if you are wrong and realize it on the spot, admit it.

If there are weaknesses in your position that you know about in advance, it is often a good idea to admit them in advance and say that you are working on them. Then your presentation is stronger.

Define your terms. When requested to define your terms (and when not requested, if you have reason to think that the others might otherwise be confused), do so. Your terminology might be different from that of other people. If someone requests a definition, it is often easiest to produce an equivalent-expression definition (Chapter 12), starting with the expression in which the term was embedded in your presentation. Because your definition, whatever its form, is likely to be one you have to formulate on the spot, and because definition hawks can often find fault with definitions presented in universal terms, it might help to add the phrase *roughly speaking* to introduce your definition. Ordinarily, the goal is to give sufficient meaning to facilitate communication rather than to give a universally applicable definition. Classification definitions (as contrasted with equivalent-expression and range definitions—Chapter 12) without the phrase *roughly speaking* are especially dangerous in difficult situations because it is usually possible to defeat them and divert attention from the important things at hand.

Respond appropriately to a challenge to your analogy. Suppose someone challenges your analogy by saying that the cases are different and then states what appears to be a difference. Of course, every analogy includes a difference in at least some respect, so the crucial issue here is whether the difference is relevant. If so, is it a significant relevant difference in the situation?

Suppose you have argued that the world of today is like eighteenth-century central North America, so the countries of the world would be better off united under one central government, just as the thirteen colonies were better off united under one central government. Suppose further that someone in response points out that the world has no outside enemies, whereas the colonies did, so the cases are different. What do you do? You have several choices.

First, you can say that you are just using the analogy to make your point more clear. Second, you can deny that the alleged difference is a difference. In this case, you might say that there is an outside enemy (such as large-scale violence, slavery, or environmental disaster). Third, you can try to show that the difference is insignificant. This last is often difficult to achieve. To avoid a shouting match ("Yes it is!" "No it isn't!" "Yes it is!") you might need to resort to a more straightforward value argument (Chapter 11), deductive or loose derivation argument (Chapters 5–7), or inductive argument (Chapters 8–10).

Sometimes, however, analogies are used like counterexamples to arguments, that is, to show that someone else's argument is defective by offering a similar argument that is obviously defective. Suppose someone had claimed that there is no such thing as general critical thinking ability, using as a reason the fact that all instances of critical thinking are thinking about a specific topic or thing. Suppose you responded by showing an analogous argument to be fallacious and claiming that therefore the original argument is fallacious. The analogous fallacious argument could be that because all instances of reading are reading of a particular set of words and are about some particular topic, there could then be no such thing as general reading ability[2] (and, it is assumed, there is such a thing as general reading ability).

If the original arguer then pointed out that reading and critical thinking are dif-

---

2. I am indebted to Richard Paul for this example.

ferent, what should you do? Here you are in a stronger position than with the previous analogical argument. You can say that your analogy shows that a particular generalization is false (a generalization that the original argument appeared to be assuming), and then you can ask the original arguer to produce an alternative generalization or some other assumption that would justify the original argument. Here is the generalization that the analogous argument showed to be false: "If a series of activities with the same name focuses on different things, then there is no general ability to do those things." You can ask for an alternative and, if it is provided, check to see whether it will do the job for the original argument, and whether it is immune to your counterexample or some other counterexample.

In sum, defending analogical arguments is sometimes tricky because so much is left unsaid in analogical arguments. But you are likely to be in a stronger position if your analogy is used to counter another argument than if yours is used directly to buttress your own position. Furthermore, your analogies will probably be quite helpful in clarifying your position or point of view.

Responding When Things Seem to Be Going Wrong

Although not totally different from the response strategies just presented, these strategies express more suspicion of the motives or strategy of the challenger. They are appropriate when something seems awry.

The challenge or question presupposes a proposition that actually is at issue in the situation, or is false. An example that illustrates the problem is, "Have you stopped beating your child?" This question presupposes that you have been beating your child —and that you have a child. Instead of answering the question "Yes" or "No," you should reject the question (assuming that you have not been beating your child or have no child).

Another example: In the presidential election of 1960, there was much discussion about who was responsible for the missile gap (the superiority of the Soviet Union in missiles). It has since turned out that the discussion falsely presupposed that there was a missile gap. The argument about responsibility inevitably made the incumbent administration look bad because it was fairly directly involved in day-to-day military activities.

Response strategy: Challenge the question, if it has a false presupposition. Even more important, be on the alert for false or dubious presuppositions. The most difficult thing in dealing with them is noticing them in the first place.

The questioner attributes a false assumption to your position, an assumption to which your position is not committed. Although your position might depend on false assumptions, it is well to be wary of this move. Your position might not depend on the alleged assumption.

Strategy: If you are confident that you do not need the assumption, then just say so, and show how your position can be defended, even though the proposed assumption is false. If you are in doubt, then you might ask why the questioner thinks that your position needs that assumption.

The questioner seems to assume implicitly a misdescription of your position. This problem shows itself when the other person starts to attack a position that is not yours but acts as if it is yours. Realizing that this has happened is often difficult.

Strategy: Be on the alert to make sure that the challenge applies to your position, not some other position.

Someone explicitly misdescribes your position (or someone's position that you are defending or investigating). Strategy: When it happens to you, just restate your position. If the difference is complicated, then you might also restate the misdescription and point out the difference.

Note: These first four problems are examples of the straw-person fallacy (formerly called the *straw-man fallacy*). To commit the *straw-person fallacy* is to misinterpret or misdescribe a person's position and attack the resulting easy target. The fourth way of committing the straw-person fallacy (the direct misstatement) is the easiest to detect, but is still not easy because so much is going on at once.

The person changes the subject. Sometimes the person starts addressing a different point. The difficult thing to do here is to realize that the subject has been changed. Be on the alert.

Sometimes the subject is changed by someone's making a personal attack on you. This is difficult to handle because you feel obliged to defend yourself rather than the point you are making. The attack on you might even cause you to forget the point. But beware. Some personal attacks are relevant, including any that impugn your credibility as a source (see Chapter 3) or the dependability of your observation (see Chapter 4). Then you must deal with the attack, and consider whether your credibility or dependability are justifiably impugned. If not, defend them.

It is often difficult to detect the change of subject that shifts the meaning of the words of the conclusion, but uses the same words. This is one way of interpreting what happened in Check-Up Item 14:14.

General strategy: Ask for the relevance of the challenge, given the real issue at hand. (See Chapter 13 for further advice.)

The questioner provides an abstract question or point, the import of which you do not see. Strategy: When this happens, ask for an example—or ask for an example of the application of this question or point in some practical context that present company agrees is important.

The questioner asks for an unneeded definition. It is difficult to respond to a request for a definition of a basic term, the meaning of which is implicitly known by all concerned, but which is very difficult to state. Here is an example: "You just said that it is true that the same side of the moon always faces the earth. What do you mean by *true?*" Another: "You just said that the short circuit caused the fire. What do you mean by *caused?*" Any attempt to define precisely the terms *true* and *caused* in contexts like those is very likely to founder. It will probably be open to counterexamples.

Strategy: One thing to do is to give a brief equivalent-expression definition (Chapter 12) that is fairly uninformative, but that is good enough for the situation: "When I said that it is true that the same side of the moon always faces the earth, I only meant that, roughly speaking, there can be no doubt about that." When your subject is astronomy, you do not need to argue the philosophical problem of the meaning of *truth.* It is similar with *cause.* If your subject is the burning of the house, you can say, "When I said that the short circuit caused the fire, I only meant that the short circuit produced the fire." If the discussant wants to pursue the philosophical question of the meaning of *truth* or of *cause,* and if the primary concerns, for example, are astronomy or the house fire, then ask the discussant to postpone that discussion.

On the other hand, if someone requests a definition of a term that is crucial to your argument (for example, *faces the earth* and *short circuit*), then you should proceed to be as clear about it as you can. See Chapters 12 and 13.

The other person offers a definition embodying a position, sometimes undefended, and acceptance of the positional definition hurts your position. Strategy: The thing to do here is to ask why we should accept that definition (as with the *freedom* definition given earlier). Perhaps you might also offer an alternative definition—and defend it. See Chapter 13.

You are asked a hypothetical question: "What would you do if. . . ?" It is often dangerous to give an answer to hypothetical questions because there are so many details about the hypothesized situation that you do not know. You have experienced that problem in doing some of the practice items in this book.

Strategy: One way to answer the question is to point out that many things could be different, so you cannot be sure, but that you might do such and such. Another way is to clarify the question by asking for more details about the situation. A third way that is sometimes used is flatly to refuse to answer the question, saying "That's a hypothetical question." This last strategy could work well with experienced people well-versed in the political process (such as newspaper reporters and judges), but some people will think that you are hiding something. So you must judge how to respond on the basis of your appraisal of the situation.

Presenting Your Own Position

I have postponed the discussion of presenting your own position because a main consideration in presenting your own position is the avoidance of the problems mentioned earlier. Now that you know them, I can give the general advice: Try to present your view in a way that minimizes the likelihood of legitimate challenges and questions. That is, try to be clear in your statement, giving definitions and examples where necessary, usually stating your thesis, your main point, at the beginning and at the end of your presentation. Define your terms, if necessary. Give your reasons, and avoid claiming more strength for your argument than it has. However, not all legitimate challenges and clarification questions can be avoided. Be resigned to that. It is often a good idea to admit difficulties in advance.

Chapters 1, 7–9 and 11–13 contain sections devoted to organizing and writing a position paper. These suggestions, together with those in this chapter, hold in general for making an oral presentation, although they must be adjusted for the situation (the amount of time available, the interests and background of your audience, etc.). However, giving concrete examples is almost always helpful.

Usually an oral presentation must be simpler than a written presentation, and most audiences (and speakers) do not understand, relate, or communicate well when a paper is read. Communication and rapport are usually better when the speaker comments from notes or comments on something everyone can see or hear. On the other hand, reading a paper enables you to say more in a specific period of time and to say exactly what you mean, so reading of papers is common in academic settings.

Large-Group Presentations

A major difference among presentation situations is to be found in your role in the situation, which is related to how much time you have and to how many other people are around. If you are the principal presenter for a large audience, then you can make a major point and buttress it with assorted reasons, examples, perhaps graphics, and responses in advance to major challenges to your view. Try to satisfy the position-paper criteria listed in Chapter 1 (except possibly the one about headings).

At the other extreme, if you are one member of a large audience making a point, you should probably try to limit yourself to one clear point. Give one or a few supporting reasons, repeating your point at the end of your presentation.

A danger in both situations is to wander around and introduce irrelevant ideas or ideas that are not clearly relevant to the audience. Ask yourself about each thing you say: "Is this relevant to the main point?" and "Am I showing how this is relevant to the main point?" To avoid wandering around, try to make your one point very simple, especially when you are in a large audience. It is amazing how often an audience participant fails to make clear the point he or she is trying to convey. When you are the presenter, start by making an assortment of notes to yourself, but then organize them into a coherent whole so that each part leads to the next. In either case, make sure that you summarize at the end.

Small-Group Presentations

On the other hand, in a small group (especially a group of two—you and one other), there is much more back-and-forth discussion, so you often do not need to summarize your point unless it is complicated. You can usually tell right away whether your point has been understood. Try to present things so that challenges and questions are avoided in advance, but again, you cannot avoid them all. There will always be legitimate challenges and questions that can be offered. Respond to them in the ways I have suggested under "Responding."

In a small group, there is more chance that the discussion will stray off the point. Be sure to keep the main point in mind, and do not be fooled into thinking that the main point has been proved—or disproved—just because some irrelevant point has been proved or disproved. All of the other advice given earlier in this chapter—for seeking clarification, challenging, and responding—hold in the small group situation.

Discussion in a small group is good practice for discussion in a larger group. Take advantage of your opportunities for such practice, and think about the process.

Check-Up 14D

True or False?
If false, change it to make it true. Try to do so in a way that shows that you understand.

14:27 Only rarely should you restate another person's question because it is the other person's responsibility to state it clearly in the first place.

14:28 When offering a challenge in a large group, it is usually best to offer as many as you can think of at the same time because you might not get another chance.

14:29 If you cannot remember the source of your information when asked, it is usually best to withdraw your claim.

14:30 When giving a definition on demand, the equivalent-expression form accompanied by *roughly speaking* is usually safer than the classification form.

14:31 In dealing with a question with a false presupposition, it is better to reject the presupposition rather than give a negative answer to the question.

14:32 A person committing the straw-person fallacy misrepresents a position in a way that makes it appear weaker and more vulnerable to attack.

14:33 Attributing an unneeded false assumption to a position is an example of the straw-person fallacy.

14:34 Personal-attack arguments are sometimes appropriate and sometimes inappropriate.

14:35 Circular arguments are fallacious.

14:36 Analogical arguments tend to be stronger if they are used to refute a position than if used to support one.

14:37 Because hypothetical questions are usually so simple, it is usually best to give a quick straightforward answer to them.

14:38 When making a presentation, it is generally a good idea to summarize.

Discussion Practice

14:39 Find a partner. Select one of the arguments in Items 14:12–14:14, or somewhere else in this book, that you have not yet used for practice. One of you adopt the argument first. The other should then offer challenges one by one that invite each of the sixteen types of responses discussed in this section. Give the appropriate response. Exchange roles after the first eight. Do them one at a time, and discuss each before going on to the next. Write out answers to the following questions:

    a. Which argument(s) did you choose? Describe the situations you have imagined.

    b. What response types seemed most useful? Why?

    c. What response types seemed least useful? Why?

14:40 Do the same thing for a new argument from a newspaper editorial page, a magazine article, a talk show, a debate, a discussion with a friend, or a meeting you attended. Try to find an argument about an issue about which you and your partner disagree.

Summary

This chapter began with advice for conducting the overview in FRISCO. It emphasized the interdependence of the parts and suggested the successive application of standards for credibility, observation, value judging, deduction, loose derivation, and induction (both generalization and best-explanation). It suggested caution, looking at things from others' points of view, and awareness of one's own deep assumptions.

In the section on discussion strategies, you received three general pieces of advice: Practice, keep track of many things at once, and be open-minded and otherwise disposed as suggested in the list of critical thinking dispositions.

You saw examples of the following specific kinds of questions of clarification: main point, reason-seeking, connection-seeking, word-meaning-seeking, and significance-seeking. You also saw three general types of clarification questions: "Why?," "What do you mean?," and "Would you say more about that?"

You saw a number of types of challenges to a position, including these: counterexample, inconsistency, dubious reasons or evidence, weak source, false or dubious assumption, circular argument, change in the subject, insufficient reason (for a variety of possible reasons: plausible alternative explanation, undefended positional definition, overgeneralization, oversimplification, emotional language without sufficient reason, faulty analogy, neglect of a point of view, and an apparent failure to follow), and equivocation.

You saw numerous strategies for responding to challenges, including restating the question, dealing with questions one at a time, summarizing your answer, admitting weaknesses in your memory but promising to try to supply the requested information, defining your terms, dealing with analogical arguments, denying false presuppositions embedded in the challenge, challenging the claim that the alleged assumption is needed, rejecting false descriptions of your position, keeping the discussion on the subject, asking for the relevance of a point, requesting an example, responding to a request for an unneeded definition, challenging undefended positional definitions, and rejecting hypothetical questions sometimes. You can add more, if you like, but these cover most of the common situations arising where the assumed standard is rational discussion, and where the major concern is whether the conclusion is justified.

Presenting your own position was discussed last because so much of it depends on foreseeing the kinds of challenges and questions of clarification presented earlier. Planning the presentation of your position can involve the quick scribbling down of some ideas, organizing them, and cutting them down to fit the situation. If there is a large group meeting in which you have no special place in the discussion, and others are anxious to join the discussion, it is often wise to limit yourself to one well-developed point. In any case, it is usually a good idea to state your thesis at both the beginning and end of your argument.

In a small group discussion, there is more chance for straying from the main point, but in any case, all of the previous pieces of advice for questioning, challenging, and responding hold.

Suggested Answers for Chapter 14

Check-Up 14A

14:1 F	14:2 F	14:3 T	14:4 F	14:5 T	14:6 T
14:7 T	14:8 T	14:9 F	14:10 F	14:11 T	

14:1 Inductively valid arguments are good arguments, even if they are deductively invalid.

14:2 Even if a reason is false, an argument might be strong enough to be a good one—without the reason.

14:4 After the conclusion is identified, the situation is still of interest in judging the meaning of the terms, in judging whether something should count as an exception, in deciding what standard of proof to use, etc.

14:9 Change *only at the end of* to *throughout*.

14:10 Change *independent* to *interdependent*.

14:12–14:14 These are up to you. Keep practicing.

Check-Up 14B
14:15-14:19 These are up to you. Keep practicing.

Check-Up 14C
14:20 F   14:21 T   14:22 T   14:23 T   14:24 F

14:20 Challenging a position often results in valuable clarification.

14:24 Some fallacy labels do not imply that a mistake has been made.

14:25–14:26 These are up to you. Keep practicing.

Check-Up 14D
14:27 F   14:28 F   14:29 F   14:30 T   14:31 T
14:32 T   14:33 T   14:34 T   14:35 T   14:36 T
14:37 F   14:38 T

14:27 You often should restate the question; otherwise, if the question is not clear, the others will not understand it, and you might not understand it yourself.

14:28 In a large-group situation, it is usually best to limit yourself to one challenge at a time.

14:29 In such a situation, it is usually best to give yourself time to think more about it, perhaps to look it up.

14:37 Beware of hypothetical questions; it is usually best to answer them, but with qualifications that protect you against unsuspected changes in the situation.

14:39–14:40 These are up to you. Remember to think about your challenges and responses and to continue to practice.

You Have Reached the End of This Book

This book has not given you a mechanical formula for critical thinking because there is none. After you have followed all the advice contained herein, you must still use your own good judgment. I wish you success. Remember to practice, practice, and practice some more, consciously employing the critical thinking dispositions listed in this chapter. Please go back and look at them now.

Epilogue

In case it is not clear how the trial turned out, here is a quick summary: We unanimously voted her not guilty of murder because we felt that the pathologist's moderate force conclusion showed that the state had not proven beyond a reasonable doubt the complicated second condition for murder. (The conditions for murder given us are listed in Chapter 7, Check-Up Item 7:8.) But we unanimously voted her guilty of voluntary manslaughter because we felt that the state had proven beyond a reasonable doubt all four conditions for voluntary manslaughter (listed in Chapter 7, Example 7:1).

Most of the discussion about voluntary manslaughter concerned the meaning of *proven beyond a reasonable doubt* and the question of whether the fourth condition for voluntary manslaughter had been proven beyond a reasonable doubt. This condition was that the defendant was not justified in using the force she used. Because we felt that she had a nonviolent alternative (escaping to her parents' room), we felt that it was proven beyond a reasonable doubt that she was not justified in using the force she used. In discussions of this trial since then, some people have held that the jurors made a faulty assumption. It is that a woman who is physically threatened by a man should pursue a nonviolent solution, if it is available. What do you think? How would you have voted? Why? Your answer is an argument. Apply FRISCO to it!

Can you think of any other assumptions we made in concluding that she was not justified in using the force she used? Are they justified? Apply FRISCO.

Basic Glossary of Critical Thinking Terms

A few of these terms are embedded in a larger framework with which you might not yet be familiar, so if you do not understand a definition here, look up the term in the index and go to the section where it is discussed.

Affirming the antecedent is the step in a deductive argument from the affirmation of the antecedent to the affirmation of the consequent. Affirming the antecedent is a deductively valid move.

Affirming the consequent is the step in a deductive argument from the affirmation of the consequent to the affirmation of the antecedent. Affirming the consequent is a deductively invalid move.

Analogical reasoning is reasoning in which a person infers that two things are alike in some respect from the fact that they are alike in at least one other respect. Not all reasoning by analogy is fallacious. Reasoning by *faulty analogy* is of course fallacious.

The **antecedent** of a conditional proposition is the part introduced by the word *if.*

An **appeal to authority** is a move in an argument that in effect says that because the authority says that something is so, it is so. *Appeal to authority* is one of the fallacy labels. Whether appealing to an authority is actually a fallacy depends on whether the alleged authority is actually an authority on the matter at hand. In a research paper, citation of a source in order to establish a point made by the source is one type of appeal to authority, often not fallacious.

An **arbitrary stipulative definition** is one that is to be judged only by the convenience it affords. It does not incorporate a substantive position on an issue, nor imply that the stipulative definition conforms to current usage of the term.

An **argument** is an attempt to support a conclusion by giving reasons for it.

An **assumption** is a proposition that is taken for granted in a situation and that backs up a conclusion. (In this book, the word *assumption* is used in this way. However, in every-day English, the word *assumption* is often also used as a label for propositions judged dubious, and is sometimes used to refer to a conclusion that is not fully established.)

Best-explanation reasoning is reasoning that is to be judged by the ability of its conclusion to best explain the facts. The conclusion must avoid being inconsistent with the facts, all of its competitors should be inconsistent with the facts, and it should be plausible.

Circularity. To reason so that you end up concluding something you assumed at the outset is to commit the fallacy of *circularity,* or to engage in *circular reasoning.* A *circular definition* is one that fails to communicate because it uses the term being defined to define itself. *Circularity, circular reasoning,* and *circular definition* are fallacy labels. Basically, to say that something is circular is to say that it gets nowhere because it repeats itself.

A **classification definition** is one that provides a general class and distinguishing features, with the intention that just the things that are in the general class and have the distin-guishing features are appropriately labeled by the term being defined.

Class logic is the type of deductive logic concerned with the relationships among classes and with individuals.

A **conclusion** is a proposition that someone is trying to justify or prove in a given situation.

A **conditional proposition** is one consisting of two other supposedly related propositions, one of which is introduced by the word *if* or some similar term. *If Ben is a cat, then Ben is an animal* is a conditional proposition.

The **consequent** of a conditional proposition is the part introduced (or introducible) by the word *then.*

Contraposition is the exchanging of the antecedent and consequent in a conditional proposition while also negating both the antecedent and consequent. Contraposition is a deductively valid move.

A **control group** in an experiment is the group in which a change is not introduced so as to serve as a basis for comparison with the experimental group.

Conversion is the exchanging of the antecedent and consequent in a conditional proposi-tion. Conversion is a deductively invalid move.

A **counterexample** is a case that counts against some proposition, usually either a general-ization, hypothesis, or definition.

The **credibility** of a source for a given statement is the degree to which that source deserves to be believed in the making of that statement.

Critical thinking is reasonable reflective thinking that is focused on deciding what to believe or do.

Deduction is reasoning in which the conclusion is supposed to follow necessarily from the reasons.

Deductive validity. To say that an argument is *deductively valid* is to say that the conclusion follows necessarily from the reasons offered. It is not to say that the conclusion is true. (Logicians and philosophers generally use *validity* as a technical term to refer to deductive validity, but that is not done in this book in order to stay close to natural language. See also *validity.*)

A **definition** is an attempt to state the meaning of a word.

Denying the antecedent is the step in a deductive argument starting from a denial of the antecedent, and concluding with the denial of the consequent. Denying the antecedent is a deductively invalid move.

Denying the consequent is the step in a deductive argument starting from the denial of the consequent, and concluding with the denial of the antecedent. Denying the consequent is a deductively valid move.

A **dependent variable** is one that an experimenter observes, in order to learn the effects of the manipulation of another variable, the independent variable.

Either–or **reasoning.** To assume that there are only two alternatives is to engage in *either–or* reasoning. Sometimes it is fallacious, depending on whether there really are only two alternatives. *Either–or reasoning* is a fallacy label.

An **equivalent-expression definition** is one that puts a term in a larger expression and equates that larger expression with another expression. (The definitions of *deductively valid, either–or reasoning, equivocate, proposition, random assignment,* and *valid* are equivalent-expression definitions.)

To **equivocate** is to shift word meanings in midargument, and to exploit the shift in reaching a conclusion. *Equivocation* is a fallacy label, and is by definition fallacious.

An **experiment** is an attempt to discover something by deliberately introducing a change in a situation and observing to see what happens.

An **experimental group** (to be contrasted with a control group) is the one in an experiment in (or for) which a change is introduced to see whether and how the group is affected.

A **fact** is a proposition that is true.

The **fact–opinion** distinction is a distinction that divides all beliefs into two groups: facts and opinions. The distinction is often misleading because it combines and confuses the distinctions between factual statements and value statements, observation statements and conclusions, and things well-established and not well-established. The distinction among *fact, opinion,* and *reasoned judgment* is preferable, though it neglects the distinction between *fact* and *factual.*

Fallacious thinking is thinking that contains an error of some significance.

Fallacy labels are terms used to identify fallacious thinking, although not all thinking appropriately labeled by each of these terms is fallacious. Fallacy labels defined in this glossary include *appeal to authority, circularity, either–or, equivocation, faulty analogy, gambler's fallacy, glittering generality, impact equivocation, namecalling, non sequitur, personal attack, overgeneralization, post hoc, straw person, streak theory, testimonial* and *transfer*.

FRISCO is a methodical approach to developing, formulating, and checking a conclusion and reasoning. The letters stand for *Focus, Reasons, Inference, Situation, Clarity*, and *Overview*.

The **gambler's fallacy** is the error of thinking that the similarity of a series of events increases the likelihood that a different type of event will appear next. For example, "I have had a series of bad hands, so I am due for a good hand (at cards)." *Gambler's fallacy* is a fallacy label, and examples are fallacious when they deal with honest decks of cards, dice, and lotteries.

A **generalization** is a proposition to the effect that a number of things have something in common.

A **glittering generality** is a laudatory term offered without backing or support. *Glittering generality* is a fallacy label, though the use of a glittering generality is not always fallacious.

Hearsay is the type of testimony that reports what someone else said, and that is offered in support of the truth of what the other said.

A **hypothesis** is a proposition that, in a given situation, is subject to test.

Impact equivocation is an unintentional shifting of word meanings in such a way that it has the impact of equivocation in an argument.

An **independent variable** is one that the experimenter manipulates in a situation in order to see whether and how it affects another variable, the dependent variable.

Induction is reasoning that is either generalizing or best-explanation reasoning (or both).

To **infer** is to reason from some proposition(s) to another, that is, to draw a conclusion on the basis of reasons. Inference is thus a process. (Sometimes, though not in this book, the word *inference* is used as a label for the result of this process, that is, as a label for a conclusion.)

Namecalling is the use of a pejorative term without backing or support. *Namecalling* is a fallacy label, although calling something by a bad name without offering support is not always fallacious.

A **non sequitur** is an inference in which the conclusion fails to follow. *Non sequitur* is a fallacy label. Non sequitur inferences are by definition fallacious (assuming the everyday sense of *follow*).

To **observe** is to notice or perceive something (contrasted with *infer*).

An **overgeneralization** is a generalization that goes beyond the data without justification. *Overgeneralization* is a fallacy label and overgeneralization is by definition fallacious.

A **personal attack argument** is one in which the arguer tries to discredit a position on the basis of an attack on the person offering the position. This move is sometimes called *argumentum ad hominem*. *Personal attack argument* is a fallacy label, although not all personal attack arguments are fallacious. For example, challenging the credibility of a witness, though often amounting to a personal attack, is often appropriate.

A **persuasive definition** is a positional definition offered in an attempt to persuade someone to accept a position underlying the definition.

A **positional definition** is one that incorporates a position on an issue.

Post hoc reasoning is reasoning to the conclusion that one thing caused another, simply because the first thing occurred before the other did. The term comes from the Latin *post hoc, ergo propter hoc*, which means *After this, therefore because of it. Post hoc reasoning* is a fallacy label, and all post hoc reasoning is fallacious. Some reasoning may appear to be post hoc, but is not, because factors other than the time sequence are implicitly taken into account.

A **presupposition** is a proposition that must be true in order that another proposition make sense in a situation. It is one kind of assumption.

Proposition. Roughly speaking, to call a set of words a *proposition* is to say that they express a complete thought, can meaningfully stand alone, and consist of a subject and predicate.

Propositional logic is the type of deductive logic concerned with the relationships between propositions connected by or attached to such terms as *if, then, or, and,* and *not*.

Random assignment to experimental and control groups is an assignment such that each member has an equal chance of being in either group.

Random sampling is sampling such that each member of the sampled population has the same chance of being selected as any other member.

A **range definition** is one that makes the vagueness of a term explicit, and still provides equality between the term and its definition.

A **reason** is a proposition that is offered in support of a conclusion.

Relativism is, in its simplest form, the position that what is justified, true, or good justifiably varies with the background beliefs or framework of the person doing the judging. There are several varieties of relativism. See Chapter 11 for some.

A **reported definition** is one that is intended to report usage accurately.

A **straw person** argument is one in which a position is significantly misdescribed and the misdescribed position is challenged. *Straw person* is a fallacy label, and straw person arguments are by definition fallacious.

The **streak theory** is the view that the similarity of a series of events makes it more likely that the next one will be similar. *Streak theory* is a fallacy label, but not all examples are fallacious. They are fallacious when they deal with honest decks of cards, dice, and lotteries.

Testimonial is the attempt to support a position on the basis of testimony in its favor. *Testimonial* is a fallacy label, but not all testimonials are fallacious.

Transfer is the accepting of a person's claim in one area because the person is an expert in another area. *Transfer* is a fallacy label, and examples are usually fallacious.

Validity. To say that an argument (or statement) is *valid* (in the everyday sense of the term *valid*) is to say that the argument is conclusive (or that the statement is true). Philosophers generally limit the application of the words *valid* and *invalid* to deductive arguments. (See also *deductive validity.*)

Value judging is the process of inferring to a value judgment. A *value judgment* is a claim about the worth or value of something.

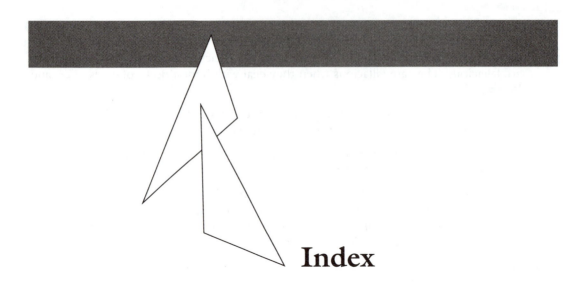

Index

Notes:

1. Refer also to the Glossary, which is not represented in this index.

2. Definitions are cited here in boldface.